Being Subordinate Men

Being Subordinate Men

Paul's Rhetoric of Gender and Power in 1 Corinthians

Brian J. Robinson

LEXINGTON BOOKS/FORTRESS ACADEMIC
Lanham • Boulder • New York • London

Published by Lexington Books/Fortress Academic
An imprint of The Rowman & Littlefield Publishing Group, Inc.
4501 Forbes Boulevard, Suite 200, Lanham, Maryland 20706
www.rowman.com

6 Tinworth Street, London SE11 5AL, United Kingdom

Copyright © 2019 The Rowman & Littlefield Publishing Group, Inc.

All rights reserved. No part of this book may be reproduced in any form or by any electronic or mechanical means, including information storage and retrieval systems, without written permission from the publisher, except by a reviewer who may quote passages in a review.

British Library Cataloguing in Publication Information Available

Library of Congress Cataloging-in-Publication Data

Names: Robinson, Brian J. (Adjunct Faculty Member), author.
Title: Being subordinate men : Paul's rhetoric of gender and power in 1 Corinthians / Brian J. Robinson.
Description: Lanham : Lexington Books-Fortress Academic, 2018. | Includes bibliographical references and index.
Identifiers: LCCN 2018041394 (print) | LCCN 2018046248 (ebook) | ISBN 9781978703346 (Electronic) | ISBN 9781978703339 (cloth : alk. paper) ISBN 9781978703353 (pbk : alk. paper)
Subjects: LCSH: Bible. Corinthians, 1st—Criticism, interpretation, etc. | Masculinity—Biblical teaching. | Masculinity in the Bible.
Classification: LCC BS2675.52 (ebook) | LCC BS2675.52 .R64 2018 (print) | DDC 227/.209—dc23
LC record available at https://lccn.loc.gov/2018041394

To Marie and Rob, for your encouragement to go out and explore the world, however strange and mysterious she might be.

To Laurie and Sam, for your love, support, and sacrifice, without which none of this would be possible.

Contents

Preface and Acknowledgments		ix
Abbreviations		xi
1	Uncovering Paul's Body	1
2	The Body, Masculinity, and Power	19
3	Reconstructed Masculinity	65
4	Paul's Subordinate Masculinity	113
5	Manifestations of Subordinate Masculinity in Paraenesis	159
6	Summary and Test of the Argument	213
Bibliography		231
Subject Index		255
Author Index		259
Ancient Sources		261
About the Author		269

Preface and Acknowledgments

The book that you presently hold, or perhaps view on your screen, began as a question. It is the question first raised by Beverly Gaventa about what to do with Paul's maternal imagery. This question birthed research that resulted in the present volume. I did not know where, if ever, this process would end when I began researching and writing. Neither did I know just how timely a book on masculinity, especially one that addresses how a Christian text that models a subordinate masculinity that imitates the broken and penetrated body of Christ, would be for the world in the 21st century. One of the most important things that I learned watching the 2016 U.S. presidential election and the response by American evangelicals is that, like Paul learning of the factionalism in Corinth, we have much work to do in confronting hegemonic and destructive forms of masculinity. The unlikely ascent of Donald Trump, built on demeaning the appearance and intelligence of his female opponents, emasculating his male opponents, and boasting about the size of his own penis as evidence that he is man enough to be president, exposed American evangelicalism's inability to resist the type of men that thrive within patriarchal systems and forms a startling parallel with the type of toxic masculinity that Paul attacks as incompatible with the gospel. For far too long Paul's writing has been misread and abused by those who wish to accumulate power in the service of their own needs and desires while oppressing the bodies of Others. It is my hope that the present book plays some small role in resisting such abuses.

There are many who have co-labored with me to deliver the present volume, and, without whom the work would have surely not come into existence. I want to first acknowledge Dr. Daniel Kirk, whose creativity and penchant for wanting to explore those queer places in texts that do not fit the current paradigms pushed me to develop the project, especially my method, in ways that were invaluable to me as I worked through text after text after text. Without Daniel this project would have unraveled; he is truly a man attested by God. Dr. Love Sechrest encouraged and prodded me to bring the wide-ranging and unwieldly argument into a more cohesive whole. Love's expertise on identity and power have been invaluable to me both as I worked on the current project and experienced these dynamics in my professional life and the classroom. I consider it a privilege and a tremendous gift to have had two colleagues who are not only outstanding scholars but outstanding human beings and whose work is more necessary now than ever. Dr. David Downs made sure that I kept the full range of 1 Corinthians in mind and that I took a fuller account of Paul's use of his own body. Finally, Dr. Dale Martin provided invaluable insight and critique of my project. I am so thankful for the guidance these four individuals gave to a careful and considered critique of my work, and any deficiencies that remain are my own.

I also want to thank my teachers, colleagues, and students who have inspired, listened to, and sharpened many of the ideas and arguments found in this book. Steve Taylor caused me to fall in love with the study of Paul. Zachary Smith introduced me to Dale Martin's *The Corinthian Body* while I was learning about Michel Foucault and encouraged me to read them together. My students have patiently listened to and questioned the main tenets of my arguments about gender identity and how Jesus and Paul model subordinate forms of masculinity. Ryan Newson read an early draft of this work and offered helpful feedback as it came into its present form. Brittany Wilson and Davina Lopez, each of whose work on gender and the New Testament was critical in opening my eyes to the importance of queer bodies and spaces, provided much appreciated support and encouragement for this work early in its development. The community of All Saints Church in Pasadena supported this work in many ways, not least of which was by modeling a religious community that understands the gospel's call to deconstruct oppressive systems while seeking to embody a radical equality. I also want to thank Neil Elliott, Judith Lakamper, and the editorial team at Lexington Books/Fortress Academic for their guidance and support of this project.

Finally, I want to thank my family: my parents, Marie and Rob, who support everything I've ever done, even if they aren't exactly sure why I do it; my son, Sam, whose refusal to long suffer the boredom of my work while there was playing to be done helps me remember the importance of fun; my partner, Laurie, who has journeyed with me through the craziness of several advanced degrees and the uncertainties of life and has shouldered much while I studied and wrote. I would not have been able to complete the present work without their love, trust, support, and encouragement.

Abbreviations

AFS	*Australia Feminist Studies*
AJAH	*American Journal of Ancient History*
Ar	*Arethusa*
Art	*Art Journal*
Bib	*Biblica*
BICS	*Bulletin of the Institute of Classical Studies*
BJCP	*British Journal of Clinical Phycology*
BJS	*The British Journal of Sociology*
CA	*Classical Antiquity*
CCJ	*Cambridge Classical Journal*
CJ	*Classical Journal*
ConBNT	*Coniectanea biblica: New Testament Series*
CP	*Classical Philology*
CQ	*Church Quarterly*
CSCA	*California Studies in Classical Antiquity*
GRBS	*Greek, Roman, and Byzantium Studies*
GS	*Gender and Society*
Hesperia	*Hesperia: Journal of the American School of Classical Studies at Athens*
ICS	*Illinois Classical Studies*
JFSR	*Journal of Feminist Studies of Religion*
JH	*Journal of Homosexuality*
JHS	*Journal of the History of Sexuality*
JP	*The Journal of Philosophy*
JRAIGBI	*Journal of the Royal Anthropological Institute of Great Britain and Ireland*
JTS	*Journal of Theological Studies*
KEKNT	*Kritisch-exegetischer Kommentar über das Neue Testament*

MDATC	*Materiali e discussioni per l'analisi dei testi classici*
MM	*Men and Masculinities*
Neot	*Neotestamentica*
NovT	*Novum Testamentum*
OEBGS	*The Oxford Encyclopedia of the Bible and Gender Studies*
PCPS	*Proceedings of the Cambridge Philological Society*
P&P	*Past and Present: A Journal of Historical Studies*
PP	*Political Psychology*
PSB	*Princeton Seminary Bulletin*
Sch	*Scholia: Studies in Classical Antiquity*
SemeiaSt	*Semeia Studies*
SP	*Social Problems*
TAPA	*Transactions and Proceedings of the American Philological Association*
TS	*Theory and Society*

Chapter One

Uncovering Paul's Body

Much has recently been made of finding new perspectives on the work of the Apostle Paul; taking a fresh look at phrases and images worn smooth by centuries of Christian interpretation and asking about the function of such language and images within Hellenistic Judaism or the urban environments of the early Principate. The current project is no different and will adopt techniques familiar to many readers. My specific goal, however, is less familiar; I seek the excavation of Paul's body. To pick it up, dust it off, and see how it performs when set within the apostle's socio-historical context and dances across the stage of his argument. While other scholars have made notable progress in understanding certain aspects of Paul's use of his body and the bodies of his audience, I will pay specific attention to the intersection of gender and power as Paul presents his own body and, then, how he calls his audience to imitate it. Ultimately, I conclude that Paul intentionally misperforms Hellenistic and Roman discourses of masculinity so as to limit the use and abuse of patriarchal systems and institutions that oppress those of lower social standing. Paul's goal for such a misperformance of masculinity is both the imitation of Christ and the antidote for the factionalism that threatens the concord of the believing community in Corinth.[1]

The current project assumes, rather than argues for, the unity of 1 Corinthians and its rhetorical goal as overcoming factionalism within the community.[2] This introduction will review how works like Margaret Mitchell's *The Rhetoric of Reconciliation* have shifted scholarship on 1 Corinthians to more willingly accept the text of 1 Corinthians as a unified whole rather than a pastiche created from other letters.[3] Mitchell's most significant contribution is her demonstration that the disparate sections of 1 Corinthians each serve a common rhetorical goal related to achieving and maintaining concord, or unity, in the believing community. The unity of both letter and rhetoric promoting concord stands in contrast to scholarship that approaches 1 Corinthians as a composite letter addressing a list of disparate issues. Such a shift away from the partition theory of 1 Corinthians also means that the main rhetorical goal of 1 Corinthians should no longer be sought in the dim light filtered through the lines and cracks of Paul's argument or in any single answer that he provides or opponent that he might identify. Rather, the goal becomes the concord of the community, which, as Mitchell demonstrates, is the focus of the argument's thesis and a theme throughout the letter. Paul's antagonist, then, becomes whatever groups or dynamics work against that concord by separating members of the community from one another or placing them in hierarchical relationships which assume the power of some members over others. I will not attempt to re-create specific personalities or beliefs of particular groups of the community other than those necessary to set the details of the text in their socio-historical context so as to glimpse how issues of identity and social position help either to separate or to unify the community.

Shifting the reader's gaze away from the specters of possible antagonists outside the text reveals the prevalence of Paul's body and the surprising ways that he misperforms discourses of masculinity within the text. Beverly Gaventa was among the first to notice such oddities of gender related to Paul's self-presentation.[4] For example, what are we to make of Paul using his own body to nurse his audience (e.g., 1 Cor 3:2)? Although she begins by simply noting the unexpected presence of feminine imagery in the Pauline corpus, Gaventa ultimately concludes that such imagery is not incidental to Paul's writing but serves key rhetorical functions within.[5] Her work raises questions about the effect of appropriating feminine imagery for a male author in the first century, hinting at the unusual nature of such a rhetorical move, but she leaves the details of such a move and its rhetorical force unexplored.

The current project developed out of my questions about what it would mean for a male authority figure in the first century to appropriate such feminine imagery in his self-presentation. In order to answer these questions, I develop an approach that is anchored in feminist and queer theory in order to decipher the relevant gendered discourses contemporary with Paul and the language deployed in them. Gender, as with race and other socially constructed categories, is about how contexts create, distinguish, and police bodies. Exploring questions about appropriate masculine and feminine behavior in Greek and Roman texts reveals a system of gender that clearly associates masculinity with being active, self-controlled, and powerful while femininity is associated with being passive, chaotic, and weak. The result is that any act that requires, or is thought to require, masculine characteristics such as temperance or advanced study becomes the domain of men while women are assumed to be naturally incapable of such acts and are, consequently, excluded. Quintilian's comments on training an orator offer a notable example of such assumptions.

> So, since the orator is a good man (*vir bonus*), and the concept of a good man (*virtutem*) is unintelligible apart from virtue (*virtus*), and since [virtue], though it derives some impulses from nature, has none the less to be perfected by teaching, the orator must above all else develop his moral character by study, and undergo a thorough training in the honourable and the just, because without this no one can be either a good man (*vir bonus*) or a skilled speaker. (Quintilian, *Inst.* 12.2.1–2, trans. Russell, LCL)

Notice that in Quintilian's logic, being a man (*vir*) is not just a matter of gender or sexuality but of virtue (*virtus*; i.e., morality).[6] Being a man might begin with nature but is "perfected" by conforming to contextually specific discourses. By connecting masculinity, or being a man, with virtue and then defining virtue by certain characteristics such as emotional restraint or particular movements of the body (Quintilian, *Inst.* 11.3.76–129), Quintilian exemplifies the connection between masculinity and performance that made certain occupations the exclusive domain of men (e.g., oratory). Women were, therefore, excluded since they were thought incapable of adequately performing such occupations because of the assumed limitation of their gender.[7] Furthermore, for a man to fail to be an orator or to demonstrate virtue was understood as failing to exemplify masculinity. Such a man would not be considered a true man. Dio Chrysostom recoils at the thought of a city devoid of true men because all of the men suddenly acquired women's voices and, consequently, were no longer able to speak in a manly fashion (Dio Chrysostom, *1 Tars.* 38). Dio's anxiety indicates a context where gender exists as a spectrum rather than a binary, a space in which a man whose oratory failed was understood as a failed, or feminized, man who had moved away from the masculine ideal and toward the feminine.[8] Gaventa and scholars like Susan Eastman point toward the possibility that such behavior would have significant, almost always disastrous, consequences for such a man.[9] As I will demonstrate in my examination of Paul's self-presentation, a man who fails to live up to the ideals of masculinity and, thus, to occupy the corresponding positions of power is predominantly how Paul describes himself in 1 Cor 1–4.

Greek and Roman constructions of gender also intersect social status and the economic and social realities that accompany them. If, as Quintilian indicates in the text quoted above, a man had to be able to speak well, and speaking well requires training, then only those boys whose families can afford to send them for such training could ever hope to become real men and hold the social and political positions reserved for real men (Libanius, *Or.* 13–15; cf.

Quintilian, *Inst.* 5.7.23–24 for a connection between class and virtue).[10] For the men in Paul's audience, then, a failure or inability to correctly embody discourses of masculinity came with tangible consequences. In the following chapters, I will describe how Paul's rhetoric in 1 Corinthians subverts masculine ideals and intentionally recasts the appropriate masculinity and status of the men in the community in order to promote unity in the face of increasing factionalism. As such, I will show how four of Paul's commands relate to institutions or practices that were exclusively or predominantly the domain of men, such as Paul's commands to become fools (1 Cor 3:18), to abstain from taking other members of the community to court (1 Cor 6:1–8), to submit their bodies to their wives (1 Cor 7:3–5), and to adopt the diets of the weak (1 Cor 8:1–11:1). Understanding the connection between masculinity and these commands, especially the commands on speaking and eating, requires the contemporary reader to continually recall the conceptions of gender that would have been "natural" for readers in a first-century Roman city. Rather than behaving as hegemonic or complicit men who seek increased status and power through reinforcing their masculinity through patriarchal institutions, Paul wants the men in his audience to behave as failed, or subordinate men, and to resist such power games.

CONTEMPORARY SCHOLARSHIP ON THE CORINTHIAN CORRESPONDENCE RELEVANT FOR THIS STUDY

1 Corinthians has long been viewed as a composite text, stitched together from letters that Paul sent to the believers in Corinth. Beginning with the work of Johannes Weiss, changes in tone, focus, and style along with the identification of syntactical clues led scholars to posit the use of two, three, or even more letters. Weiss's initial work argues that 1 Cor 6:12–20; 10:1–22; 10:23–30; 11:2–24; and 2 Cor 6:14–7:1 comes from a single text, Letter A, while the rest of 1 Cor comes from a second text, Letter B.[11] The driving assumption of such theories was that Paul must have a unifying theme for any of his letters, but, because scholars could not find a unifying theme that spanned the disparate sections, 1 Corinthians must be a later creation. The result was that scholars compartmentalized the sections, such as those on wisdom, marriage, and spiritual gifts, in order to focus more narrowly on the language and argument of each. Martinus C. de Boer is representative of scholars who sought a middle position, arguing that 1 Corinthians is a single text but suggesting a disjointed writing process.[12] De Boer argues that Paul wrote 1 Cor 1–4 in response to an initial report from Chloe's people but, then, had to resume composing the text after he was informed of other issues

affecting the community.¹³ Such an argument begins to make sense of how each section relates to Paul without asking how the sections relate to each other. Although I disagree with some of De Boer's conclusions and his assumption that the sections do not share a common theme, his work is important because of the way he attempts to find unity in Paul's work while also giving attention to the diversity of topics and issues covered. Such a balance resists elevating any one section as primary and forces an examination of how the letter functions as a rhetorical whole.

Margaret Mitchell's *The Rhetoric of Reconciliation* marks a major turning point in understanding the unity, and therefore the purposes, of 1 Corinthians. Mitchell's insights come from utilizing comparative rhetorical structures to demonstrate that the letter functions as a cohesive piece of deliberative rhetoric.¹⁴ Although Mitchell was not the first to apply rhetorical analysis to New Testament texts in general and 1 Corinthians specifically,¹⁵ her work represents a key transition in the use of rhetorical analysis. Previous rhetorical analysis focused on understanding how a text argues whereas Mitchell focuses on the use of rhetoric so as to identify the goal of the argument. Mitchell's work makes such a shift in readings of 1 Corinthians by finding unity in the purposes of each section rather than in the specific details within them. The result also turns attention away from describing a specific group or groups that stand behind the issues affecting the Corinthian congregation as Paul's opponents. The reason for this shift is that the details of a particular section, such as Paul's discussion of wisdom that dominate the first four chapters, are not taken as an end in themselves that are aimed at a particular group but function as part of a broader critique of the use of public rhetorical performances to secure an elevated social status. Paul's critique of the manipulation of markers of elevated status are then situated within the broader argument against factionalism which can be found in each section of the letter. The focus shifts from behind the letter to within as the details in each section are analyzed as part of Paul's more explicit goal of overcoming factionalism and achieving concord.

Mitchell's rhetorical analysis highlights Paul's call in 1 Cor 1:10 to put an end to divisions and live in unity as the argument's thesis statement and focal point to which each section relates. Indubitably, Paul's discussion of how the Corinthian believers divide based on party allegiance or division between rich and poor at the Lord's Table addresses factions within the community, but Mitchell's work goes further by demonstrating that even sections like Paul's discussion of lawsuits and head coverings contain rhetorical critiques of factionalism and repeatedly emphasize the ideas of advantage, imitation, and stability of the group, ideas which are commonly used in deliberative arguments for harmony.¹⁶ Mitchell's extensive treatment of discussions of how to achieve and maintain harmony in groups of various sizes provides invaluable background that shows Paul, like Cicero and others, engage a wide range of topics to convince their audiences to reimagine an individual's advantage as inextricably bound up with that of the collective.

Although Mitchell demonstrates *that* the disparate sections of the letter cohere, her analysis does not consistently describe *how* such commands will produce and reinforce the desired unity. The closest that Mitchell gets to describing the how of Paul's argument is her analysis of the way that Paul reframes an individual's personal advantage (συμφέρει and συμφέρον; e.g., 1 Cor 6:12 and 7:35, respectively) in terms of the advantage of others, especially those of lower status.[17] While this is true, Mitchell's analysis does not provide a clear set of criteria or mechanisms to adjudicate how one reframes their understanding of advantage of the other. Understanding the how more precisely requires social-scientific analysis which explores the possible social and political consequences for the original author or audience.[18] Gerd Theissen's social-scientific analysis of 1 Corinthians is a key turning point for both social-scientific analysis and the study of 1 Corinthians because it demonstrates that the letter not only contains language related to how social status was assessed in an urban Roman setting but, more importantly, interacts with conventions of how status was assessed in such a context.[19] One of Theissen's most significant contributions comes in his description of how the conflicts addressed in 1 Corinthians correspond to conflict between those of high and low status and that a significant number of the Corinthian believers are of low status.[20] Furthermore, rather than understanding connections to social context as incidental or unrelated to the gospel, Theissen moves beyond the work of earlier social-scientific scholarship, e.g., Deissmann, by demonstrating that Paul's engagement with his context as seen in his commands, language, and outlook is rooted in his understanding of the gospel. The impact of Theissen's work can be seen in the development of Anthony Thiselton's approach to 1 Corinthians.

> Although I argued in 1978 that the unifying issue in 1 Corinthians was that of an overrealized eschatology, I should now wish to qualify this in spite of reaffirming this emphasis. The triumphalism of many Christians at Corinth was certainly encouraged and supported by an overrealized eschatology which in turn led to a distorted view of what constitutes "being spiritual," or a "person of the Spirit" . . . *Nevertheless I now perceive how this theological misperception combined with the seductive infiltration into the Christian church of cultural attitudes derived from secular or non-Christian Corinth as a city. Concerns about self-promotion, the psychological insecurity generated by status inconsistency, competitive pragmatism, and the radical pluralism . . . all encouraged concerns about "high status" as "people of the Spirit who were gifted" within a Christian subculture with its own autonomous value system.*[21]

Thiselton's comments demonstrate that thoroughly grounding the biblical text in its historical context reveals that concepts and discussions that were previously thought to be uniquely Christian or theological are shown to be inextricably embedded in the language, thought, and concerns of the author and audience. Paul does not have a theology that is abstracted from the symbols and discourses of his context but a theology that is itself a reworking of those symbols. To understand Paul's theology requires attending to how those symbols function in the broader context.

Immediately following the above passage, Thiselton praises Dale Martin, who demonstrates how concerns of status addressed in 1 Corinthians correspond to two competing ideologies of the physical body.[22] The two approaches to the physical body, however, do not just represent disagreements on biology or physiology. Rather, Martin demonstrates that the two competing ideologies of the body arise from the particular concerns of people living in distinct social locations.[23] The basic difference between the social locations outlined by Martin turns on whether a person's body is susceptible to exploitation, thus making it liable to control by a foreign agent. As I will demonstrate in the following chapter, being in control of your body is one of if not the most important criteria for determining a person's gender and social location. This concern with control is also why pollution in the forms of food and sex occupies such a prominent place in Paul's arguments (e.g., 1 Cor 5, 6, 7, 8–10, 11). The first ideology of the body applies a hierarchical understanding to the body, understanding higher-status bodies as more stable, balanced, and, therefore, less vulnerable to the influence of foreign agents. These bodies need not be concerned with the threat of pollution that accompanies the indiscriminate eating of food sacrificed to idols or sexual activity. Such an understanding corresponds to individuals whose elevated social location provides them more control over their lives. Martin argues that these are the bodies that Paul deems as "the strong" in the discussion of food (1 Cor 8–10).[24] The second ideology understands the body as vulnerable and in need of proper protection from pollution.[25] Such an ideology of the body reflects the concerns of individuals of a lower social status who have little if any control over their lives and must constantly enlist the help of others for protection. Martin argues that Paul's commands and discussions consistently frame the present body, as opposed to the resurrection body (cf. 1 Cor 15), as vulnerable, porous, and susceptible to pollution and, therefore, is an ideology that coheres with the position of lower status members of the community who, like the vulnerable body, are in need of protection.[26] In effect, Paul tells the higher-status members of the community to adopt the mindset and corresponding practices of lower-status members of the community. Martin, therefore, succeeds in extending and clarifying Theissen's insights on the gospel's focus on those of lower social status by highlighting the importance of bodies and how those bodies function in society.

Identifying a common ideology of the body that holds together the diverse topics addressed in 1 Corinthians represents a significant advance in the social-scientific treatment of 1 Corinthians. By anchoring Paul's language, i.e., discourses, within ideologies of the body that are broadly attested, Martin can describe the social implications of Paul's vision for the community without becoming hopelessly entangled in conjectures about his opponents or invisible forces that lie behind the text. Understanding Paul's approach to the body and the way such a vulnerable body needs to be protected also indicates what type of community Paul envisions as the ideal for the believing community. Such a group adopts the ideology of those of lower status, seeking to protect one another rather than abuse positions of power in order to take advantage of others. Such a move is not incidental to Paul's understanding of the gospel but arises from his imitation of a Christ (cf. 1 Cor 11:1).[27]

Martin's use of ideologies of the body and argument that Paul commands the community to adopt the ideology of the weak compliments and extends Mitchell's approach to 1 Corinthians since it more directly accounts for how Paul's body language and commands fit together in an argument for concord (*homonoia*). The behavior of the higher-status members, such as eating meat sacrificed to idols, creates division within the community because lower-status members are unable or unwilling to participate in such behavior since they fear the pollution that might result. Mitchell demonstrates that the various subjects that Paul addresses contain *topoi* relating to factionalism; Martin extends this analysis by showing that not only do these arguments address factionalism but that they do so by arguing for a common understanding of the body. Paul's primary tool in avoiding factionalism and achieving concord is to have all the members of the believing community adopt the same understanding of the body that will prevent higher-status members of the community from using their positions in ways that will harm the lower-status members of the community. Martin shows that conceptions of the body sit at the heart of how Paul reframes the idea of advantage, thus more clearly delineating the how of Paul's deliberative argument.[28]

Analysis of the use of the body also highlights the presence and use of Paul's own body within 1 Corinthians as an example for his audience to imitate.[29] This alone makes studying the performance of Paul's body intriguing, but its importance is heightened by realizing that Greek and Roman authors strategically use their authorial presence and self-references to construct a *persona* for specific rhetorical effect. V. Henry T. Nguyen demonstrates that Paul's self-presentation in 2 Corinthians follows the many of the conventions and terminology of authorial self-presentation in order to situate Paul's self-presentation as a carefully constructed part of his argument.[30] Nguyen's argument provides helpful balance to the work of Elizabeth Anne Castelli, who argues that Paul's language of mimesis, or imitation, functions as a move of domination.[31] Castelli's point, building on the work of Michel Foucault, argues that truth claims access not objective realities or facts, but discourses that reveal the constraints of a community. These truth claims take on power as people respond to them and assume they are natural.[32] Truth claims, therefore, serve to grant and reinforce the authority of members of the community who are most able to control them. Castelli argues that Paul makes just such a move to reestablish his authority by presenting himself as the model for his audience to imitate.[33] Nguyen's analysis confirms that Greek and Roman authors would intentionally construct personas that would serve to reinforce their authoritative position, which should command their audience's obedience, while outlining the rules that governed such practices.[34] The surprise is not that Paul included such rhetorical moves in 1 Corinthians but the fact that his language and method of such self-presentation represents a clear and consistent violation of the discourses of masculinity that were the explicit goals of such presentations. Paul intentionally fails to present himself as a masculine man even while arguing that his audience should imitate his behavior. Even while presenting himself in authority over the Corinthians, Paul resists adopting a hegemonic masculinity.

Michael Gorman further nuances Paul's call to imitation by demonstrating how Paul's use of the crucifixion shapes the appropriation of other cultural symbols.[35] That is, the image of the cross plays such a key role in Paul's gospel that it bends other symbols in his theological discourse to conform to certain key elements associated with Jesus's crucifixion. Becoming cruciform, or seeing these symbols through the lens of the cross, often requires the inversion of such symbols. For example, Paul's discussion in 1 Corinthians 1–4 appropriates the symbols of weakness and strength through the cross in such a way that weakness becomes strength and strength becomes weakness (1 Cor 1). Power in the kingdom of God is cruciform, or cross-shaped, power which appears as weakness from the world's perspective.[36] Although I fully agree with Gorman's point on the cruciform character of Paul's gospel and the various elements found within it, I do not think that Gorman goes far enough in locating the image of the cross and the resulting shame within the context of the early Principate. Indeed, highlighting the shame associated with the cross does not restrict the idea of cruciformity but shows that it affects almost every detail and discussion in Paul's letters. The current project will demonstrate how Paul's self-presentation as a failed orator, a wet nurse, and a celibate man each function in the inverted logic of the cross and, ultimately, demonstrate Paul's cruciform understanding of gender.

A major goal of the current project is to bring Martin's work on the social function of bodies into conversation with Mitchell's argument for a common rhetorical goal of concord. In agreement with Mitchell and those who build upon her rhetorical analysis, I will analyze texts throughout 1 Corinthians as parts of a consistent argument for unity as a means of overcoming the factionalism. In agreement with Martin, I approach Paul's argument with an eye to its consistent and coherent connections to the perception and function of the body. In bringing these two lines of analysis together, I argue that the factionalism that threatens the community replicates the social hierarchy that dominated urban Roman environments during the Principate. Paul's remedy for such factionalism is not to say that such a hierarchy does not exist, but to problematize the hierarchy's structure by pressing those members of the community who can access positions of elevated status to adopt behaviors that would align them with the lower-status members of the community. Because of the interdependence of status and gender, commanding a change in status in this way also involves a change in gender, that is, from hegemonic to subordinate masculinity. Demonstrating that Paul embodies such a failed masculinity and commands his audience to as well is the burden of the current project.

WHAT HAPPENED TO THE CORINTHIAN WOMEN PROPHETS?

Readers familiar with discussions of gender in 1 Corinthians might rightly wonder how a focus on masculinity will address the work of Elizabeth Shüssler Fiorenza and Antoinette Clark Wire, two feminist scholars whose work on gender and rhetoric profoundly influenced the study of the Corinthians correspondence.[37] Schüssler Fiorenza's application of a "hermeneutics of suspicion" resisted an uncritical acceptance of an author's framework and descriptions because of the way oppressive systems, such as patriarchy, can influence how a person perceives, describes, and adjudicates an event.[38] Such a suspicion can detect the distorting influence of bias in both ancient and contemporary writers and readers of texts,[39] which makes it an invaluable contribution to my analysis of first-century discourses of gender and the way that gendered language in 1 Corinthians has been understood. For example, by carefully attending to gender and social practices, Schüssler Fiorenza demonstrates that women in Corinth could use celibacy as a mechanism for liberation from "the confines of the patriarchal family."[40] The observation that celibacy has the potential to liberate women becomes a key part of Wire's argument that Paul's main targets are powerful women prophets who take advantage of their experience of newfound liberation within the believing communities.[41] Like Schüssler Fiorenza, Wire not only approaches Paul's argument, but Paul himself, with suspicion, and argues that Paul attempts to rein in women who seek to take the liberating experiences of the early Christian gatherings into other areas of their lives.[42] One of the significant strengths of this approach to 1 Corinthians is that it unifies the letter's disparate sections; Paul's degradation of the wisdom of the world can even be understood within this model by framing it as an attack on women's use of Sophia (wisdom) as an equalizing force. As noted above, such a reading is part of a broader movement toward the unity of 1 Corinthians and helpfully incorporates gender as a key category.

I essentially agree with such feminist insights and the understanding of how women's equal access to the Spirit and prophecy had to the potential to be profoundly liberating within the early believing communities. I disagree, however, with Schüssler Fiorenza and Wire on two main points; the result of which is a rather different picture of Paul and his goal for the Corinthian believers. First, I do not take Paul's commands about head coverings in 1 Cor 11:2–16 to be restrictive of women's freedom and authority but actually encouraging such it. Such an examination will have to wait until the final chapter of the present volume. Second, I understand Paul as critiquing destructive and oppressive forms of *masculinity*, often using the feminine in positive ways that reframe how men should behave. In other words, rather than Paul needing to counter out-of-control women, I think Paul needs to counter out-of-control men. Such a reading fits with more current feminist approaches to 1 Corinthians such as that of Gillain Townsley, who also understands Paul as confronting destructive forms of masculinity rather than out-of-control women.[43] Although Townlsey articulates Paul's goal as lesbianising the men in the community whereas I use the language of embodying a subordinate masculinity, our vision for Paul's language and its effects on the men in the believing community are quite similar.[44] In our analysis, Paul does not try to restrain women, prophetic or otherwise, but upends the gendered discourses that are threatening the stability of the believing community.

OVERVIEW OF THE CURRENT PROJECT

The current project will proceed in four parts. The second chapter will review the development of gender criticism out of and in conversation with feminist studies. The evolution of first-, second-, and third-wave feminist studies provides the necessary methodological grounding for an examination of masculinity in the context of the urban setting of first-century Roman Corinth.

Such an examination pays close attention to the interplay of gender and sexuality in the early Principate and to how specific discourses that govern and delineate masculinity and femininity inscribe power based on the body and behavior. The work of Michel Foucault, David Halperin, and Amy Richlin will be of utmost importance as I survey the intersection of physical bodies, power, and gender in the Greek and Roman discourses of masculinity. The main takeaway from this chapter is that rhetoric in Paul's context inextricably binds together masculinity and socio-political power in ways that marginalize bodies that were liable to feminine characteristics.

The third chapter will discuss ways that three male authors who were near contemporaries of Paul respond to attributes that would have been read as feminine and which, therefore, undermined their ability to function as men. Favorinus is a congenital eunuch whose powerful oratorical abilities were in conflict with his physical body. Although he spoke and defeated opponents like a man, his body did not conform to the assumptions of a masculine body. This discursive break threatened his status as a real man (*vir bonus*). In his response, Favorinus articulates a new vision for masculinity that emphasizes his strengths while minimizing and reframing the liabilities of his physical body. Likewise, Philo's *Gaius* engages discourses of masculinity and femininity to show that the native Egyptians, not the Jews, are responsible for undermining Rome's hegemony in Alexandria. Philo accomplishes this by situating the Jews as complicit men who are not masculine enough to challenge Rome's control but not feminine enough to bring chaos to the city. The native Egyptians, on the other hand, are too feminine to be trusted and must be ruled harshly in the same way that the masculine must rule the feminine. Josephus's *Wars of the Jews* makes a similar argument in situating the Jews as complicit men by blaming the revolt of 67 C.E. on a small group of Jewish men whose femininity sparks the rebellion and is not indicative of other Jewish men. This chapter shows that issues of gender and status were widespread and critical enough that near contemporaries of Paul intentionally engage them within their writings for specific rhetorical purposes. They also provide a critical contrast to Paul, who embraces such femininity rather than explaining away or limiting feminine attributes.

The fourth chapter will focus on key aspects of Paul's self-presentation in 1 Corinthians that intersect discourses related to masculinity. I will examine Paul's presentation as a failed orator, a wet nurse, a shamed father, and a celibate man in connection with discourses of gender relevant to each. The result will be the demonstration of a consistent emphasis on femininity, either through an intentional failure to perform masculine discourses correctly or through appropriating feminine discourses. The result of Paul's performance is to make him a subordinate man. I will situate such a move within first-century rhetoric which demands that authors carefully attend to their self-presentations so that an audience would know what kind of man the author was. I will connect Paul's subordinate masculinity with his imitation of Christ and broader understanding of the gospel's implications for life in the midst of the present age. Conforming to the image of the crucified Lord means adopting a persona that the broader world would be read as a subordinate, i.e., failed, masculinity.

The fifth and final chapter demonstrates the continuity between a selection of Paul's commands and his own subordinate masculinity as he calls the men in the audience to imitate him. These commands call the male believers to misperform discourses of hegemonic masculinity that encourage people to separate and compete with each other for increased status and power. I show that Paul subverts the use of gender and power as mechanisms of elevating oneself over others and, thereby, undermines the factionalism that threatens to tear the community apart. In its place, Paul offers a model for behavior that gives away power and seeks the benefit of others. Such behavior is in opposition to discourses of masculinity and ask that his audience become subordinate men as they imitate Paul, who imitates Christ (cf. 1 Cor 16:13 and 11:1; respectively).

The conclusion will provide a review of key aspects of my argument and an interpretive exploration of Paul's comments on head coverings (1 Cor 11:2–16). I save these commands for last because not only are they enigmatic but their interpretation is so thoroughly wrapped up with the subordination of women that it is difficult to read the passage otherwise or attend to important details like the fact that Paul also addresses men in the passage.[45] Rather than address this line of interpretation, I will assume that the logic of subordinate masculinity that I demonstrate elsewhere in 1 Corinthians is also present in the commands on head coverings. I then argue that Paul's commands on head coverings restrict the manipulation of head coverings as markers of prominence in a religious setting. Such a line of thinking brings this passage into rhetorical continuity with the rest of 1 Corinthians and explains Paul's command to give a symbol of authority to those members of the community whose bodies make them the most vulnerable. Ultimately, this analysis will demonstrate the importance of humility in addressing issues that pertain to factionalism, which is the very thing that Paul says in the thesis of his argument (cf. 1 Cor 1:10).

NOTES

1. I use the term patriarchy to describe a series of gendered discourses that privilege men and the masculine over women and the feminine. My use of the term, however,

must always be understood within a broader system that Elizabeth Schüssler Fiorenza labels kyriarchy; see *But She Said: Feminist Practices of Biblical Interpretation* (Boston: Beacon, 1992), 103–32. Schüssler Fiorenza uses the term to describe the intersectional nature of discourses in creating and sustaining power imbalances. To this end, I will demonstrate the way that sex, race, economic status, education, and legal status intersect and function together within first-century Jewish, Greek, and Roman conceptions of gender, hence my choice of patriarchy rather than kyriarchy.

2. Johannes Weiss was not the first to suggest a composite theory for 1 Corinthians, but his work did spark the modern proliferation of such theories; *Der erste Korintherbreif* (Göttingen: Vandenhoeck & Ruprecht, 1910), xli. I will review the development and consequences of such theories in chapter 4 of the present volume.

3. Margaret M. Mitchell, *Paul and the Rhetoric of Reconciliation: An Exegetical Investigation of the Language and Composition of 1 Corinthians* (Louisville, Ky.: Westminster/John Knox, 1993). Mitchell's use of the category of deliberative rhetoric has been critiqued by scholars such as S. M. Pogoloff (*Logos and Sophia: The Rhetorical Situation of 1 Corinthians* [Atlanta: Scholars Press, 1992], 151–52) for misunderstanding the goal of Paul's use of deliberative rhetoric. Such a critique, however, does not question the use of deliberative rhetoric or its usefulness in arguing for concord in a community. For a helpful review of the issues surrounding rhetoric in 1 Corinthians, see Anthony C. Thiselton, *The Fist Epistle to the Corinthians: A Commentary on the Greek Text* (NIGTC Grand Rapids: Wm. B. Eerdmans, 2000), 41–46.

4. Beverly Roberts Gaventa first raised the issue of Paul's appropriation of feminine imagery in his self-presentation in "The Maternity of Paul: An Exegetical Study of Galatians 4:9," in *The Conversation Continues: Studies in Paul and John in Honor of J. Louis Martyn* (ed. Robert T. Fortna and Beverly Roberts Gaventa; Nashville: Abingdon, 1990), 189–201. Gaventa developed the question beyond Galatians in "Our Mother St. Paul: Toward the Recovery of a Neglected Theme," *PSB* 17 (1996): 29–44. This article was later included and expanded in *Our Mother Saint Paul* (Louisville: Westminster John Knox, 2007).

5. Gaventa, *Our Mother Saint Paul*, 48.

6. Simone de Beauvoir famously makes the distinction between gender and sexuality in that a body's sex describes what can be thought of as physical characteristics while a body's gender describes, among other things, how those characteristics are coded within a particular discursive context; *Le deuxième sexe* (Paris: Gallimard, 1949), repr. of *The Second Sex* (trans. Constance Borde and Sheila Malovany-Chevallier; New York: Alfred A. Knopf, 2010), 62–265.

7. I discuss the restrictions on women and speaking publicly in chapter 5.

8. Such connections will be demonstrated in the second chapter, where I discuss the connection between gender, the body, and power.

9. Gaventa, *Mother*, 48; emphasis added. Susan Eastman makes a suggestion similar to Gaventa's but leaves the comment as speculation without fleshing out the details; "Imagery, Gendered: Pauline Literature," in *The Oxford Encyclopedia of the Bible and Gender Studies: Vol 1* (ed. Julia M. O'Brien; Oxford: Oxford University Press, 2014), 379–80.

10. Maud W. Gleason, *Making Men: Sophists and Self-Presentation in Ancient Rome* (Princeton: Princeton University Press, 1995), 161–64.

11. See Weiss's discussion under the heading "Der Brief des Paulus" in *Der erste Korintherbreif*, xxxix–xliii.

12. Martinus C. de Boer, "The Composition of 1 Corinthians," *NTS* 40 (1994): 229–45.

13. de Boer, "The Composition of 1 Corinthians," 229–30.

14. Mitchell, *Rhetoric*, 25–38.

15. G. A. Kennedy is often credited with the rise of interest in rhetoric in studying the New Testament; see, *New Testament Interpretation through Rhetorical Criticism* (Chapel Hill; NC: University of North Carolina Press, 1984). The immediacy and scale of Kennedy's work can be seen in the fact that only four years after its publication, there was already a need to organize and catalog rhetorical approaches to biblical texts; see Duane F. Watson, "The New Testament and Greco-Roman Rhetoric: A Bibliography," *JETS* 31 (1998): 465–72. The methodological development of rhetoric in the interpretation of biblical texts can be traced in the series of five volumes: Stanley E. Porter and Thomas H. Olbricht, eds., *Rhetoric and the New Testament: Essays from the 1992 Heidelberg Conference* (JSOTSup, 90; Sheffield: JSOT Press, 1993); Stanley E. Porter and Thomas H. Olbricht, eds., *Rhetoric, Scripture and Theology: Essays from the 1994 Pretoria Conference* (JSNTSup, 131; Sheffield: Sheffield Academic Press, 1996); Stanley E. Porter and Thomas H. Olbricht, eds., *The Rhetorical Analysis of Scripture: Essays from the 1995 London Conference* (JSNTSup, 146; Sheffield: Sheffield Academic Press, 1997); Stanley E. Porter and Dennis L. Stamps, eds., *The Rhetorical Interpretation of Scripture: Essays from the 1996 Malibu Conference* (JSNTSup, 180; Sheffield: Sheffield Academic Press, 1999); Stanley E. Porter, Dennis L. Stamps, and Thomas H. Olbricht, eds., *Rhetorical Criticism and the Bible: Essays from the 1998 Florence Conference* (JSNTSup, 195; London: Sheffield Academic Press, 2002). These five edited volumes along with the voluminous secondary literature with which they engage, show a transition in rhetorical criticism focusing on *how* a text communicates to *what* it communicates. Vernon K. Robbins is representative of such a transition in his understanding of textuality, rhetoric, and the ways that a single text can apply multiple discourses in order to create a rhetorical tapestry (i.e., socio-rhetorical interpretation); see *The Tapestry of Early Christian Discourse: Rhetoric, Society, and Ideology* (New York: Routledge, 1996) and *Exploring the Texture of Texts: A Guide to Socio-Rhetorical Interpretations* (Harrisburg; PA: Trinity Press International, 1996). Mitchell's work marks a similar transition since she not only focuses on how 1 Corinthians argues through examining Paul's individual arguments for concord but brings these arguments together to show that Paul counters factionalism within the community; *The Rhetoric of Reconciliation*, 182–84.

16. Mitchell, *Rhetoric*, 20–64.

17. The centrality of Paul's use of and reframing the concept of advantage is a key piece of Mitchell's evidence for labeling 1 Corinthians as deliberative rhetoric; Ibid., 33–39.

18. See John Elliott's helpful introduction and overview of social-scientific approaches to the New Testament; *Social-Scientific Criticism of the New Testament: An*

Introduction (London: SPCK, 1995). More recently, Elliot traces the development of social-scientific analysis from the earlier work of Adolf Deissmann, who was more concerned with situating biblical material within its context, to more recent scholarship that uses social-scientific analysis to understand the effects of the biblical material with its context; "From Social Description to Social-Science Criticism," *BTB* 38 (2008): 26–36. Although Deissmann's comparative work on non-literary Greek texts makes significant advancements in situating the early Christian movement in its social context, his goal is to look beyond such similarities in order to find the uniqueness of the Christian proclamation. The language and ideas that anchored the biblical texts in their social context, then, were not where the gospel is to be found. Rather, Deissmann finds Christianity's uniqueness in the aspects of the one God, Jesus and his return, and a strong morality which attends to the guilty soul. In short, Deissmann does not thoroughly examine how the early Christian's experiences of God, Christ, and their experience of the kingdom of God impact how they interact with their social context. The result can be seen in Deissmann's assessment that the uniqueness of the gospel most clearly found in 1 Corinthians comes in Paul's discussion of love in 1 Cor 13; see *Light from the Ancient East: The New Testament Illustrated by Newly Discovered Texts of the Graeco-Roman World* (trans. Lionel R.M. Strachan; 4th ed.; London: Harper & Brothers, 1927), 252–392, esp. 378–91. Deissmann makes similar moves in his assessment of Paul by thoroughly anchoring his reasoning and use of Scripture in first-century Judaism, then using such a connection to look elsewhere for the uniqueness of the gospel; see *Light from the Ancient East*, 381–82. Albert Schweitzer takes a nearly identical approach in his work on the historical Jesus by thoroughly locating Jesus's life and teaching within first-century Judaism and, then, by arguing that Jesus's intentions fail on the cross, points to his unexpected impact on history as what makes him "the one immeasurably great Man"; see *The Quest for the Historical Jesus: A Critical Study of Its Progress from Reimarus to Wrede* (trans. W. Montgomery; London: Adam and Charles Black, 1910), 368–69. Schweitzer and Deissmann each make valuable contributions to situating the biblical texts in their context, but they each also make a similar mistake of looking beyond those common elements for the impact of the gospel. The historical significance of German New Testament scholars from the late 19th and early 20th centuries divorcing Christianity from its Jewish roots cannot be overemphasized.

19. Theissen's work is a critical advance since it brings the search for the impact of the gospel to those elements shared by both the biblical texts and their context. Many of his key essays are collected in *The Social Setting of Pauline Christianity: Essays on Corinth* (ed. and trans. John H. Schütz; Eugene, Or.: Wipf & Stock, 2004).

20. Gerd Theissen, "Soziale Schichtung in der korinthenischen Gemeinde: Ein Beitrag zur Soziologie des hellenistischen Urchristentums," *ZNW* 65 (1974): 232–72.

21. Anthony C. Thiselton, *The First Epistle to the Corinthians: A Commentary on the Greek Text* (NIGTC; Grand Rapids: Eerdmans, 2000), 40; emphasis original.

22. Dale B. Martin, *The Corinthian Body* (New Haven: Yale University Press, 1995).

23. Ibid., xv.

24. Ibid., xv, 55–68.

25. It is not entirely clear whether "the weak" in Corinth have a distinct ideology that sees all bodies as vulnerable or whether they have adopted the hierarchical ideology of the body and understand their lower social position to mean that their bodies are likewise in a vulnerable state. What is clear is that Paul wants everyone in the community to understand their present bodies as vulnerable which requires the avoidance of practices that threaten to pollute the body.

26. Martin, *The Corinthian Body*, 196–96.

27. It is important to note that an emphasis on conforming one's mindset and practice to the needs of the weaker members of the community also appears at key points in other Pauline texts (e.g., Rom 14:1–15:8, Phil 2:1–11).

28. Although this is not a main thrust of Martin's work, he makes the point in several places; e.g., ibid., 39, 77.

29. Paul also commands his audience to imitate him in Phil 3:17, 1 Thess 1:6, and 2 Thess 3:7. Commands to imitate God come in Eph 5:1 and 1 Thess 1:6. While other texts implicitly contain the concept of imitation (e.g., Phil 2:5), Castelli demonstrates that the language of *mimesis* has specific functions related to the use of power in Greek and Roman rhetoric; see *Imitating Paul: A Discourse of Power* (Louisville: Westminster John Knox, 1991), 59–88. Note that 1 Thess 1:6 combines imitation of Paul and of God in a manner like that of 1 Cor 11:1 but with two important differences. First, 1 Thess 1:6 commands imitation of God while 1 Cor 11:1 commands imitation of Christ. Second, 1 Thess 1:6 commands imitation of Paul *and* God while 1 Cor 11:1 commands imitation of Christ through the imitation of Paul. This final detail is one of Castelli's most convincing points since it gives Paul a mediatorial role between the community and Christ. The fact that Paul commands imitation of Christ in 1 Cor becomes all the more interesting in light of the way that Christ's crucified and, then, resurrected bodies function in the rhetoric of 1 Cor 1–4 and 15, respectively.

30. V. Henry T. Nguyen, *Christian Identity in Corinth: A Comparative Study of 2 Corinthians, Epictetus and Valerius Maximus* (WUNT 2/243; Tübingen: Mohr Siebeck, 2008).

31. Elizabeth Anne Castelli, *Imitating Paul: A Discourse of Power* (Louisville: Westminster/John Knox, 1991), 21–34.

32. Castelli, *Imitating Paul*, 56–58.

33. Ibid., 22.

34. Nguyen, *Christian Identity in Corinth*, 10–51.

35. Michael J. Gorman develops and traces the implication conforming to the image of the cross and its implications, or what Gorman refers to as cruciform(ity), in several volumes: *Cruciformity: Paul's Narrative Spirituality of the Cross* (Grand Rapids: Eerdmans, 2001); *Apostle to the Crucified Lord: A Theological Introduction to Paul and His Letters* (Grand Rapids: Eerdmans, 2004); *Inhabiting the Cruciform God: Kenosis, Justification, and Theosis in Paul's Narrative Soteriology* (Grand Rapids: Eerdmans, 2009).

36. Gorman, *Apostle of the Crucified Lord*, 240–43.

37. There are many other important feminist scholars who both contribute to and develop the work of Schüssler Fiorenza and Wire whose work I will not discuss at this point. I do this because they share the assumption that Paul focuses on reinforcing a

kyriarchical understanding of gender that privileges the male over the female. As will become clear throughout the present volume, I argue that whenever possible, Paul undermines such a kyriarchy by encouraging a form of masculinity that could not occupy a privileged position over others. For example, Lone Fatum, "Image of God and Glory of Man: Women in the Pauline Congregations," in *The Image of God: Gender Models in Judaeo-Christian Tradition* (ed. Kari Elisabeth Børresen; Minneapolis: Fortress Press, 1995), 50–133; Elizabeth A. Castelli, "The *Ekklēsia* of Women and/as Utopian Space: Locating the Work of Elisabeth Schüssler Fiorenza in Feminist Utopian Thought," in *On the Cutting Edge The Study of Women in the Biblical World: Essays in Honor of Elisabeth Schüssler Fiorenza* (ed. Jane Schaberg, Alice Bach, and Esther Fuchs; New York: Continuum Press, 2004), 36–52. Mary Rose D'Angelo, "Women Partners in the New Testament," *JFSR* 6 (1990): 65–86. Jurunn Økland, "Feminist Reception of the New Testament: A Critical Reception," in *The New Testament as Reception* (ed. Mogens Müller and Henrik Tronier; JSNTSup 269; London: Sheffield Academic, 2002), 131–56.

38. Elizabeth Schüssler Fiorenza, "Remembering the Past in Creating the Future: Historical Critical Scholarship and Feminist Biblical Interpretation," *Feminist Perspectives on Biblical Scholarship* (ed. Y. A. Collins; Atlanta: Scholars Press, 1985), 55–63.

39. Schüssler Fiorenze, *But She Said*, 84.

40. Elizabeth Schüssler Fiorenza, *In Memory of Her: A Feminist Theological Reconstruction of Christian Origins* (New York: Crossroad, 1985), 220–26.

41. Antoinette Clark Wire, *The Corinthian Women Prophets: A Reconstruction through Paul's Rhetoric* (Minneapolis: Fortress Press, 1990).

42. Ibid., 72–115.

43. Gillian Townsley, *The Straight Mind in Corinth: Queer Readings across 1 Corinthians 11:2–16* (SemiaSt 88; Atlanta: Scholars Press, 2017), 110–115. Townsley primarily focuses on 1 Cor 11:2–16 and only briefly mentions the rest of 1 Corinthians, whereas the present volume focuses on key texts in the rest of 1 Corinthians and only briefly examines 1 Cor 11:2–16 in the final chapter. Our studies are mutually reinforcing rather than simply overlapping examinations of masculinity in 1 Corinthians.

44. Ibid., 113–115.

45. Thiselton addresses the way the interpretive history of the passage overlooks key details within it; see *First Corinthians*, 800–801.

Chapter Two

The Body, Masculinity, and Power

This chapter will introduce gender studies and describe the ways it conceptualizes masculinity. It will then provide a thorough examination of masculinity, and gender more broadly, in ancient Greek and Roman literature. This will begin with Foucault and develop through scholars who engage his work. One of the points which will surface is the critique that Foucault focused on too narrow a selection of sources and so overlooked the diversity in conceptions of gender within Greek and Roman literature. As a result, Foucault was unaware of the positive assessments of femininity which occur in certain authors (e.g., Plutarch, *Mulier. virt.* 242E–F) or in certain subordinate/deviant masculinities (e.g., Favorinus, *Cor. orat.*). The diversity points toward the shifting and competing discourses of masculinity and the changes in masculinity which accompanied the shift from the Republic to the Principate. Despite this diversity and the competing conceptions of masculinity, there are common assumptions about masculinity that pervade Greek and Roman discourses of gender. I will demonstrate these commonalities and show how they connect the body, power, and hierarchy in patriarchal systems that legally and socially privilege men and the masculine over women and the feminine. The result will be a map of how Roman society during the early Principate conceived of gender in ways that favored a particular construction of masculinity and attributed power according to a person's ability or failure to conform to that form of masculinity. The following chapter will further nuance this patriarchal system by distinguishing hegemonic, complicit, and subordinate masculine identities and how they function within these power relationships. This will allow me to explore the lengths to which male authors would go in constructing a specific masculine identity and the purposes for which they would use such an identity. Certain male authors, such as Favorinus, address apparent lapses in their masculinity by attacking their opponents in an attempt to reaffirm their identity as hegemonic men and present their body as the masculine ideal. Other male authors, like Josephus and Philo, present themselves as sufficiently masculine to be complicit within the patriarchal structure of the Principate but not masculine enough to threaten Rome's domination. What a man presented about himself depended on what he hoped to accomplish. Situating the rhetorical construction and use of a specific masculine identity will allow me to examine how Paul engages with and renegotiates masculinity through the manipulation of key discourses of gender to present himself as a subordinate, or failed, man.

THE DEVELOPMENT AND INFLUENCE OF GENDER STUDIES

The study of gender in the writings of Paul typically focuses on the portrayal, status, and regulation of women in the churches to which he writes as well the underlying assumptions which inform his thinking. By focusing only on women, scholars implicitly accept men, and the masculinity which they embody, as a stable, monolithic norm. The problem is that not only do Paul's letters evidence a conflict over appropriate male identities but, also, that Paul appears to renegotiate his own masculinity in ways that are problematic in both Hellenistic Jewish and urban Roman contexts. Questions about gender in Paul's writings are further complicated by Paul's apparent inconsistency on matters of gender roles and decorum. Though there are times when Paul promotes a level of equality between men and women (e.g., 1 Cor 7:1–4), more often he *appears* to reinforce gender and social hierarchies which assume male headship by appealing to both Jewish writings and the conventional wisdom of his day (e.g., 1 Cor 11:2–16). Such tension appears to typically lead a reader to simply elevate those passages that most agree with their presuppositions and discount those that do not.[1] But to understand Paul's comments on gender, as with his comments on other topics, his writing must be set within its socio-historical context and understood in relation to his role with and desires for his audience.[2] In order to understand Paul's use of gender effectively, I will first trace the development of gender studies with a focus on its origin, assumptions, and method for analyzing gender and the discourses which create, sustain, and police gender. I will then use this broader discussion of gender studies to understand the study of masculinity in Hellenistic texts primarily ranging from 200 B.C.E. to 200 C.E. with particular attention to issues of hierarchy and power. This will allow me to survey the study of masculinity within biblical studies and highlight the under-explored aspects of subordinate masculinities as I explore the construction of Paul's masculinity in 1 Corinthians.

Gender studies originates from feminist scholarship, particularly second wave feminist scholarship, which highlights the way women were constructed, manipulated, and maligned by men and androcentric institutions and cultures.[3] As feminist scholars came to understand the construction and deployment of discourses which focus on women, they noticed that these same insights also apply to men. Although scholars were quite obviously aware of the presence and influence of men, they had not applied the same critical sensibilities to understand the construction and manipulation of men or the ideas of male or masculinity as gendered terms but assumed their stability, rationality, and normalcy.[4] Judith Shapiro characterizes this shift as a transition from an implicit to an explicit confrontation with the social and cultural dimensions of masculinity and how they impact women.[5] This awareness opened the way for historical and ethnographic studies that analyze the influence of masculinity on topics ranging from the modern workforce to wartime behavior to gay culture. Beginning with the work of Peter Filene and Peter Stearns, sociologists observed key shifts in how men were supposed to behave in different spheres of life, relate to other men as opposed to non-men, and reinforce their own masculine identity.[6] Masculinity could no longer be thought of as a stable, universal category. These studies, and others like them, indicate that there is just as much that distinguishes the concept of masculinity through time and across cultures as unifies it. Take the concept of male, or homosocial bonding. In ancient Greece, men spent time together bathing and exercising in the nude. This practice was thought both practical for men and vital for boys since the best way to boost one's masculinity and learn how to be a man was from close, often intimate, contact with other men. In many contemporary, Western contexts, however, hearing of a group of men who exercise and bathe together in the nude would not immediately connote maintaining or promoting social ideals of masculinity but, more likely, notions of homosexuality that, in certain contexts, would carry connotations of effeminacy. Todd W. Reeser makes the point that this divergence indicates that what is considered natural and "taken for granted is not at all a given, but a fabrication or a construct of a given historical and cultural context."[7] Once the stability of the "normal" is problematized, masculinity becomes a gender open for investigation and critique on the same level as femininity. As Gardiner puts it, "Misogyny created feminist theory, and feminist theory has helped create masculinity."[8]

But labeling masculinity as a socially constructed gender which is open to investigation does more than allow for comparative work; it also illuminates the connection between masculinity and power as masculinity functions as part of a person's identity that situates him within a society. Being a man requires fulfilling certain roles and gives the person who correctly acts the part a certain amount of power. The perpetuation of pay inequality and a dearth of female C.E.Os and world leaders can be taken as evidence of a continued, contemporary connection between power and masculinity.[9] When women do ascend to the heights of power in the political or economic worlds, their violation of the connection between power and masculinity causes them to often be demonized or categorized in male terms.[10] As such, scholars note that attention to masculinity becomes increasingly acute in periods of social change when identity and roles are threatened, giving rise to a crisis in a culture's discourses of masculinity. Attention to just such a period of crisis helps explain some of the transitions in masculinity which accompanied the shift from the Republic to the Principate and will be important as I examine the renegotiation of masculinity in the first-century texts discussed below.[11]

Not only does the concept of masculinity change across time, but it can also take varied and sometimes competing forms within a particular context. R.W. Connell, who coined the term hegemonic masculinity, argues that hegemonic masculinities form when cultural ideals and institutional power coalesce into a particular, typically exclusive, image of masculinity.[12] The "Three-Fifths Compromise," which stated that men of color were only to be counted as a three-fifths of a *man* in determining political representation, was a crucial step in passing the U.S. Constitution and represents just such a convergence. Men of color were recognized as men, as opposed to women and children, but were not given worth equal to that of white men.[13] White men, and more particularly those who owned land, occupied the hegemonic position because of their increased social and political power. This provision further solidified the connection between the ideal of the white, male citizen and the power of the federal and local governments and institutionalized the inferiority of non-white, male bodies as a subordinate masculinity. This subordination did not fully negate their masculinity since they were still able to exercise male authority in some circles, but it did reinforce their legal and social exclusion from full membership in the masculine identity to which white men could lay claim.

With such diversity, can the study of masculinity as a gender fall within the purview of feminist studies? The interdisciplinary, philosophical, and linguistic turns which helped give rise to masculinity studies and came to inform certain strains of feminist studies require a shift in terminology from feminist studies *and* masculinity studies to something which expresses a more fully gender-critical perspective. Deryn Guest argues that the label gender studies helps capture this idea by highlighting the insufficiency of only focusing on the discourses which create and control female bodies without simultaneously accounting for how these same discourses create and control male bodies.[14] This methodological double vision will also help me account for how the subordinate masculinities explored in the following chapters blur the lines between masculine and feminine.

Yet gender studies did not just emerge from feminist studies or come to be its complementary partner. Part of the reason for this asymmetry is that much of feminist studies works to give women the same status, and hence power, as men, but masculinity is not a monolithic category and oftentimes a man's identity has more to do with his relationship to other men than to women. Understanding the diversity of masculine identities and how they structure relationships between men is one of gender studies key insights. In imperial Rome, for instance, some men are taken as exemplary while others represent various levels of deviancy. A Roman senator in good standing had control of his own body and household and, consequently, was seen as manly (*virtus*); a gladiator, although physically powerful, had little if any control over his body and life and so was seen as less masculine. This emphasis on self-control as a quintessential characteristic of masculinity will resurface throughout my examination of Greek, Roman, and Jewish texts. Such a connection between being a man (*vir*) and dominating, or controlling others, rather than being dominated by them is a key theme in Roman imperial propaganda during the first century.[15] This is just the first of many examples which will be offered below to demonstrate that not only does male identity vary from context to context and across time, but it can also have multiple manifestations within a particular context since "masculinity, too, is a gender and therefore men as well as women have undergone cultural processes of gender formation that distributes power unevenly."[16] Interrogating the cultural forces which construct masculine identities and distribute power accordingly requires gender studies to take a multidisciplinary approach which includes postcolonial studies, critical race studies, cultural studies, and queer theory.[17] The benefit of this multidisciplinary approach is that it accounts for the fact that identity, which includes gender, is created and policed not only through attention to a person's biological sex but also through socially constructed discourses related to perceptions of race, class, and other categories which situate a person within a society.

Theorizing that masculinity, as a gender, is socially constructed and contextually specific led to further work showing that all bodies could be feminized, not just those biologically recognizable as female. Furthermore, labeling certain bodies as feminine serves to reinforce their social locations not just to make a statement about biology. This was an important step in perceiving the connection between power and gender and the regulation of this relationship in texts. Eve Kosofsky Sedgwick's point that female and male are not binary opposites but orthogonal, in that they are their own continuums which intersect so that a person could be high on one scale and simultaneously low on the other, recognizes that the use of feminine ideals becomes another tool for enticing participation in patriarchal systems.[18] A woman or a slave conforming to feminine characteristics, such as obedience, would be seen as proper or natural while those characteristics also served as "evidence" of their inferiority. To be a good slave (i.e., subordinate man) or a good woman required the person to fail to be masculine.

Judith Butler was one of the first and most powerful voices to make use of the way that gendered discourses police bodies and behavior as part of the constructivist turn. Butler's work, beginning with her seminal *Gender Trouble*, begins with the idea that gender is not an essential or stable part of a person's identity. Butler more clearly connects gender and systemic imbalances of power by examining the ways in which gender requires ongoing performance. One of the most significant results of this approach to gender is that overcoming misogyny, or any systemic power imbalance, does not require rallying around *the* female identity but misperforming female gender in such a way as to subvert oppressive discourses on gender which require female bodies to look and act certain ways. If women are systemically oppressed, as they are in any patriarchal system, then moving toward equality cannot mean conforming to such a context's expectations of the feminine. This approach builds on Foucault's notion that the power of discourses is to both create and discipline subjects, and Butler's insight is to refuse to fully hand *the body* over to the power of others.[19] By refusing to be the type of subjects required by a discourse, people could potentially negate the discourse's power to control them. Butler's work represents a dramatic departure from traditional feminist assumptions which defended the inherent value of feminine identities. Butler's work makes clear that gender is an effect of culturally bound performances and not a stable, ahistorical given. This requires distinguishing a person's gender from what could be considered his or her biological sex.[20] Butler's work also points to the subversive power of mis-performing a gender, which will be a key component of my analysis of Paul's portrayal of his own gendered identity.

Butler's insights about the performative and citational nature of gendered identities along with Sedgwick's understanding of how these performances contextualize both masculine and feminine bodies, form the main tenets of queer theory, which is one of if not they key methodological component of gender studies. As discussed above, within the purview of queer theory, masculinity and femininity are not inherent traits a person possesses at birth. Rather, these qualities are attributed as a body acts, or performs, in accordance with socially determined discourses. Queer theory does not stop at pointing out the arbitrary, socially constructed nature of gender discourses and the power invested in them. Rather, building on post-structuralist insights, queer theory points to the gaps in gendered discourses, places where assumptions conflict. In other words, queer theory not only points out that every individual exists outside the definition of normal, i.e., is queer, but also that the gendered discourses are not fully coherent and deconstruct under the right critical pressure. David Halperin argues that illuminating the mechanics of gendered discourses and their failure to form fully coherent narratives gives queer theory the potential "to startle, to surprise, to help us think what has not yet been thought."[21] For example, Chet Meeks and Arlene Stein utilize queer theory to provide a possible path beyond "normalization" or rejection as the LGBT community thinks about appropriating marriage without reinscribing the patriarchal baggage that often accompanies the institution.[22] Reconceptualizing the expectations and assumptions of bodies means that institutions that bring bodies together can also be reconceptualized toward more just and equitable arrangements. In other words, Meeks and Stein argue that queer theory's ability to interrogate socially inscribed and attributed male-female differences can help achieve more just and equitable unions for marriages of all formulations, even those deemed "normal."

The idea that there can be divergent understandings, or performances, of gender, both masculine and feminine, will be a key focus of this investigation as Paul can be seen doing masculinity differently, or queerly, by positively incorporating aspects of femininity. Ken Stone, one of the leading practitioners of gender criticism within biblical studies, lays out the contours of a gender-critical investigation by asking,

> What norms or conventions of gender seem to be presupposed by this text? How might attention to the interdisciplinary study of gender allow readers of the Bible to tease out such presuppositions? How are assumptions about gender used in the structure of a particular plot, or manipulated for purposes of characterization? How is gender symbolism related to other types of symbolism in the text? How does the manipulation of gender assumptions in a text relate to other textual dynamics, including not only literary but also theological and ideological dynamics? Which characters embody cultural gender norms successfully, and which characters fall short of such norms or embody them in unexpected ways? Might a character's success or failure at embodying gender norms result from strategy to cast that character in a particular light, whether positive or negative?[23]

Stone's questions make clear that gender studies does not simply determine whether characters perform a gender but why they perform and how this performance relates to the broader ideological intentions of the text.

Within the broader purview of gender studies, the concept of masculinity within the current study "refers to a complex of values and ideals more profitably analyzed as a cultural tradition than as a biological given: what it is to be fully gendered as a 'real man' as opposed to simply being assigned to the male sex."[24] To understand the process of gendering requires accounting for the ways in which the body and behavior function within the gender discourses of a particular context. Following Butler, I will argue that which bodies, physical or textually inscribed, matter and how they matter is not inherent within the body but depends on how that body's performance is assessed within particular discursive contexts.[25] Identifying which bodies matter and how they are assessed within a first-century, urban, Roman city will be the focus of a later section of the current chapter.

DOVER, FOUCAULT, AND THE STUDY OF MASCULINITY IN THE ANCIENT MEDITERRANEAN WORLD

The critical examination of ancient Mediterranean masculinity begins with the work of Kenneth J. Dover, who reappraised the assessment of sexuality and gender by problematizing the use of contemporary discourses of sexuality to understand ancient artifacts.[26] He accomplished this by offering the first significant critique of the static and binary frameworks of sexuality which modern, European scholars had imposed on classical texts.[27] For example, Dover examines ancient Greek texts and artifacts, mostly vases, in order to demonstrate that the primary concern for Greeks relating to sex was not with whom one had sex but a person's self-control and role as either the penetrator, i.e. active, or the penetrated, i.e. passive. A man's masculinity was not determined by whether he had sex with men or women, rather, a man's masculinity was primarily determined by his self-representation and self-control, seen in both his control of his passions and his ability to avoid the penetration of his body by either men or women. A man could have sex with women or males, usually free boys or male slaves of any age, without endangering his sexuality. However, if a man demonstrated femininity in action, sexual or otherwise, assessments of his sexuality could change. Evidence like this leads Dover to conclude that words like μαλακός (soft) were not descriptive of a person's sexual orientation, as is typical in modern thought, but of their inability to reflect an ideal of masculinity.[28] The susceptibility of a person's masculinity to corruption (i.e., feminization) and the relationship between masculinity and power meant that a man needed to publicly demonstrate his masculinity in order to maintain his gendered, and therefore his social, position. So although Dover's work begins with the modest aim of describing "those phenomena of homosexual behavior and sentiment which are to be found in Greek art and literature,"[29] by uncovering such divergent assessments of sexuality, his work ultimately serves as the initial overture in a movement which leads to a reappraisal of sexuality and gender in the ancient Mediterranean world.

Michel Foucault develops Dover's insights into the social construction of male sexuality by arguing that the history of sexuality is intimately related to power.[30] Foucault accomplishes this by analyzing the way power functions to construct and regulate subjects in societies through discourses which pertain to various aspects of a person. Foucault's first volume on the history of sexuality begins to treat sexuality in a similar vein as that in which he had dealt with mental illness, modern medicine, and discipline in his previous works. That is, sexuality is not something that is distorted or repressed by socially constructed discourses or is subject to the whims of taboo. Rather, discourses which appear to merely govern sexuality actually create it through describing the very body which they are to regulate.[31]

Foucault begins by investigating the sciences and institutions which created and regulated the idea of sexuality, but, later, he shifts to investigate how people regulate their own desires. This is why Foucault focuses on the Greek and Roman emphasis on self-control (ἐγκράτεια). This control became the goal for every aspect of life, including one's sexual practice, and was the normal state to which people should aspire. In male dominated societies, the normal is also associated with the masculine. The focus on self-control is the chief reason why masculine behavior was not determined by the sex of one's partner but by one's self-control in the sexual act itself. So, Foucault argues, there is no difference between having sex with a woman or a boy as long as the man maintained control, or the active/penetrative role, in sexual acts. A man could demonstrate masculinity while having sex with another man and a man could demonstrate femininity while having sex with a woman. Matthew Kuefler demonstrates that, during the first two centuries C.E., the rise of the Roman emperor and the increased use of eunuchs, traditionally seen as effeminate, in positions previously reserved for men led to an increased focus on self-control in aspects of life that had not previously been the focus of demonstrating masculinity.[32] Elite men could no longer use military conquest and political power to demonstrate their masculinity which led them to seek other avenues for self-presentation.

Foucault's approach to Greek and Roman sexuality had an immediate and noticeable impact on the works of classicists.[33] David M. Halperin, in particular, developed Foucault's insights about the discontinuity between contemporary and classical constructions of sexuality. In "Why Is Diotima a Woman?," Halperin applies the active-passive hierarchy to Plato's discussion of erotic love in order to show how validating a woman as a legitimate object represents a radical departure from ancient Greek literature and philosophy (*Symp.* 201–12).³⁴ In the process Halperin demonstrates the viability of the Greek notion that "men are not born but made" and pederasty, as Diotima argues in the work, plays a necessary role in masculinizing the undeveloped body of the youth.³⁵

Foucault's model of connecting gender and power in ancient Greece and Rome, however, can be critiqued on several counts. First, Foucault relies too heavily on penetration without adequate attention to how the context of the act determines its implications for the gender of those involved in the act.³⁶ Not only were views on penetration more diverse than Foucault allows, but the implications of penetration were related to the age, class, and emotional state of those involved. A man penetrating a male slave could demonstrate either masculinity or femininity depending on whether the penetrator was overcome with *pathos* or maintained control over himself. Second, Foucault assumes too high a degree of continuity between Greek and Roman sexual discourses. One key example is the distinctive understandings of pederasty offered in Greek and Roman contexts. The Greeks saw the man-child relationship as the most natural way to instill masculinity in youths while the Romans passed laws which prevented elite male youths from being permanently feminized by sexual liaisons with older men. Plutarch, writing from a Greek perspective within the Roman Empire, provides a full-length treatment of the subject in his *Amatorius*, a full-length treatment of the question of whether love between a man and a woman is better than love between men. The dialogue is essentially framed as Greek versus Roman conceptions of love and propriety as characters discuss whether it is better for a man to be in sexual relationships with a powerful woman or with another man. Third, frameworks of sexuality which focus predominantly on penetration tend, almost by definition, to elide women. Though a singular focus on men is the logical conclusion of Foucault's model, it cannot account for important material and textual evidence which indicates a necessary role for the feminine and diverse forms of masculinity, particularly within Roman contexts.³⁷ This latter point will be particularly relevant for my work since Paul adopts feminine attributes into his portrayal of masculinity.

MASCULINITY AND BIBLICAL STUDIES

To a degree, biblical scholars have been engaged in the study of masculinity since they first recognized the presence of and differentiation between men and women in the biblical texts. Although these earlier studies can be important in their own right, the present review of scholarship will focus on work which engages biblical texts following the publication of Michel Foucault's

The History of Sexuality and the scholarship which develops and critiques his work. As I discussed in the previous section, Foucault's work represents a methodological turning point in the study of gender by furthering our ability to trace the relationship between gender and power as well as perceive more subtle manipulations of gender in texts and artifacts. Foucault's influence is particularly strong in New Testament studies since his second and third volumes address sexuality in Greece and Rome, respectively, and make an indelible mark on classicists whose work often informs historical-critical examination of biblical scholars.

Howard Eilberg-Schwartz was one of the first to examine masculinity in relation to biblical texts in *God's Phallus*.[38] He argues the provocative thesis that God's masculinity both inscribes masculinity as the ideal state and problematizes the masculinity of male Israelites. The issue is that "When a man confronts a male God, he is put into the female position so as to be intimate with God. . . . [W]hen Israelite men had to face God, their masculinity was made uncertain."[39] The intersection of God's masculinity and a heterosexual ideal resulted in the feminization of male Israelites and all Israel more broadly because it placed Jews as an object of love and desire by the supreme male, God. Eilberg-Shwartz's examination of God's control over the reproductive power of Israelite men through circumcision (cf. Exod 4:21–26) and how the feminization of Moses corresponds to his role as God's partner in leading Israel (Num 11:4–15) informs my analysis of Paul's subordinated self-understanding as one of God's feminized messengers (1 Cor 4:9).

David J. A. Clines closely followed Eilberg-Shwartz's work with an article examining the construction of masculinity in the character of David and has continued to work on masculinity in both Jewish and Christian texts.[40] Though his work evidences a close reading of the text with careful attention to the depiction of masculinity, Clines's inductive approach to the portrayal of masculinity means that his conclusions are never contrasted with other ancient conceptions of masculinity which could inform how the text was heard by ancient audiences.

In contrast to Clines, Michael Satlow works deductively, demonstrating congruency between Jewish and Greco-Roman conceptions of masculinity and exploring developments in Jewish conceptions of masculinity in light of the subjugation of Jews by Greek and Roman imperial powers.[41] The rabbis, Satlow argues, adopt the basic male/female antithesis and, like the Stoics, understand masculinity primarily through the demonstration of self-restraint. However, the rabbis understood the application of self-restraint to apply primarily to the study of Torah. Though the rabbinic sources Satlow examines postdate Paul by nearly two centuries, the anxieties over Jewish masculinity reflected in them as well as their process of constructing an appropriate

Jewish masculinity share striking similarities with earlier Jewish writers like Philo and Josephus. Though later Jewish sources cannot be used for direct parallels, they offer examples of Jewish men having to renegotiate their masculinity in the face of socio-political subjugation.

Daniel Boyarin offers a developed and methodologically robust analysis of conceptions of the body, sex, and gender within Hellenistic and rabbinic Judaism.[42] Boyarin argues that Rabbinic Judaism broadly avoids the high degree of allegorization and use of Platonic models of gender that are found in many Hellenistic Jewish texts (e.g., those of Philo and Paul), which allows rabbinic Judaism to more directly deal with the flesh (i.e., the carnal body).[43] Boyarin proposes a "generous critique" that can critically examine texts with a sensitivity to contemporary concerns without demonizing previous people and perspectives for failing to hold contemporary values.[44] This generous critique is effectively applied in Boyarin's ensuing work that argues that Jewish masculinity, beginning with trends in Hellenistic Judaism, developed as a more compassionate approach to women that does not simply envision femininity as failed masculinity as does much of Greek and Roman thinking on gender.[45] Judaism is still patriarchal, but it is a form of patriarchy that limits a man's power by placing him in a subordinate position to God because, in Judaism, God assumes many of the roles that Greek and Roman thinking reserves for the male head of the family.[46] This approach shares much with that of Eilberg-Schwartz, which I discuss above, since both understand the subordination of Jewish men to God as having left a profound impact on Jewish conceptions of masculinity, most notably the ability to positively assess the feminine.[47] Boyarin, however, goes further in demonstrating that Jewish conceptions of masculinity also developed in response to the various Hellenistic and Roman forms of domination.[48] Although Boyarin's analysis makes many meaningful contributions to the study of gender in Judaism, his portrayal of Judaism's more compassionate patriarchy overlooks the fact that it rarely empowers women in ways that makes them equal to men or operative outside the authority of men; masculinity might be softer, but it still dominates. In terms that I will develop in the following chapter, Boyarin understands Jewish masculinity as complicit, not subordinate, and, therefore, still able to participate in and benefit from patriarchy.

The comparative approach to the study of masculinity found in Satlow and Boyarin is further developed in Stephen Moore's and Janice Capel Anderson's edited volume *New Testament Masculinities* which serves as a touchstone for the study of masculinity in the New Testament and biblical studies more broadly.[49] Moore's introduction surveys the methodological diversity in the small number of studies on biblical masculinity which existed up to that point and contrasts it with the "emergence of a more unified methodological front in the study of early Christian masculinities" which characterizes the essays in the volume.[50] The volume's methodological uniformity largely follows a comparative approach to understanding masculinity influenced by classicists following Foucault as outlined in an earlier article they coauthored.[51]

One of the more exciting developments in this volume is the awareness in certain essays that some of the masculinities presented in the biblical texts subvert hegemonic forms of masculinity. Such subversive masculinities, however, are typically restricted to examinations of Jesus and the canonical Gospels. Anderson and Moore, for example, trace the way that the Gospel of Matthew's emphasis on child-likeness and abandoning possessions is "a reversal of traditional [Greek and Roman] hegemonic masculine values—indeed they entice the male reader/hearer with an irresistible reward for abandoning all ambition to head a household (19:27–29)."[52] Of particular importance is the way that the work in this volume begins to grapple with the way that the malleability of masculinities can be exploited by authors wishing to instill a particular vision for a community's life and practice. Jennifer Glancy, for example, argues that the masculinity of the Pastoral Epistles not only conforms to "a protocol of masculinity informed by contemporary codes of masculinity," but that it does so in contrast to the subversive masculinity of Jesus, John the Baptist, and the authentic Pauline Epistles.[53] Glancy's work, both here and elsewhere, highlights the way that some authors of the New Testament, particularly Paul, incorporate and elevate what would have been considered deviant behavior for men.[54] Glancy's argument that Paul reverses discourses of masculinity by extolling his physical vulnerability, i.e., his boasting of being beaten, coheres with the broader presentation of Paul's masculinity in the present volume. At this point, however, the language of hegemonic and subordinate are only loosely connected with Connell's work as outlined above and so lack descriptive clarity. Nevertheless, perceiving the discursive rift between a biblical text and contemporary conceptions of masculinity and working to identify the broader, ethical consequences for the original audience represents exciting progress which will be important as I explore how seemingly unrelated behavior coalesces into a subordinate masculinity in 1 Corinthians.

Ovidiu Creangă's edited volumes *Men and Masculinity in the Hebrew Bible and Beyond* and *Biblical Masculinities Foregrounded* build on the methodological advances and critiques and witnesses to the maturation of the study of masculinity in biblical studies.[55] *Men and Masculinity in the Hebrew Bible and Beyond*, the first of these volumes, brings together essays that examine the construction, instability, and deployment of various masculinities within the Hebrew Bible. The preponderance of these essays, following Foucault's insights, use the active/passive antithesis and the instability of masculine identities as the basis for identifying and analyzing issues of gender and power and demonstrate similarities between conceptions of gender in the Jewish texts they examine and the surrounding cultures even as those texts sought to retain various Jewish particularities.[56] Susan Haddox argues that the Hebrew Bible utilizes subordinate masculinities to portray key figures (e.g., the patriarchs and Moses in the Torah) which subvert the hegemonic portrayals of masculinity while concurrently developing a "Jewish" model of masculinity.[57] So although Genesis's portrayal of Abraham bending to the will of Sarah might present problems for his masculinity, the story manages to fix this by presenting it as obedience to God (i.e., a subjugated masculinity). Sandra Jacobs develops a picture of masculinity which shows significant overlap with the earlier work of Eilberg-Schwartz in understanding Jewish masculinity, particularly that of the rabbis, as primarily seen in relation to the dominant male in the universe, God.[58] As Moore notes, this type of masculinity is inherently "queer" since it subverts expectations of the hegemonic masculinity, i.e., any form of masculinity which promotes the inherent dominance of a particular ideal of masculinity over those who deviate from the ideal, found throughout both the ancient Near East and Greco-Roman world.[59] Though the Greek and Roman gods were capable of emotion, these emotions were typically directed to single people or to other gods. The idea that a whole group of people could be described in feminine terms and made the object of their god's love and erotic intentions places Jewish masculinity in a precarious position (e.g., Isa 54:5 MT but not the LXX, 61:10 in both MT and LXX; Eze 16; Hos 2:16–20). The most illustrative example of this is the Song of Solomon, which, according to Jewish tradition dating back at least to Rabbi Akiva, portrays God as a bridegroom in passionate pursuit of and possibly consummating his love with his bride, Israel.[60]

The essays contained in *Biblical Masculinities Foregrounded* do not pursue the inductive constructions of masculinity which contain the underlying assumption that we can or should uncritically adopt portraits of masculinity from the biblical texts. Also, the authors appropriate the language of hegemonic and subordinate masculinities with far more nuance, reflecting developments in gender studies which account for the multiplicity of masculinities within a single context, the ways which hegemonic masculinities control power and inscribe alterity in subordinate masculinities, and the way these power dynamics are institutionalized and reinforced through stereotypes and language. Susanna Asikainen, in particular, shows the interpretive possibilities of these categories as she explores the function of the Gospel of Matthew's positive assessment of eunuchs to encourage Christian men to embody a subordinate masculinity which will bring them into conflict with the standards of the broader culture.[61] By undermining the discursive practices which exclude eunuchs from positions of power and positively reinforcing their identity as one which others should imitate, Matthew not only opens the possibility of more just relationships between masculinities but, also, more just ways of conceiving of those masculinities in the first place.

The subversion of hegemonic forms of masculinity surveyed above demonstrate the ways in which Israel's traditions queer, or challenge, the dominant or ideal conceptions of masculinity as well as resist attempts to coopt Israel's worship of YHWH in order to reinforce hegemonic masculinities. In other words, the inherently feminine aspects of Jewish masculinity preclude Jews from *fully* adopting the hegemonic masculinities of the empires which often dominated the Jewish people. This final point will be important for understanding the shape of Paul's subordinate masculinity and the type of community which embodies it in their interactions with others.

HOW TO "READ" ANCIENT MEDITERRANEAN MASCULINITIES

The trajectory of the study of masculinity in biblical texts raises four key questions that I will address in the current section before moving to the details of masculinity in the ancient Mediterranean world, during which I will focus my comments on Corinth and other urban, Roman environments but will need to include a broader range of sources to fill out certain details. First, are concerns about masculinity restricted to elite texts and artifacts or do they pervade texts and artifacts that are more broadly accessible to people outside elite settings? Second, how diverse are conceptions of masculinity? Third, what are the consequences for a man whose masculinity deviated from the ideal? Fourth, how, if at all, are we to understand the importance of gender in texts that do not *appear* to directly address gender? Answering these questions is critical to the current investigation because Paul's audience is not predominately of elite social standing, which requires me to establish the possibility that such an audience would be able to perceive Paul's interaction with and renegotiation of masculinity in 1 Corinthians and understand its significance. The current section addresses these four questions and points to the scope and importance of gendered discourses, showing that gendered discourses pervade elite and non-elite texts in ways that indicate that most people would have the requisite knowledge to read their meaning and consequences. The remainder of this chapter continues to develop these ideas to show that conceptions of masculinity were widespread, pertained to behaviors that a contemporary reader would likely not naturally associate with gender, and that how one's gender was read had profound legal and social effects for the individual. The following section on the body and masculinity answers the question of how Greeks and Romans understood what made a body masculine or feminine (i.e., the gendering of the body) and how, beginning with conception and continuing through death, people perceived and conformed to expectations of gender. The closing section in this chapter demonstrates that these gendering discourses do not just describe bodies but arrange them in a hierarchy that bestows legal and social privileges on the masculine over the feminine (i.e., these gendered discourses form a patriarchy). Chapter 3 will examine how near contemporaries of Paul manipulate gendered discourses for specific rhetorical goals. Chapters 4 and 5 will highlight aspects of the language and rhetoric in 1 Corinthians to show that the text makes a conscious engagement with gendered discourses and that understanding how Paul's use of gender would have been heard in first-century Roman Corinth has significant payoff for contemporary reading and appropriation of the text.

The rules governing and consequences of public oratory provide one of the clearest examples of the power of gendered discourses in the ancient world. Aristotle's influence on both Greek and Roman oratory makes him a suitable place to begin.[62] Although Aristotle cautions against simply identifying a particular aspect of a person with his character (Arist. *Rh.* 1369a13–19), he does defend the use of stereotypes and description of vices to cast an opponent in an unfavorable light (Arist. *Rh.* 1356b30–34, 1388b12–1391b17, 1417a3–8). Yet Aristotle does not indicate that describing or even embellishing an opponent's sexual proclivity or gambling habits deceive the audience through rhetorical flair; rather, such practices convey the excellence, or not, of an argument by connecting it with the person presenting it and contrasting it to an opponent and his position. Embellishing was acceptable as long as it was done to elucidate the type of person making an argument because Aristotle assumes an intimate connection between the goodness of the person, behavior, and social position (i.e., of form and content). The apparent strength of such a connection can be more important than fastidiously working through each detail of the argument itself. In a comment on the requirements of diverse types of rhetoric, Aristotle emphasizes restraint since, "it is more fitting that a virtuous man should show himself good than his speech should be painfully exact" (Arist., *Rh.* 1418b14–15). Quintilian, at the beginning of his panoramic treatment of rhetoric, makes a similar connection,

> I am proposing to educate the perfect orator, who cannot exist except in the person of the *good man* (*vir bonus*). *We therefore demand of him not only exceptional powers of speech, but all the virtues of character as well.* I cannot agree that the principles of upright and honorable living should be left to the philosophers. *The man who can really play his part as a citizen,* who is fit for

the management of public and private business, and who can guide cities by his counsel . . . is surely no other than our orator. (Quintilian, *Inst.* 1.9.9–11, trans. Russell; emphasis added)

Combining the body delivering the argument with the argument itself means that ancient rhetoric was not just a matter of truth or fiction, success or failure, but a matter of ethics which includes the orator *him*self as an object for evaluation. What makes rhetoric true, then, is not some fact abstracted from the orator but the orator's ability to participate in and embody gendered discourses which equate masculine behavior with virtue, goodness, and truth. As Erik Gunderson puts it, "Truth's antonym is vice," or, building on the Greek and Roman construction of the feminine as the opposite of the masculine, truth's antonym is effeminacy.[63]

Although the majority of the evidence for understanding ancient masculinities comes from texts written by men of the upper echelons of Greek and Roman society to men of similar standing (i.e., elites writing or performing for other elites), there is a significant amount of non-elite literary sources and material artifacts which demonstrate similar gendered discourses that are found in the elite literature. Dover's work on masculinity, discussed above, began by studying depictions of people on Greek vases in order understand the social function of portrayals of sex without the intrusion of modern, moral evaluations.[64] Diachronic analysis of the depictions of bodies and acts further supports Dover's argument about the influence of gendered discourses. For example, Greek vases showing pederastic acts rarely show anal penetration because the youths in these relationships, conforming to Greek expectations of masculinity where the boys were taught to be men through pederastic relationships, were not supposed to experience pleasure while Roman vases, though less commonly depicting pederastic acts, are more graphic because the boys are assumed to be slaves or members of the lower class who could not grow up to be real men.[65]

The use of gendered discourses on items found in non-elite homes indicate their prevalence but does not necessarily indicate that they were understood by the people who owned and used the artifacts.[66] The prevalence and influence of visual manifestations of gendered discourses can be traced through both Greek and Roman settings and, as Davina Lopez demonstrates, often served as propaganda directed to the predominantly non-elite masses.[67] Lopez shows how including performances such as penetration, receiving tribute, weeping, and being held captive serve to conform the depiction of Roman bodies to masculine ideals while simultaneously feminizing and Other-ing the depiction of non-Roman bodies.[68] The combined imagery establishes a clear hierarchy which places the conquering, Roman, penetrating, male body at the pinnacle of power while showing the domination and control over other, penetrated, feminized bodies. The consistent use of these images in Roman Imperial propaganda points toward an intentional use of gender that could be broadly understood. This power dynamic fits the more nuanced expressions of hegemonic and subordinate masculinity discussed above. While public imagery within Roman cities could be seen by travelers, its main audience would be residents of the cities. Although the majority of the observers would find themselves somewhere between the hegemonic masculinity which was only attainable for a select few and the subordinate masculinity of the feminized Other, they would "read" these images as not-so-subtle encouragement to obediently participate in the system that supports the hegemonic ideal of Rome or suffer the fate of the feminized Other. The *pax augusta*, which is the genesis for the period of the early Principate defined by the *pax romana*,[69] captures this dynamic nicely with the offer to accept the peace of Rome or suffer military subjugation. This theme is manifest in Augustus's account of his military campaigns that "extended the boundaries of all the provinces which were bordered by races not yet subject to our empire. The provinces of the Gauls, the Spains . . . I reduced to a state of peace" (Augustus, *Res gest. divi Aug.* 1.26; Shipley). "Peace" with Rome meant subjugation to Roman rule, either willingly or through military conquest, and is depicted as feminization since the conquered people are no longer exercising self-control.[70]

The use of gendered discourses in the Roman theater, both tragedy and comedy, offers another important witness to the pervasiveness of gendered discourses and supports the idea that a non-elite audience would be equipped to understand their meaning and rhetorical effect.[71] Like the imperial propaganda discussed above, these plays were written to be decipherable by non-elite audiences. The use of these gendered discourses with little if any context shows how easily the playwright thought they would be understood as well as their power in communicating a specific point. Plautus, a Roman playwright infamous for the use of sexual imagery, has a slave insulted with the line, "When the soldier went out at night on guard duty and you went with him, did his sword fit into your sheath?" (Plautus, *Pseud.* 1180–1181). Such a joke brings together assumptions about the sexual availability of slaves to their masters with the shame of a man who submitted to penetration. Such an intersection points to the way that slaves were assumed to not be real men because of the actions required by their status. Plautus ends *Casina*, a comedy where a husband's pursuit of a young slave girl is foiled by his wife, with a call for applause that contains a complex use of the play's content that also engages the assumed marital relationships of the audience. An actor speaks directly to the audience and encourages the men to applaud as loud as they can in order to fool their wives into thinking that they appreciate such a story so that the men can continue to have sex with slaves and prostitutes without their wives becoming suspicious (Plautus, *Cas.* 1015–1018). The use of such discourses to engage the audience in what was might well have been a rather uncomfortable joke points to the prevalence of such ideas. Gendered discourses also pervade Roman tragedy. Seneca's *Thysetes* depicts the disastrous consequences when men are overcome by their desires and passions, seen most strikingly when desire leads Atreus to cook and feed Thysetes's children to their drunk father (Seneca, *Thy.* 4).[72] Atreus becomes a warning to the men in the audience to not succumb to their passions lest they are led to commit truly abominable acts.

Now to address the second question regarding the diversity in gendered discourses. One example comes from the depiction of pederastic relationships, mentioned above, that evidence changes from Greek to Roman contexts that correspond to changes in the gendered discourses accepted in each setting. More broadly, during the Principate, Roman authors frequently portray Greece and its cultural artifacts as effeminate and posing a political threat to Rome. The invective follows the logic that Rome's power derives from the masculinity (virtue, strength, impenetrability, autonomy, etc.) of Roman men. Livy comments that in comparison to Rome "no state was ever greater, none more righteous or richer in good examples, none ever was where avarice and luxury came into the social order late, or where humble means and thrift were so highly esteemed and so long held in honour" (Livy, *Hist.* I.11–12, Foster). Greek culture, on the other hand, is said to feminize men which is why the Greek cities eventually lost their autonomy and were subjugated (i.e., were penetrated) by other, more masculine, people. Plutarch highlights these suspicions in commenting that "the Romans used to be particularly suspicious of rubbing down with oil, and even today believe that nothing has been so responsible for the enslavement and effeminacy of the Greeks as their gymnasia and wrestling schools" (Plutarch, *Quaest. rom.* 273D).[73] In the same passage, Plutarch mentions that the anxiety around these suspicions was great enough to even prevent priests from publicly anointing themselves with oil because it might give the appearance of being too Greek.

The interaction of competing conceptions of masculinity demonstrates both their discursive differences as well as how those differences can be leveraged to attack the masculinity of others and brings the investigation to a third question about the consequences for a man whose masculinity failed to embody the ideal. The Roman polemic against Greek masculinity, discussed in the previous paragraph, offers one example of this as Roman authors sought to explain and legitimate their domination over Greece and its former territories. The conflict between Favorinus and Polemo, which I will discuss in more detail below, serves as another key example of these dynamics since it manifests the public and personal consequences of problematizing an orator's masculinity as well as how an orator could defend his masculinity. Favorinus's reputation and authority in Corinth were both denigrated by Polemo, convincing the Corinthians that Favorinus was not a real man and, therefore, should not be held in esteem or hold authority in the city. To substantiate such allegations, Polemo points to Favorinus's soft skin, lazy eyes, exuberant hand motions, and falsetto voice as indicating that he "surpassed in all wickedness all the wild beasts and evil men of his time, while surpassing the stupidity of all idiots in his generation" (*Phys.* 65, 1.280F). The removal of Favorinus's statue from Corinth is just one indication that Polemo's use of gendered discourses to undermine Favorinus was successful since it indicates the Corinthians no longer see Favorinus as manly enough to serve as a model to be imitated. The fact that the masculinity of his statue is the focus of his writing to the Corinthians further supports this reading. Polemo successfully convincing a general audience through appeals to physiognomy shows the flexibility and diversity of discourses of masculinity as well as the consequences for those involved. As is the case with Favorinus, a man whose masculinity was successfully problematized could lose his social and/or legal standing.

The consequence of being associated with a failed masculinity is broadly evidenced by the Roman anxiety of being too closely associated with Greek activities. Such anxiety appears in the limitation or avoidance of actions which resemble Greek customs and in the criticizing of a person or a group for flagrantly mimicking Greek customs.[74] The presence or criticism of facial hair offers one example. Hadrian's ascension as emperor changed a centuries-old custom of Roman elites being clean-shaven. Hadrian's beard began a century-long tradition of Roman emperors and elites donning Greek-style beards. The anxiety caused by the apparent imitation of the Greek philosopher king appears in writings ranging from Seneca's advice on grooming to Julian's satirical self-portrait in the *Misopogon* (Beard-Hater) and eventually caused the emperors in the fourth century to once again appear clean-shaven (Seneca, *Ep.* 5.2; cf., Julian *Misopogon*).

Greek authors living within the Roman Empire offer various defenses for a viable masculinity constructed with the tools of Greek culture. Plutarch is a prime example since he seeks to navigate the intermingling of the two cultures through Hellenism yet avoids collapsing them together. While I will examine the way Plutarch constructs his masculinity by restructuring how key Greek concepts are assessed in terms of masculinity and effeminacy, it is important to note how he utilizes the concept of *paideia* in his writing since this will also shed light on the instability of the Roman invectives against Greek culture.[75] For Plutarch, as well as many other Greek and Roman rhetoricians and orators during the Principate, *paideia* was not merely the acquisition of knowledge but the cultivation of the civilized man who establishes "the undisturbed peace in the household and in societies" (Plutarch, *Mor.* 146; 452c–d). In such a context, being able to control or represent masculinity was a potent political tool for self-promotion as well as attacking an opponent since non-men represented social and political instability.

Although the harsh rhetoric which Roman authors direct toward Greek culture and customs could be taken to indicate a clean separation between Greek and Roman cultures, the reality is far more complicated. For elite Roman men, knowledge of and engaging in Greek culture, and specifically the idea of Greek *paideia*, was a means to distinguish oneself as more masculine. Cicero writes of Roman citizens, even elite men, who don Greek attire and surround themselves with aspects of Greek culture when they are outside the city of Rome (Cicero, *Rab. Post.* 26–27). Publicly, the works of Homer and Plato combined with Greek-style physical training to mold upper-class youths so that "social superiority [would] appear 'natural' . . . rooted in the personal skills appropriate to superior persons."[76] In other words, demonstrating *paideia* was a method of establishing one's place among those men who wield political power and demonstrating one's masculinity, and thus functions as a badge of hegemonic masculinity. Yet this was a sign of masculinity that had to be performed carefully, lest it be seen as a sign of being too Greek (i.e., feminine).

The discussion of *paideia* has introduced the fourth and final question for this section that asks how to understand the function of gendered discourses when gender does not obviously appear in the text. As the above discussion indicates, the socially ascribed connections between gender and particular activities or ideas are so strong that gender can be discussed without ever being directly addressed. A helpful example comes from the prosecution and defense of Murena, whose acquittal evidences a delicate manipulation of the associations between dancing, deviancy, and masculinity without ever explicitly mentioning gender.[77] In the trial, Cicero defends Murena against Cato's charge that Murena is a dancer, a charge which Cicero refers to as "strong language and forceful prosecution" (Cicero, *Mur.* 13). Cicero refers to the charge of being a dancer as such because it is a direct assault on Murena's masculinity and, therefore, makes him liable to the political corruption which is the actual charge for which Murena is on trial.[78] Cicero rebuts Cato's charge by arguing that if Murena really was a dancer then Murena would naturally exhibit other feminine activities such as "soft living" and cowardice in battle (Cicero, *Mur.* 12–13). Cicero's point is that Murena cannot be guilty of political deviancy because that would mean that Murena's masculinity had failed, and, since there are no other signs that Murena's masculinity had failed, he can still be considered a "good man" (*virum bonum*) who would not be liable to charges of bribery (Cicero, *Mur.* 14). Gender is the point, even when it is being discussed through associated activities or ideas. The next section will more closely detail the connections between the body and masculinity.

THE BODY AND MASCULINITY

In order to understand the complexity of Roman thinking on masculinity, I will begin with what might appear as the most basic and natural site for determining gender, the body. This will provide a foundation for the next section that traces the intersection of gender, hierarchy, and power. Contemporary readers might assume that determining gender simply requires reading the body through examination of certain features, notably the genitalia. However, assigning gender in both the ancient and modern worlds involves the interpretation as well as manipulation of physical features, including but not limited to the genitalia, in coordination with varying and contextually specific expectations of what is natural and acceptable for each gender.[79] As Butler's work makes clear, these expectations produce a person's gender as the physical body performs or misperforms culturally specific gendered discourses. The physical body matters in determining gender and, therefore, placement within society, but how the physical body matters involves a complex interaction of flesh and context, of material body and discourse.[80] If gender was simply a matter of physical features, then calling a girl a tomboy or telling an adult male to act like a man would cease to make sense. These locutions have power because the gendered idea of a girl or a man is not just about the body but about how society expects those bodies to behave.

Greek and Roman texts evidence attempts to explain and determine gender beginning at the moment of conception. The two main views on this process differ mainly in their understanding of the contributions of the man and the woman but not on the elements which affect gender.[81] Aristotle proposes that the man provides the semen which serves as the active element in conception while the female provides the substance/matter, menses or menstrual blood, which is shaped by the active semen (*Gen. an.* 727a32–35; 729a20–33). He understands the conception of a male child resulting from strong, masculine semen from the man mixing with the warm menstrual blood of the woman. A female child, on the other hand, results from some combination of imperfect conditions (e.g., weak semen from an effeminate male or the woman's womb being too cold). The other view, known as a pangenesis and appearing more frequently in Hippocratic texts, posits that the man and woman both contribute semen in the act of conception (e.g., *On Generation* 8.1–2; *The Seed*).[82] Since women were assumed to be weaker and cooler, the female semen was weaker than the male semen and, as a result, had less influence on the development of the child (Galen, *De usu partium* 14.6–7; *De semine* 2.5). Some adherents combined this with the idea that semen is only released during orgasm to argue that the women needed to orgasm before the man. This would allow her semen to slightly warm her womb, so that when the man's semen entered her uterus it would not be overly cooled by her naturally colder body (Hippocrates, *Genit.* 4.2). The importance of temperature is crucial since cooler semen would produce a cooler, i.e., feminine child, either an effeminate boy or a girl.[83] Another implication of connecting the female orgasm to the release of the woman's semen is that women needed to orgasm in order to conceive. A Jewish text found at Qumran goes so far as to portray Bitenosh, Lamech's wife, successfully defending herself from charges of infidelity by describing a recent orgasm she had with her husband as proof the child must be his (1QapGen^{ar} ii, 1–17).[84] Both approaches demonstrate an application of the active-passive distinction as mapped onto gender and understand that the manipulation of masculine and feminine characteristics will produce a specific, gendered result.

The process of molding a baby's body to fit a desired gender continues immediately after birth. Soranus describes strenuous massages which are meant to contour the knees, back, buttocks, and head so as to "mold every part according to its natural shape . . . [so that] if something has been twisted in the time of delivery, one must correct it and bring it into its natural shape" (*Gynecology* 2.9.14; see also 2.16.32–33 for texts on massaging).[85] Although certain aspects of swaddling and care apply equally to both male and female babies, there are distinct actions appropriate for preparing each gender to develop according to the respective ideals of masculine and feminine. In both genders the left arm is to be swaddled for a longer period of time to encourage the dominance of the right arm, but swaddling the thorax differs "in females binding the parts at the breast more tightly, yet keeping the region of the loins loose, *for in women this form is more becoming*" (*Gynecology* 2.9.15; emphasis added). The shaping of the male body, as might be expected, focuses on the penis, including a process for "lengthening" the foreskin by pulling or tying with string (*Gynecology* 2.16.34). These texts frame the processes of molding the baby's body as restoring what has been misshapen, not creating an illusion of what was never there. A nurse could not, in Soranus's thinking, shape a feminine child so as to develop into a masculine child because this would be unnatural. As Martin notes, the concept of natural refers to the esthetic ideals of the upper classes, whose energy for properly shaping the child is motivated by an understanding that a child who does not appropriately embody their gender will be disadvantaged in both personal and public life.[86]

Molding and developing continues through childhood with an added emphasis on hardening the male in both mind and body. Galen discusses the job of nurses and those who care for the child as "schooling the body to good health and condition and at the same time schooling the mind to obedience and self-control" (Galen preserved in Oribasius, *Incerta* 17.5). Correctly maturing the male's body requires proper balance and timing between hard and soft as well as hot and cold. If the body is not gradually hardened it will remain soft and effeminate, but if it is hardened too quickly then it will not properly grow and develop. This is seen in Galen's justification for delaying a male's first cold bath until he is 25 since application of a cold treatment hardens the skin and would restrict growth by diminishing the heat necessary for masculine attributes (Galen, *Hygiene* 3.4). Girls, since they are naturally softer and colder than boys and are desired to remain as such throughout their lives, are only allowed moderate amounts of activity and drink which might raise their temperature thereby masculinizing them.[87]

The guidance of the body so as to fully embody a particular gender is also marked by anxiety over possible causes for failing to attain and maintain the desired gender. One notable source of anxiety is the treatment of the free born male, also known as the *praetextatus*, who is on his way to being a man but has not yet arrived. The discussion above notes that the bodies of developing boys were understood as feminine since they are soft and cool, but should these bodies be treated like other feminine bodies or did they warrant special protection since they had the potential to become men? Walters discusses the issue in terms of the "bodily inviolability" of a man which protected him from sexual penetration and liability to physical beating.[88] A *praetextatus* would wear a special amulet, a *bulla*, and refrain from certain gestures and styles of walking which would signal his availability for penetration, sexual and otherwise (Plutarch, *Quaest. rom.* 101, 288a; Cicero, *De or.* 3.216). A *praetextatus* occupies a sexual and social location more akin to a noblewoman. He is still under the control of another man and seen as part of another's household. While this status is appropriate for his youth, he must take care not to be(come) overly feminine otherwise this status will become permanent, preventing him from appropriating the status of a man. Seneca the Elder scorns the effeminacy of the young men and notes that they, "mold their voices until they are as sweet as those of women, in order to compete with women in the softness of their bodies. . . . All their lives they remain as weak and soft as the day they were born" (*Contr.* I, 1.1.8–9, 10). Seneca goes on to say that failure to attain the true form of masculinity has left them "men only in their lusts" (*Contr.* I, 1.1.10). The effects of feminine behavior during youth, therefore, could stunt the development of masculinity or permanently feminize a body even into adulthood. In fact, charges of youthful effeminacy, particularly sexual indiscretions with older men, are so common in political invective that they become a well-worn rhetorical trope.

Developing the boy into an adult male also requires developing the voice and mannerisms in order to perform masculinity properly in a way that demonstrates their superiority, control, and dominance. Quintilian directly contrasts his formation of oratory as a virtue (*virtus*) with those who expend great time and effort memorizing declamation but without correctly shaping the orator (*Inst*. 2.20.3–5). The goal is to shape what is naturally present, not change the nature of a person. For Quintilian, imitation without formation of the boy into a man is a "pointless imitation" and a "vain labor" and brings the youth perilously close to being identified as the lowest of all public performers, an actor (*Inst*. 1.11.3). At all costs, boys should be wary of using their voice in "a sing song manner which is the chief problem . . . in every school nowadays" (*Inst*. 11.3.57). If a boy adopts such a voice, or even uses it casually, there is a danger he could permanently feminize his voice, preventing him from ever developing a masculine persona and becoming a man in the public sphere (*Inst*. 1.11.1; 11.3.28). The suspicion of actors and their practices also derives from the fact that they can trick an audience into thinking they are something other than they are.[89] In fact, anxiety that non-men could learn the arts of rhetoric simply by studying textbooks like Quintilian's caused many authors to exclude key material. Even though these non-men could not actually become men, there was a fear that they could dupe untrained observers.[90]

Even after becoming an adult, a man's masculinity required constant maintenance and defense. Decisions about massages and bathing provide one avenue for maintaining or restoring the right balance of heat, increasing or decreasing the body's density, and manipulating the composition of the body by enlarging or shrinking pores which facilitate the release or retention of various vapors.[91] Whether a man chose a firm or gentle massage, before or after bathing, frequent or sporadic depends on how a person needs to manipulate the body. If a man's body is in danger of becoming soft, then repeated vigorous massaging will harden his body with the goal of returning it to its natural condition (Galen, *Hygiene* 2.3).[92] Galen's discussion of the effect food has on the body exhibits a consistent motivation to restore a person's natural, balanced condition;[93] honey is said to be beneficial for older men with lazy lifestyles but harmful for a young man who endures daily hardship (Galen, *On the Properties of Foodstuffs* 1.471–472). Galen's point in the text is to critique a simplistic approach to understanding the effect of food on the body which does not account for the interaction with substances like bile and mucous or how the food will react with the specific condition of each body. As with massage, the goal is to demonstrate the key traits of masculinity, control and protection of the body.

Cultivating and maintaining a masculine identity also requires the proper presentation and use of the adult, male body. A man needed to know which hand gestures, facial features, hairstyles, manner of walk, and sexual behaviors were appropriate since deviating from these norms would signal effeminacy. Seneca writes, "A sexually impure man is revealed by his gait, his gestures, sometimes by his answers, by his finger touching his head, and by the shifting of his eyes" (*Ep.* 52.12, trans. Gummere). Though these actions form a well-known discourse of masculinity as found in more elite texts such as Seneca's and the rhetorical training manuals discussed above, they are also represented in more popular settings such as the performance of comedies and satires as well as in public graffiti.[94] A character can defend his own masculinity by claiming, "I have absolutely no idea how to use a twittering voice or walk about in effeminate style, with my head tilted sidewise like all those pathics that I see here in the city smeared with depilatories."[95] The rhetorical effect of the actor distancing himself from accusations of effeminacy requires a non-elite audience to be conversant with the significance of these gendered symbols of voice and walk without requiring further explanation.

Physical demonstrations of masculinity could also involve the proper use of the penis. Although the requirement of a penis might appear obvious, the way the penis and testicles function in establishing or violating masculinity is far more nuanced and surprising than a modern reader might expect and will be important in discussing Paul's commands and limitations on sex (1 Cor 5, 7).[96] A congenital eunuch, like Favorinus, or one who becomes a eunuch at some later point is vulnerable to being assigned a legal and social status akin to that of a woman. Catullus captures this transformation by describing the reflections of Attis, a young man who castrates himself for the goddess Cybele (Catullus, *Poems* 63). Attis transforms himself from an elite male youth into a "spurious woman" and mourns the loss of the public spaces and social positions his now-departed masculinity had afforded him. Gardner's examination of Roman legal texts shows that even a man who becomes impotent through disease or old age is in danger of losing his masculinity.[97] The incorrect use of the penis could also bring a man's masculinity into doubt. Although certain philosophical traditions, for example the Stoics represented by Seneca and Musonius Rufius,[98] argue for a more restrained sexuality which confines both partners to sex within marriage, a man's sexual behavior was generally limited only by social position and quantity.[99] As long as the man maintained a dominant position during sex and his partner was of lower social status than himself, his masculinity was not brought into question and the social hierarchy remained intact.[100] It did not matter to his status as a man whether his partner was a lower-class woman or a male slave. What would jeopardize his masculinity was if he took a submissive sexual role, either to a man or a woman or engaged in sexual liaisons with a man of equal status. Also, since control of one's body was a primary characteristic of masculinity, having too much or too little sex could jeopardize a man's masculinity.[101] A man who was overly consumed with the pursuit of sexual liaisons, either with men or women, was liable to the charge of succumbing to womanly passions. A man was even liable to charges of effeminacy for excessive passion toward his own wife. Tacitus describes Otho as losing his masculinity when his passion for Poppaea Sabina, his wife, causes him to lose control over his own body (Tacitus, *Ann.* 13.45). Suetonius reports that Nero was able to use this excessive passion as a legal pretense for banishing Otho under the charge of being "an adulterer of his own wife" (Suetonius, *Otho* 4.1). The cultural logic at work is that Otho's passion impedes his self-control, which in turn threatens his status as *paterfamilias* (i.e., his masculinity) which, in turn, undermines the hierarchy of his household, thereby making it a threat to the stability of the empire.

The inspection of the male body includes any scars and injuries suffered by the body.[102] Josephus recounts Antipater's defense before Caesar where the former "threw away his garments, and showed the multitude of the wounds he had, and said, that, as to his goodwill to Caesar, he had no occasion to say a word, *because his body cried aloud, though he said nothing himself*; When Caesar heard this . . . he bestowed the dignity upon him; so [Anitpater] was constituted procurator of all Judea" (Josephus, *J.W.* 1.197–199; emphasis added). Although Anitpater's example shows a gesture succeeding because a person's past actions and loyalty can be taken as evidence of future action and loyalty. But scars can also speak to other aspects of a person's identity and character, or what I have described as masculinity. For as much as Quintilian emphasized oratorical skill, he notes the power of physical displays in swaying a courtroom by recounting Antonius's defense of Manius Aquilius of the charge of extortion:

> [Antonius] tore open his client's clothes *and disclosed the scars he bore in front, earned in his country's service*, and thus, instead of relying on his own eloquence, delivered a shock to the eyes of the people of Rome, who, we are led to believe, were chiefly moved to acquit him by the mere sight. (Quintilian, *Inst.* 2.15.7–8; emphasis added)

Aquilius's fidelity to Rome, a masculine quality, is imprinted on his body in the form of frontal scars (i.e., scars earned facing an opponent in battle as opposed to scars on the back which could signal retreat). The court acquits Aquilius since such a manly man (*vir*), with all the accompanying connections of propriety, is understood as incapable of such an unmanly act as extortion. But it is not just the presence of scars but, as Quintilian notes, their location and how they are received. Aquilius's front-facing battle scars are efficacious in his defense because they are located on the front of his body and were received in service of Rome. In fact, the assumed differences in meaning between front and back scars is so strong that Livy recounts how the presence of scars on the front and the back of the same body sends a crowd into an uproar because such signs were assumed to be incongruous (Livy, 2.23.4–7). Scars on the back were typically associated with punishment or cowardice in battle, both of which were problematic for a person's masculinity.[103] Philo recounts Flaccus beating Jews on the back with implements used specifically for lower-status individuals as a sign of Flaccus's degradation of the Jewish people as a whole (Philo, *Fla.* 75–80). Philo's statement also indicates that the act whereby a person received the scar matters just as much as where they are. Cicero's prosecution of Verres involves an telling scene where, after earlier referring to the aforementioned scene involving Antonius and Aquilius, Cicero asks if Verres would dare "show the people of Rome his scars—scars made by women's teeth, the imprinted records of lechery and foulness?" (Cicero, *Verr.* 2.5.33; cf. 2.5.3). Each example further testifies to the connection between the body, the character or masculinity of the person, and the consequent status and treatment. Furthermore, the rhetorical use connections between the body, performance, and masculinity, support my argument that Paul makes similar moves in 1 Corinthians.

A man's masculinity was not only based on his control over his own body but also on his ability to maintain control over the bodies of the people within his household. The head of the household, the *paterfamilias*, demonstrated this control through the exercise of *patria potestas*, a legal right which guaranteed him nearly unquestioned authority over the family's social, economic, and legal decisions.[104] Adult males who were married and had children could still find themselves subject to the economic decisions of their father. Though the image of the *paterfamilias* wielding absolute control over his household does not seem to be the reality for most Roman families, the *potestas* a father exercised over his household established a clear hierarchy, which paralleled the broader social hierarchy evident during both the Republic and the Principate. Dionysius of Halicarnassus records that these powers were instituted by Romulus to the first generation of Roman fathers and that the severity of paternal authority was necessary to "restrain the folly of youth and . . . to give self-control to those who have been heedless of all that is honourable" (*Ant. rom.* 2.26.2–4, Cary). By locating *patera potestas* in Rome's storied beginnings, adherence to this authority and the social hierarchy it maintained became a form of *pietas*, a discursive symbol which represents fidelity to all that makes Rome superior to other people.[105] In fact, the evidence suggests that the more extreme rights of *patria potestas* were only used when the father acted on behalf of Rome or a family member had threatened the stability of Rome.[106]

Furthermore, an attack or violation of the bodies within a man's household is a challenge to that man's control over his house and, therefore, a challenge to his masculinity. A slave's body, for example, could be penetrated or beaten by his or her owner, but any violation of the slave's body without the owner's consent was problematic and required the master's response in order to reestablish his authority over the slave's body.[107] The same dynamic appears in texts dealing with adultery. A cuckolded husband must reestablish his masculinity by dominating, either sexually or through beating, the man he catches with his wife.[108] An attack on a man's control over his household could also come from the members of his household, a dynamic which could lie behind the situation in 1 Cor 5 where Paul discusses a man sleeping with his mother-in-law. Martial, a first-century Roman poet, reflects this hierarchy and the fear of losing his position of power in the household when he says, "You all ask why I don't marry a rich wife? I don't want to be my wife's wife. The matron, Priscus, should be below her husband. That's the only way man and woman can be equal" (*Ep.* 8.12, Bailey). Plutarch expresses a similar idea in describing Fulvia as desiring to "rule a ruler and command a commander" (*Ant.* 10.3). Diana M. Swancutt argues that statements like those above reflect the instability of the gendered hierarchy in the household which produce the anxiety that a wife could jeopardize her husband's masculinity by upsetting that hierarchy.[109] A woman who seeks to dominate a household, particularly if it a politically prominent household, is portrayed as introducing chaos and threatening the Empire.[110] Pliny notes that a bad wife can ruin a man's reputation and "denies [the man] complete success as citizens" (*Pan.* 83.4). Since the structuring and stability of each household was, at least in theory, seen as reflecting that of the Empire, a threat to a household's structure and stability also threatened the Empire, a connection which was at the heart of Augustus's legal reforms in 18 B.C.E. of marriage (*lex Julia de maritandis ordinibus*) and adultery (*lex Julia de adulteriis*).[111]

The bodies of adult women were also subject to standards of appearance and behavior which correlate to their position in the family and, therefore, Roman society as a whole. Judith Lynn Sebesta demonstrates that the woman's body came under heightened scrutiny following Augustus's moral reforms and use of the female body as political propaganda.[112] Augustus framed these reforms as devotion (*pietas*) to the moral values which led to Rome's dominance but where abandoned during the latter years of the Republic, leading to social and political instability. Rather than relegating a woman's place to the private sphere as was common in Greek culture, Augustus's reforms brought women into the public sphere as the *custo domi* (preserver of the household). This status required her to publicly embody the characteristics of chastity and restraint, both sexually and socially, through submission to her husband. This was demonstrated by covering of the body with a white *stola*, braiding the hair with woolen bands (*vittae*), not being overly consumed by luxury items such as perfumes and foreign food, and proper behavior at public gatherings. These symbols transformed the wife into a physical representation of her husband's masculinity. Violations of dress and behavior, then, represent a threat to his control over his household and, therefore, the stability of the Empire.[113] Valerius Maximus reports that Sulpicius Gallus divorces his wife after she goes "about publicly with an uncovered head" and that her actions are "to be associated with suspicion and culpability" (Valerius Maximus, *Memorable Deeds and Sayings* 6.3.10). In fact, in an earlier period a woman's body was so commodified as her husband's property that seeing a woman naked could be prosecuted as stealing property from the husband and an attempt to usurp his status over her (cf. Herodotus, *Hist.* 1.10).

MASCULINITY, HIERARCHY, AND POWER

The current section will develop the social and political implications of assigning the labels masculine and feminine onto bodies as discussed in the previous section. Masculinity, in Greek and Roman contexts, can be conceptualized as a series of pairs which follow a type-antitype pattern. In this pattern masculinity is the type and femininity, or effeminacy, forms the antitype. One of the ways to act like a man, then, is to not act like a woman. In order to determine what is masculine from what is feminine, the Greeks and Romans attribute gender to characteristics and activities in ways which often surprise modern readers. This system characterizes men as dominant, active, self-controlled, hard, hot (temperature), dry, and reserved in emotion. Women, needing to represent the other end of the spectrum, are submissive, passive, out of control, soft, cold, damp, and excessive with their emotions.

> The male is physically stronger and braver, less prone to defects and more likely to be sincere and loyal. He is more keen to win honor and he is worthier of respect. The female has the contrary properties: she has but little courage and abounds in deceptions. Her behavior is exceptionally bitter and she tends to hide what is on her mind. She is impulsive, lacks a sense of justice, and loves to quarrel: a blustering coward. (Polemo, *Physiognomy* 1, 1.191–94F)

Polemo's description of masculine and feminine proceeds in terms of ethics and behavior with only brief mention of what could be considered a biological manifestation of gender. As discussed above, these characteristics even apply to the conditions of conception. Galen comments that a male child is conceived only from a masculine environment, when the womb has sufficient heat to coagulate the seed from both the mother and father together (Galen, *De usu partium* 14.6–7; for a parallel account of seeds in animals and plants which follows a similar pattern see Galen, *Nat. Fac.* 1.6). The father's masculinity was also thought to influence the masculinity or effeminacy of the child.[114] A father whose conduct in public and during intercourse displays self-control and dominance (i.e., displays masculine characteristics) will produce masculine children. One consequence of such descriptions is that, from the moments of conception, the male is associated with the normal and socially superior while female becomes the abnormal and socially inferior; a woman, then, is a failed man.[115] Another consequence is that males who do not exemplify masculine characteristics or who appear feminine are failed men and unable to assume the full identity of a man.

This dynamic is evident throughout the work of Polemo, an orator during the second century whose writing will resurface in my discussion of Favorinus, and other treatments of physiognomy which study physical characteristics in order to determine whether the masculine or feminine dominate in a person. The labels of masculine and feminine, however, are not just descriptive but carry prescriptive power and influence a person's position in society. The power of such connections is seen in the discussion of physiognomy which can be traced back to Aristotle and reaches a heightened state during the Principate.[116] Polemo's comments are illustrative:

> You may obtain physiognomic indications of masculinity and femininity from your subject's glance, movement, and voice, and then, from among these signs, compare one with another until you determine to your satisfaction which of the two sexes prevails. For in the masculine there is something feminine to be found, and in the feminine something masculine, but the name masculine or feminine is assigned according to which of the two prevail. (Polemo, *Phys.*, 2, 1.192F)

Notice that Polemo is aware that there is not a firm distinction between masculine and feminine. Yet this blurring does not prevent a judgment about whether masculine or feminine prevail. A trained eye can weigh the signs and label the body. This labeling, as noted above, carries particular judgments about the person. A man labeled as feminine for his walk or love of dancing would be liable to other feminine characteristics such as passivity which indicates an inability to defend oneself, one's home, and the country.[117] The public and political consequences of such labeling have been thoroughly documented and show the anxiety over and socio-political consequences for a man being perceived as feminine.[118]

Even though the details of masculinity differ, distinguishing bodies as masculine or feminine based on a distinction of active-passive or control-uncontrolled functions in connection with social norms to form a gendered hierarchy. This hierarchy places some men at the apex of power by defining them as the ideal of masculinity, non-ideal men and elite women occupy a middle position, and women, slaves, and all lower-class men occupy the bottom position.[119] The result is a pyramid where the top represents a concentration of power in the smallest group comprised exclusively of elite men. The result is a form of hegemonic masculinity, as defined by Connell, which coopts social norms and the idea of nature to limit access to masculinity and simultaneously attribute it a disproportionate amount of social and legal power.

At the top of the Roman gender hierarchy is the *vir*. While *vir* can be translated as man, it more precisely defines an adult, freeborn, Roman, male citizen who maintains good social standing by demonstrating appropriate masculine characteristics.[120] The connection between *vir* and *virtus* (virtue) is not accidental and shows that virtue is an inherently masculine characteristic (e.g., Cicero, *Sest.* 93; Virgil, *Aen.* 1.566–7). But the appropriate external features, whether biologic or social, are not themselves the point; rather, their importance lies in their ability to indicate the type of person. A man is not just a body with a penis but a person who demonstrates the masculine characteristics necessary to rule his household, govern society, and maintain social stability. The tension between the external and the internal features can be found in the writing of Seneca, who can encourage the examination of a man's external appearance to discern his character (*Ep.* 52.12–14) while also emphasizing the need to avoid confusing the external façade constructed by some men for their actually being a *vir* (*Prov.* 6, 2–5; cf. Cicero, *Off.* 1.129).

A man's failure to embody the virtues of a *vir* could be used to attack his political position or prove his guilt in a crime. For example, during the struggle for control following the assassination of Julius Caesar, Antony and Octavian were each accused of sexual excess and luxury in order to portray them as effeminate and unable to lead the empire.[121] These attacks on an opponent's virtue build on the logic that "[t]hose who could not govern themselves, whose desires were uncontrollable . . . were not fit to control the state."[122] I need to emphasize that what a modern reader would consider the primary, or even exclusive, determining factor of the masculine gender, biological sex, is only one facet of the gendered category *vir*. This is especially true for men whose jobs were in the public eye since one of the more expedient ways to depose a rival or gain political standing was to ferret out effeminate men who did not belong in public office. Cicero exhorts his son to emulate the characteristics of honesty and impartiality consistently even if judging the case of a friend, in order to show himself to be a man (*vir*) by controlling his emotions and consistently working for the best interests of society (*Off.* 3.43–44). Cicero's instructions also emphasize that failing to keep the public's interest was not just a moral failure but a collapse of masculinity which would threaten the person's status as a man and the other social powers that that title provides.[123] Disparaging a man's masculinity would cause him to slip down the gendered hierarchy and take the position closer to that of a woman. As I will discuss in the next chapter, Favorinus's questionable masculinity lies at the heart of the political attacks leveled against him by Lucian and Aristides.

Men who cannot fully demonstrate the ideals of the *vir* are *homines*. The semantic change is not, however, just a matter of language but representative of a separate socio-political reality occupied by such non-men. These non-men are seen as passive (feminine) in contrast to the active (masculine) "nature" of the *vir*. These men were seen as effeminate as much as they demonstrated feminine characteristics rather than masculine ones. The assumption is that active bodies are those which desire to act, or penetrate, while passive bodies seek out penetration. This is one reason why equating a *cinaedus*, a man who was sexually penetrated by either a man or woman, with the modern usage of homosexual or gay is so problematic;[124] a man who had sex with other men could still be a *vir*, and not a *cinaedus*, as long as he played the active or penetrating, role (Seneca, *Ep.* 83.20). A *vir* is "able to protect [his] body from assault even as a punishment; the mark of those of low status was that their body was available for invasive punishment."[125] This distinction explains why Paul can avoid corporeal punishment by stating that he is a Roman citizen (Acts 22:25–29) and why being beaten is seen as lowering oneself and taking the position of a non-*vir* (*Dig.* 2.9.5; 49.14.12).

Those individuals who did not possess the status of a *vir* were governed by different legal standards. Certain elite women (*matron*) were able to operate with similar freedoms as freeborn boys (*praetextatus*) who are potential *viri*. Unlike many Greek conceptions which see women as objects to be controlled by men and attribute little if any benefit to female sexuality or personality, Rome during the Principate saw women as embodying a vital, albeit subordinate, role in promoting the stability and greatness of Roman society. The protected status of these women as well as freeborn youths who are potential men can be seen in the laws which govern their sexual availability and call for the severe punishment for any who seduce, attempt to seduce, or are accomplices to such actions (Paulus, *Sent.* 5.4.14). Similar consequences attend the rape or seduction of an elite woman; these consequences do not apply, however, if the woman has lowered her social status through previous acts of *stuprum*, that is, any act which threatens her chastity or the perception of her husband's control over the household (*Dig* 25.7.1).[126] In fact, prostitution was only a crime if the woman was from an elite family, and the punishment for raping or propositioning an elite woman was less severe if her dress did not clearly demonstrate her status (*Dig* 47.10.15).[127] In the same way that not all women's bodies were equal, not all men's bodies were equal. In the eyes of the law, the body of a male freedman, a slave who had been manumitted, was seen more like the body of a woman than that of a *vir*. The problem is that slaves, youths, and women have the potential to occupy similar social and legal space. The need to distinguish, for example, freeborn from lower-status youths and elite from lower-class women led to the use of particular styles of dress, articles of clothing, and the use of amulets to indicate a body's gender and, hence, how it should be treated (Plutarch, *Quaest. rom.* 101, 288).[128]

As discussed above, there was not uniform acceptance of such systems of assessing masculinity, a tension which was exacerbated by a "crisis of masculinity" during the first three centuries C.E.[129] This crisis resulted from men having to adjust their masculinity in light of the emperor's status and power. No longer could an elite man rely on amassing wealth and political power as a means of demonstrating his masculinity since these could be perceived as threats to the emperor and result in exile or death. Furthermore, Roman society was restructured with the emperor as the headman. This forced all other men to take subordinate positions below the emperor. Furthermore, people who had previously been assessed as non-men and, therefore, excluded from positions of power came to dominate those positions. During the Principate, eunuchs came to fill political offices previously reserved for elite men because they posed less of a political threat than men from elite, established households. Eunuchs were not legally recognized as men, Roman law prevented them from taking heirs which prevented them from passing on property or titles.[130] As a result they posed little threat of forming a dynasty to rival the emperor's family.

Along with positions of political power, military service had been a key avenue for achieving masculinity for elite men during the Republic. However, the increased need for a standing army under the emperors, the lack of a political future resulting from such service, and military service no longer being framed as defense of Rome meant that military service was less desirable for elite youths.[131] Instead, these positions were filled with non-elite youth and foreigners, the very people who were supposed to be incapable of the virtues required of soldiers. Also, as the typical soldier shifted from youth who came from families with land and money to youths who might enlist out of financial desperation, the image of the soldier became less desirable and even detestable (Sallust, *Bell. Cat.* 11.7, 37.6; Cicero, *Planc.* 72). This discursive breakdown between the soldier and the ideology of the *vir* became so great that Augustus instituted reforms to the military to restore the *virtus* of the soldier. Richard Alston highlights this as one reason that Virgil's *Aeneid* focuses on *pietas*, particularly as a duty to the state (6.676, 875).[132] The *Aeneid* exposes Aeneas, its protagonist, to taunts of being a "half-man" and ridiculed as soft, liking luxurious clothes, and indulging in dancing, all things which feminize a man, yet Virgil maintains that Aeneas is still a true *vir* despite these characterizations (e.g., 4.215–17, 9.614–20).[133] A man could still be a man even if he did not fulfill all of the traditional discourses of masculinity. Written during the reign of Augustus, the moralizing intent of the work is clear in its direct references to Augustus and that expressing devotion (*pietas*) to him was a chief characteristic of masculinity (6.790–95, 8.675–80).

The Asiatic rhetoricians of the Second Sophistic, of which Favorinus was a member, are just one example of a group who sought to renegotiate their place in society by introducing new norms for masculinity. It is important to note that these attempts to redefine masculinity retain the basic active-passive framework along with the key concepts like ethics, freedom, and paideia which are associated with it. These authors also show a greater willingness to attribute positive, that is male, virtues to women. Plutarch takes up this issue at length in order to show that women, under the right conditions, can embody masculine virtues such as bravery, self-control, and governance of a city (*Mulier. virt.* 257C–D, 261D, 257E, respectively). Note that Plutarch does not elevate femininity in general since men can still be mocked for acting like women (246A, 258E–F). Rather, he argues that people beside elite, Roman men can demonstrate masculinity.

Hellenistic Jewish and Christian authors evidence a similar approach as they demonstrate that their group's values and history provide them a unique ability to embody masculinity, even as they redefine the contours of masculinity and effeminacy in ways which deviate from the general conventions of their day.[134] Attributes or practices which would otherwise feminize them are reconceptualized so as to demonstrate their masculinity. *The Letter of Aristeas* presents King Ptolemy questioning a group of Jewish elders on matters of governing, life and the Torah. The answers given by the Jewish elders shows how Jewish wisdom, even in those commandments pertaining to apparently arbitrary distinctions between clean and unclean, "were made for the sake of righteousness *to aid the quest for virtue and the perfecting of character*" (144, emphasis added). I also want to point out that the text participates in other gendered discourses, especially in its portrayal of women as weak and not able to demonstrate self-control:

> After listening to this man, the king asked the next [elder] in order how he could live amicably with his wife? And he answered, "By recognizing that womankind are by nature headstrong and energetic in the pursuit of their own desires, and subject to sudden changes of opinion through fallacious reasoning, and *their nature is essentially weak*. It is necessary to deal wisely with them and not to provoke strife. For the successful conduct of life the steersman must know the goal toward which he ought to direct his course. It is only

by calling upon the help of God that men can steer a true course of life at all times." (250–51, emphasis added)

Notice, again, that dynamics between masculine and feminine are couched in terms of domination and submission, ruling and being ruled. This is yet another example of the "natural" way a hierarchical gender structure reinforces hegemonic masculinity for some while confining others to positions of subordination. Nature makes women and weak men incapable of self-rule so it is only proper for real men to exercise control over them. These Jewish texts not only transform what would otherwise be a potential matter of shame, feminization throughout irrational limitation on what a man can eat, into an aid in demonstrating characteristics associated with masculinity, but they also evidence a broad acceptance of gendered discourses in the treatment of women and kingship. The apologetic pattern that seeks to transpose issues of Jewish particularity into the gender and moral discourse of the surrounding culture can be found throughout the text and also appears in other Hellenistic Jewish documents.[135]

Christian authors demonstrate a similar situatedness within the first-century gendered discourses. Brittany Wilson has recently offered a masterful treatment of Luke's portrayal of Zechariah, Jesus, Paul, and the Ethiopian Eunuch which demonstrates that not only do Luke and Acts interact with the gendered discourses I outline above but that Luke intentionally portrays these characters in unmanly ways. Demonstrating that Paul's first letter to the Corinthians also engages these gendered discourses will be the focus of my fourth chapter, but in the next chapter I will discuss alternative masculinities which are evident in other first- and second-century C.E. texts.

NOTES

1. For example, Gillian Townsley demonstrates how assumptions about homosexuality drive many readings of 1 Cor 11:2–16 without ever asking or defending the legitimacy of using homosexual as a category within a first-century text; *The Straight Mind in Corinth: Queer Readings across 1 Corinthians 11:2–16* (SemiaSt 88; Atlanta: Scholars Press, 2017), 62–79.

2. Cynthia Long Westfall addresses some of the disastrous results of imposing modern assumptions of gender and sexuality on Pauline texts; *Paul and Gender: Reclaiming the Apostle's Vision for Men and Women in Christ* (Grand Rapids: Baker Academic, 2016), 1–6. Her work represents an important step toward a more appropriate understanding of gender in the Pauline corpus that seeks to set issues of gender, the body, and power within first-century discourses.

3. Deryn Guest, *Beyond Feminist Biblical Studies* (Sheffield: Sheffield Phoenix, 2012). Elisabeth Schüssler Fiorenza, "Between Movement and Academy: Feminist

Biblical Studies in the Twentieth Century," in *Feminist Biblical Studies in the Twentieth Century: Scholarship and Movement* (ed. Elisabeth Schüssler Fiorenza; Atlanta: Society of Biblical Literature, 2014), 1–20. Susanne Scholz, "Second Wave Feminism," in *OEBGS* 1:242–51 (ed. Julia M. O'Brien, et al; Oxford: Oxford University Press, 2014).

4. As R.W. Connell and others note, this turn coincided with a blunting of the political edge which was a hallmark of the early feminist movement; *Gender in World Perspective* (2nd ed.; Cambridge: Polity, 2009), 32–37. 72–93, 134–51.

5. Judith Shapiro, "Cross-Cultural Perspectives on Sexual Differentiation," in *Human Sexuality: A Comparative and Developmental Perspective* (ed. Herant A. Katchadourian; Berkeley: University of California Press., 1979), 269; R.W. Connell, *Masculinities* (2nd ed.; Berkeley: University of California Press, 2005), 269–308.

6. Peter Filene, *Him/Her/Self: Sex Roles in Modern America* (2nd ed.; Baltimore: Johns Hopkins University Press, 1986); Peter Stearns, *Be A Man! Males in Modern Society* (New York: Holmes and Meier, 1986).

7. Todd W. Reeser, *Masculinities in Theory: An Introduction* (Malden; MA: Wiley-Blackwell, 2010), 2.

8. Judith Kegan Gardiner, "Men, Masculinity, and Feminist Theory," in *Handbook of Studies on Men and Masculinities* (ed. Michael S. Kimmel, Jeff Hearn, R. W. Connell; Thousand Oaks; CA: Sage Publications, 2005), 36.

9. Virginia Valian, *Why So Slow? The Advancement of Women* (Cambridge, Mass.: MIT Press, 1998), 125–86.

10. Karrin Vasby Anderson examines the way that Hillary Rodham Clinton was characterized because of her "aggressive" behavior, which was essentially no different than that of her male colleagues; "'Rhymes with Rich': 'Bitch' as a Tool of Containment in Contemporary American Politics," *RPA* 2 (1999): 599–623. Sheila Jeffreys makes a broader analysis of how fashion and the male gaze "hobbles" women even as they reach the top levels of the business world; *Beauty and Misogyny: Harmful Cultural Practices in the West* (2nd ed.; New York: Routledge, 2015).

11. Matthew Kuefler, *The Manly Eunuch: Masculinity, Gender Ambiguity, and Christian Ideology in Late Antiquity* (Chicago: University of Chicago Press, 2001), 37–69.

12. Connell, *Masculinities*, 45–88.

13. Paula S. Rothenberg, *Race, Class, and Gender in the United States: An Integrated Study* (2nd ed.; New York: St. Martin's, 1992), 454–55.

14. Guest, *Beyond Feminist*, 150–64.

15. Craig A. Williams, *Roman Homosexuality* (2nd ed.: Oxford: Oxford University Press, 2010), 145–50.

16. Judith Kegan Gardiner, "Introduction" in *Masculinity and Feminist Theory: New Directions* (New York: Columbia University Press, 2002), 11.

17. P. Essed, D. H. Goldberg, and A. Kobayshi, "Introduction: A Curriculum Vitae for Gender Studies," in *A Companion to Gender Studies* (ed. P. Essed, D. H. Goldberg, and A. Kobayshi; Oxford: Blackwell, 2005), 8.

18. Eve Kosofsky Sedgwick, *Between Men: English Literature and Male Homosocial Desire* (New York: Columbia University Press, 1985).

19. The connection between discourse and the creation and control of particular bodies is a key theme in much of Foucault's work; see part 3 in *Discipline and Punish: The Birth of the Prison* (trans. Alan Sheridan; New York: Vintage Books, 1995), 135–230. Butler's critique that Foucault pushes the constructivist argument too far can be found in her essay "Foucault and the Paradox of Bodily Inscriptions," *JP* 86 (1989): 601-07.

20. Note that even the binary pair male/female is a construct that Sedgwick and others consider part of a heteronormative framework. This framework fails to account for bodies that do not fit a clear male or female distinction, or the fact that even those bodies which might appear male could, for genetic reasons, later manifest as female. I retain the male/female pairing since it reflects both Hellenistic Jewish and Roman assumptions.

21. David M. Halperin, "The Normalization of Queer Theory," *JH* 45 (2003): 343.

22. Chet Meeks and Arlene Stein, "Refiguring the Family: Towards a Post-Queer Politics of Gay and Lesbian Marriage," in *Intersections between Feminist and Queer Theory* (ed. Diane Richardson, Janice McLaughlin, and Mark E. Casey; New York: Palgrave MacMillan, 2006), 136–55.

23. Ken Stone, "Gender Criticism: The Un-Manning of Abimelech," in *Judges and Method: New Approaches to Biblical Studies* (2nd ed.; ed. Gale. A. Yee; Minneapolis: Fortress Press, 2007), 192.

24. Craig A. Williams, *Roman Homosexuality* (2nd ed.: Oxford: Oxford University Press, 2010), 4.

25. Butler, *Bodies that Matter: On the Discursive Limits of Sex* (2nd ed.; New York: Routledge, 2014), 27–56.

26. Kenneth J. Dover, "Eros and nomos (Plato, *Symposium* 182A–185C)," *BICS* 11 (1964); *Greek Homosexuality*, (2nd ed.; Cambridge; Mass: Harvard University Press, 1989). For a detailed treatment of the transition from earlier views on sexuality, specifically homosexuality, in ancient Greece, which is critical of Dover and Foucault, see James Davidson, "Dover, Foucault, and Greek Homosexuality: Penetration and the Truth of Sex," *PP* 170 (2001): 3–51. Davidson critiques Dover and Foucault for oversimplifying the picture of sexuality in ancient Greek sources since it was the context of the act, not the act itself, which determined its implications for the person(s) involved.

27. Dover, *Eros*, 31–42; *Greek Homosexuality*, 50. Dover's examinations coincide with other works which argue for the modern, social construction of the categories heterosexual and homosexual; see Mary McIntosh, "The Homosexual Role," *SP* 16 (1968): 182–92. Much of this work references the work of Alfred Kinsey, who documented the fluid nature of sexuality throughout the lives of people in twentieth-century North America.

28. Dover, *Greek Homosexuality*, 79.

29. Ibid., vii.

30. Foucault, *History vol 1*, 3–13.

31. Foucault, *History vol 1*, 68.

32. Kuefler, *Manly Eunuch*, 37–104.

33. David M. Halperin, *One Hundred Years of Homosexuality: And Other Essays on Greek Love* (New York: Routledge, 1990); David M. Halperin, John J. Winkler, and Froma I. Zeitlin, eds., *Before Sexuality: The Construction of Erotic Experience in the Ancient Greek World* (Princeton: Princeton University Press, 1990); David Konstan and Martha C. Nussbaum, *Sexuality in Greek and Roman Society* (Providence: Brown University Press, 1990); John J. Winkler, *The Constraints of Desire: The Anthropology of Sex and Gender in Ancient Greece* (New York: Routledge, 1990).

34. David M. Halperin, "Why Is Diotima a Woman? Platonic *ERŌS* and the Figuration of Gender," in *Before Sexuality: The Construction of Erotic Experience in the Ancient Greek World* (ed. David M. Halperin, John J. Winkler, and Froma I. Zeitlin; Princeton: Princeton University Press, 1990), 257–308.

35. Halperin, "Diotima," 286.

36. Amy Richlin, "Not before Homosexuality: The Materiality of the Cinaedus and the Roman Law against Love between Men," *JHS* 3 (1993): 523–77.

37. Carol L. Meyers, "Was Ancient Israel a Patriarchal Society?" *JBL* 133 (2014): 8–27.

38. Howard Eilberg-Shwartz, *God's Phallus and Other Problems for Men and Monotheism* (Boston: Beacon Press, 1994).

39. Howard Eilberg-Shwartz, "Unmanning Israel," in *Men and Masculinities in Christianity and Judaism: A Critical Reader* (ed. Björn Krondorfer; London: SCM, 2009), 167.

40. David J. A. Clines, "David the Man: The Construction of Masculinity in the Hebrew Bible," in *Interested Parties: The Ideology of Writers and Readers of the Hebrew Bible* (JSOTSup, 205; ed. David J. A. Clines; Sheffield: Sheffield Academic Press, 1995), 212–43.

41. Michael Satlow, "'Try To Be A Man': The Rabbinic Construction of Masculinity," *HTR* 89 (1996): 19–40; "Jewish Constructions of Nakedness in Late Antiquity," *JBL* 116 (1997): 429–54.

42. Daniel Boyarin, *Carnal Israel: Reading Sex in Talmudic Culture* (Berkeley: University of California Press, 1993); *Unheroic Conduct: The Rise of Heterosexuality and the Invention of the Jewish Man* (Berkeley: University of California Press, 1997).

43. Boyarin, *Carnal Israel*, 3–9.

44. Ibid., 21.

45. Boyarin, *Unheroic Conduct*, 10–23.

46. Ibid., 9.

47. Ibid., 12.

48. Ibid., 95–97.

49. Stephen D. Moore and Janice Capel Anderson, eds., *New Testament Masculinities* (Atlanta: Society of Biblical Literature, 2003).

50. Stephen D. Moore, "'O Man, Who Art Thou . . .?': Masculinity Studies and New Testament Studies," in *New Testament Masculinities* (ed. Stephen D. Moore and Janice Capel Anderson; Atlanta: Society of Biblical Literature, 2003), 17.

51. Stephen D. Moore and Janice Capel Anderson, "Taking It Like a Man: Masculinity in 4 Maccabees," *JBL* 117 (1998): 249–73; Cline's essay in the volume is

the exception which proves the rule. Clines argues that "the Paul we meet in the New Testament is more of a man than we have been inclined to notice. His masculinity is pretty normal and, at least in the aspects I have been considering, not particularly culturally conditioned. But it is quite palatable, and it permeates the characterization of him." While some of the other essays, Jerome Neyrey's "Jesus, Gender, and the Gospel of Matthew," for example, argue the masculinity of a biblical text conforms to contemporary standards, Clines appears to assume an ahistorical masculinity by which he can judge Paul.

52. Janice Capel Anderson and Stephen D. Moore, "Matthew and Masculinity," in *New Testament Masculinities* (ed. Stephen D. Moore and Janice Capel Anderson; Atlanta: Society of Biblical Literature, 2003), 90

53. Jennifer A. Glancy, "Protocols of Masculinity in the Pastoral Epistles," in *New Testament Masculinities* (ed. Stephen D. Moore and Janice Capel Anderson; Atlanta: Society of Biblical Literature, 2003), 235–64.

54. Jennifer A. Glancy, *Corporal Knowledge: Early Christian Bodies* (Oxford: Oxford University Press, 2010), 24–28.

55. Ovidiu Creangă, ed., *Men and Masculinity in the Hebrew Bible and Beyond* (Sheffield: Sheffield Phoenix Press, 2010).

56. Ela Lazarewica-Wyrzykowska, "Samson: Masculinity Lost (and Regained?)," *Men and Masculinity in the Hebrew Bible and Beyond* (ed. Ovidiu Creangă; Sheffield: Sheffield Phoenix Press, 2010), 171–88.

57. Susan E. Haddox, "Favored Sons and Subordinate Masculinities," in *Men and Masculinity in the Hebrew Bible and Beyond* (ed. Ovidiu Creangă; Sheffield: Sheffield Phoenix Press, 2010), 2–19.

58. Sandra Jacobs, "Divine Virility in Priestly Representations: Its Memory and Consummation in Rabbinic Midrash," in *Men and Masculinity in the Hebrew Bible and Beyond* (ed. Ovidiu Creangă; Sheffield: Sheffield Phoenix Press, 2010), 146–70.

59. Moore, "Masculinity," 251.

60. The interpretation of the Song has been a source of debate and a significant issue in the book's acceptance. The final acceptance of the book appears to have occurred with the caveat that anyone who took the song to portray human love would have no place in the kingdom of heaven. The debate is recorded in Yadayim 3.5.

61. Susanna Asikainen, "'Eunuchs for the Kingdom of Heaven': Matthew and Subordinate Masculinities," in *Biblical Masculinities Foregrounded* (ed. Ovidiu Creangă and Peter-Ben Smit; Sheffield: Sheffield Phoenix Press, 2014), 156–88.

62. Allison Glazebrook, "Sexual Rhetoric: From Athens to Rome," in *A Companion to Greek and Roman Sexualities* (ed. Thomas K. Hubbard; Oxford: Blackwell, 2005), 431–32.

63. Erik Gunderson, *Staging Masculinity: The Rhetoric of Performance in the Roman World* (Ann Arbor; Mich.: University of Michigan Press, 2000), 5.

64. Dover, *Greek Homosexuality*, 2.

65. Marilyn B. Skinner, *Sexuality in Greek and Roman Culture* (Malden, MA: Blackwell, 2005), 265–66.

66. For example, just because I own a copy of *A Brief History of Time* does not mean that I understand the problems of combining classical and quantum mechanics. Own-

ing and understanding an artifact are two separate things. Stephen W Hawking, *A Brief History of Time: From the Big Bang to Black Holes* (Toronto: Bantam Books, 1988).

67. Davina C. Lopez, *Apostle to the Conquered: Reimagining Paul's Mission* (Minneapolis: Fortress, 2008), 19.

68. Lopez, *Conquered*, 26–118.

69. See Ali Parchami's discussion of the development of the *pax romana* as a tool of Roman propaganda and its relation to subjugating through military force; *Hegemonic Peace and Empire: The Pax Romana, Britannica, and Americana* (New York: Routledge, 2009), 15–58.

70. I will discuss the connection between Roman conquest and the feminization in my discussion of Josephus, below.

71. Williams, *Roman Homosexuality*, 35–40.

72. Cedric Littlewood, "Seneca's *Thysetes*: The Tragedy with No Women?" *MDATC* 38 (1997): 57–86.

73. Catherine Edwards, *The Politics of Immorality in Ancient Rome* (Cambridge: Cambridge University Press, 2002), 92–97; Williams, *Roman Homosexuality*, 62–95; 125–59.

74. Benjamin H. Isaac, *The Invention of Racism in Classical Antiquity* (Princeton: Princeton University Press, 2004), 381–405.

75. Ewen Bowie, "The Greeks and their Past in the Second Sophistic," *PP* 46 (1970): 3–41; Rebecca Preston, "Roman Questions, Greek Answers: Plutarch and the Construction of Identity," in *Being Greek Under Roman Rule: The Second Sophistic and the Development of Empire* (ed. Simon Goldhill; Cambridge: Cambridge University Press, 2001), 86–119.

76. Peter Brown, *Power and Persuasion in Late Antiquity: Towards a Christian Empire* (Madison; Wis: University of Wisconsin Press, 1992), 41.

77. See Christopher P. Craig for a helpful overview of the charges, apparent guilt, and politics surrounding Murena's trial; "Cato's Stoicism and the Understanding of Cicero's Speech for Murena," *TAPA* 116 (1986): 229–39.

78. Anthony Corbeill, "Dining Deviants in Roman Political Invective," in *Roman Sexualities* (ed. Judith P. Hallett and Marilyn B. Skinner; Princeton: Princeton University Press, 1997), 105–7.

79. Skinner, "Introduction," 3–4. Virginia Burrus, "Mapping as Metamorphosis: Initial Reflections on Gender and Ancient Religious Discourses," in *Mapping Gender in Ancient Religious Discourses* (ed. Todd Penner and Caroline Vander Stichele; Leiden: Brill, 2007), 2–4. Maria Wyke, *Parchments of Gender: Deciphering the Bodies of Antiquity* (Oxford: Clarendon, 1998). Emma Dench, "Austerity, Excess, Success, and Failure in Hellenistic and Early Imperial Italy," in *Parchments of Gender: Deciphering the Bodies of Antiquity* (ed. Maria Wyke; Oxford: Clarendon Press, 1998), 121–24, 137–46.

80. Butler discusses the importance of the body as the meeting of textual and material; *Bodies that Matter*, esp. 28–31.

81. Jan Blayney, "Theories of Conception in the Ancient Roman World," in *The Family in Ancient Rome: New Perspectives* (ed. Beryl Rawson; Ithaca, NY: Cornell University Press, 1987), 230–36.

82. Pieter W. van der Horst, *Studies in Ancient Judaism and Christianity* (Leiden: Brill, 2014), 8–11.

83. Thomas W. Laqueur, *Making Sex: Body and Gender from the Greeks to Freud* (Cambridge: Harvard University Press, 1990), 25–62. Corbeill, "Dining Deviants in Roman Political Invective," 108–10.

84. Pieter W. van der Horst, "Bitenosh's Orgasm (1QapGen 2:9–15)," *JSJ* 43 (2012): 613–28.

85. The text comes from Owsei Temkin *Soranus' Gynecology* (Baltimore; MD: Johns Hopkins Press, 1956), 84.

86. Martin, *Corinthian Body*, 26–29; Gleason, *Making Men*, 70–71.

87. Martin, *Corinthian Body*, 224–26.

88. Jonathan Walters, "Invading the Roman Body: Manliness and Impenetrability in Roman Thought," in *Roman Sexualities Roman Sexualities* (ed. Judith P. Hallett and Marilyn B. Skinner; Princeton: Princeton University Press, 1997), 33–37.

89. Corbeill, "Dining Deviants," 115.

90. Gleason, *Making Men*, 90–91.

91. Corbeill, "Dining Deviants," 114.

92. Galen, *Hygiene* (trans. R. M. Green; Springfield; Ill: Thomas, 1951).

93. Galen, *On the Properties of Foodstuffs* (trans. O.W. Powell; Cambridge: Cambridge University Press, 2003).

94. Gleason, *Making Men*, 67–68. Amy Richlin, "Slave-Woman Drag," in *Women in Roman Republican Drama* (ed. Dorota Dutsch, et all.; Madison; Wiss.: University of Wisconsin Press, 2015), 37–67; *Sexuality in the Roman Empire*, 330–33. Barbara Gold, "'Vested Interests' in Plautus's *Casina*: Cross-Dressing in Comedy," *Helios* 25 (1998): 17–30. Kristina Milnor, *Graffiti and the Literary Landscape of Roman Pomepeii* (Oxford: Oxford University Press, 2014), 191–98.

95. Kock, CAF 3.470, quoted by Clement in *Paidagogos* 3.11.69.

96. Foxhall, Introduction, 4–5.

97. Gardner, *Sexing*, 139–40.

98. The restrained sexuality taught by many prominent Stoics during the first and second centuries C.E. can be correlated with their arguments for equality between the sexes in other areas such as education. See Martha C. Nussbaum, "The Incomplete Feminism of Musonius Rufus, Platonist, Stoic, and Roman," in *The Sleep of Reason: Erotic Experience and Sexual Ethics in Ancient Greece and Rome* (ed. Martha C. Nussbaum and Juha Sihvola; Chicago: University of Chicago Press, 2002), 283–326.

99. Williams, *Roman Homosexuality*; 18–19, 177–245.

100. Myles McDonnell, *Roman Manliness: Virtus and the Roman Republic* (Cambridge: Cambridge University Press, 2006), 166–68.

101. Ibid., 169–70. Edwards, *Politics*, 85–86.

102. Glancy argues this point persuasively in *Corporal Knowledge*, 24–47.

103. Ibid., 31–32.

104. Wilson, *Unmanly Men*, 73–75. Richard P. Saller, *Patriarchy, Property, and Death in the Roman Family* (Cambridge: Cambridge University Press, 1994), 102–32.

105. Saller, *Patriarchy*, 105-09. Richard P. Saller, "*Pietas*, Obligation and Authority in the Roman Family," in *Alte Geschichte und Wissenschaftsgeschichte: Festschrift fur K. Christ* (ed. P. Kneissl and V. Losemann; Darmstadt, 1988), 393–410.

106. William V. Harris, "The Roman Father's Power of Life and Death," in *Studies of Roman Law in Memory of A. Arthur Schiller* (ed. Roger S. Bagnall and William V. Harris; Leiden: Brill, 1986), 81–96.

107. The body of a slave was understood as a piece of property, similar to "four-footed cattle which are kept in herds such as sheep, horses, mules, and asses" (*Dig.* 9.2.2.2; cf. 47.10.25 for a discussion of the sexual violation of another's slave). That the bodies of slaves were used sexually by their masters pervades literary texts (Horace, *Sat.* 1.2.114–19; Martial 1.84; Catullus, *Poems* 7.47; Musonius Rufus 12; Lutz). Seneca comments about a slave's sleepless nights, dividing time between serving wine and serving the lust of his master (Seneca, *Ep.* 47.7). Masters could even expect this sexual access to a former slave's body after he or she had been manumitted (Seneca, *Controv.* 4.10). Plutarch describes the use of amulets (bullae) for the purpose of distinguishing between sexually available slave children from freeborn children who are off limits (Plutarch, *Quaest. rom.* 101). Yet the sexual use of slaves still follows the gender hierarchy where the husband could seek out other sexual partners but his wife could not. The elder Seneca records a wife successfully defending against charges of adultery with a male slave by arguing that the male slave was in her bed only because the husband had invited the slave for his own sexual use (Seneca, *Controv.* 2.1.34–35). It was legal for the husband to use the slave's body for sex, but it was illegal for the wife to do so.

108. Apuleius provides an account of the sexual domination by the cuckolded husband, even it is while Lucius is in the form of an ass (Apuleius, *Metam.* 9.28). Martian describes a husband who looks forward to exacting this revenge on his wife's younger lovers (Martial 2.49). Horace provides a list of possible punishments for adulterers that includes being raped by stableboys or castrated (Horace, *Sat.* 1.2.44–45). Lysias, although writing in the 4th cent. B.C.E., offers one of the fullest accounts of a husband's defense for killing his wife's lover. The husband states that the man "had an intrigue with my wife, and not only corrupted her but inflicted disgrace upon my children and *shamed* me by entering my house" (Lysias, 1.4; emphasis mine). A similar point is made in the Digest that removes guilt and liability for killing a slave from a husband who catches his wife having sex with the slave of another (*Dig.* 9.2.30.1).

109. Diana M. Swancutt, "Still before Sexuality: 'Greek' Androgyny, the Roman Imperial Politics of Masculinity and Roman Invention of the *Tribas*," in *Mapping Gender in Ancient Religious Discourses* (ed. Todd Penner and Caroline Vander Stichele; Leiden: Brill, 2007), 35–37.

110. Sandra R. Joshel, "Female Desire and the Discourse of Empire: Tacitus' Mesalina," in *Roman Sexualities* (ed. Judith P. Hallett and Marilyn B. Skinner; Princeton: Princeton University Press, 1997), 239–49.

111. Amy Richlin, "Approaches to the Sources on Adultery at Rome," *Women's Studies* 8 (1981): 225–50.

112. Judith Lynn Sebesta, "Women's Costume and Feminine Civic Morality in Augustan Rome," *Gender and History* vol. 9 (1997): 529–41. See also Molly Myerowitz Levine, "The Gendered Grammar of Ancient Mediterranean Hair," in *Off with Her Head!: The Denial of Women's Identity in Myth, Religion, and Culture* (ed. Howard Eilberg-Schwartz and Wendy Doniger; Berkeley: University of California Press, 1995), 102-05. Anne Carson, "Putting Her in Her Place: Women, Dirt, Desire," in *When Men were Men* (ed. by Lin Foxhall and John Salmon; New York: Routledge, 1998), 135–69. L. William Countryman, *Dirt, Greed, & Sex: Sexual Ethics in the New Testament and Their Implications for Today* (Philadelphia: Fortress, 1988), 147–67.

113. Susan Fischler, "Imperial Cult: Engendering the Cosmos," in *When Men Were Men: Masculinity, Power and Identity in Classical Antiquity* (ed. Lin Foxhall and John Salmon; New York: Routledge, 1998), 169–71.

114. Kuefler, *Manly Eunuch*, 28–29.

115. See the discussion in Peter Brown, *The Body and Society: Men, Women, and Sexual Renunciation in Early Christianity* (New York: Columbia University Press, 1988), 9–11.

116. Maud W. Gleason, "The Semiotics of Gender: Physiognomy and Self-Fashioning in the Second Century C.E.," in *Before Sexuality: The Construction of Erotic Experience in the Ancient Greek World* (ed. David M. Halperin, John J. Winkler, and Froma I. Zeitlin; Princeton: Princeton University Press, 1990), 389–416; idem, *Making Men: Sophists and Self-Presentation in Ancient Rome* (Princeton: Princeton University Press, 1995).

117. Corbeill, "Dining Deviants," 99–128.

118. Amy Richlin, *The Garden of Priapus: Sexuality and Aggression in Roman Humor* (Oxford: Oxford University Press, 1992). Edwards, *The Politics of Immorality*, 137–72.

119. Holt N. Parker, "The Teratogenic Grid," *Roman Sexualities* (ed. Judith P. Hallett and Marilyn B. Skinner; Princeton: Princeton University Press, 1997), 47–63.

120. Walters, "Invading the Roman Body," 32. Brittany Wilson, *Unmanly Men: Refigurations of Masculinity in Luke-Acts* (Oxford: Oxford University Press, 2015), 42–43. Ross Sheperd Kraemer, *Unreliable Witnesses: Religion, Gender, and History in Greco-Roman Mediterranean* (Oxford: Oxford University Press, 2011), 12–13. Francesco Santoro L'Hoir, *The Rhetoric of Gender Terms: 'Man,' 'Woman,' and the Portrayal of Character in Latin Prose* (Leiden: Brill, 1992).

121. Most notable is Cicero's accusation that Antony took the role of bride and slave boy (Cicero, *Phil.* 2.44–45). Plutarch records accusations that Octavian was in the habit of sleeping with twelve men (Plutarch, *Ant.* 59.4). See the discussion by Judith Hallett, "Perusinae Glandes and the Changing image of Augustus," *AJAH* 2 (1977): 151–71.

122. Edwards, *Immorality*, 26.

123. Anthony Corbeill, *Nature Embodied: Gesture in Ancient Rome* (Princeton: Princeton University Press, 2004), 71, 107–39.

124. Williams, *Roman Homosexuality*, 139–47, 195–97.

125. Walters, "Invading the Roman Body," 38.

126. Williams, *Roman Homosexuality*, 104–5.

127. Bruce W. Winter, "You Were What You Wore in Roman Law: Deciphering the Dress Codes of 1 Timothy 2:9–15," *SBL Forum*, n.p. [cited June 2015]. Online: http://sbl-site.org/Article.aspx?ArticleID=277

128. See the discussions of the various styles and articles of clothing and how they used gendered discourses to express the social and legal standing of the body wearing them in "Public Dress and Social Control in Late Republic and Early Imperial Rome," in *Roman Dress and the Fabrics of Roman Culture* (Toronto: University of Toronto Press, 2008), 21–46.

129. Kuefler, *The Manly Eunuch*, 70–104.

130. Jane F. Gardner, "Sexing a Roman: Imperfect Men in Roman Law," in *When Men Were Masculinity, Power and Identity in Classical Antiquity* (ed. Lin Foxhall and John Salmon; New York: Routledge, 1998), 136–52. For an extended treatment of the increasing role of eunuchs during the Principate as well as the shift in masculinity their presence helped bring about, see Kuefler, *The Manly Eunuch*, 31–37.

131. Kuefler, *Manly Eunuch*, 37–69; Richard Alston, "Arms and the Man: Soldiers, Masculinity and Power in Republican and Imperial Rome," in *When Men Were Men: Masculinity, Power and Identity in Classical Antiquity* (ed. Lin Foxhall and John Salmon; New York: Routledge, 1998), 205–23.

132. Alston, "Arms," 212–13.

133. Eve Adler, *Vergil's Empire: Political Thought in the Aeneid* (New York: Rowman & Littlefield, 2003), 220.

134. See the above discussion in the section Masculinity and Biblical Studies for examples of how Jewish and early Christian sources adapted masculinity in light of changing socio-political realities. My work in chapters 4 and 5 of the present volume will argue that Paul's argument in 1 Corinthians engages in a similar process of renegotiation of masculinity.

135. John M. Barclay, *Jews in the Mediterranean Diaspora: From Alexander to Trajan (323 B.C.E.–117 C.E.)* (Edinburgh: T&T Clark, 1996).

Chapter Three

Reconstructed Masculinity

The previous chapter examined the way Roman society during the Principate conceived of gender, specifically in terms of a dominant form of masculinity, and distributed power according to a person's ability or failure to attain to that masculinity. The current chapter will build on these insights by more clearly defining masculinity in terms of hegemonic, complicit, and subordinate masculinities with particular attention to the capacity of subordinate masculinities to function as sites of resistance and counter-narratives. I will first need to define the terms "hegemonic," "complicit," and "subordinate" masculinities since their appropriation in biblical studies typically lacks methodological precision, and are often used as vague descriptors of social dominance or domination.[1] I will then show how this power structure could influence a man's public self-presentation, his *persona* or *aspectus*. Finally, I will offer examinations of this process in the writings of Favorinus, Josephus, and Philo to show how each author engages in a process of reframing problematic aspects of his masculinity in order to transform what could be a subordinate masculinity into a hegemonic or complicit masculinity. The investigation offered in this chapter will prepare us for the following chapters, which will offer a more nuanced understanding of Paul's self-presentation of his masculinity and its social, political, and theological consequences for his Corinthian audience.

DISTINGUISHING MASCULINITIES: HEGEMONIC, COMPLICIT, AND SUBORDINATE

Hegemonic masculinity was first applied to the sociology of gender and sexuality in an attempt to understand the intersection of feminism, "men's liberation," and the development of gay activism.[2] In their original articulation of hegemonic masculinity, Tim Carrigan, R. W. Connell, and John Lee define hegemonic masculinity in terms of its political power and the ability to establish and maintain social discourses of gender which legitimize the dominance of a particular group of men and the subordination of men who fail to meet the ideal as well as women in general.[3] Hegemonic masculinity, then, is not defined by numerical superiority. Rather, hegemonic masculinity is defined as a form of masculinity which restricts social and political power through the manipulation of cultural and legal discourses in such a way that only a small number of elite men have access to any significant power.[4] Because hegemonic masculinity perpetuates the dominance of men, it is inherently connected to patriarchy and the subordination of the feminine, among both men and women.[5] The posthumous deification of Julius Caesar intensified the hegemonic masculinity of Rome since it further restricted claims to rule to those men who had familial connection to him.

To account for the numerical majority of men who do not embody the hegemonic ideal, Carrigan, Connell, and Lee also articulate the categories of complicit and subordinate masculinities. A complicit masculinity is a form of masculinity which, although failing to attain the hegemonic ideal by lacking key markers of hegemonic masculinity, nevertheless demonstrate enough masculine traits to participate in the patriarchal structures created by the hegemonic ideal.[6] Those men identified within complicit masculinities often vastly outnumber those men thought to attain to the hegemonic ideal and still benefit from the systems of patriarchy which the hegemonic creates, even though they are excluded from the zenith of social and political power.[7] These men might lack the proper pedigree or education necessary to hold powerful positions in society, but they are still the most powerful members of their households. Lower-class freemen of the Roman Empire, for example, can be seen as complicit since they hold some amount of political power and benefit from the subordination of women and slaves yet cannot hope to attain the level of political power available to men of senatorial and other higher ranks.

Subordinate masculinity, like complicit masculinity, represents a form of masculinity that fails to embody the hegemonic ideals, but, in contrast to complicit masculinity, men who fall within subordinate masculinity are so deviant, typically by the manifestation of feminine characteristics, that they may not fully participate in or benefit from patriarchal structures of power. This leaves out men who are labeled as effeminate and, therefore, incapable of occupying positions of power within patriarchal systems that idealize masculine traits as the good and ideal form of humanity.[8] These men cannot demonstrate the markers their specific context deems necessary to perform as a man (e.g., physical strength, intellectual ability, social status, financial means, etc.). Such men are labeled as effeminate and treated like women, holding positions at the bottom of patriarchal power structures. Attis, a young man who castrates himself in a night of drunken worship, laments the fact that losing his penis means that he also loses access to the spheres of power which provide men opportunities for political and economic advancement (Catullus, *Poems* 63). Attis is still a man, but his new effeminacy means that he is no longer masculine enough to hold or utilize power over others. Catullus signals this transformation by shifting between masculine and feminine pronouns for Attis after his castration and circumscribing Attis to feminine social spheres. As a subordinate man, not only can Attis not hold political office, he cannot even act as a man within his own household. This final point represents the key difference between subordinate and complicit masculinities.

The concepts of hegemonic and subordinate masculinities have undergone critique and revision since they were first put forward. The most salient critiques have come from a wide range of scholars but can be summarized in the work of Mike Donaldson, Christine Beasley, and Mimi Schippers.[9] Donaldson helpfully traces the origin of the term hegemony within the academic discipline of sociology to the work of Antonio Gramsci, something not done in Carrigan, Connell, and Lee's original article even though they implicitly draw on Gramsci's insights.[10] Gramsci develops the notion of class hegemony by discussing the links among politics, class solidarity, and the transfer and maintenance of political power.[11] One class, although being a minority in terms of number, can effect dominance over another through manipulating systems of political power and education.[12] Yet Gramsci understands that the spheres of politics, education, and economics coalesce to form a coherent, though not structurally unified, hegemony, or bloc, which forms the basis for a discursive ideal which then dominates groups that fail to embody those ideals.[13] Donaldson also makes an important critique of Connell's use of hegemonic masculinity in that Connell overlooks the structural breakdown of masculinity in certain settings, notably within evolving family relationships.[14] Beasely furthers this line of critique by arguing that Connell is too committed to structural stability, which prevents adequately addressing discursive violations of patriarchal structures, such as when a man who otherwise embodies a complicit masculinity adopts an egalitarian relationship with his wife within their household.[15] Schippers's work emphasizes the role of the feminine in constructing patriarchal relationships as well as the ability of the feminine to serve as a site of resistance of patriarchy.[16] By focusing on the distribution of power, Schippers effectively deploys the concept of hegemony to both masculinity and femininity so as to analyze the discursive formation of relationships within a given context.[17]

Connell and James W. Messerschmitt respond to the critiques cited above and, in so doing, arrive at a more nuanced and focused understanding of hegemonic, complicit, and subordinate masculinities.[18] In order to understand the creation and perpetuation of hegemonic masculinity, the focus must be on how the relationality between gendered groups forms hierarchies of actualized power. To be hegemonic, a form of masculinity must establish a legal or social precedent for its domination, not merely exercise dominance over other masculine or feminine identities. Ronald Weitzer and Charis Kubrin demonstrate that hip-hop music creates a hegemonic masculinity since it creates and disseminates a pattern of patriarchal expectations, legitimizing men's objectification of women and women's subordination, which men and women accept and embody as requirements for participating in hip-hop culture.[19] One key indication of this process is the marginalization and vilification of dissenting voices which transgress the established patterns of patriarchy. Weitzer and Kubrin examine female rappers who resist the objectification of women necessary to sustain the hegemonic ideal and note that they are censured and often portrayed as deviants.[20] Notice that this way of identifying hegemonic masculinity does not address numerical greatness or forms of dominance which do not establish rules or patterns. Rather, it focuses on how a specific form of masculinity creates a system that secures its dominance and reinforces the subordinate position of another group.[21]

The fact that subordinate groups have a degree of agency in performing in accordance with the rules which support the patriarchal systems which dominate them also means that they have the potential to utilize that agency in order to resist and disrupt those oppressive discursive systems.[22] Judith Butler's analysis of (mis)performances as subversive acts which demonstrate the arbitrary and tentative nature of gendered categories engages this dynamic and describes how misperforming gender can undermine patriarchal systems.[23] Increased attention to the agency of subordinate groups and the ways that agency functions within specific social and legal patterns highlights the need to understand the full range of categories, such as race or sexuality, which are also applied in order to define a group's subordinate position.[24]

The consistent logic of masculinization as increasing power and feminization as restricting power and, thereby, marginalizing effeminate men which is evident throughout the overview of masculinity in Roman literature presented in the previous chapter makes the categories of hegemonic, complicit, and subordinate masculinities appropriate categories to apply to the study of first-century texts. Although it was the emergence of gay activism as a response to the political, social, and legal marginalization of gay men which provided the groundwork for illuminating the presence and machinery of hegemonic masculinity, the framework of hegemonic, complicit, and subordinate masculinities can apply to any particular group of men "whose situations are related in different ways to the overall logic of the subordination of women to men."[25] I will most closely follow the dynamics of local and regional hegemonic masculinities since the authors I will examine operate within a single system which involves the direct representation of either themselves or an opponent (i.e., face-to-face). At the forefront of my investigation will be examining how an author represents the feminine and positions himself in relation to it. Does an author reformulate masculinity around his identity or does the author destabilize patriarchy by undermining its positioning of men and women? If an author undermines the current system, what type of system do they offer in its place? The authors examined below all engage these ideas in different ways as they renegotiate their own masculinity within the Roman Empire.

Although the nature of the discussion and sources require that I focus most of my attention on men, women and their perceived capacities or deficiencies as legitimate members of society and the household will play an important role in assessing the way the authors discussed below conceive of their own masculinity. This is because the ability to create and sustain patriarchal systems of inequality is one of the key features of hegemonic masculinity.[26] This means that destabilizing patriarchy is crucial for overcoming hegemonic masculinity and the oppression it legitimates. As noted in the previous chapter, one of the main critiques of Foucault's work is his erasure of women's identity as a legitimate, and not merely deviant, identity.[27] Attention to discussions of and treatment of women is crucial because they often serve as discursive windows into how an author who fails to embody key aspects of masculinity will legitimize his own identity.

(RE)PRESENTING MASCULINITY

In this section, I engage the intersection of gender, text, and authorial identity in order to demonstrate how pervasive issues of gender are in texts and how gender is at stake even when it is not directly mentioned. This last point is of particular importance since, following Connell's and Messerschmitt's focus on social relationships discussed above, I will argue that the construction of masculinity primarily happens through the analysis of social relationships which might otherwise appear unrelated to gender. As evident in the Greek and Roman literature discussed in the previous chapter, gender was not an isolated part of a person's identity but was integrated into how the person as a whole was perceived and located within society. As a result, I will need to attend to the how the person as a whole would be presented, viewed, and critiqued before I can focus on how gender functions in relation to the types of masculinity outlined above.

In Greek and Roman literature, the presentation or conceptualization of a person occurs through the idea of the πρόσωπον or *persona*. The term πρόσωπον functions as the Greek equivalent to *persona*, covering a similar semantic range and conveying the sense of the person as a whole through the idea of the face.[28] Though having a broad semantic range and complex etymological development, the Latin term *persona* functions as the Latin equivalent to πρόσωπον and derives from the idea of a mask with the function of demonstrating a character's role in a public performance.[29] It could refer to a mask, a role or character, a person's place in society with the expectations attached to it, or the person's individuality, and it could carry the legal sense of a person's rank or official status.[30] Understanding the significance of the use of a term for a mask or face for a person as a whole requires attending to the relationship between form and content which was a perennial issue in Greek philosophy and rhetoric. For example, Aristotle's argument that a speaker should choose the type of argument (i.e., form or rhetoric) based on what was to be argued (i.e., the content) influences Quintilian's understanding that the form of the orator (i.e., bodily deportment) must correspond to the content of his speech.[31] The connection between form and content also provides the basis for the physiognomic examination discussed in the previous chapter since the form of a person, or what is observable, conveys information that would otherwise be hidden to the observer. This is why Polemo can observe a man's walk (i.e., the form) and from it determine if the man could function as a man (i.e., content) in other settings (e.g., ruling a household, holding political office, etc.).

The usage of *persona* and πρόσωπον, however, do not just describe a person's identity in the abstract but, often, describe what modern sociologists refer to as a person's social identity.[32] By social identity, scholars mean to describe how different traits and descriptors coalesce to determine to what groups a person belongs, what status a person holds within those groups, and what actions are therefore permissible based on this status and membership.[33] In other words, social identity seeks to understand how a particular identity functions socially in relationship and often in competition with other identities within a particular socio-historical context. Henry Nguyen effectively argues that the terms *persona* and πρόσωπον convey these key aspects of social identity since determinations of a person's *persona* affect legal standing, social mobility, and social and political obligations within the Greek and Roman worlds.[34]

Nguyen points to Cicero's discussion of *persona* in *De officiis* as key support the connection between *persona* and social identity since it explicitly describes four different *personae*, how they determine the appropriate duties (*officiis*) of an individual, and their corresponding role in society (*decorum*)

(*Off.* 1.105–25).³⁵ The first *persona* is the ability to reason, which all people have the opportunity of performing (*Off.* 1.105–7). Although the universal availability of this *persona* appears to give it a unifying effect, Cicero emphasizes that people who abandon reason are "men in name only" and are indistinguishable from senseless animals that are controlled by their passions (*Off.* 1.105). In other words, a person who fails to don and perform this mask commensurate with their position in society will be excluded from any benefits which correspond to the position Cicero justifies such a statement in that reason allows people to determine what is moral and decorous in accordance with their position in society, abandoning decorum corresponds to abandoning reason, which thereby removes a person from society (*Off.* 1.107). The second *persona* is that of personal ability and physical endowments, among which Cicero lists speed, strength, appearance, wit, and eloquence (*Off.* 1.107–8). The point is not to decipher the best attribute since Cicero describes how each can function to benefit the individual and society; rather, as with the first *persona*, Cicero emphasizes the need to understand one's own attributes and how they position a person within society so he may act accordingly (*Off.* 1.109–10). The third and fourth *personae* Cicero lists are the socio-political circumstances of a person's family and his choice of profession, respectively, and includes everything from nobility and status to possible civic duties a person could pursue (*Off.* 1.115–16). As in the discussion of the second *persona*, Cicero emphasizes that a person apply reason in order to understand how nature positions them in society (e.g., noble birth, wealth, etc.) and what types of lives they may therefore pursue. Cicero brings his argument full circle in arguing that reason allows a person to evaluate their form (e.g., a noble-born man with intellect or a peasant woman) and pursue a life (i.e., content) that is appropriate to that form. Notice the use of the correlation between form and content or *persona* and social identity.

Cicero also discusses how correctly identifying the *personae* of others by observing their behavior and form allows his reader to judge how the behavior of others corresponds with or betrays a person's place in society along with the corresponding consequences (*Off.* 1.110–14, 118–24). Like actors who are not skilled enough to play the most eloquent or demanding roles, some people must take a sober assessment of their *personae* and play the less honorable parts in society with as little impropriety as possible (*Off.* 1.115). Cicero concludes this section by describing the different roles and expectations of magistrates, citizens, and foreigners, positions which a person can identify by the different *personae* just elaborated (*Off.* 1.124–25). The key difference Cicero gives to how these three groups should conduct themselves pertains to how they relate to political power and the running of a society where magistrates are in control, citizens support the magistrates, and foreigners are excluded. These categories and their relation to positions of political power closely correlate to the categories of hegemonic, complicit, and subordinate as reviewed in the previous section. Bringing together Cicero's comments on the different "faces" or aspects which coalesce to form a person's identity, the connection between *persona* and social identity appears justified since a *persona* situates a person in a specific social role which carries expectations particular to it. This also shows how a *persona* can be examined in relation to modern constructions of gender and power.

Cicero connecting gender and background in the determination of *persona* points toward a key connection between what contemporary readers would think of as ethno-racial background and gender. This connection assumes that a person will embody certain masculine or feminine traits simply by knowing where they were raised or their ethno-racial background.[36] Sallust offers a clear example of the application of this trope in *The War with Catiline*. Sallust first traces the origin of Rome's greatness to the mental strength and self-control of its founders and how it was passed on and instilled in each household by true, male citizens (*Cat.* 6.1–9.5). He then describes how Rome's men were corrupted by Eastern, feminine traits such as avarice and an insatiable appetite that characterize men from Asia (*Cat.* 10.1–13.5). For example, "Avarice implies a desire for money, which no wise man covets; steeped as it were with noxious poisons, it renders the most manly body and soul effeminate; it is ever unbounded and insatiable, nor can either plenty or want make it less" (*Cat.* 11.3). Catiline represents the zenith of this feminization and quickly undermines the morality of every Roman who comes into contact with him (*Cat.*, 14.1–7). Sallust, then, characterizes Catiline as a threat to the masculinity that established and safeguarded Roman domination, a perfect literary framing to portray Catiline's rebellion as a threat to Rome rather than the legitimate heir to Sulla's power.[37]

Despite repeatedly emphasizing the inherent nature of one's *persona*, Cicero and other authors evidence concern over the construction, practice, and loss of a *persona*, with a noted emphasis on policing elite status. After describing the different roles in society, Cicero immediately distinguishes masculine from feminine behavior, speech, and dress and warns his audience to avoid the feminine (*Off.* 1.128–32). If a person's role and behavior were indeed naturally given and inherent in one's *persona*, then there would be no need to give instruction on it since the person should naturally perform accordingly. Julius Caesar's regulation of clothing based on one's *persona* demonstrates the same anxiety as does Suetonius's placement of this detail within a list that represents Caesar's administration of justice (Suetonius, *Jul.* 43.1). Clothing is not actually connected to behavior but reveals a sociopolitical agenda based on Caesar's claims to justice. Augustus's legal reforms have a similar focus on dress and other symbols of status in relation to the maintenance and stability of the social hierarchy which are couched in terms of maintaining the "natural" order of the world (e.g., *Aug.* 40.5).[38] I will argue that Paul's commands for the Corinthians to behave in ways that are appropriate to their new identity, or *persona*, follow the same discursive pattern.

The proper embodiment and presentation of one's *persona* presents unique challenges for authors since they cannot rely on an audience's direct gaze to identify visible cues and they occasionally need to adopt different *personae* for rhetorical purposes.[39] Although direct observation functions as the most reliable means of assessing a subject's *persona*, the evidence shows that Greek and Roman audiences assume that the text provides just as accurate a presentation of its author where descriptions of status, actions, discourse, and the impressions of other characters serve to present the author's *persona*.[40] The assumed connection between who an author is, his or her *persona*, and what the author writes is assumed to be so strong that even genres which intentionally engage material outside of an author's lived experience cannot shield the author's *persona* from the audience's gaze. Cicero, discussing Greek poetry, asks, "Lastly, what disclosures do men of the highest culture and poets of supreme merit make about their own life in their poems and songs?" (*Tusc.* 4.71). In the same verse, Cicero goes on to note how an author's literary *persona* can reveal otherwise hidden details about the author's actual identity such as practicing pederasty or being overcome by love. In this example, otherwise manly authors are uncovered as effeminate. Authors could even be charged with holding points of views expressed by characters in the text and be thought to hide their own views behind the masks of their characters. Pliny the Elder states that Horace found eggs of a particular shape to be more appealing even though Horace was only relaying the view of one of his characters (*Nat.* 10.145). Especially relevant are Quintilian's comments that authors will hide their views behind the masks of characters and that he can unmask the author attempting such a trick (*Inst.* 10.3.1–2 and 10.5.2; respectively).[41] Here, a master of rhetoric claims to see through the literary mask of a character to the author who stands behind it. Similarly, we will see in Polemo an astute observer who can interpret the outward signs in order to determine if a person is masculine or feminine.

Greek and Roman audiences assume such a tight connection between what an author writes and the author's *persona* that authors were often held liable for writing about the inappropriate or scandalous.[42] Ronald Mayer reviews notable instances in the writings of Catullus, Ovid, and Martial where the authors' choice of subject material left them open to attack and critique by their readers. Furius and Aurelius take Catullus's descriptions of love and passion as indicating that he is effeminate; a charge which, as discussed above, carries serious social and legal consequences. Catullus responds with a stinging critique of their masculinity which includes the assertion that his masculinity is sufficient to dominate Furius and Aurelius sexually for an entire night.

> I'll bugger you and stuff you, you catamite [*pathice*] Aurelius and you passive man [*cinaede*] Furius, who have supposed me to be immodest, on account of my verses, because these are rather naughty. For the sacred poet ought to be chaste himself, though his poems need not be so. Why, they only acquire wit and spice if they are rather naughty and immodest, and can rouse with their ticklings, I don't mean boys, but those hairy old men unable to stir their arthritic loins. Because you've read my many thousand kisses, do you think I'm less virile on that account? Yes, I'll bugger you and stuff you all night. (Catullus, *Poems*, 16; Cornish)

Note how charges of effeminacy cause Catullus to respond with accepted demonstrations of masculinity which not only prove his masculinity but do so at the expense of his opponents' masculinity. Favorinus will make a similar move in defending his own masculinity. Like Catullus, Ovid's *Tristia* shows the author feverishly attempting to distance his social identity from that of his literary *persona* since Augustus has apparently read and condemned Ovid's work (*Tr.* 2.497–540).[43] Ovid directly references Augustus's gaze (*vidisti*) to make the point that since Augustus does not punish actors who perform indecent acts he should not punish someone who writes about them (*Tr.* 2.514–515), an argument which falters since actors were indeed liable to charges of effeminacy for the actions they portrayed. An author's liability for the perceived intentions or positions of his literary persona could even result in the author's death.[44] It is important to note that even as authors like Ovid and Catullus who attempt to distance their identities from the literary *personae* found in their writing, themselves never make that same distinction about the work of other authors; rather, they assume that identifying literary *personae* is tantamount to seeing the author.[45] The fact that this would then influence an author's position in society and hold them legally responsible shows that literary *personae* can be understood as influencing an author's social identity. The assumption that a text contains the author's literary *persona* and that this reveals the author's actual social identity appears to be an inescapable and, at times, a disastrous reality for Greek and Roman authors.

The benefits and dangers of an author's self-presentation, then, are pervasive and require authors to select carefully what they write and how they write it. This same concern appears in manuals on public oratory which warn students against impersonating the wrong types of people or lower forms of rhetoric. An orator or writer who could effectively present and wield a masculine *persona* would have certain social and legal privileges available to him. Conversely, and as is evident in the above discussion of Cicero and Ovid, an author who left himself open to charges of effeminacy could suffer the social and legal consequences associated with a failed masculinity. This connection between identity and masculinity is why Catullus responds by adopting a hyper masculine *persona*; by establishing or defending the masculinity of his literary *persona*, he can save his social identity and avoid the consequences of being labeled effeminate. The importance and consequences of authorial self-presentation help us better understand the gravity of Paul's disclosure of his suffering, his weaknesses, and his expectation that the Christian community would imitate him in such a scandalous display of downward mobility (e.g., 1 Cor 4:10–16).

But not all authors respond to charges of effeminacy or other critiques of their identity by asserting their masculinity by replicating the categories of the hegemonic ideal and attacking their opponents. Some authors compete for a hegemonic masculine identity by reframing aspects of their identity which can be read as feminine (i.e., weak) as sources of masculinity (e.g., self-control, social dominance, etc.). These authors leave the basic discourse of masculinity in place but switch what characteristics best embody it. Favorinus is representative of this approach as he defends his statue, and therefore himself, to his Corinthian audience and offers a new paradigm of masculinity while still leaving traditional assumptions about the function of a masculine identity intact.[46] Other authors take a different approach of defending against a failure of masculinity by presenting their identity as a complicit masculinity. That is, they do not compete for dominance but show that they support those in positions of power and that whatever feminine attributes they possess do not threaten social stability. As I will show below, Philo and Josephus are examples of authors who fall into this category. Philo retains an understanding of female subordination, going so far to deploy the "disease of effeminization" to men he feels have abandoned their proper place in society (*Abr.* 136). Philo's articulation of Jewish masculinity, as will be discussed below, is more appropriately categorized as complicit since it does not undermine the patriarchal system of the first century but fits Jewish masculinity within that system. Examining the approaches of these authors will serve to frame the radical approach of the Apostle Paul who leaves the assessment of his body as feminine intact and embraces that effeminacy within a distinct paradigm of identity and power, one in which the discourse of gender and power is inverted wherein strength as masculinity is weakness and weakness as effeminacy is strength.

FAVORINUS

The question of Favorinus's masculinity, its influence on his identity, and, by implication, its impact on his public career makes him an exemplary candidate with which to begin my examination of reconstructed masculinity.[47] Favorinus was born in Arles toward the end of the first century and described as double-sexed, bearing both male and female sexual characteristics (Philostratus, *Vit. Soph.* 489). Although such gender ambiguity could result in being exposed at birth as a *monstrum*, Favorinus would go on to study under such figures as Dio Chrysostom in his pursuit of mastering *paideia* and become part of a movement of orators who sought to elevate Greek language and culture as a paradigm for masculinity, a movement which Philostratus labels the Second Sophistic (*Vit. Soph.*, 481).[48] Throughout his life, Favorinus would hold positions of public significance, at times be labeled a philosopher and at others a sophist, and find himself locked in a dispute over the nature of identity with Polemo, one of the second century's most astute physiognomists and Favorinus's chief competition for public honor and identity. The fact that Favorinus could ascend to the heights of Greek philosophy and rhetoric despite not being born a Greek and that he would hold powerful public positions which were traditionally reserved for elite men even though his gender was a perennial question shows the degree to which Favorinus was able to construct his identity effectively. Yet Favorinus could never fully secure his identity, and questions about his public legitimacy and gender demonstrate just how precarious an endeavor Favorinus undertook in attempting to turn a foreign, effeminate, peculiar body into a quintessential example of Greek masculinity. I will begin by examining what type of masculine identity Favorinus appears to construct for himself. I will then show how Favorinus's origin and body left this identity vulnerable to critique in terms of effeminacy and, finally, how Favorinus defends his masculinity in a speech to the Corinthians.

During the Second Sophistic, orators like Favorinus seized upon a moment of cultural change when long-standing Roman discourses of masculinity were renegotiated as a result of socio-political evolution. As mentioned in the previous chapter, the change in Roman masculinity primarily stems from the dominance of the emperor and the institution of a professional army, both of which limited the opportunities for elite men to achieve and display their masculinity.[49] The erosion of the standard vehicles for the display of masculinity provides these public orators the opportunity to present other paradigms for masculinity based on mastery of *paideia* (i.e., Greek language, culture, and rhetoric). This change did not shift the goal of masculinity, since, as Tim Whitmarsh demonstrates, the new presentation of masculinity continued to replicate earlier ideologies of dominance over feminized others.[50] The goal was still a hegemonic masculinity which would place them in key political positions and allow them to increase their wealth and power. In the process, these men exchanged wars waged on battlefields for those waged in public forums and traded their horses and swords for words, rhetorical flourishes, and appeals to the exemplary figures of Greek tradition. As with demonstrations of military prowess, public oratory required an opponent to demonstrate successfully one's dominance. Maud Gleason emphasizes that the public and competitive nature of sophistry at this time was such that "If they had had no rivals, they would have created them to define themselves."[51]

From all surviving accounts, Favorinus applies his extensive learning in Greek culture and oratorical skill to embody the life of a sophist, a public intellectual who blurred the lines between philosopher and orator.[52] Since a successful sophist was to be a person of extensive learning, rhetorical dominance, and public power, a sophist had to be a man and questions of a person's masculinity could impugn one's status as a sophist. The bulk of this section will focus on Favorinus's success or failure in attaining the identity of sophist and the crucial role Favorinus's gender played in this endeavor. Philostratus provides one of the clearest pictures of Favorinus, labeling him a philosopher and saying that he was proclaimed a sophist because of his "charm and the beauty of his eloquence" (*Vit. Soph.* 489). Favorinus's own works show him engaged in precarious debates over the etymologies of Latin words and other matters of minutia which were typically the domain of philosophers. Dio's account of Favorinus's conflict with Hadrian, himself a well-known devotee of Greek culture, centers on Favorinus more fully embodying Greek ideals than the emperor (*Roman History* 69.3.1–5). Dio also reports that Hadrian sought to overthrow Favorinus and other men who rivaled Hadrian's mastery of Greek culture and learning by "elevating their antagonists," a comment which appears to explain why Polemo was the object of such imperial benevolence (*Roman Histories* 69.3.4).

The competition between Favorinus and Polemo also demonstrates Favorinus's identity as a sophist since the two men strive with one another for the honor of cities and elite men in Rome (*Vit. Soph.* 490–491). Philostratus says that the mere fact that Favorinus competes with Polemo places his identity as a sophist beyond dispute because the fact that "[Favorinus] had quarreled with a sophist was evidence enough; for that spirit of rivalry . . . is always directed against one's *competitors in the same craft*" (*Vit. Soph.* 491; emphasis added). Even the accounts of Lucian and Polemo, both of whom openly attack Favorinus, demonstrate him operating as a sophist. In Lucian's *Demonax*, to which I shall return below, Favorinus is described as a failed sophist, but a sophist nonetheless, since he gives public lectures and engages in public competitions with Demonax over the nature of their learning and ability to speak (*Demon.* 12–13). Likewise, Polemo offers faint praise for Favorinus's style before quickly moving to a physiognomic examination of his eyes and body which reveal that Favorinus is too effeminate and, therefore, morally dubious to stand as a masculine ideal for others to emulate (*Phys.* 1.160–61). Polemo's need to argue that Favorinus cannot stand as an ideal of Greek masculinity due to certain effeminate characteristics only makes sense if Favorinus was functioning as such through the vocation of a sophist, a point made clear in Philostratus's account of their conflict.

As noted in the preceding paragraph, Favorinus's status as a sophist is vigorously disputed by his opponents often by critiquing his masculinity. Demonax's dispute with Favorinus begins with a quarrel over their rhetorical and philosophical abilities, but Demonax's ultimate critique of Favorinus's ability to act as a sophist centers on Favorinus's effeminacy. The exchange shows how crucial gender could be in discussions of legitimate identity.

> When Favorinus was told by someone that Demonax was making fun of his lectures and particularly of the laxity of their rhythm, saying that it was vulgar and effeminate and not by any means appropriate to philosophy, he went to Demonax and asked him: "Who are you to libel my compositions?" "A man with an ear that is not easy to cheat," said he. The sophist kept at him and asked: "What qualifications had you, Demonax, to leave school and commence philosophy?" "Testicles," he retorted. (Lucian, *Demon.* 12, Harmon)[53]

A contemporary reader might wonder how a rhythm could be effeminate, but the rhetorical instructions offered in the first century, like those reviewed in the previous chapter, clearly distinguish between proper, masculine cadences and uses of the voice and effeminate ones which could alter the student's gender and prevent him from being able to speak and function as a man. Favorinus's need to respond to Demonax's slander represents the type of public competition which was typical of the sophists. Demonax's response of pointing to the visible masculinity of his own body and ability to avoid deception, two quintessential traits of masculinity, makes the case that he has the correct traits to be a public man and challenge Favorinus. In the next line, Favorinus does not question Demonax's body, that is, his ear, but his training, an important distinction for Favorinus since his own body could not support such scrutiny. This is precisely the point Demonax makes in his response by, yet again, pointing to his body, this time to his testicles, something Favorinus could not do. A similar dynamic plays out in another exchange between the two men, this time centering on Favorinus's inability to grow the beard which was seen as necessary for a philosopher (*Demon.*, 13). Whereas Favorinus wants to establish a masculine identity though matters of status and training, Demonax repeatedly points to the masculinity which can be read right off his body and contrasts it to the physical indicators of effeminacy which Favorinus cannot hide.

Polemo's description of Favorinus also demonstrates the penetrating power of the gaze to literally un-man an opponent by pointing to the body.[54] Polemo begins by describing how to examine a person's eyes in order to determine character, of which his final example is the man who lacks modesty (*Phys.* 1.151). Polemo immediately moves to disqualify this person's masculinity by stating that he is not like other men and, then, specifically identifying the person as a congenital eunuch. Though Polemo never mentions Favorinus by name, he clearly has him in mind since he says that he has only ever seen one example of such a person "from the land called Celtas" (*Phys.* 1.152). This connection to Favorinus's homeland and the ensuing description of effeminate speech and mannerisms which match Polemo's explicit references to Favorinus leave little doubt as to the object of his invective.[55] The description begins by labeling him "greedy and immoral beyond all description" and then making numerous comparisons between Favorinus's body and that of a woman (*Phys.* 1.152–56). Favorinus's effeminacy is then said to be manifest in a lack of self-control and debauchery both in his own behavior and that which he inspires in others (*Phys.* 1.157–60). Polemo's use of physiognomy to correlate Favorinus's appearance with an identity that feminizes Favorinus and those around him is a direct attack on Favorinus's identity as a sophist.

Although Favorinus's direct responses to the attacks of Lucian and Polemo have not survived, Favorinus's letter to the people of Corinth shows him self-consciously working through the apparent discrepancy between problematic aspects of his identity, primarily his effeminate body, and the necessary masculinity for his identity as a sophist embodying Greek culture, the very type of attack which Lucian and Polemo level against Favorinus.[56] Since self-praise was typically unacceptable,[57] Favorinus seizes upon the removal of his statue from public display in Corinth to launch his self-defense. Throughout the speech, Favorinus works to blur the lines between himself and his statue, at times referring to the statue as if it was a person and using statuesque language for himself (cf. *Cor. orat.* 22, 23, 25, 32, 46). Indeed, the Corinthians' action of erecting the statue as a stand-in for Favorinus follows the same logic of equating a statue with its model since they originally erect the statue in order to serve as a stand-in for Favorinus after they could not convince him to remain in the city (*Cor. orat.* 8). They cannot have Favorinus so they will take a copy which Favorinus describes as "a mute semblance of my eloquence," in other words, in embodiment of his ability to perform as a sophist (*Cor. orat.* 46). This overlap between Favorinus and his statue allows Favorinus to defend himself by defending his statue.

While Favorinus never explicitly states the reasons for his falling out of favor with the Corinthians, he alludes to slander and a rumored feminine transformation in Rome where he lost the favor of Hadrian and, therefore, the masculine ability to perform as a sophist and wield political power. If Favorinus is to protect his statue and reputation in Corinth, then he must defend the masculinity of his *persona*. After articulating his success in attaining a Hellenistic identity, a point to which I will return, Favorinus addresses the Corinthians,

> Therefore, knowing all this as you do, are you surprised if there has been spread abroad against this man too some censure, a thing which absolutely none of those who have lived distinguished lives has had the power to escape, but which in his case is based upon the charm of his eloquence, or whatever one should call that gift to which you yourselves, along with women and children, give approval? Will you not consider the matter? . . . Then do you believe that the man who has lived a decent life in Greece, in the midst of greater license and indulgence, has suffered transformation in Rome, in the presence of the Emperor himself and the laws? Why, that is very much as if one were to say of the athlete that, though privately he keeps the rules, in the stadium and in the presence of the Master of the Games he violates the code! (*Cor. orat.* 33–34, Crosby; cf. 32)

Favorinus's description of an attack based on his eloquence fits the model of competition evidenced in the preceding discussion of Lucian and Polemo, a pattern which Favorinus says is so common that no one of renown can escape. When Favorinus alludes to the "transformation in Rome" we can surmise that the issue is that the Corinthians now believe, likely through slanderous rumors, that Favorinus was transformed in Rome from a true man, demonstrating the masculine characteristics of self-control and eloquence, into an effeminate person, demonstrating the feminine characteristics of indulgence and lack of power. These remarks likely refer to Hadrian's disfavor with Favorinus when Favorinus appeared before him, which becomes the reason the Athenians remove their statue of Favorinus (cf. Philostratus, *Vit. Soph.*, 490–491).[58] The loss of status and identity means this transformation would represent a loss of the hegemonic masculinity which had allowed Favorinus to function as a sophist and thus inhabit masculine ideals.

As I discuss above, attacks on Favorinus center on his foreign origin and effeminate body. Since Favorinus cannot hide either of these apparent truths, he, instead, turns them into sources of strength which demonstrate the true greatness of his identity and ability to wield power, in other words, his masculinity. The process of defending his masculinity begins with his reference to the Corinthians erecting a statue of him for the purpose of honoring his work for the city and to "most effectively stimulate the youth to persevere in the same pursuits as myself" (*Cor. Orat.*, 8). Favorinus's logic is that the Corinthians must have seen him as an exemplary *man* to which future men should mold themselves. Favorinus will go on to outline his pursuit as the transformation of a non-Greek body into the pinnacle of Greek culture, which Favorinus describes in terms of speech, thought, and form (*Cor. Orat.*, 25). The use of speech, thought, and form are no accident since they function as key markers of masculinity; the Corinthians' recognition of him as an exemplary man confirms his claims to be able to speak and act like a man. Favorinus will go on to draw a parallel between the Corinthians' purpose in setting up the statue and the gods divinely equipping him as a model of Greek culture designed to encourage Greeks everywhere to fully embody their heritage as well as to show that non-Greeks, even Celts, can "seem and be Greek" through proper training (*Cor. orat.* 25–27). Favorinus even faintly mocks an instance when someone of Greek heritage is honored for their ability to speak Doric as honoring something which is not really an accomplishment (*Cor. orat.* 24). In other words, Favorinus's ability to embody the best of Greek culture despite his foreign status and seemingly effeminate body demonstrates just how powerful and masculine he really is. He not only applies his redoubtable knowledge of Greek culture and history to provide examples for his argument but to construct a *persona* which epitomizes the masculine characteristics of learning and oratorical dominance which are necessary for the identity of a sophist. If Favorinus is successful, it means he effectively argues that to be a man, to embody the characteristics and privileges associated with that status, does not require such seemingly necessary accoutrements as testicles, a deep voice, or the masculine bodily movements exhorted by Quintilian.

Furthermore, if the Corinthians balk at Favorinus's claim that an effeminate, non-Greek body can truly represent the best of Greek culture, then the Corinthians themselves are in danger of losing their claim to being a chief representative of Greek culture. Favorinus says "though Roman, he has become thoroughly Hellenized, even as your own city has" (*Cor. orat.* 26), a remark which highlights the fact that by the second century C.E. Corinth had been rebuilt as a Roman city and then tried to recapture its Greek heritage.[59] Like Favorinus, the city was "born" a Roman but tried to make itself Greek. If Favorinus's origins and effeminate body prevent him from passing as a Greek, something similar is true of Corinth.[60] Favorinus tries to secure a hegemonic masculinity by connecting the Corinthians' authority and status to his own. If they want to retain their power and position in the world then they will continue to ascribe power and position to Favorinus.

In summary, Favorinus provides a witness to an attempt to renegotiate a person's masculinity following the apparent failure of his masculine identity. The accounts provided by Lucian and Philostratus show Favorinus competing for an identity as a sophist which requires a masculine *persona*. These accounts also show that Favorinus's opponents could not critique his learning or oratorical abilities so they challenge his status as a man by highlighting his foreign birth and the fact that he is a congenital eunuch, characteristics which threaten to make Favorinus a subordinate man by removing him from the public arena and any exercise of power. If they successfully undermine his status as a man then they would also successfully undermine Favorinus's identity as a sophist. Favorinus defends his masculinity to the Corinthians by demonstrating that his physical body which appears to undermine his claims to being able to function as a sophist actually demonstrates the chief characteristics of masculinity and, thereby, secure his identity as a sophist. By using himself as a model of masculinity given by the gods for others to imitate, Favorinus seeks to reclaim the power and authority which accompany a hegemonic masculinity.

PHILO

Beginning with the work of Richard A. Baer, the philosophical use of Philo's application of the categories male and female has been widely acknowledged.[61] More recently, scholars have recognized the ways in which Philo's use of male and female correlate with discourses of gender like those presented in the previous chapter, often serving rhetorical goals related to social and natural hierarchies.[62] Sharon Lea Mattila's distinction between Philo's use of male and female in regard to sex in contrast with his use of male and female in regard to gender is particularly insightful since it clarifies what Baer originally described as Philo's "second usage" where "Philo refers to the sense-perceptible world as female and the realm of the mind as male, however, it is clear that [Philo] is using the categories male and female quite differently [than to refer to anatomical sex.]"[63] This "second usage" is what I describe above as gender that is socially constructed as opposed to what could be thought of as anatomical or biological understandings of sex. I note this to point out that Philo's use of socially constructed discourses of gender, like when Philo associates men with the realm of the mind and Logos and then deduces a closer relationship between men and God (e.g., *Sacr.* 103), is so pervasive that Baer perceived Philo's application of them before such gender-critical categories and analysis were well-known. The following excerpt shows both usages at work in the same passage.

> And since the elements of which our soul consists are two in number, the rational and the irrational part, the rational part belongs to the male sex, being the inheritance of intellect and reason; but the irrational part belongs to the sex of woman, which is the lot also of the outward senses. And the mind is in every respect superior to the outward sense, as the man is to the woman; who, when he is without blemish and purified with the proper purifications, namely, the perfect virtues, is himself the most holy sacrifice, being wholly and in all respects pleasing to God. (*Spec.* 1.201; trans. Yonge)

Philo simultaneously uses categories of sex, distinguishing man from women, and categories of gender, associating the rational with the male and irrational with the female in order to align the subordination of women with the subordination of irrational thought. The result is a clear and consistent gendered hierarchy which assumes the superiority of the male and the necessity of female subordination, in other words, patriarchy.[64]

Mattila and Dorothy Sly each apply a more developed gender critical lens in order to further Baer's initial insights into Philo's use of gender categories.[65] In doing so, each argues that what appear to be deep incongruities between Philo's use of sex and gender are different perspectives on a single gender hierarchy which manifests a consistent focus on control and order. Such apparent incongruities appear in Philo alternating the gender of personified wisdom from female to male. This gender switching follows a consistent approach to a hierarchy focused on control which maintains the dominance of the masculine. So God (masculine) exercises control over wisdom (feminine) because wisdom is closer to creation and, therefore, more feminine than God (e.g., *Her.* 127; *Cher.* 49; *Ebr.* 30–31). Yet wisdom (masculine) exercises control over people (feminine) since people are further removed from God and, therefore, are relatively more feminine than wisdom (*Fug.* 51–52).[66]

> How, then, can the daughter of God, namely, wisdom, be properly called a father? Is it because the name indeed of wisdom is feminine but the sex masculine? For indeed all the virtues bear the names of women, but have the powers and actions of most full-grown men, since whatever is subsequent to God, even if it be the most ancient of all other things, still has only the second place when compared with that omnipotent Being, and appears not so much masculine as feminine, in accordance with its likeness to the other creatures; for as the male always has the precedence, the female falls short, and is inferior in rank. . . . [W]isdom . . . is both male and a father, and that it is that which sows the seed of, and which begets learning in, souls, and also education, and knowledge, and prudence, all honorable and praiseworthy things. (*Fug.* 51; Younge)

A system which assumes that the feminine must, in order to maintain the created and social order, be subordinate to the masculine manifests a patriarchy which not only subordinates women but all that is associated with the feminine and threatens the masculinity of men who manifest feminine characteristics.

Another example of a possible incongruity are the places where Philo applies aspects of the gendered category of male to praise a particular woman, such as Sarah who demonstrates the masculine characteristics of mastering her passions and jealousy by becoming fully subordinate to her husband (*Abr.* 245–52). The point is not that women, although irrational by nature, cannot demonstrate rational thought but that they can only demonstrate such an inherently masculine characteristic when taking a subordinate position to a man.[67] Using a logic like that in the passage from *De fuga et inventione* quoted above, the masculine must have precedence and control over the feminine. It is Sarah's obedience to Abraham's control that allows her to exercise masculine virtues in overcoming her feminine passions. Philo always reserves such praise for situations when women subordinate themselves to the control of men.[68] So even though Philo can speak positively of particular women, his use of gender follows the discourses of gender outlined above by consistently assuming that "the male is active, rational, and more akin to mind and thought" and that the female represents its antithesis (e.g., *Q.E.* 1.8).

One key implication of the ubiquity of Philo's gendered hierarchy is that Philo can invoke the categories of male and female and the discourses he associates with them even when masculinity or femininity does not appear to be an issue or necessary for his argument.[69] This is why Philo can ascribe gender to a concept like nature or wisdom based on certain characteristics and, then, associate other characteristics of that ascribed gender or argue against a conclusion based on an obvious characteristic. The following passage illustrates this dynamic.

> [F]or in the marriage of the bodies it is the male partner which sows the seed and the female which receives it, but in the union which takes place with regard to the soul it is quite the contrary, and it is virtue (ἡ ἀρετή) which appears to be there in the place of the woman, which sows good counsels, and virtuous speeches, and expositions of doctrines profitable to life; but the reason (ὁ λογισμός) which is considered to be classed in the light of the man receives the sacred and divine seed . . . for certainly, in the grammatical view of the words, the word reason is masculine, and the word virtue has a feminine character. But if any one, discarding the considerations of the names which tend to throw darkness over the subject, chooses to look at the plain facts without any disguise, he will know that virtue is masculine by nature, inasmuch as it puts things in motion, and arranges them, and suggests good conceptions of noble actions and speeches; but reason is feminine, inasmuch as it is put in motion by another, and is instructed and benefited, and, in short, is altogether the patient, as its passive state is its only safety. (*Abr.* 101-02; trans. Yonge)

Note that Philo argues against what might be considered the obvious gender of each word based on its grammatical gender because of his understanding of the characteristics associated with the concept. This is all the more striking since, elsewhere, Philo uses grammatical gender and etymology to substantiate his rhetorical uses of a word, name, or concept. For example, Philo uses the Hebrew meaning of Leah's name "faint and rejected" to argue, "therefore the sacred scriptures represent Leah as hated, and on this account it is that she received that name; for Leah, being interpreted, means 'repudiating and laboring,' because we all turn away from virtue and think it a laborious thing" (*Mut.* 254; cf. *Cher.* 41). Leah's connection with rejection not only allows Philo to associate her with virtue but, also, to ascribe to Leah other masculine attributes related to virtue, like self-control and denial of passion through perpetual virginity, which seem to conflict with a natural reading of the biblical account (*Mut.* 132–33, 254; compare with Gen. 29:23, 32; 30:16).[70] The point is that, for Philo, one key characteristic of masculinity or femininity is enough to apply an entire discourse of masculinity or femininity, even when doing so appears to contravene evidence and attribute characteristics unsubstantiated by the biblical account.

Philo's discussions of masculinity and distinguishing men as masculine or feminine demonstrate the same dynamics as those discussed above which focus on women. Philo's discussion of the differences between virtuous and wicked minds ascribes masculinity and all the good attributes that come along with it to the virtuous mind and femininity and all the depraved things which come along with it to the wicked mind.

> [W]e shall say . . . that to bring forth is peculiar to the female sex, as to beget is the office of the male: therefore God wills in the first place to render the mind, which is filled with virtue, like to the male sex rather than to the female, thinking it suited to its character to be active, not passive. In the second place both do generate, both the virtuous mind and the wicked one: but they generate in a different manner, and they produce contrary offspring, the virtuous mind producing good and useful things, but the depraved or wicked mind producing base and useless things. (*Q.G.* 3.18; trans. Yonge)

Philo understands that men who do not attain the chief characteristics of masculinity are failed men and inclined to act as women, a process which Philo describes as "being *castrated* and mutilated of all the *masculine* and generative parts of the soul" (*Dues.* 1.111; emphasis added). Philo comments that if he forgets to allow reason to guard his mind at dinner parties, then he will become a "slave to luxury . . . being under the guidance of masters who could not be tamed" and overwhelmed by his passions, both of which are common feminine characteristics (*Leg.* 3.156; trans. Yonge). Philo's conflation of the feminine ideas of luxury and passion with subordination is a clear manifestation of the patriarchal gender hierarchy and a warning of the dangers of effeminacy. Philo also presents Esau as indicative of what happens if a man surrenders to passion, which represents a loss of self-control, being unmanly, and an inability to correctly discern virtue from folly. Esau is said to be "slave to the pleasures of the belly" that produces passion and shame which manifest in the redness of his complexion (*Q.G.* 4.167–68; trans. Yonge). Elsewhere,

Philo links Esau's proclivity to vice, ignorance, and rudeness with his subservience to passion and Jacob's wisdom and virtue with his position of dominance over his brother (*Leg.* 3.2; cf. 3.88).[71] As I will show in my analysis of Josephus, correlating certain behaviors or characteristics with masculine or feminine identity and then importing those assessments into a patriarchal context makes the subjugation of people with feminine characteristics "natural" and part of maintaining social order.

Philo's discussion of the dangers he faces at dinner parties and Esau's loss of his birthright are indicative of the dangers effeminacy poses to all men, seen most strikingly in Philo's discussion of men who trade their masculinity for effeminacy. Philo describes such men as "those who are afflicted with the disease of effeminacy, men-women, who, having adulterated the coinage of nature, are willingly driven into the appearance and treatment of unrestrained behavior of women" (*Spec.* 1.325; trans. Yonge). Philo can build on such a label in order to apply other feminine attributes such as lack of self-control, subordination, loss of rationality, love of luxury, being overcome by passions, and bringing about chaos (e.g., *Virt.* 18–21; *Spec.* 2.50, 3.37–42; *Somn.* 1.22–23; *Prob.* 1.124; *Contempl.* 60). For Philo, such men represent the end result of a process of surrendering masculine control over their bodies and passions for effeminizing subordination to desires and passions. These men-women also threaten the natural ordering and, therefore, stability of society since they have perverted the natural place of their own bodies.

> As men, being unable to bear discreetly a satiety of these things . . . become stiff-necked, and discard the laws of nature, pursuing a great and intemperate indulgence of gluttony, and drinking, and unlawful connections; for not only did they go mad after women, and defile the marriage bed of others, but also those who were men lusted after one another, doing unseemly things, and not regarding or respecting their common nature . . . and so, by degrees, the men became accustomed to be treated like women, and in this way engendered among themselves the disease of females, an intolerable evil; for they not only, as to effeminacy and delicacy, became like women in their persons, but they made also their souls most ignoble, *corrupting in this way the whole race of man*, as far as depended on them (*Abr.* 135–36, emphasis added; trans. Yonge).[72]

Philo goes on to address the fatal consequences that such effeminate men pose to their societies since they can no longer protect and lead since they lack the masculinity required to operate at the top of a patriarchal system.

Philo also uses these discourses of gender to portray Jewish men and the nation as a whole as a model of masculinity with an eye toward appeasing Roman suspicions. Mary Rose D'Angelo demonstrates that, throughout Philo's writings, gender "manifests [his] political investments that originate from his engagement with the Roman imperial order."[73] Of importance is the resemblance between Philo's use of the Greek εὐσέβεια to the Latin *pietas*, a term which under Augustus's moral reforms came to be closely associated with the manly characteristic of *virtus* as loyalty to the imperial order. To be a man, then, meant faithfully fulfilling one's social position and supporting the emperor and failing to embody this masculinity posed a threat to the man as well as those around him. With this connection in mind, Philo's use of "the disease of feminization" provides an extreme example of the danger such men pose to Rome since they undermine the patriarchal stability the reforms were meant to ensure. Philo's discussions of the management of the household which affirm male domination and control of its members show that the Jewish law and society embody these characteristics (e.g., *Decal*. 126–31; *Opif*. 167; *Leg*., 3.40; *Contempl*. 33). D'Angelo shows that Philo's language and arguments on household order follow the patterns of Roman laws in such a way that Jews emerge as a people uniquely shaped to function within Roman society.[74] One of the most striking examples D'Angelo highlights is Philo's development of Deut 24:1–4 in terms of the effects on the cuckolded husband (*Spec*. 3.30–31).[75] Philo applies the charge of προαγωγείαν, the Greek equivalent to the Latin *lenocinium* (pimping), and the same type of feminization, "softness and unmanliness" (μαλακίας καὶ ἀνανδρίας), to the cuckolded husband if the offense goes unpunished. These details are missing from the Mosaic commands but directly parallel the Roman law. Philo is not inventing new laws or inserting Roman misogyny but contextualizing and developing the Jewish law in such a way that it would present the Jewish people in a favorable light to Rome. The political purposes of such a move will be explored below.

Philo's account of the pogrom in Alexandria under the Roman governor Flaccus offers a unique look into how Philo rehabilitates Jewish masculinity in light of its apparent failure. Philo recounts how the Jews were slandered as being detriments to Alexandria's status, derided for their synagogues and Torah, physically overcome by their enemies, and then confined to a single quarter of the city. Each of these issues reads as a sign of the effeminacy of the Jewish nation as a whole and Jewish men in particular. In light of the above discussion about how even a single feminine characteristic could leave a person or group liable to charges of effeminacy, Philo appears to take on the challenge to rehabilitate Jewish masculinity which was seen in Josephus's *Jewish War*. Although Philo does not provide an introduction like the one Josephus includes in *Jewish War*, Philo's direct connections between justice, God's protection, and the Jews as noble citizens in *Flaccus* 170–73 evidences a clear need to defend the Jews against disenfranchisement of their status as citizens.[76] As I will show in Josephus, Philo's rehabilitation of Jewish masculinity requires that he feminize another group. For Josephus this will be the rebels who follow John of Gischala; for Philo this will be Flaccus and the Egyptians who corrupt Flaccus's masculinity. This follows the type of competition for masculinity found in the Greek and Roman sources discussed in the previous chapter and seen in Favorinus. In other words, demonstrating one's masculinity often requires feminizing an opponent.

In order to defend Jewish masculinity, Philo applies masculine language and characteristics to the Jews in order to demonstrate that they embody a complicit masculinity through their obedience to and support of the emperor, their *pietas*. Although this subservience could be read as feminine, *pietas* marked by submission to Rome and the emperor became key markers of subordinate masculinity for both Romans and foreigners as they demonstrated self-control through understanding and occupying their proper place in society. To this end, Agrippa is a model Jewish man. He obeys Gaius's commands and looks upon the emperor as "his master" (*Fla.* 25). Although the rhetoric of obedience to another could be read as feminine, as I discussed above the use of obedience to express piety to the emperor became a key marker of masculinity in the Principate. Agrippa is also modest in his conduct, not entering or living in Alexandria with too much extravagance or luxury (*Fla.* 27–29). In light of Philo's anxiety over the feminizing effects of luxury as seen in his discussion of the dangers of a dinner party, this shows that Agrippa's masculinity is not in danger of being compromised, which is a key issue because Flaccus's engagement with luxury begins to soften his masculinity. Finally, Agrippa listens to the Jewish case against Flaccus and appeals to Caesar on their behalf (*Fla.* 103), something which Flaccus had earlier refused to do (*Fla.* 23–24). As I previously demonstrated with Favorinus, being able to effectively represent a city or people before the emperor was a key avenue of demonstrating masculinity and acquiring honor. Agrippa, therefore, consistently manifests masculine characteristics and a resistance to potentially feminizing influences while still maintaining a clear subordination to Gaius.

These descriptors of obedience and aversion to luxury are consistent with Philo's portrayal of the Jewish nation as a whole. Philo's main complaint about the destruction of Jewish synagogues in Alexandria is that it prevents the Jews from displaying their "εὐσάβειαν (piety) towards their benefactors," that is the imperial household, an event Philo describes as worse than "suffering ten thousand deaths" (*Fla.* 48–49). Philo specifically describes the synagogues as instrumental in this obedience since "[o]ur houses of prayer are manifestly incitements to all the Jews in every part of the habitable world to display their piety and loyalty towards the house of Augustus" (*Fla.* 49). This obedience, Philo argues, is part of the Jewish law and customs and manifests in all the countries where Jew settle (*Fla.* 46–47). By situating the Jews as obedient members of the imperial household, Philo makes a key point for the complicit masculinity of the Jewish people.

Philo also frames the Jewish laws and way of life as facilitating a complicit masculinity that is confirmed by Augustus, resisting luxury, and maintaining proper boundaries between men and women. Philo describes the Jewish law as "our own laws which Augustus himself is in the habit of confirming," and asks how the Jewish people could be liable to punishment since they "obey [them] in every way" (*Fla.* 50). Philo also describes how Augustus was directly involved in establishing the Jewish system of governance which Flaccus violates (*Fla.* 74). Philo's description of the Jewish people as making "no pretense to magnificence or delicate luxury; the nature of which things is to engender satiety, and satiety is apt to engender insolence, which is the beginning of all evils" applies the idea of a progressive feminization which endangers society and shows that Jewish people act as a safeguard against that feminization (*Fla.* 91). This is in direct contrast to Philo's description of those men like Isidorus, who feminize Flaccus and, as a result, undermine Roman hegemony.

> There are a vast number of parties in the city whose association is founded in no one good principle, but who are united by wine, and drunkenness, and revelry, and the offspring of those indulgencies, insolence; and their meetings are called synods and couches by the natives. In all these parties or the greater number of them Isidorus is said to have born the bell, the leader of the feast, the chief of the supper, the disturber of the city. (*Fla.* 136–37; trans. Yonge)

Philo feminizes men like Isidorus by connecting them to behavior associated with excess such as drinking. At the beginning, Flaccus's masculinity is intact and he can resist and control such femininity, but, at the end, he has become the subject and is under the control of such effeminate men (*Fla.* 4). As I will discuss in the following section on Josephus, this portrayal of the feminine foreigner who threatens Roman masculinity is a common trope in Roman self-presentation. When Flaccus orders the searching of Jewish households for weapons which would indicate an intention to rebel against Rome, Philo reports that the soldiers barely found knives necessary for the preparation of food (*Fla.* 90). Not only does this dispel rumors of Jewish rebellion, it also reinforces the simplicity of the Jewish lifestyle which contrasts with the drunken dinner parties associated with the rebels and which breed feminine behavior. Philo also notes that the search forces all the Jewish women out into the "public gaze" of men which scandalizes them, indicating that they were accustomed to the private spaces appropriate for women (*Fla.* 89). Rather than revealing Jewish sedition, the search indicates that the structure of the

Jewish way of life maintains clear boundaries between masculine public spaces and feminine private ones, resists luxury, and does not entertain dissention against Rome, all things Flaccus fails to do (e.g., *Fla.* 91; more on this below). As a whole, Philo uses these common discourses of masculinity to present Judaism as fully complicit with the mechanisms of Roman imperial power yet without giving any indication that the Jews desire to seize control of those mechanisms for themselves or embody feminine characteristics that could undermine Roman masculinity.

In contrast to Agrippa and the Jews, Flaccus and the Egyptians of Alexandria are consistently portrayed as feminine, primarily seen by their undermining Roman control of the city, lack of self-control, and excess. Philo begins by describing the near perfection of Flaccus's masculinity at the beginning of his governance over Egypt (*Fla.* 1–4).

> This Flaccus . . . being a man who at the beginning, as far as appearance went, had given innumerable instances of his excellence, for he was a man of prudence and diligence, and great acuteness of perception, very energetic in executing what he had determined on, very eloquent as a speaker, and skillful too at discerning what was suppressed as well as at understanding what was said . . . [H]e pulled down the over proud, he forbade promiscuous mobs of men from all quarters to assemble together; and prohibited all associations and meetings which were continually feasting together under pretense of sacrifices, making a drunken mockery of public business, treating with great vigor and severity all who resisted his commands. (*Fla.* 2, 4; trans. Yonge)

At the beginning, Flaccus is energetic, eloquent, wise, able to resist manipulation, consistent in executing justice, resistant to the feminizing effects of sumptuous feasts and luxury, and firm in maintaining Roman hegemony by forbidding the types of mobs and public behavior which will later threaten Rome's representatives (cf. *Fla.* 33–34). Philo notes that he needs to go out of his way to praise Flaccus's greatness to emphasize just how wicked he becomes throughout the story (*Fla.* 8). Although beginning as an exemplary man, Flaccus's pessimism over Gaius's ascent to power leads Flaccus to "utterly abandon all other hope for the future, and was no longer able to apply himself to public affairs as he had done before, being weakened and leaky (διαρρέων) in spirit" (*Fla.* 16). Philo consistently uses διαρρέω for souls or men that weaken their masculine nature and display the feminine characteristics of being vulnerable to passions and lacking reason (e.g., *Sacr.* 80; *Fug.* 199–201; *Spec.* 2.19, 4.91). Philo makes this connection explicit in stating,

> And he, again, who encounters what is disagreeable to be born with fortitude and manly perseverance, is taking the best road to happiness; for it is not the nature of virtue to abide with those who are given up to delicacy and luxury,

and who have become effeminate in their souls, and whose bodies are leaky (διαρρέουσιν) by the incessant luxury which they practice every day. (*Mos.* 2.184; trans. Yonge)

Note the connection between luxury's effects on making a person effeminate and leaky and how virtue, a key masculine characteristic, is not to abide with them. With these connections in mind, Philo's comments indicate that Flaccus's former masculine state has been feminized.

With his masculinity compromised, Flaccus loses control of his emotions and begins associating with Egyptians who are now able to deceive and manipulate Flaccus in order to "became executors of all the plans which they had devised, treating him like a mute person on the stage," (*Fla.* 17–21). A man losing the ability to speak was a major sign of effeminacy, especially for a public official like Flaccus,[77] and Philo uses the connection between muteness and effeminacy to describe how Flaccus is now under the control of the Egyptians. The subjects have now become the masters, effectively compromising and reversing the political hierarchy which maintains Roman sovereignty. After these same Egyptians turn on Flaccus, Philo makes the shame and subordination explicit in stating, "But nothing is so terrible as for men who have been the more powerful to be accused by their inferiors, and for those who have been rulers to be impeached by their former subjects, which is as if masters were being prosecuted by their natural or purchased slaves" (*Fla.* 127). As noted in the previous chapter, the images of being ruled and of losing a public contest are implicitly linked with femininity. This femininity, then, is the primary threat to Roman hegemony, a problem which is at least partially overcome by the complicit masculinity of the Jews, which is a significant focus in Philo's presentation of the Jewish people as discussed above and in *The Embassy to Gaius*.

As indicated above, Philo consistently portrays the Egyptian people as feminine in action, specifically in their attempts to undermine Roman hegemony. This not only allows Philo to draw a sharp contrast with Jewish masculinity but, more importantly, to show that Jews are complicit with Roman rule and cannot be blamed for the political unrest of Alexandria. Philo describes his Egyptian opponents as,

> [T]he [Egyptian] mob which, out of its restlessness and love of an unquiet and disorderly life, was always filling every place with tumult and confusion, and who, because of their habitual idleness and laziness, were full of treachery and revolutionary plans, they, flocking to the theater the first thing in the morning, having already purchased Flaccus for a miserable price, which he with his mad desire for glory and with his slavish disposition, condescended to take to the injury not only of himself, but also of the safety of the commonwealth. (*Fla.* 41; trans. Yonge)

Descriptions like this occur throughout the work and attribute the feminine characteristics of laziness, love of luxury, loss of control, being ruled by passions, inclination toward sedition, inability to control their speech, inability to learn, and creativity in acting contrary to nature (*Fla.* 17, 33–34, 43, 92, 125–26, 135). In contrast to the Jewish people who are obedient and embody a simple life, "the Egyptian disposition is by nature a most jealous and envious one and inclined to look on the good fortune of others as adversity to itself" (*Fla.* 29). King reaches a similar conclusion regarding the use of gendered tropes and notes that the rhetorical effect of "Philo's argument is that the Jews should be ranked higher [than Greeks and Egyptians] due to their superior continence and masculinity, and their ethnic privileges restored and protected."[78] If the Jews demonstrate their masculinity through their obedience, then the Egyptian inclination toward sedition is a clear manifestation of the trope of the effeminate barbarian who threatens Rome's dominance (i.e., masculinity) (e.g., Juvenal, *Sat.* 3.109–14 and Tacitus, *Ann.* 14.35.1), which is clearly the dynamic at work in Philo's portrayal of their gaining control over Flaccus and throwing Alexandria into chaos.[79] The Jews should be seen as having a complicit masculinity within Roman hegemony while the Egyptians manifest a subordinate masculinity since they exhibit and spread an effeminacy that threatens Roman masculinity. Yes, the Jews are not as manly as the Romans, but they do not evidence the effeminacy of the Egyptians.

As in my examination of Josephus which follows, Philo evidences a concern to address challenges which threaten to feminize the Jewish *persona*. Also like Josephus, Philo argues that the Jewish way of life and law provide the Jewish nation, and Jewish men in particular, with a complicit masculinity that allows them to function appropriately without challenging Roman hegemony. For Philo, this is specifically set in contrast to the Egyptians in Alexandria whose effeminacy is so toxic that it feminizes a truly great Roman man, Flaccus. Even though Philo does not go as far as Josephus does in feminizing his opponents by saying that they dress as women and seek women's roles in sex, the abundance of feminine characteristics that Philo applies to his opponents like Flaccus and Isidorus gives a clear indication that he utilizes discourses of femininity which render his opponents women and unable to function as men.

JOSEPHUS

The apologetic and polemical contours of Josephus's writings in both his direct confrontation with those who attack Judaism (e.g., *Ag. Ap.*) as well his reconstruction of the past (e.g., *Ant.*, *J.W.*) are well documented.[80] Josephus's use of gendered stereotypes and tropes as rhetorical tools, however, is not as thoroughly explored and will be the focus of this section as I examine how Josephus applies discourses of gender to characters in *Jewish War* and the rhetorical effects of such presentations in his overall argument. Due to the length of *Jewish Wars* and the text's less prominent use of explicitly gendered language,[81] I will focus more narrowly on those instances when gender is clearly deployed rather than attempt to show how Josephus maintains a consistent gendered vision for the Jewish nation as I did for Philo's *Flaccus*. Here, I demonstrate that Josephus, a near contemporary of Paul, associates gender with other characteristics which contemporary readers would not naturally link with gender, and that he manipulates gender for rhetorical purposes. Because Josephus's most stereotypical presentations of gender correspond with his rhetorical goals as stated in the preface to *Jewish Wars*, I will begin with the main claims in the preface and demonstrate how Josephus applies gendered tropes and discourses to characters in order to substantiate his claims about the masculinity of each and what that masculinity means for how they should be treated by the Romans.

Before moving to Josephus's claims, however, I first need to outline the trope and stereotypes that stands behind those claims, that of Roman masculinity dominating the effeminate barbarian.[82] It is helpful to begin by recalling the previous chapter's discussion that being a man (*vir*) did not simply denote biological maleness but the traits of masculinity such as valor, virtue, and self-control which were associated with it. For example, a gladiator, regardless of whatever feats of strength and bravery he could demonstrate in the arena, was not a true man (*vir*) and was liable to the effeminate charge or softness (*mollis*) and lack of self-control because he was subjected to the whims of others and acted as a public entertainer.[83] Seneca associates becoming a gladiator with being castrated while Juvenal relates it to men becoming brides and subjecting themselves to the domination of other men (Seneca, *Nat.* 7.32.4; Juvenal, *Sat.* 2.143–45). The association between masculinity and the domination of that which is deemed effeminate coalesce into a trope that pervades texts ranging from Cicero's philosophical reflection of the domination that the mind should exert over the emotions to Augustus's self-presentation of how he brought peace and order by subjecting the world to Roman domination (Cicero, *Tusc.* 2.47–48; *Res gest. divi Aug.* 26–33).[84] The association between Roman domination (*imperium*), peace (*pax*), and conquest becomes explicit in Augustus's description of closing the gates of the Temple of Janus three times during his reign, an action which demonstrates Rome's fulfillment of its divinely given mandate to bring order to the world by dominating it (*Res gest. divi Aug.* 13).[85] Colleen Conway argues that awarding Augustus the title *patrem patriae* (father of the country) makes explicit the connection between masculinity and domination which point to Augustus as *the* man which all other men should imitate;[86] a point that Augustus expresses since, "I (Augustus) restored many traditions of our ancestors and which were falling into disuse, and I myself set precedents in many things for posterity to imitate" (*Res gest. divi Aug.*, 8, Shepley; cf., 13). The connection between Rome's leaders and its divine mandate to take the masculine position of exerting power and bringing order to the world by subduing it is a major focus of such important presentations of Roman self-understanding as the Virgil's *Aeneid*, Livy's *History of Rome*, and Dionysius of Halicarnassus's *Roman Antiquities*.[87] In a move similar to that of Sallust that I discussed above, Juvenal uses this trope to demonstrate the dangers of Roman men not fulfilling their divinely given mandate to dominate effeminate foreigners and, consequently, allowing the foreigner's effeminacy to "conquer" Rome by feminizing Roman youths, thereby making the youths unable to lead Rome.

> [He] who was more effeminate than all other Eastern lads, is said to have yielded himself to an impassioned tribune. Look at the effects of international relations: he had come as a hostage, but here we create—human beings! And if such boys put on Roman ways by staying here longer, they'll never lack a lover. . . . That's how they take teenage Roman morality back in triumph to Artaxata. (Juvenal, *Sat.* 2.165–70)

Bringing together Augustus's comments with Juvenal's warnings makes clear the importance of Roman masculinity, seen most clearly in the masculinity of the "father" of the country, in dominating effeminate barbarians, thereby maintaining the divinely established gender/ethnic hierarchy of the world.[88]

If Roman domination of the world was thought to be natural, and if domination shared an essential connection with masculinity, then the nations which the Romans subjugated were necessarily seen as effeminate and Roman subjugation of them as maintaining the natural, patriarchal order of the Roman world. This connection pervades Roman texts and iconography in the form of portraying other people groups with effeminate characteristics (e.g., small, kneeling, bound, chaotic, uncivilized, etc.) or simply as women.[89] Virgil refers to the Trojans as soft and effeminate "half-men" (*semiviri*) who cannot possibly hope to fend off the attacks of real men (Virgil, *Aen.* 4.215; cf. 12.99).[90] The effeminacy of foreign peoples even pervades Roman ethnographies such as Diodorus's description of the Galatian men as having "very little to do with them (their women), but rage with lust, in outlandish fashion, for the embraces of men. . . . And the most astonishing thing of all is that they have no concern for propriety, but prostitute out their bodies easily, nor do they consider this disgraceful" (Diodorus, 5.32.7). As demonstrated in the previous chapter and in the discussions of Favorinus and Philo, such behavior makes people, regardless of their biological sex, effeminate and liable to the other characteristics associated with femininity. Furthermore, the portrayal of such effeminacy as deviating from natural, read Roman, gender norms threatens Roman masculinity and the hegemony that masculinity supports and, thus, requires Rome to maintain stability by exerting dominance over them. Note how Plutarch frames Rome's dominance over their effeminate neighbors as following the natural order of the world in terms of dominate/submissive which itself is based on masculine/feminine.

> You march against these peoples, and if they will not share their goods with you, you enslave them, despoil them, and raze their cities to the ground; not that in so doing you are in any way wise or cruel or unjust, but you are obeying the most ancient of all laws which gives to the stronger the goods of his weaker neighbors, the world over, beginning with God himself and ending with the beasts who perish. (Plutarch, *Cam.* 27.3–4, Perrin)

In a system where strength and weakness were essentially gendered categories, such statements carry a clear gendered bias and reinforce Rome as the masculine dominator and the foreigner as the submissive feminine.[91]

Such foreign effeminacy did not just require that Rome subjugate those peoples, it also threatened to feminize Roman masculinity. This was part of the point of Juvenal's critique that I quote above. In a manner similar to Juvenal, Horace describes Marc Antony's feminization by his relationship with Cleopatra as a mighty Roman warrior being enslaved to a drunken woman and her shriveled eunuchs (Horace, *Epod.* 9.12–14). Cato is consistently called upon to decry the destruction of Rome from the inside by the feminizing effects of foreign dress, foods, and other manners of foreign indulgence on Roman men (e.g., Polybius, *Hist.* 31.25.5; Plutarch, *Cat. Maj.* 8.2). Cicero, likewise, compares the truly manly men of the past to contemporary Roman men who

> [C]annot bear a pain in the foot, or a toothache (but suppose the whole body is in pain); the reason is that there is a kind of womanish and frivolous way of thinking exhibited in pleasure as much as in pain, which makes our self-control melt and stream away through weakness, and so we cannot endure a bee-sting without crying out. (Cicero, *Tusc.* 2.52)[92]

The older Seneca makes a similar accusation of Roman men and elaborates that "these effeminates" transform themselves into women by "[b]raiding the hair, refining the voice till it is as caressing as a woman's, competing in bodily softness with women, beautifying themselves with filthy fineries. . . . Which of your contemporaries . . . is sufficiently a man?" (Seneca, *Contr.* 1.1.8–9). The feminizing effects of such foreign influences is why Augustus's moral reforms which sought to reinstate the traditions of the ancestors, those Roman men who were truly masculine because they had not succumbed to foreign influences, serve as key demonstration of his masculinity and effort to ensure the masculinity of Rome. Cicero applies these gendered tropes in his characterization of Catiline who, although being of higher birth than Cicero, manifests the various foreign sexual vices related to passivity that feminize Roman men and threatens the stability of the empire (Cicero, *Cat.* 2.7–11).[93]

Augustus's presentation of the nations also distinguishes those nations that can be treated with clemency because they seek to be saved by Roman friendship (i.e., domination) and those that need to be crushed because they refuse Roman friendship through military opposition. "The foreign nations which could with safety be pardoned I preferred to save rather than destroy" (*Res gest. divi Aug.* 3). By "saving," Augustus means incorporating into Roman rule as a subjugated foreign nation which must look up to Rome as a wife looks up to her husband.[94] Such a gendered dynamic becomes more pronounced in visual representations of Rome's interactions with other nations where, as Lopez points out, foreign nations are either described with effeminate characteristics or simply presented as women.[95] A nation could be saved by proactively seeking Roman friendship (i.e., rule), by negotiations, or by surrendering after some initial fighting:

> The Parthians I compelled [through negotiation] to restore to me the spoils and standards of three Roman armies, and to seek as suppliants the friendship of the Roman people. . . . Kings of the Parthians, Tiridates, and later Phrates, the son of King Phrates, took refuge with me as suppliants. . . . Phrates, son of Orodes, king of the Parthians, sent all his sons and grandsons to me in Italy, not because he had been conquered in war, but rather seeking our friendship by means of his own children as pledges. And a large number of other nations experienced the good faith of the Roman people during my principate who never before had had any interchange of embassies or of friendship with the Roman people (*Res gest. divi Aug.* 29, 32; trans. Shipley).

Lopez points to such variegated hierarchies in *Res Gestae* that relate how some foreigners can be effectively included in Rome's household through different means of subjugation, while other nations are so unruly that they must be destroyed to bring about world peace, as part of Rome's imperial propaganda of encouraging submission to Rome and justifying the destruction of any people that refused Rome's friendship.[96] Applying the gendered ideology of Roman imperial domination as discussed above shows that the more resistant a group is to Roman control the more effeminate are their descriptions. Such a distinction is important as Josephus pointedly describes the rebels who cause the war as acting like women.

Josephus's use of discourses of gender must be fit within his overall rhetorical goals in *Jewish Wars* as indicated in the preface to the work.[97] Josephus begins by contesting other accounts which do not accurately present the significance of the war, both in terms of the ferocity of the battles or the cost to the Jews and Romans. Josephus laments that these other accounts undermine their goal "to demonstrate the greatness of the Romans" because these accounts "diminish and lessen the actions of the Jews" (*J.W.* 1.7). Josephus makes the point that for the Romans to be truly great, they cannot only conquer those who are weak but must be shown to overcome truly powerful enemies (*J.W.* 1.8). The greatness of the Romans will be demonstrated through the "length of the war, the multitude of the Roman forces who so greatly suffered in it, or the might of the commanders whose great labors about Jerusalem will be deemed inglorious if what they achieved be reckoned but a small matter" (*J.W.* 1.9). Josephus, then, calling the war between the Romans and the Jews the "greatest of all those [wars], not only that have been in our times, but, in a manner, of those that ever were heard of" functions to rehabilitate Jewish identity despite the loss to the Romans and reinforce Roman greatness and sovereignty in ways similar to the presentation in *Res Gestae* that I discussed above (*J.W.* 1.1).

Such a presentation would locate the Jews as one of the great nations against which Rome establishes its identity as proper ruler of the world. Josephus makes this point explicit in Agrippa's lengthy attempt to dissuade the Jewish rebellion. Agrippa systematically discusses the Roman subjugation of foreign nations in a manner that evokes of Augustus's presentation in *Res Gestae* since it deals with characteristics of each nation and how they resist or accept Rome's peace (*J.W.* 2.356–88).[98] Caryn Reeder makes a similar point in examining the way Josephus portrays the Jewish and Roman characters throughout the *Jewish Wars* as conforming to masculine ideals.[99] While Reeder focuses more broadly on the way Josephus reconstructs Jewish masculinity through attributing masculine attributes to various Jewish characters by applying the categories of masculinity and femininity, I will look more narrowly on how characters and groups are situated within the gendered trope as discussed above. It will, therefore, be important to note how Josephus conforms Jews and Romans to gendered tropes as he presents them as truly great people or those who are responsible for causing the war.[100] This will be seen in Josephus's presentation of Jewish and Roman leaders as exemplary men by conforming them to standards of masculinity, Jewish women as the epitome of appropriate femininity, and the rebels as out of control effeminates. Most Jewish men, then, are portrayed as complicit men.

Josephus's most obvious application of gendered language comes in his descriptions of the rebels who follow John of Gischala, those tyrants that

Josephus repeatedly blames for causing the war (cf. *J.W.* 1.10, 11, 24, 27).[101] Rather than Roman aggression or a widespread rebellion by the Jewish people, "it was a seditious temper of our own that destroyed it; and that they were the tyrants among the Jews who brought the Roman power upon us, who unwillingly attacked us" (*J.W.* 1.10). Not only do these tyrants provoke the Romans to attack the Jews (*J.W.* 1.10), but the tyrants' barbarity causes internal fighting amongst the Jewish people (*J.W.* 1.24). Jason von Ehrenkrook notes that it is this "tyranny which emerges as the central antagonist in [Josephus's] narrative" as it threatens to undermine Roman sovereignty and destroy Jewish society.[102] Josephus is clear that the Romans are not guilty of unjust aggression but "pitied the people who were kept under by the seditious, and did often voluntarily delaye the taking of the city, and allowed time to the siege in order to let the authors have the opportunity for repentance" (*J.W.* 1.10; cf. 1.27). The depiction of a chaotic or unruly group of foreigners who require the disciplined and just Romans to bring peace and stability through restrained and just conquest corresponds to the gendered ideology of Rome's imperial propaganda as presented above. Philo applies nearly identical language to depict Augustus saving the world from utter destruction and chaos and as one "who gave freedom to every city, who brought disorder into order, who civilized and made obedient and harmonious, nations which before his time were unsociable, hostile, and brutal" (*Legat.* 143–47).

Corresponding to this description in the preface, Josephus paints the rebels as overcome by effeminacy. They fight other Jews rather than defend Jerusalem (*J.W.* 5.72–74), they do not defend their women and children (*J.W.* 4.107, 4.118), and they murder real men out of envy and fear with the hopes of removing the men who demonstrate masculinity by protecting the land (*J.W.* 4.357–60). This description makes a sharp contrast to the masculine actions of Caesar, whose masculine place as the *patrem patriae* extends peace and justice to the world. Most explicitly, to complete their effeminate characterization, John of Gischala and his followers are overcome by their passions, dress as women, use makeup, and seek the passive role in sexual acts (*J.W.* 4.559–62). The account begins with them being "permitted to do all the things that any of them desired to do" (*J.W.* 4.559). The giving of oneself over to the control of passion and desire is one of the quintessential markers of effeminacy.[103]

> with freedom feminize themselves to the full with long hair, putting on women's clothing, pouring ointments so as to appear beautiful, and painting under their eyes and not only imitated the ornaments but, also, the lusts of women, and were guilty of such excessive debauchery, that they invented unlawful pleasures of that sort. And they wallowed in the city as in a brothel (πορνείῳ), and defiled it entirely with their impure actions; nay, while their faces looked like the faces of

women, they killed with their right hands: and when their walk was effeminate, they presently attacked men, and became warriors, and drew their swords from under their finely dyed cloaks, and ran everyone through whom they came to. (*J.W.* 4.561–62, trans. Whiston)

Josephus's description of the transformation of masculine bodies into effeminate ones through the use of feminine adornments and actions mirrors the transformation which Josephus elsewhere ascribes to eunuchs (cf. *Ant.* 4.290–91). Most shockingly, the excessive passion and pleasure leads them to invent new forms of feminine excess which ultimately feminizes the city by making it like a house of πορνεία. In striking contrast to the way masculinity is portrayed as maintaining the order of a city and protecting its inhabitants, these rebels feminize themselves and the city, plunging it and the people into danger. Recalling the physiognomic discussions from Polemo and the previous chapter makes the description of the rebels' walks and faces as effeminate all the more jarring since it shows that they are not merely pretending but are thoroughly effeminate; they might as well be women. Making the connection with Josephus's comments in the preface about tyrants clearly portrays their effeminacy as thoroughly intertwined with their rejection of Roman rule. The feminine disobedience of this small group does not, therefore, problematize the masculinity of other Jewish men who demonstrate masculinity and, therefore, can be loyal to Rome.

Josephus goes to great lengths to associate the Jewish people as a whole and exemplary Jews like Herod and himself with masculine characteristics, a move which would prevent the Jewish people from suffering the institutionalized marginalization which could result when a people fell out of favor with Rome.[104] The two main challenges that Josephus faces in this endeavor are that he cannot rewrite history to say that the Jews won the war and that he cannot masculinize the Jews to the extent that he threatens Rome's dominance (i.e., feminizes Rome). This renegotiation of masculinity without relying on physical dominance in combat is seen in a wide variety of Greek and Roman texts beginning in the first century as Rome's military shifted from a necessary means for elites to establish their political careers to primarily drawing from the lower classes and no longer necessary for political advancement. Masculinity for the preponderance of men, then, was framed in terms of complicit masculinity since it was associated with obedience to the emperor, or virtue (ἀρετή), and living within one's proper place in society.

Josephus's use of virtue in connection with key terms of masculinity demonstrates his application of this discourse and simultaneously manifests what other characteristics Josephus associates with masculinity. In the *Jewish War*, Josephus utilizes many of the key terms for masculinity to describe Herod. Herod displays courage (ἀνδρεία) and virtue (ἀρετή) in coming to the aid of Antony in battle (*J.W.* 1.321–22); terms which the previous chapter demonstrated were key markers of masculinity. Josephus's writings also show a consistent association between these terms in marking the masculinity of key men (e.g., *Ant.* 3.58; 6.160); a roman soldier's courage (ἀρετή) in battle inspires other Roman soldiers to become (γίνομαι) manly (ἀνδρεία) (*J.W.* 5.314). Herod displays an astonishing degree of self-mastery over his passions and body by shortening his mourning over his brother's death and completing a march that exceeds his physical capabilities (*J.W.* 1.328–29). The ensuing description of Herod avenging his brother's death, repeatedly defeating enemies in battle through feats of courage, retaking Jerusalem, and instilling courage (ἀνδρεία) in his soldiers through great speeches all fit the model of a masculine leader (*J.W.* 1.330–80). Within this section of the narrative, one of the key moments is when Herod prevents his own forces, many of whom are non-Jews, from destroying the Jewish temple and looting the city (*J.W.* 1.354–55). Josephus has already used the masculine characteristic of being active, a term Josephus uses in conjunction other masculine characteristics such as bravery and the ability to speak (*J.W.* 1.283; 4.230, 392, 624), in describing Herod as a leader who protects his people from brigands and inspires others to restore order in Jerusalem (*J.W.* 1.204–5). In fact, the rhetorical force of Herod's plea to Caesar after Antony's defeat hinges on Caesar recognizing Herod's friendship (i.e., loyalty and support) to his Roman benefactor rather than the fact that Herod's benefactor had been Antony (*J.W.* 1.386–90). Caesar's recognition of Herod's virtue causes him to engage him as a friend and secure Herod's kingship (i.e., status as a powerful man since losing this position would be seen as feminizing Herod). Recalling the use of friendship in *Res Gestae* shows us how Josephus has used such language and masculine characteristics to position Herod as one of the people that Rome should save, not destroy.

Although Herod does evidence some feminine qualities in *Jewish War*, these are minimized in comparison with Josephus's description of him in *Jewish Antiquities* and relate to dangers which threaten men in general. One of the main exceptions to Herod's masculine characterization comes as a result of his love for Mariamne which renders him unable to speak (*J.W.* 1.437–38). The silencing of men is a common trope of feminization throughout Hellenistic, Jewish, and Christian literature.[105] Elsewhere, Josephus notes the potential feminizing effect of beauty on those who observe it (*Ant.* 1.162, 4.129), particularly beautiful women like Mariamne (cf. *Ant.* 15.23), and so it does not appear to be a slight against Herod's masculinity in particular but a warning in general to all men. Although beauty can be a positive characteristic, like Moses's beauty as a baby which attracts people to follow the child (*Ant.* 2.230–31), it has the potential to make people vulnerable to their passions and, therefore, to feminization. This connection appears to drive Josephus's warnings about eunuchs "for it is evident that while their soul becomes effeminate, they have transfused that effeminacy to their body also" (*Ant.* 4.291). This is the same type of feminization which requires Josephus to lock the women of the city in their houses lest they feminize the men and prevent them from defending the city (*J.W.* 3.263). So Herod's characterization in *Jewish War* is not only predominantly masculine, but significantly more masculine than his characterization in Josephus's other writings.

Even though the Jews lost the war, Josephus can still utilize the battlefield to highlight the virtue and, therefore, the masculinity of the Jews. Josephus's emphasis on the length of the war, the number of Romans necessary to conquer the Jews, and the ability of Titus and Vespasian who lead the Roman forces indicates that the Jews are manly, but not as manly as the Romans, and that this masculinity reinforces Rome's greatness.[106] The Jewish soldiers are able to rally each other from passively watching the Romans building their camp to fighting bravely against them (*J.W.* 5.73–75; cf. 6.69–80 and 6.152–55). Although these displays of masculinity temporarily overwhelm the Romans, the Roman commanders are able to threaten the soldiers with effeminacy in order to spur them to bravery and overcoming the Jewish attacks. Seeing the possibility of defeat, Titus "reproached [his Roman soldiers] for their lack of manhood (ἀνανδρίαν) and brought those back that were running away" (*J.W.* 5.81). This threat spurs the Romans to bravely fight and overcome the Jews. Their masculinity overcomes that of the Jews. In fact, the Jews demonstrate such remarkable courage in the face of near certain defeat that they spur the Roman soldiers to a greater display of courage (*J.W.* 3.152–53).[107] Josephus presents Jewish masculinity in such complicit terms that even when it might otherwise challenge Roman dominance, it only serves to reinforce and strengthen Rome's hegemonic masculinity.

Josephus's self-presentation embodies this same dynamic. He clearly positions his masculinity below that of the Romans by stating that although he did not defeat the Romans, his military prowess lengthened the time needed to defeat the Jews and is recognized by the Roman soldiers which calls to mind Titus's recognition of Herod's masculinity discussed above (*J.W.* 3.464; 4.9). Josephus is careful, however, to not portray his masculinity as rivaling that of the Romans since Josephus's defense are "strongly fortified . . . though not as strongly as Tiberius" (*J.W.* 3.364). While still fighting with the rebellion, Josephus exhorts his fellow Jews that, "Now is the time to begin to fight in earnest, when there is no hope of deliverance left. It is a brave thing to prefer glory before life" and then attacks the Roman encampment, causing the Roman soldiers shame at the losses they suffer (*J.W.* 3:204–6). The display of courage despite the near certainty of defeat is a well-established means of demonstrating masculinity and one Josephus also uses for the Romans (*J.W.* 3.276). Herodotus's account of the Greeks holding off the Persians at Thermopylae refers to the courage and ferocity of the Greeks despite the certainty of their dying in the process as demonstrating their greatness (*Hist.* 7.222–24).[108] This courage is even recognized by the Romans. Nicanor, on behalf of Vespasian himself, tells Josephus that, "[Josephus] had behaved himself so courageously (ἀρετήν), that the commanders rather admired than hated him that the general was very desirous to have him brought to him, not in order to punish him, for that he could do though he should not come voluntarily, but that he was determined to preserve a man of his courage" (*J.W.* 3.347–48). Like Herod, Josephus's masculinity is so plain that the Romans not only spare his life but welcome him into friendship, a relationship which would safeguard Josephus from suffering the same type of marginalization suffered by the Egyptians under the *idios logos*, laws which were established by Augustus and prevent Egyptians from assuming public roles of power, serving in the military, gaining citizenship, and other manifestations of masculinity.[109] These Egyptians are in vivid contrast to the Jewish rebels who, although appearing to act bravely by jumping into a burning tower, are cast as effeminate since they are simply being deceptive because they were protected in a hidden vault (*J.W.* 5.330).

Josephus also rehabilitates Jewish masculinity by conforming Jewish women to stereotypical discourses of femininity. Josephus omits accounts of Jewish women fighting alongside men, which are found in Tacitus's account of the Jewish rebellion where the Jewish "men and women [who defend Jerusalem] showed the same determination" (*Hist.* 5.13). When Josephus does portray women fighting the Romans, they do so in the most feminine way possible by throwing domestic objects from their roofs while the "men of power" fight in the streets (*J.W.* 3.303). William Barry demonstrates that the portrayal of women, youths, and slaves defending their homes by throwing domestic materials, primarily tiles from the roof, is a common trope for appropriate military activity of feminine people.[110] Although women fighting in battle might be thought to interfere with the gendered discourse that fighting was an exclusively masculine activity, these texts maintain the basic gendered framework of public and private spaces and what is appropriate for the masculine and the feminine by only portraying women and effeminate men fighting in and around the domestic sphere.[111] Furthermore, in Josephus's account, as soon as the Jewish men are defeated by the Romans the fighting is over and the women are taken captive (*J.W.* 3.304); the women cannot fight on their own, only aid the fighting of the men. This represents a dramatically different portrayal than that of Tacitus, who blends Jewish men and women together during the siege of Jewish cities.

Josephus also conforms Jewish women to other gendered stereotypes which emphasize their passive nature. During the height of a particularly gruesome battle, Josephus says that the Jewish women cry so loudly that they rival the sound of the battle (*J.W.* 3.248). The uncontrolled display of emotion the women demonstrate was typically associated with effeminacy. Josephus also presents Jewish women and children at the mercy of the direction of Jewish men. In such accounts, their obedience to men reinforces the dominance of the men. This is even the case when the men choose to kill the women rather than let them be captured by the Romans (*J.W.* 3.248, 4.70–83, 4.106–10). As with the descriptions of bravery despite the certainty of defeat, men killing their women rather than let them fall into the hands of their enemies was a sign of masculinity.[112]

Josephus's rehabilitation of Jewish masculinity, then, shows that Jews conform to appropriate gender stereotypes while remaining obedient to Roman dominance. As discussed at the beginning of this chapter, such a location within a gendered hierarchy fits the model of complicit masculinity since Josephus argues that the Jews, in general, demonstrate sufficient masculinity to be pious members of the Empire. Whatever effeminacy that caused the war between the Romans and the Jews can be assigned to the rebels who, because of their inability to conform to standard models of masculinity, need to be subordinated. The effect is to encourage the Romans to treat Jews as appropriate members, albeit subjugated members, of the Roman household as they seek Roman favor and protection in Judea and throughout the empire.

CONCLUSION

The current chapter has addressed the way different forms of masculinity relate to power. In order to accomplish this, I began by discussing hegemonic, complicit, and subordinate forms of masculinity as formulated in modern sociological investigations and how each form of masculinity controls, restricts, promotes, or lacks power. Before turning to examples of these forms of masculinity at work in ancient literature, I examined the idea of *persona* in ancient Greek and Roman texts. This examination argued that how an author presented himself, what the author said, and even how the author said it could have significant influence on the perception of the author's masculinity or lack thereof. The importance of an author's *persona* and its connection to his masculinity was crucial because of the legal consequences such perceptions held for the author. The importance of this section is that, in my final investigation of specific texts, I needed to be able to argue that the authors being examined could expect that their audiences would make significant determination about their masculinity based on their texts, even with respect to obscure details which could be read as masculine or feminine, and especially when using well-established discourses of gender. Since each of the authors evidence a concern over how their masculinity was perceived, it is not unreasonable to expect that they would go to significant lengths to rehabilitate their masculinity and that of the group with which they are associated.

After applying a gender critical analysis to Favorinus, Philo, and Josephus in order to investigate how each author invokes and manipulates discourses of gender for specific aims, it is clear that each author can be associated with either hegemonic or complicit masculinity. Favorinus seeks to renegotiate the contours of masculinity around his own problematic body in such a way that not only are his opponents subordinated to him but that he aspires to a position of dominance over his audience and any who might challenge him. Favorinus's argument for his status as the pinnacle of masculinity and the way that status should allow him to exert dominance over his audience fit the chief characteristics of a hegemonic masculinity. Josephus and Philo, on the other hand, go to great lengths to distance the Jewish people from charges of sedition by feminizing a particular group and demonstrating that the Jewish law and customs make the Jews complicit members of the Roman Empire. For both authors, the Jews are not only innocent of threatening Roman dominance (i.e., masculinity), they actually serve to secure it. Their work to show that Jewish masculinity supports, rather than threatens, Roman dominance while they simultaneously feminize their opponents in such a way that their opponents could not function within Rome's hierarchy fits the description of complicit masculinity.

The methodological approach and conclusions of this chapter will need to be kept in mind as I turn to enact a similar examination of Paul's first letter to the Corinthians. How does Paul present himself, the Corinthian Christians, and outsiders? Do these descriptions demonstrate a pattern consistent with any of the discourses of gender examined so far? If there is a pattern, is the gender and position to power consistent with how Paul situates any of these groups vis-a-vis any other groups? Finally, how does Paul's use of gender and power correspond with his vision of the kingdom of God and its place in the world?

NOTES

1. For example, although Susanna Asikainen's analysis of the use of eunuchs in Matthew 19 is helpful in terms of gender deviance, her work lacks a focus on how the terms hegemonic and subordinate apply specifically to power and the legitimization of group relations and patriarchy; "'Eunuchs for the Kingdom of Heaven': Matthew

and Subordinate Masculinities," in *Biblical Masculinities Foregrounded* (ed. Ovidiu Creangă and Peter-Ben Smit; Sheffield: Sheffield Phoenix Press, 2014), 161–69.

2. Tim Carrigan, R.W Connell, and John Lee, "Toward a New Sociology of Masculinity," *TS* 14 (1985): 551–604. Susan Haddox provides one of the most thorough evaluations of a biblical text in light of Carrigan's, Connell's, and Lee's use of hegemonic and subordinate masculinities; see "Favored Sons and Subordinate Masculinities," in *Men and Masculinity in the Hebrew Bible and Beyond* (ed. Ovidiu Creanga; Sheffield: Sheffield Phoenix, 2010), 2–19. I largely agree with her usage, but, as will be clear below, I also adopt the more recent term "complicit" to help better understand the power relations between different forms of masculinity.

3. Ibid., 552, 592–99.

4. Ibid., 590.

5. R. W. Connell and James W. Messerschmidt, "Hegemonic Masculinity: Rethinking the Concept," *GS* 19 (2005): 832–833.

6. Ibid., 592–93.

7. R. W. Connell, *Masculinities* (2nd ed.; Berkeley: University of California Press, 2005), 76–77.

8. Carrigan, Connell, and Lee, Toward, 587–88.

9. Mike Donaldson, "What is Hegemonic Masculinity?" *TS* 22 (1993): 643–57; "Studying Up: The Masculinity of the Hegemonic," in *Male Trouble: Studying Australian Masculinities* (ed. Stephen Tomsen and Mike Donaldson; Melbourne: Pluto Press, 2003); Christine Beasley, "Re-Thinking Hegemonic Masculinity in a Globalizing World," *MM* 11 (2008): 86–103; "Problematizing Current Men/Masculinities Theorizing: The Contribution of Raewyn Connell and Conceptual-Terminological Tensions Today," *BJS* 63 (2012): 747–65. "Mind the Gap? Masculinity Studies and Contemporary Gender/Sexuality Thinking," *AFS* 28 (2013): 108–24. Mimi Schippers, "Recovering the Feminine Other: Masculinity, Femininity, and Gender Hegemony," *TS* 36 (2007): 85–102. Some critiques of this literature appear to stem from confusion over the scope of the terms due to not properly understanding their origin. For example, *The Handbook of Language, Gender, and Sexuality* (2nd ed.; ed. Susan Ehrlich and Miriam Meyerhoff, and Janet Holmes; Oxford: John Wiley & Sons, 2014) traces the origin of hegemonic masculinity to the first edition of Connell's *Masculinities* (Berkeley: University of California Press, 1995). The result is that scholars often critique Connell and others for not specifying a focus on power or the diversity within masculinity even though the original article by Carrigan, Connell, and Lee discussed above clearly outlines hegemonic masculinity in these terms.

10. Donaldson, "Hegemonic," 645.

11. Antonio Gramsci, *Prison Notebooks, Volume 1* (trans. Joseph A. Buttigieg; New York: Columbia University Press, 1992), 137, 350.

12. Gramsci, *Prison Notebooks*, 152–53.

13. See the discussion in Richard Howson, *Challenging Hegemonic Masculinity* (New York: Routledge, 2006), 22–28; "Hegemonic Masculinity in the Theory of Hegemony: A Brief Response to Christine Beasley's 'Rethinking Hegemonic Masculinity in a Globalizing World,'" *MM* 11 (2008): 109–13.

14. Donaldson, "Hegemonic," 650–52.

15. Beasley, "Mind," 109–11.
16. Schippers, "Recovering," 87–88.
17. Ibid., 100–101.
18. R. W. Connell, James W. Messerschmidt, "Hegemonic Masculinity: Rethinking the Concept," *GS* 19 (2005): 829–859; James W. Messerschmidt, "And Now the Rest of the Story: A Commentary on Christine Beasley's "Rethinking Hegemonic Masculinity in a Globalizing World," *MM* 11 (2008): 104-08; *Hegemonic Masculinities and Camouflaged Politics* (Boulder, Colo.: Paradigm, 2010); "Engendering Gendered Knowledge: Assessing the Academic Appropriation of Hegemonic Masculinity," *MM* 15 (2012): 56–76;
19. Ronald Weitzer and Charis Kubrin, "Misogyny in Rap Music: A Content Analysis of Prevalence and Meaning," *MM* 12 (2009): 3–29.
20. Weitzer and Kubrin, "Misogyny," 22–24.
21. Messerschmidt, "Engendering," 4.
22. Connell and Messerschmidt, "Hegemonic," 847–49.
23. Judith Butler, *Gender Trouble: Feminism and the Subversion of Identity* (2nd ed.; New York: Routledge, 1999), 101–80.
24. Messerschmidt, "Engendering," 4. More recent discussions highlight the differences between local, regional, and global constructions of hegemonic masculinities; see Beasley, "Re-Thinking," 1–18. The main difference between these constructions is that local and regional hegemonic masculinities propagate on a more direct, personal basis within a particular society whereas global hegemonic masculinities cross national borders and often create systems which manipulate and export regional hegemonic masculinities.
25. Carrigan, Connell, and Lee, "Toward," 587.
26. Messerschmidt, "Engendering Gender Knowledge," 56–76;
27. Richlin, "Not Before Homosexuality," 532–40.
28. Since the terms *persona* and πρόσωπον function as near equivalents, I shall hereafter use *persona* except when the term πρόσωπον appears in the primary source. For a discussion of the semantic equivalence between *persona* and πρόσωπον, see V. Henry T. Nguyen, *Christian Identity in Corinth: A Comparative Study of 2 Corinthians, Epictetus, and Valerius Maximus* (WUNT 243; Tübingen: Mohr Siebeck, 2008), 16–20; Liddel, Scott, and Jones, *A Greek-English Lexicon*, ad loc.
29. Nguyen, *Christian Identity*, 14–16. For other examinations of *persona* and its effects on a person's public or legal identity, see Anna McCullough, "Gender and Public Image in Imperial Rome" (Ph.D. diss., University of St. Andrews, 2007), 54–74; Erik Gunderson, "Discovering the Body in Roman Oratory" in *Parchments of Gender: Deciphering the Bodies of Antiquity* (ed. Maria Wyke; Oxford: Clarendon, 1998), 169–89.
30. This selection of some of the more common and useful meanings of the term comes from Glare, *Oxford Latin Dictionary*, ad loc; Lewis and Short, *A Latin Dictionary*, ad loc.
31. For Aristotle's discussion of the matching the form of rhetoric, or *topos*, to the content being argued, see *Rhet.*, I. For Quintilian's use of Aristotle's *Rhetoric*, see

Inst. orat., 5.10.17 which refers to *Rhet.*, II.12–17; William M.A. Grimaldi, *Aristotle, Rhetoric II: A Commentary* (New York: Fordham University Press, 1988), 3–4.

32. The initial explorations of the idea of social identify are found in S. Schlossmann, *Persona und ΠΡΟΣΩΠΟΝ im Recht und christlichen Dogma* (Kiliae: Lipsius and Tischer, 1906); M. Mauss, "Une catégorie de l'esprit humain: La notion de personnne, celle de 'moi,'" *JRAIGBI* 68 (1938): 263–81. Social identity later developed into Social Identity Theory in the 1970s and 1980s with the work of H. Tajfel, "Social categorization, social identity and social comparison," in *Differentiation Between Social Groups: Studies in the Social Psychology of Intergroup Relations* (ed. H. Tajfel; London: Academic Press, 1978), 61–76; "Individuals and Groups in Social Psychology," *BJSP* 18 (1979): 183–90. See Mark Rubin and Miles Hewstone for a helpful review of the key tenets of Social Identity Theory and critique of some of its applications; "Social Identity, System Justification, and Social Dominance: Commentary on Reicher, Jost et al., and Sidanius et al.," *PP* 25 (2004): 823–44.

33. Rubin and Hewstone, "Social Identity," 824–25.

34. Nguyen, *Christian Identity*, 12–13, 21–51.

35. Nguyen, *Christian Identity*, 22–23.

36. See the discussion in the previous chapter regarding the connection between the body and gender.

37. Skinner, *Sexuality in Greek and Roman Culture*, 197–99.

38. Edwards, *Politics*, 34–62; Karl Galinsky, *Augustan Culture: An Interpretive Introduction* (Princeton: Princeton University Press, 1996), 58–79.

39. Adopting the *persona* of another was a common practice in rhetorical education and carried similar dangers; see W. Martin Bloomer, "Schooling in Persona: Imagination and Subordination in Roman Education," *CA* 16 (1996): 57–78.

40. Ronald G. Mayer, "Persona Problems: The Literary Persona in Antiquity Revisited," *MDATC* 50 (2003): 55–80; Diskin Clay, "The Theory of the Literary Persona in Antiquity," *MDATC* 40 (1998): 9–40.

41. Ibid., 63.

42. Ibid., 67–73.

43. Although the reason for Ovid's exile is not known, he appears to respond to charges of effeminacy. See the discussion in G. P. Goold, "The Cause of Ovid's Exile," *ICS* 8 (1983): 94–107.

44. Ibid., 77.

45. Clay, "Literary Persona," 39–40; Mayer, "Persona," 79.

46. This will be demonstrated in the following section, which focuses on Favorinus's *Corinthian Oration*.

47. For a treatment of the history of Favorinus's writing, much of which survives as attributed to other authors or in their recollections and quotations of his work, see Adelmo Barigazzi, *Favorini di Arelate Opere* (Florence, 1966); E. Mensching, *Favorin von Arelate: Der erste Teil der Fragmente* (Berlin: Walter de Gruyter, 1963); Leofranc Holford-Strevens, *Aulus Gellius* (Chapel Hill: University of North Carolina Press, 1988), 81–83. G. W. Bowersock's treatment of Philostratus as the biographer of the sophists provides a helpful framework within which to read the work of Philostratus

and other authors who wrote about the sophists; *Greek Sophists in the Roman Empire* (Oxford: Clarendon, 1969), 1–16, 89–109; see also C. P. Jones, "The Reliability of Philostratus," in *Approaches to the Second Sophistic* (ed. G. W. Bowersock; University Park, Pa: American Philological Association 1974), 14.

48. For an overview of Favorinus's upbringing and educational pedigree, see Gleason, *Making Men*, 1–6.

49. McDonnell, *Roman Manliness* 1–72; Foxhall, *Introduction*, 3–4.

50. Tim Whitmarsh, "Thinking Local," in *Local Knowledge and Microidentities in the Imperial Greek World* (ed. Tim Whitmarsh; Cambridge: Cambridge University Press, 2010), 1–16.

51. Gleason, *Making Men*, 28.

52. Simon Goldhill's edited volume examines the benefits and problems with the use of the single term sophists in describing writers with interests as varied as geography and medicine who never refer to themselves as part of a self-conscious movement; *Being Greek under Rome: Cultural Identity, The Second Sophistic and the Development of Empire* (ed. Simon Goldhill; Cambridge: Cambridge University Press, 2001).

53. Harmon's translation in the LCL of ὄρχεις as "Those you lack" is a curious circumlocution of for ὄρχις, the most common and, in light of the discussion on in the intersection of power and masculinity, most plausible meaning of which is testicles. I replace this with testicles in order to emphasize the connection between the physical body, masculinity, and oratory. See *LSJ* for a list of such uses.

54. I follow Robert Hoyland's translation of *Physiognomy* found in *Seeing the Face, Seeing the Soul: Polemo's Physiognomy from Classical Antiquity to Medieval Islam* (ed. Simon Swain; Oxford: Oxford University Press, 2007), 329–464.

55. Gleason, *Making Men*, 46–47. An anonymous Latin manuscript which comments on physiognomy makes direct reference to this section of Polemo's *Physiognomy* and states that, "[Polemo] did not write down his name, but it is understood that he was talking about Favorinus. He assigned the other signs of this type of body to this man" (*Anon. Lat.* 40); see Ian Repath, "Anonymous Latinus, *Book of Physiognomy*," in *Seeing the Face, Seeing the Soul: Polemo's Physiognomy from Classical Antiquity to Medieval Islam* (ed. Simon Swain; Oxford: Oxford University Press, 2007), 583.

56. The text for Favorinus's *Corinthian Oration* has been preserved in the work of Dio Chyrsostom, Favorinus's teacher. The text is universally hailed to be the work of Favorinus. For a history of the text see Barigazzi, *Favorino*, 298–300. Barigazzi argues that it was Favorinus's quarrel with Hadrian that led the Corinthians to remove the statue of Favorinus. Although Philostratus indicates that this is the reason for the Athenians removing a statue of Favorinus, there is no direct evidence for this being the case in in Corinth. Gleason, avoids speculation on the providence of the text; *Making Men*, 8. Swain argues that it was on account of Favorinus's apparent adultery with the wife of a man of counselor rank which resulted in the Corinthians removing his statue; *Favorinus and Hadrian*, 154–55.

57. See Gleason's discussion on the problems of self-praise and Favorinus's use of a defense of his statue in order to avoid directly praising himself; *Making Men*, 9, 16–17, 104, 149–50.

58. Gleason, *Making Men*, 146–47.

59. Jason König, "Favorinus's *Corinthian Oration* in Its Corinthian Context," *CCJ* 47 (2001): 141–71.

60. Ibid., 160–71.

61. Richard A. Baer, *Philo's Use of the Categories of Male and Female* (Leiden: Brill, 1970). See the discussion in Loader, *Philo, Josephus*, 4–5.

62. Dorothy Sly, *Philo's Perception of Women* (BJS 209; Atlanta: Scholars Press, 1990); Judith Romney Wegner, "Philo's Portrayal of Women: Hebraic or Hellenic?," in *"Women Like This": New Perspectives on Jewish Women in the Greco-Roman World* (ed. A.-J. Levine; SBLEJL 1; Atlanta: Scholars Press, 1991), 41–66; Sharon Lea Mattila tackles the apparent incongruity between Philo's consistent use of gendered stereotypes in presenting people and his use of gender to personify concepts like wisdom; "Wisdom, Sense Perception, Nature and Philo's Gender Gradient," *HTR* 89 (1996): 103–29; Annawies van den Hoek, "Endowed with Reason or Glued to the Senses: Philo's Thoughts on Adam and Eve," in *The Creation of Man and Woman: Interpretations of the Biblical Narratives in Jewish and Christian Traditions* (ed. G. P. Luttikhuizen; *Themes in Biblical Narrative* 3; Leiden: Brill, 2000), 63–75; Leslie Baynes, "Philo, Personification and the Transformation of Grammatical Gender," *Studia Philonica Annual* 14 (2002): 31–47; Colleen Conway, "Gender and Divine Relativity in Philo of Alexandria," *JSJ* 34 (2003): 471–491; Holgar Szesnat, "'Pretty Boys' in Philo's De Vita Contemplativa," *Studia Philonica Annual* 10 (1998): 87–107; Colleen Conway, "Gender and Divine Relativity in Philo of Alexandria," *JSJ* 34 (2003), 471–91; David Lincicum, "Philo and the Physiognomic Tradition," *JSJ* 44 (2013), 57–86. Karen L. King, "Comparative Study of Gendered Strategies to Represent the Sacrality of the Group: Philo of Alexander and a Korean-American Presbyterian Church," in *Bodies, Borders, Believers: Ancient Texts and Present Conversations* (ed. Anne Hege Grung, Marianne Bjelland Kartzow, Anna Rebecca Solevåg; Eugene, Or: Penwick, 2015), 3–21.

63. Baer, *Philo's Use*, 49. Mattila, "Philo's Gender Gradient," 104-05. Loader makes a similar point in his analysis of Philo's use of sex and gender; e.g., *Philo, Josephus*, 31–32.

64. Loader, *Philo, Josephus*, 31–40, 45–55; Sly, *Philo's Perception*, 122.

65. Mattila, "Philo's Gender Gradient," 105-07; Sly, *Philo's Perception*, 43–58.

66. Mattila, "Philo's Gender Gradient," 108–10, 126–27.

67. Sly, *Philo's Perception*, 145–54.

68. Sly, *Philo's Perception*, 220.

69. See Mattila's discussion of Philo attributing gender to wisdom and nature in "Philo's Gender Gradient," 108–12, 120–25.

70. See Sly's discussion of Phil's surprising description of Leah and Rachel which appears to conflict with the biblical account's portrayal of the two women; "Philo's

Perception," 163–74. Loader demonstrates that this process of attributing a host of feminine or masculine characteristics based on a single observation is widespread in Philo's writings; *Philo, Josephus*, 31–55.

71. Haddox provides a similar evaluation of the biblical account of Esau as found in Genesis; see "Favored Sons," 10–14.

72. See Szesnat's discussion on the progression of unnatural acts and its consequences, "Pretty Boys," 93–95.

73. Mary Rose D'Angelo, "Gender and Geopolitics in the Work of Philo of Alexandria: Jewish Piety and Imperial Family Values," in *Mapping Gender in Ancient Religious Discourses* (ed. Todd Penner and Caroline Vander Stichele; Leiden: Brill, 2007), 66.

74. Ibid., 70–88.

75. Ibid., 77–78.

76. Torrey Seland, "Philo as a Citizen: *Homo politicus*," in *Reading Philo: A Handbook on Philo of Alexandria* (ed. Torrey Seland; Grand Rapids: Eerdmans, 2014), 70.

77. Brittany E. Wilson, "Unmanly Men: Refigurations of Masculinity in Luke-Acts" (Ph.D. diss., Princeton Theological Seminary, 2012), 117–29.

78. King, *Gendered Strategies*, 15.

79. Lopez, *Apostle to the Conquered*, 101-017.

80. See the review in Aryeh Kasher, "Polemic and Apologetic Methods of Writing in *Contra Apionem*," in *Josephus' Contra Apionem: Studies in Its Character and Context with a Latin Concordance to the Portion Missing in Greek* (ed. Louis H. Feldman and John R. Levinson; Leiden: Brill, 1996), 143–86.

81. Caryn A. Reeder, "Gender, War, and Josephus," *JSJ* 46 (2015): 70.

82. Williams, *Roman Homosexuality*, 145–150; Davina Lopez, *Apostle to the Conquered: Reimaging Paul's Mission* (Minneapolis: Fortress Press, 2008), 26–55, 86–118; Colleen M. Conway, *Behold the Man: Jesus and Greco-Roman Masculinity* (Oxford: Oxford University Press, 2008), 15–48; Harry O. Maier, "A Sly Civility: Colossians and Empire," *JSNT* 27 (2005), 323–29; Eleanor Winsor Leach, "Horace Carmen 1.8: Achilles, the Campus Martius, and the Articulation of Gender Roles in Augustan Rome," *CP* 89 (1994): 334–43. Matthew Kuefler shows how a crisis in the assumed masculinity of the Romans and the effeminacy of foreigners in terms of military prowess led to a renegotiation of the discourses of masculinity; *The Manly Eunuch: Masculinity, Gender Ambiguity, and Christian Ideology in Late Antiquity* (Chicago: University of Chicago Press, 2001), 37–69.

83. Williams, *Roman Homosexuality*, 83–84, 154–56.

84. Philo shares Cicero's understanding of the necessity of the mind's masculinity in exerting control over emotions (*Her.* 1.274). Philo goes so far as to describe the mind which is enticed by luxury to give into softness as abandoning its nature and becoming like a eunuch.

85. Lopez offers an excellent analysis of how the stories of Rome's founding and history reinforce the divine mandate to bring order to the chaotic world through military dominance; *Apostle*, 56–86.

86. Conway, *Behold the Man*, 46–48; Bonnie J. Flessen makes a similar point in Augustus as moral and masculine exemplar intended for imitation; *An Exemplary Man: Cornelius and Characterization in Acts 10* (Eugne; Or.: Pinwick, 2011), 116–18. Michael Peachin argues that *Res Gestae* presents Augustus as an ideal father who demonstrates extreme self-control in not exercising authority too quickly as part of the text's legitimation of the titles given to Augustus (cf., *Res gestae divi Aug.*, 35); "Rome the Superpower: 96–235 C.E.," in *A Companion to the Roman Empire* (ed. David S. Potter; Oxford: Blackwell, 2006), 148.

87. See Lopez's discussion of the key role played by Roman domination in each of these texts; *Apostle*, 56–86.

88. Amy Richlin put the point of the imagery rather sharply as, "The Roman projection of Rome as a male fucking the rest of the world"; "Not Before Homosexuality: The Materiality of the Cinaedus and the Roman Law against Love between Men," *JHS* 3 (1994): 553.

89. For a discussion of the feminization of non-Roman people groups and its connection with Roman masculinity in imperial propaganda, see Lopez, *Apostle*, 17–21, 26–48.

90. Although the LCL translation of *semiviri* as "eunuch" accurately relates the connection between a eunuch as a person who lacks the adequate characteristics of masculinity to be a full *vir*, it misrepresents the point of Virgil's slanderous jab. The point is that the natural softness of these non-Romans makes them effeminate and unable to defend themselves from the domination of true men.

91. Such a gender bias pervades imperial Roman iconography; see Lopez, *Apostle*, 26–55.

92. Juvenal and Seneca make similar comparisons as they bemoan the feminizing influence of foreigners and the moral destruction of Rome's masculinity (e.g., Seneca, *Ben.*, 4.2.4; Juvenal, *Sat.*, 2); cf., Williams, *Roman Homosexuality*, 69–77, 148–51.

93. Erich S. Gruen offers a convincing argument that Cicero's disparaging of foreigners through feminizing characterization is a rhetorical move meant to dissuade Romans from activities that Cicero believes will endanger Roman superiority and, therefore, dominance by making them less manly; "Cicero and the Alien" in *Roman Literature, Gender and Reception: Domina Illustris* (ed. Donald Lateiner, Barbara K. Gold, and Judith Perkins; New York: Routledge, 2013), 13–27.

94. Parchami presents the *Pax Augustus* as the restoration of order to the worldwide Roman "household" in *Hegemonic Peace and Empire*, 15–30. Also, Gleason notes how masculinity is linked with class under the auspices of the *Pax Romana* in a way that provides Roman men the opportunity to challenge each other's masculinity; a point which helps explain the allure of such a system which allowed competition for masculinity without the danger of slipping into to the level of the effeminate barbarian; *Making Men*, 162.

95. Lopez, *Apostle*, 26–55.

96. Lopez, *Apostle*, 94.

97. For an overview of how Josephus's presentation of the war fits with the imperial ideology presented by Vespasian and Titus, see James S. McLaren, "The

Jewish War as a Response to the Crisis of Flavian Propaganda," in *Ancient Jewish and Christian Texts as Crisis Management Literature: Thematic Studies from the Centre of Early Christian Studies* (ed. David C. Sim and Pauline Allen; London: T&T Clark, 2012), 9–28.

98. Lopez notes the use of geography and ethnicity in Agrippa's speech reflect a political vision reminiscent of Augustus's; *Apostle*, 53–54, 110–13.

99. Reeder, "Gender, War, and Josephus," 65–85.

100. That Josephus has both Jewish and non-Jewish audiences in mind can be seen in his comments in *J.W.* 1.16 where he remarks that the mouths of the Jewish leaders are "muzzled" when it comes to write about the war; a lacuna Josephus will fill.

101. Jason von Ehrenkrook, "Effeminacy in the Shadow of Empire: The Politics of Transgressive Gender in Josephus's *Bellum Judaicum*," *JQ* 101 (2011): 145–63.

102. Ibid., 150–51.

103. Dale Martin provides a helpful review of such discourses related to passion and desire in *Sex and the Single Savior* (Louisville: Westminster John Knox, 2006), 65–76.

104. See the discussion in Naphtali Lewis, *Life in Egypt under Roman Rule* (Oxford: Clarendon, 1983), 33–34.

105. Wilson, *Unmanly Men*, 117–30.

106. Though Josephus uses the language of masculinity less frequently than his Greek and Roman contemporaries, when he does deploy such language it is more often to aggrandize Roman masculinity and diminish the masculinity of those who fight against Rome; see Reeder, "Gender, War, and Josephus," 71–76.

107. Also, J.W. 5.310 where Roman manliness derives from Roman military prowess, courage, and obedience to 5.330 where the apparent masculinity of the Jewish rebels jumping into a burning tower is mere deception since they were protected in a hidden vault.

108. Reeder, "Gender, War, and Josephus," 74–75.

109. Robert K. Ritner, "Egypt under Roman Rule: The Legacy of Ancient Egypt," in *The Cambridge History of Egypt: Vol 1* (ed. Carl F. Petry; Cambridge: Cambridge University Press, 1998), 5–8.

110. William D. Barry, "Roof Tiles and Urban Violence in the Ancient World," *GRBS* 37 (1996): 55–75.

111. Ibid., 68–69.

112. Reeder, "Gender, War, and Josephus," 74–75.

Chapter Four

Paul's Subordinate Masculinity

And last of all, as though to a miscarried baby, he appeared to me also.

—1 Cor 15:8

The current chapter moves this project into the constructive phase by applying the work of the first three chapters so as to better understand Paul's self-presentation of his subordinate masculine identity. As a result, it will focus narrowly on the function of gendered discourses in 1 Corinthians where Paul either references his own behavior or places his body before the Corinthians with enough detail to draw clear connections to discourses of gender. I will examine Paul's presentation of himself as failed orator (1 Cor 1:17–18; 2:1–5), a wet nurse (1 Cor 3:1–3), a shameful father (1 Cor 4:14–15), and a celibate man (1 Cor 7:1–7). In each text, I will demonstrate that Paul either appropriates a feminine or subordinate masculine position with the gendered discourse that he engages. For a male author to adopt a feminine role is startling within ancient Greek and Roman literature because doing so would pose catastrophic consequences for his ability to function or be heard as a man. When Paul does adopt male roles, like that of a failed orator or a shameful father, he fails to perform such roles according to the standards of masculinity expected of the men who properly fulfill such roles. Taken together, the overall effect for Paul's persona is the portrayal of a subordinate masculinity that would restrict his access to institutions and relationships that reinforce patriarchy and hegemonic dominance. Such a portrayal makes Paul an ideal model for the Corinthians to imitate in their abrogation of just such oppressive socio-economic structures that threaten the unity of the Corinthian congregation. The key question at the center of the current chapter and the one that follows is how Paul can implore the Corinthians to imitate him and act like men after embodying and prescribing behavior that, from the perspective of a person living in first-century Corinth, fails to embody the dominant discourses of masculinity (cf. 1 Cor 16:13). It will be the burden of the following chapter to interrogate this self-presentation so as to understand the overall rhetorical effect of Paul's construction and use of his subordinate masculinity as the basis for his paraenesis for a particular kind of unity.[1]

Before moving forward, I need to address my reasons for not incorporating Paul's self-presentation as a worker in a field (1 Cor 3:6–8), a master-builder (1 Cor 3:10–13), and an approved steward (1 Cor 4:1–4). The main reason for not incorporating these passages into my examination is that, despite their clearly being instances of self-description by Paul, they do not offer clear enough connections to gendered discourses so as to determine how each would present Paul's masculinity. Although Paul's use of the agricultural metaphor has the most potential to be set within discourses of gender, there is not enough information provided to determine how Paul's self-presentation as a worker in a field intersects with such discourses. If Paul plants and tends his own field, then it would be possible to read such a metaphor as increasing Paul's masculinity. Cato's introduction to his handbook on agriculture says that when "they praised a good man [*virum bonum*] they praised him thus: 'good farmer and good cultivator.' A man who was praised in this way was reckoned to have been praised to the fullest" (*Agr.* 1.1). Although such a remark might appear to support understanding Paul's usage of an agricultural metaphor as supporting his masculinity, notably the connection with being a good man (*vir bonus*), the divergence between Cato's and Paul's usages should restrain any such move.[2] Cato goes onto connect the "good farmer" with those "men who are the bravest men and sturdiest soldiers" (*Agr.* 1.4). Elsewhere, Cato conjures the imagery of his own roots as a farmer as part of his ascent to Censor and his reimaging of Roman aristocrats as the heirs of the virtue, i.e., masculinity, of the self-sustaining farmers of Rome's past.[3] Cato does not laud working on a farm, especially when the farm belongs to someone else, just owning and supervising hired workers and slaves (e.g., *Agr.* 2.1–2). Conversely, Paul describes himself as God's servant who plants God's field (1 Cor 3:5–6). Paul's reference to being a worker of God's field could position him as hired worker, a slave, or a tenant farmer, positions which would likely have been less than favorable in the minds of is audience. In short, Paul could be following Cato and reclaiming the masculinity of the self-sufficient farmer-soldier of Rome's past, or he could be positioning himself in the less-than-desirable position of a farm laborer. I find the latter usage more likely because Paul refers to God as the owner of the field and source of growth (1 Cor 3:6, 9).

Paul's reference to being a master-builder has many of the same ambiguities of uncertain status as those discussed in the agricultural metaphor

(1 Cor 3:10). Jay Shanor's analysis compares Paul's usage to contracts which reflects the selection of one artisan from the group working on a construction project who would serve as the master-builder (ἀρχιτέκτων).⁴ Although such a person would exercise authority over a particular building project, such a role would not require a corresponding change in social status.⁵ If this is the context of Paul's usage, then a master-builder would not necessarily carry prestige or honor or signify a higher status. There are, however, some references to a master-builder that possibly accord honor and high status to the role.⁶ Aristotle uses the relationships of master-builders to their servants and of masters to their slaves to describe the way that an artisan uses a tool (*Pol.* 1.2.1254a). As with the agricultural metaphor, there is potential for Paul to develop such imagery with further reference to gender such as by describing his role as control over his own building, but he does not. Paul's point is to place himself in subordination to God who is the owner of the building and to frame his Corinthian audience as the object of his work. In neither case does Paul use such a presentation to claim direct authority over the community, such authority belongs to God.

Finally, Paul's identification as a servant of Christ and steward approved by his master (1 Cor 4:1–4), i.e., God, offers even less detail to situate this self-presentation within discourses of gender. As in the discussions of farming and building, Paul's appropriation of the title of steward could be read as a sign of either high or low status depending on which of the many uses of the term a reader understood in Paul's usage.⁷ A steward could wield great power and influence, as with those stewards in powerful or well-connected families (e.g., Pallas's wealth and status as referred to by Pliny in *Ep.* 7.29), but, they were still seen as inferior members of the household whose progeny bore a lower status because of their vocation (Plutarch, *Brut.* 1.7).⁸ What is clear is that Paul's self-description is consistent with his subordination under God's authority in the work with the Corinthian congregation.

PAUL'S SELF-PRESENTATION IN 1 CORINTHIANS

As I discussed in the previous chapter, the social and legal importance of one's *persona*, literary or otherwise, caused ancient authors and speakers to take great care in how they presented themselves and the lengths to which they would go in order to defend their *persona*. Strategies and an awareness of what to present about oneself, how to present it, and what rhetorical and socio-political effects such a presentation could have are found in works ranging from Quintilian to Galen.⁹ Jason König argues that the ubiquity of the tropes of self-presentation despite differences across geographical regions, chronology, and genre signal the near necessity of self-presentation for the ancient author. As seen in the popularity of physiognomy, being able to assess a person's character and ability based on observation was crucial in a world without standardized mechanisms of reference and accreditation.[10] Authors had to highlight certain characteristics while ignoring or accounting for others. Failure to construct the proper *persona* meant almost certain failure for their argument and could have social and legal consequences for an author. The one, *possible* exception to this rule is the subversion of discourses of gender in Latin love elegy that often inverted gendered discourses by portraying a male lover as subordinate to his dominant, female partner.[11] As Ellen Greene demonstrates through examinations of some of the more well-known Latin elegists such as Catullus and Tibullus, these possible feminine subversions are neutralized and men and women are ultimately brought in line to reflect "Roman realities of male domination."[12] Paul, on the other hand, does not reinstate a traditional masculinity but allows his masculinity to remain problematized. What Paul reveals about himself throughout 1 Corinthians, especially when he places himself as an example for the Corinthians to imitate, must be read against this background if we want to grasp the significance of Paul's rhetoric and the goal of his argument.

Kevin Ronald Scull brings this discussion of self-presentation to the study of the New Testament by examining its function within the Pauline corpus.[13] Scull concludes that Paul's use of self-presentation coheres with the rhetorical function and categories of self-presentation as found in other ancient authors. It situates the author in a particular frame of reference that supports the author's rhetorical goals. According to Scull, Paul diverges from conventional self-presentation in Greek and Roman literature by his descriptions of suffering and his use of self-deprecating descriptions.[14] For example, rhetoricians like Quintilian can encourage appearing unprepared or weak but only sparingly and so far as it magnifies the greatness of the orator once he overcomes his opponent or protects him from charges of self-praise (*Inst.* 11.1.21–22). In contrast, Paul's self-descriptions place him at the bottom of the socio-political hierarchy to a degree not found in any extant Greek or Roman literature, as when he portrays himself being led captive in a Roman procession and condemned to die (1 Cor 4:9).[15] Although inversions of standard conventions such as those of happiness or freedom were common enough and recognizable from public displays like those of the Stoics and Cynics, these inversions often involve reassessments of shameful characteristics as actually being honorable. While I will show that Paul does engage to this type of renegotiation to a certain extent, he also repeatedly emphasizes his identification with those characteristics and practices that locate him at the bottom of such hierarchal relationships.[16] For example, Paul repeatedly invokes the crucifixion of Jesus to emphasize the importance of this location at the bottom of such hierarchies (cf. 1 Cor 11:1). In such instances Paul does not simply invert the system; he places Jesus and himself at the bottom of it in the most shameful location. This will be a key point of comparison to keep in mind as I discuss Paul's self-presentation and its rhetorical effect in his argument. Does he, like the Cynics and Stoics, invert common labels of shame and honor in order to present himself and the gospel of Jesus as the best system for attaining happiness and moving up in the world? I will argue that he does not. Instead, Paul's use of such conventions creates a subordinate *persona* that eschews dominating through manipulation of the socio-political relationships in favor of rhetoric that encourages the Corinthians to imitate him in such feminine behavior as an antidote for their factionalism. In other words, he presents himself as a subordinate man and invites the Corinthians to imitate him as such.

1 COR 1–4: PAUL AS FAILED ORATOR, WET NURSE, AND SHAMED FATHER

Although 1 Corinthians as a whole has been subjected to numerous partition theories, the integrity of 1 Cor 1–4 has seldom been questioned. Even Johannes Weiss, whose work popularized understanding the current text of 1 Corinthians as a composite of two separate letters,[17] understands these chapters as a coherent whole which focus on Paul's confrontation with factions within the Corinthian congregation.[18] Even though I do not follow Weiss's desire to uncover the precise nature of the factions in Corinth, I agree with his assessment that these early chapters present Paul confronting factions that have split based on their aligning with different key personalities.[19] The proximity and diversity of Paul's self-presentation in the opening chapters, then, must play a key role in any approach to understanding Paul's self-presentation in 1 Corinthians more broadly.

PAUL AS FAILED ORATOR

> For Christ did not send me to baptize, but to preach the gospel—and not with learned speech, so that the cross of Christ would not become useless. For the message about the cross is foolishness (μωρία) to those who are perishing, but to us who are being saved it is the power of God.
>
> —1 Cor 1:17–18

> When I came to you, brothers and sisters, I did not come with learned speech as I proclaimed the testimony of God. For I decided to be concerned about nothing among you except Jesus Christ, and him crucified. And I was with you in weakness and in fear and with much trembling. My speech and my proclamation were not with persuasive words of wisdom, but with a demonstration of the Spirit and of power, so that your faith would not be based on human wisdom but on the power of God.
>
> —1 Cor 2:1–5

Paul's first positive self-description comes as he defines himself as one sent to preach the gospel. This initial focus on Paul's vocation in relationship to the message about Jesus, along with his earlier comments that he was not crucified for the Corinthians nor were they baptized in his name, situates Paul in a subordinate position to Jesus (cf. 1 Cor 1:13). By positioning himself along with Apollos as subordinates to Jesus, Paul also begins to counter the factionalism which Paul indicates has caused the Corinthians to divide by aligning themselves with various prominent figures (1 Cor 1:12).[20] Such factious behavior over public figures was common in urban centers throughout the Empire and, as I discussed in relation to the conflict between the sophists Favorinus and Polemo, appears to have reached particularly high levels in Corinth.[21] Dio describes Diogenes witnessing chaotic public competitions between teachers and their disciples as each school fought for dominance and how people rejected Diogenes when he refused to engage in such a spectacle (*Virt.* 8.9–11). Dio goes on to indicate that such competition continues in Corinth into his time of the first century.[22] Paul's presentation as an orator will not only intentionally position him in the disgraced position of a failed orator who cannot meet the expectations for a man who speaks publicly, it will identify such a shameful position as rooted the gospel.

The public competition of orators and teachers were not just exhibitions of rhetorical ability or learning (παιδία); they determined the teacher's social standing and ability to attract and retain students. Since the teacher's standing influenced that of the student, people had to choose a teacher carefully and defend him when necessary. As occurred with Favorinus, the Corinthians quickly disassociated with him once his socio-political standing was jeopardized. One of Favorinus's key rhetorical moves to try to reestablish his authority over the Corinthians is to bind together their fate with his own, encouraging them to come to his defense, in an attempt to reestablish his place as an exalted teacher with all of the accompanying benefits. Another notable example of the competition between teachers comes in Philostratus's account of the rhetorician Philagrus being publicly humiliated by the students of a rival, Herodes (Philostratus, *Vit. Soph.* 208, 578–580). Paul, on the other hand, undermines such factionalism and emphasizes that he and Apollos are fellow workers who share a common goal (1 Cor 3:4–9). So although Paul's characterization of himself as one who proclaims a message could be taken as situating himself within this context of public competition, his resistance to the resulting factionalism and public vitriol indicates an avoidance to the manipulation of such a system for personal glorification.

Paul goes on to further appropriate the role of a teacher in a way that not only resists the type of competition for status and authority that fuel the divisions in Corinth but ultimately locates him on the feminine end of the spectrum for analyzing an orator. Paul's statements that he did not use "clever speech" (σοφία λόγου) shows an explicit rejection of characterization as a successful teacher. The language of clever speech, usually translated as "wise words," finds a particular resonance in the public competition of sophists which was so common in Corinth. Stephen M. Pogoloff offers an insightful analysis of the phrase σοφία λόγου, and its equivalents, as conveying rhetorical abilities which were necessary for public success and, therefore, indicative of a person's social status.[23] Not only was clever speech required, not demonstrating clever speech is often connected to humiliating public defeats. Philagrus suffers just such a defeat, one from which he never recovers, when his speech violates the accepted standards of declamation in Athens (Philostratus, *Vit. Soph.* 208). As a result, Philagrus never achieves the elevated social status attributed to him in other cities. By explicitly rejecting the clever speech necessary to successfully engage in public debate, Paul deliberately accepts a lowered position as assessed by such a system.[24]

Paul further counters the Corinthians' tendency to appropriate discipleship to Christ for socioeconomic advancement by describing it as foolishness (μωρία) (1 Cor 1:18). Although readers since the time of Justin Martyr have recognized that Paul's use of μωρία signals a break between the gospel and conventional social metrics, this break has often been understood in terms of madness or a lack of logic that is meant to contrast with the learned wisdom of the world.[25] In contrast to this reading, L. L. Welborn argues that Paul's use of the language of μωρία derives from broader Hellenistic usages where the term connotes a failure to understand or live within a prescribed system and, consequently, forces the person to exist in a subordinate position.[26] For example, in the rhetorical tradition, μωρία can describe a person who fails to adopt his methods to fit his audience, almost certainly condemning the person to public failure of a type previously discussed as effeminacy (Quintilian, *Inst.* 12.10.69). Rather than focus specifically on the trope of the buffoon in terms of a lower-class μῖμος (mime) as does Welborn, I want to emphasize that in each of the contexts the point is on failing to achieve dominance, or demonstrate masculinity, within a particular system and consequently having to resort to a subordinate position. Paul, therefore, is not saying that the gospel of the crucified Christ is simply illogical to those who are perishing, though it most certainly is, but that it is utter buffoonery, fit only for those who are forced to the bottom of whichever hierarchy they happen to intersect. The world does not look on in bemused wonder but in utter contempt at those who are barely worth noticing.

It is, therefore, no coincidence that Paul combines the idea of foolishness with the image of the cross.[27] Cicero's often quoted comments help make this point "the executioner, the veiling of the head and the very word cross should be far removed not only from the person of a Roman citizen but from his thoughts, his eyes and his ears" (Cicero, *Rab. Perd.* 16). Cicero's point is that a citizen, one who by the nature of *his* identity occupies a position of privilege, should not even think about such an instrument of shame because falling victim to it would strip him of his power and privilege and transform him into a feminized body with an accompanying decrease in status.[28] This appears to be one reason why upper-class authors treat crucifixion as sparingly as they do.[29] The shame of the cross is so significant that Lucian applies it in a comical scene where the letter Sigma brings charges against the letter Tau because it served as the muse for inventing the crucifixion, something that has brought endless shame and fear to mankind (Lucian, *Jud. voc.* 12). Not only is the message of the cross heralded by a failed orator, the message itself is utter foolishness. Paul's presentation, then, does not simply remove the cross from analytical models that promote oppressive hierarchies but places the gospel within such models and emphasizes its locus on the shameful, failed, feminine end of such models.

Paul returns to the imagery of the cross and his status as a failed public speaker in 2:1–5. Here, he elaborates and describes his presence among the Corinthians as being in "weakness, and fear, and much trembling" (1 Cor 2:3). Each term represents an antithesis to the standard characterization of an orator.[30] For example, Quintilian comments that a trembling hand might be appropriate for actors but dooms an orator's presentation to failure (Quintilian, *Inst.* 11.3.103). Quintilian's point is that a trembling hand is a physiognomic manifestation of femininity and, hence, a person who is not masculine enough to succeed as an orator. The use of the technical language of rhetoric such as ὑπεροχή, πειθώ, ἀπόδειξις, πίστις, and δύναμις further indicate that Paul's description intentionally situates him in relation to other public speakers. In contrast to the manly orator who exudes strength and control, Paul represents the failed orator even before he opens his mouth. Note that Paul, unlike Favorinus, does not rework his characteristics in order to portray himself as the quintessential man in order to take on positions of power and prestige; rather, Paul assumes the standard model for oratory and masculinity, but positions himself at the bottom of it.[31] Such a move is reminiscent of Dio's account of Diogenes, who is rejected when he intentionally fails to publicly compete according to conventional standards.[32] As discussed previously, the consequences for a man who failed to embody the requisite characteristics was to be read as a failed man and be forced to occupy a subordinate position in relation to more masculine men. Paul unequivocally portrays himself as a failed orator, one with whom the Corinthians could not associate if they wanted to engage in the public competition for power and dominance. As discussed above, this locus at the feminine end of the spectrum of orators appears to be in imitation of the buffoonery of the cross. Furthermore, as I will demonstrate in the following chapter, this relegation of power is precisely the point in Paul's exhortations for the Corinthians' behavior, both when he explicitly calls them to imitate him and not.

PAUL AS A WET NURSE

> So, brothers, I could not speak to you as spiritual people, but instead as people of the flesh, as infants in Christ. I fed you milk, not solid food, for you were not yet ready. In fact, you are still not ready, for you are still influenced by the flesh. For since there is still jealousy and dissension among you, are you not influenced by the flesh and behaving like unregenerate people?
>
> —1 Cor 3:1–3

Having just outlined a distinction between the spirit of the world and the spirit of God along with the realms of knowledge that correspond to each, Paul applies these categories in terms of spiritual and fleshly people in order to make an unfavorable characterization of the Corinthian congregation (1 Cor 3:1–4). To substantiate his characterization of the Corinthians congregation as fleshly, Paul points to the presence of jealousy and dissension among them. It comes as no surprise that Paul addresses these characteristics within the opening chapters of the letter since they illuminate the factionalism which Paul confronts in his thesis statement in 1:10. Whatever Paul says, here, must be read in continuity with the broader argument of 1 Cor 1–4 and the letter as a whole.

At the center of 1 Cor 1–4 lie two points. First, Paul frames what he is able to communicate, or more accurately, what the Corinthian congregation is able to understand, in terms of the competing systems of valuation that he began to outline in 1:18 before developing the epistemological implications through the discussion 1 Cor 2. The result is a pair of hierarchies that relate to the categories of wisdom, foolishness, strength, and weakness. The first hierarchy represents the world's rubric which assigns strength based on social status and wisdom based on rhetorical abilities. The second hierarchy represents God's rubric which stands as an inverted mirror image of the worlds' hierarchy; what the world values as wisdom, God values as foolishness, and vice versa. The basis for this reversal comes from the incongruity between what the world esteems, namely wisdom and strength, and what God esteems, namely foolishness and weakness. As Margaret Mitchell persuasively argues, Paul does not discuss wisdom and strength in the abstract but specifically as they relate to the public competition for fame and power that characterize Roman competitions for masculinity.[33]

This contrast in Paul's characterization of the Corinthian congregation as people of the flesh, then, means that they are following a system of valuation oriented toward the characteristics esteemed by the world and not those esteemed by God. The fact that Paul makes such a contrast within a section which chastises the Corinthians for their factionalism makes a strong case for understanding the divisions within the Corinthian congregation as stemming from their inappropriate means of assessing value in their leaders in light of the discussion of the public competition of sophists in my opening chapter.

Second, to help elucidate the issues, Paul applies a metaphor of child development that contrasts the abilities of an infant with those of a mature person and places himself within the metaphor as the provider of nourishment. Although contemporary readers might be tempted to read Paul's use of a metaphor as merely illustrative or used for literary effect, Greek and Roman authors and orators applied metaphors and similes as key components in the development of logical or moral arguments (e.g., Seneca, *Ep.* 13.1–3). The image of a wet nurse, therefore, should not be discarded or explained away as a simple aside to Paul's care for the Corinthians.[34] The use of this metaphor is signaled by Paul's statements in 3:2 that he previously gave the Corinthians milk, in distinction from solid food, and that he still cannot give them solid food because they are not ready.[35] In other words, metaphorically they are still babies. In order to understand the rhetorical effect of the metaphor in this passage and the overall argument, we must attend to the way the metaphor would be heard by a first-century audience, especially in light of Paul's striking adaptation of donning the female persona in the metaphor.

Abraham Malherbe was one of the first to locate Paul's imagery of a nurse with her charges within Greek and Roman discourses of moral and philosophical education and does so in order to emphasize the gentleness of a nurse.[36] Dio Chrysostom relates a story of Diogenes who, after being harsh with Alexander the Great, tells him a story, mirroring the actions of a nurse who tells a story to comfort a child after punishing him (*4 Regn.* 4.74). Plutarch uses the same image of nurses who know how to balance and mix comfort and punishment (*Adul. amic.* 69C). Likewise, the author of *The Education of Children* also praises the nurse's ability to mix reproof with gentleness and applies it as a model for teachers with their students ([*Lib. Ed.*] 3C–F). Some authors, however, use the association of nurses and gentleness to criticize people who remain, or allow others to remain, in an underdeveloped state. These cases provide a negative presentation of the image of a nurse as one who obstructs growth and change by mitigating necessary amounts of suffering and hard work. The imagery of a nurse, therefore, is not necessarily the positive image that Malherbe thought.

Although Malherbe focused on 1 Thess 2, he acknowledges that the imagery and rhetorical effect of the passage mirrors that of 1 Cor 3:1–3,[37] with a key difference being that the latter does not use the term nurse (τροφός). Malherbe surveys a wide variety of sources that substantiate understanding the nurse as a figure associated with gentleness and that this image was applied to education, and his sources do so with a focus on the gentleness of a nurse as opposed to boldness (παρρησία). As Gaventa points out, although Malherbe is correct that some texts do emphasize the nurse's gentleness, the criticism of a nurse's gentleness as well as the image of a nurse as alternating boldness with gentleness makes it difficult to claim that the image of a gentle nurse forms a well-established trope.[38] Malherbe might have been on firmer ground to support the coherence of Paul's presentation of his ministry in Thessalonica as both bold and gentle without falling prey to charges of inconsistency (bold in 1 Thess 2:2; gentle in 1 Thess 2:8).[39] So although Malherbe was correct that Paul uses a contextually specific image when he brings up the image of a nurse and milk, he did not fully explore the range of contexts containing nurse imagery in Greco-Roman discourse contemporary with Paul.

A more fitting analogue for Paul's language of nursing and milk appears in discourses of moral and educational development which are found in Jewish, Greek, and Roman literature. Philo's application of the metaphor equates basic levels of teaching with milk which is only suitable for infants while more advanced teaching is associated with solid food which benefits only those who are mature. Philo's comments in *De agricultura* are worth quoting at length.

> But since milk is the food of infants, but cakes made of wheat are the food of complete men, so also the soul must have a milk-like nourishment in its age of childhood, namely, the elementary instruction of encyclical science. But the perfect food which is fit for men consists of explanations dictated by prudence, and temperance, and every virtue. For these things being sown and implanted in the mind will bring forth most advantageous fruit, namely, good and praiseworthy actions. (Philo, *Agr*. 9; trans. Yonge)

Philo begins by assuming a clear difference in the food appropriate for infants as to that which is appropriate for men. Notice also that in Philo's trajectory the body in question moves from an initial state of irrational immaturity to one of rationality and virtue. Recalling the previous discussions regarding assumptions about the intellectual and moral capabilities of men and women makes Philo's placement of complete, or truly masculine, men at the perfect end of the developmental spectrum no accident. It also frames the undeveloped state as feminine, something which is consistent with my previous observations of Philo's use of gendered discourses. Philo's coupling of the imagery of rudimentary education as milk fit for undeveloped bodies (i.e., feminine people, including women, children, and failed men) while more philosophically developed instruction befits mature bodies (i.e., men embody masculine norms) appears in two other texts.[40] "But [infant souls must first receive], in the place of milk, the soft food of instruction given in the school subjects, later, the harder, stronger meat, which philosophy produces" (*Prob.* 160; Yonge; cf. *Cong.* 19). Here, Philo also applies the imagery of weaning to signal the process of maturation, indicating self-sufficiency (i.e., the masculinization) of the body.

> Moses moreover represents two persons as leaders of these two companies. The leader of the noble and good company is the self-taught and self-instructed Isaac; for he records that he was weaned, not choosing to avail himself at all of tender, and milk-like, and childish, and infantine food, but only of such as was vigorous and perfect, inasmuch as he was formed by nature, from his very infancy, for acts of virtue, and was always in the prime and vigor of youth and energy. But the leader of the company, which yields and which is inclined to unmanly submission (εὐενδότου), is Joseph; (Philo, *Somn.* 2.10; trans. Yonge)

Philo's use of εὐένδοτος (easily yielding or morally weak) to describe Joseph helps signal the masculine/feminine contrast between the infantile, less developed person and the mature, fully developed man since Philo uses it in other texts in direct contrast to characteristics that define a man.

> But if he thinks that [suffering] is inconsistent with his destiny, then, if he be oppressed with any very terrible calamity, he will suffer the punishment of Sisyphus, not being able to raise his head, not even ever so little, but being exposed to all sorts of evils coming upon him and overwhelming him, and meeting them all with submission (εὐένδοτον), the passions of a degenerate and unmanly (ἀνάνδρους) soul. (Philo, *Cher.* 78; trans. Yonge)

Each text holds together the development of the body, progressing from milk to solid food, with the development of the mind, progressing from basic instruction to more advanced. Part of the reason that this metaphor is so powerful is that Philo sees nature working to equip the bodies of babies for milk, right down to their not being born with teeth since they would not be necessary and cause the mother pain (cf. *Spec.* 3.199–200; *Virt.* 130). He then applies this to a model of educational development that allows the mature to receive more advanced instructions, described as consisting of every virtue, with the end result of such mature instruction being correct action.

Epictetus, in discussions of moral and educational development, also applies the imagery of milk as suitable food only for a baby while more developed bodies require solid food. As part of a larger discussion about accepting those changes that are not under your control, Epictetus says, "Shall we not wean ourselves at last, and call to mind what we have heard from the philosophers?" (*Disc.* 3.24.9). The teaching to which Epictetus refers concerns the nature of the universe and the necessity of periodic changes as opposed to irrational animals and children who either cannot make appropriate attachments or cannot understand that change is necessary, respectively (*Disc.* 3.24.8–14). Weaning, the process of transitioning from milk to solid food, then, is parallel to moving from rudimentary knowledge to more developed teaching. Epictetus uses the imagery of weaning to provoke men who have already left behind milk for solid food for their physical nourishment to make the same transition in terms of how they think about the nature of the world. Epictetus's use of shame in connection with weaning as a means of spurring men to behave like men shows up in other texts. "Are you not willing, at this late date, like children, to be weaned and to partake of more solid food, and not to cry for mammies and nurses—old wives' lamentations?" (*Disc.* 2.16.39).[41] Epictetus's goading serves to encourage his audience to be like Heracles and Theseus, mature men who cleared away wickedness, before telling them to clear out their own wickedness, one of the characteristics of which is effeminacy (μαλακός) (*Disc.* 2.16.44–45).

Like Philo, Epictetus demonstrates a consistent contrast between milk as the food for children and solid food for grown or mature bodies. Also like Philo, Epictetus applies this understanding of the natural progression of bodies to the moral or educational development of men so as to represent a development from basic teachings to more advanced ones. Most importantly, Philo and Epictetus both emphasize the fact that certain actions denote an immature state while other actions denote a mature one. It is also important that both authors can apply the language of milk without having the gentleness of the nurse in view. Rather, the use of milk in contrast to solid food emphasizes, at times even shaming, the audience's need to leave childish thinking behind and to think like men so that they can act like men. This usage demonstrates that the imagery of a nurse or milk could be applied to highlight the development of the child without focusing on or even invoking the idea of gentleness. Paul does not, therefore, have to be understood as invoking the imagery of a wet nurse and milk in order to emphasize his gentleness or boldness as is the case in 1 Thess 2. Rather in 1 Cor 3:1–3, Paul may be using milk imagery to emphasize the immaturity of a person or group in order to spur on a particular course of action. Such a move equates the current state as one of immaturity and outlines what changes must be made to reach maturity. I will show that the logic in 1 Corinthians equates factionalism with immaturity and harmony with maturity.

In taking a closer look at the rhetorical use of milk, it is apparent that Greek and Roman sources do not denigrate milk for babies or basic instruction for young children; the problem is failing to progress from that state or progressing in the wrong ways. The failure to mature and, consequently, remaining in an immature, feminized state fits Paul's usage as he implores the Corinthians to partake of appropriate teaching (i.e., nourishment) and mature. As I will demonstrate below, many authors go to great lengths to emphasize the importance of finding the right kind of breast milk so as to cause the right kind of physical, moral, and educational development. In other words, concerns over a child's need for milk in order to develop coincide with concerns to find the right kind of nurse who can produce the right kind of milk that will result in the right kind of development. Aristotle makes some of the earliest known connections in Greek literature between the nurse's characteristics and the development of the child. "[D]ark women's milk is healthier than [the milk of] fair ones" (Aristotle, *Hist. an.* 3.21.523a.9–13). Aristotle also correlates the quickness with which an infant cuts teeth to the temperature of the breast milk (*Hist. an.* 7.10.587b.18–19). Note the connection between characteristics of the woman to those of her breast milk and the effect of the breast milk on a child. This basic understanding also pervades later Greek and Roman writings about breastfeeding.[42] The work of Soranus, a near contemporary of Galen and a writer who exerted a profound influence on approaches to the care of women and children, evidences a similar understanding of the connection between the woman, her milk, and its effects on the health of the infant.[43] The connection between the condition of a woman's body and the acceptability for her breast milk for nursing serves as the basis for Soranus's recommendation that mothers not nurse their own children for at least twenty days since the birthing process is so taxing on the body, as well as Soranus providing extensive instructions on how to select a wet nurse if the mother will not or cannot nurse her own child.[44]

Outside of the medical experts, Greek and Roman authors who discuss breastfeeding and milk for infants tend to focus on the connection between what we might call the morality or ethos of the provider of the milk and the development of the baby. Tacitus compares the "good old days [when] every man's son, born in wedlock, was brought up not in the chamber of some hireling nurse, but in his mother's lap, and at her knee" to the current state of families in Rome handing "our children . . . to some silly little Greek serving maid, with a male slave, who may be anyone, to help her—quite frequently the most worthless member of the whole establishment, incompetent for any serious service" (Tacitus, *Dial.* 28 and 29, respectively; Peterson). Tacitus emphasizes that a child whose mind is still "green and unformed" that spends time around such a person will lose all sense of respect or shame, the very problems that are evident in the Roman youth that Tacitus observes (Tacitus, *Dial.* 29). Quintilian makes a similar point that a child's wet nurse should, in a perfect world, be educated in philosophy but at least speak properly since she will leave an indelible imprint on the baby's young mind (Quintilian, *Inst.* 1.1.4–5). Quintilian provides the example of Alexander the Great, whose speech, even as a king, was marred by an ill-spoken pedagogue during his youth. Gellius's account of Favorinus takes the connection between the woman providing the milk and the formation of the child. Favorinus disputes with a mother-in-law over whether her daughter, a new mother in a high-ranking family, should nurse her new son or whether a wet nurse should be provided. The mother-in-law represents a position close to that advocated by Soranus, that the task of birth is so exhausting that having the mother nurse would not be beneficial. Favorinus counters by assuming that the mother and father's blood, coagulated in the form of semen that is present in both parents, cause the child's body and mind to resemble its parents, so too the milk, which is also formed from coagulated blood, will so form the body and mind of a child (Gellius, *Noct. att.* 3.1.11–15). This is especially dangerous if the wet nurse is a slave, of servile origin, or from a foreign nation since the milk causes a child to draw a "spirit into its mind and body from a body and mind of the worst character" (Gellius, *Noct. att.* 3.1.18). He goes on to make the connection between milk and formation explicit in saying,

> And there is no doubt that in forming character the disposition of the nurse and the quality of the milk play a great part; for the milk, although imbued from the beginning with the material of the father's seed, forms the infant offspring from the body and mind of the mother as well. (Gellius, *Noct. att.* 3.1.20, trans. Rolfe)

Favorinus makes a direct connection between the characteristics of the woman creating the milk and the formation of the body and the mind of the child who receives it. Favorinus's view about the deterioration of the morality of the Roman youth caused by Roman women outsourcing the nursing of their children is shared by Cicero and Tacitus (Cicero, *Tusc.* 3.1–2; Tacitus, *Germ.* 20.1). While this is a finer point on the means of the influence that the wet nurse exerts on her charges than some of the other authors I survey, it shares the assumptions about the necessity of milk for the development of the child, in both body and mind, and emphasizes the propriety of having the correct source of that milk because of the nurse's ability to pass on specific characteristics. The assumption is that drinking the milk of the nurse will form the child to be like the nurse.

Turning back to 1 Corinthians, a first-century audience, then, would almost certainly be familiar with the imagery of milk as elementary instruction in comparison to solid food as more advanced instruction, a point often made in scholarly work on the passage which then takes this to be Paul's main point.[45] What is not well explored is how imagery about the source of the milk and the failure to develop properly can influence a reading of the passage and how Paul might use the imagery as part of his larger argument against factionalism. The discussion in the previous paragraphs about the link between the moral character of the one supplying the milk and the moral formation of the one consuming it supports connecting Paul's portrayal of himself as the Corinthian believers' wet nurse with direct appeals that they imitate his actions (e.g., 1 Cor 4:16; 11:1). In other words, Paul's use of the milk imagery contains an implicit appeal to imitate and become like him. This would make Paul's point that the Corinthian congregation never developed, a point he makes explicit by pointing to their factious behavior as apparently inconsistent with the initial teaching he gave them and indicative of being people of the flesh rather than the spirit (cf. 1 Cor 3:4).[46] The problem is not that the Corinthians still want milk when they should have moved on to solid food but that the milk Paul gave them has not had its desired effect of forming and developing them into mature, or spiritual, people (cf. 1 Cor 2).[47] The imagery suggests that the Corinthians never properly ingested the milk (teaching) that Paul gave them originally, not that they are still consuming milk when they should move onto solid food. Readings that argue that the problem is that the Corinthian believers still want milk understand the milk as Paul's basic teaching and the Corinthians as not wanting to progress beyond it.[48] But these readings overlook the association between milk and moral formation and the corresponding assumption that consuming milk will shape a child to be like the one who provides the milk. If the Corinthians had consumed the milk Paul gave them (i.e., following his teaching), then they would have matured and be ready for more meaty food (i.e., substantive teaching). This is Paul's point when he says, "I fed you milk, not solid food, because (γὰρ) you were not ready, *but, even now, you are still not ready*" (1 Cor 3:2; emphasis added). Here Paul reflects on the fact that they *still* have not been formed in accordance with the milk that he had fed them. Raymond Collins makes this point in arguing that, unlike Philo and Epictetus, Paul's point is not to provide a two-stage theory of development.[49] Rather, Paul argues that they should have matured from fleshly to spiritual people but have not.[50] In other words, if the Corinthians had been consuming Paul's milk they would naturally demonstrate maturity in the form of concord.

If the passage is read with a focus on Paul's use of milk and solid food in terms of formation, the imagery makes more sense within Paul's broader call for the Corinthian congregation to imitate him, a point that he makes explicit later in the letter (cf. 1 Cor 4:16, 11:1–2). Yet Paul's use of the imagery appears to do even more than just invoke the idea that the Corinthians need to imitate him after they have obviously failed to do so. Paul's use of the imagery also makes a specific point about what imitating Paul will mean because, in a culturally and rhetorically stunning move, it frames Paul in a distinctly and unmistakably feminine role. Gaventa highlights the possibility of such a reading by focusing on the fact that Paul places himself in the position of the one who provides the milk.[51] The discomfort evidenced by the authors above over the influence of wet nurses on Roman babies indicates that wet nurses were usually of lower status and often slaves. Although wet nurses are predominantly women, there is evidence that lower-status men sometimes filled the role. Tacitus refers to a male helper for the wet nurse who assisted in the care of infants. These men ranked so low within the social and family structure that they are "the most worthless member of the household" (*Dial.*, 29). They would not, therefore, qualify as "real men" and function as the near equivalent of a female wet nurse. They would be subordinate men. I, however, think that it makes better sense to understand Paul embodying the *persona* of a wet nurse in this passage because of the connection between moral formation and the person who produced it. Male nurses would have to procure milk from another source, typically goat milk that could be mixed with honey (Galen, *On the Properties of Foodstuffs*, 7.678). This would not fit with Paul's use of the imagery of milk for moral formation since someone drinking goat milk would, at some level, take on the animal's characteristics. Writers like Favorinus and Tacitus are concerned that a Roman child nurse from a good Roman mother. By saying that he was the one who fulfilled a role which only a woman or possibly a subordinate man could, Paul would necessarily problematize his masculinity.[52]

Gaventa goes further by contextualizing such a stunning rhetorical move, stating that, "By actively taking upon himself a role that could only be played by a woman, he effectively *concedes* the culturally predisposed battle for his masculinity."[53] This "battle" is the same battle that we saw between Favorinus and Demonax and between Catullus and his accusers, Fuirius and Aurelius. It is a battle that requires a man to claim as dominant a form of masculinity as he can in order to ensure the masculinity of his *persona* and, therefore, his sociopolitical standing. For Paul to concede this battle, intentionally sabotaging the masculinity of his *persona*, would be inconceivable for someone who then wants to be taken seriously as a leader of the community. Remember that the Corinthians toppled Favorinus's statue precisely because Favorinus's masculinity had been problematized because his ability to defend the city before the emperor was jeopardized. To intentionally appropriate or cultivate feminine characteristics as Paul does in this passage would be disastrous for the masculinity of his *persona* and significantly shape the way the Corinthians perceive him. At this point, it is crucial to point out that although my review shows that use of nursing imagery and milk as teaching occurs in numerous sources, nowhere else does an author identify as the provider of the milk. While I can only speculate about exactly why an author would do or not do something, I have shown that authors intentionally avoid feminine characteristics and bombastically defend themselves from accusations of taking on feminine roles in order to secure the masculinity of their *persona*. If Paul intentionally adopts a feminine persona as part of his self-presentation, then one would want to know why and whether it is an anomaly in his self-presentation and rhetorical strategy or part of a pattern that surfaces elsewhere in 1 Corinthians. Could Paul really want the Corinthians to view him as a man who cannot measure up to the masculine standards required to ascend the patriarchal ladder of Roman politics and, therefore, cannot manipulate a position of social power over others?

PAUL AS A SHAMEFUL FATHER

> I do not write these things to shame you but to correct you as dear children. For though you may have ten thousand pedagogues in Christ, you do not have many fathers, for, through the gospel, I became your father in Christ Jesus.
>
> —1 Cor 4:14–15

Paul's use of paternal language to describe his relationship to the Corinthian community is notable both for its placement at the rhetorical crescendo of this opening section and the fact that Paul explicitly appropriates masculine imagery that would appear to require him to perform a hegemonic masculinity in his self-presentation. If there is one instance where my thesis about Paul's focus on feminine and subordinate gendered imagery would falter, it would appear to be this text. Assuming that Paul dons the *persona* of the *paterfamilias* in order to dominate his audience and solidify his position of authority is certainly a possible reading of the text.[54] Given the reading of 1 Cor 3:1–3 offered above, it is better to read this as Paul's deployment of fatherhood as a call to the type of subordinate masculinity which the Corinthians are later called to embody (cf. 1 Cor 16:13). I will demonstrate that by the time Paul applies the paternal imagery, he has so problematized and subordinated his *persona* through the characterization in 1 Cor 4:7–13, that it would be impossible for the Corinthians to read him as the type of hegemonic man that was essential to fulfill the role of father. Rather, he embodies a type of subordinate masculinity that would bring shame on the other members of his household.

Paul begins this section by framing how the Corinthians are to assess him; they are to reckon him as a servant of Christ and a steward of the mysteries of God (1 Cor 4:1).[55] Paul's point in applying such imagery appears to focus on the means the Corinthians should use in assessing Paul.[56] As Paul states, a steward is assessed on their faithfulness as determined by their employer (1 Cor 4:6), not on rhetorical ability or other displays of power or prestige. In fact, the positions of servant and steward would necessarily limit the masculinity of the men who occupy those roles since they are operating within someone else's household and under their authority.[57] Beyond shifting the means of assessment, Paul also locates the ability to judge solely with God. This is crucial because the actions and identity that he will elaborate in 1 Cor 4:9–13 would, under the model for masculinity outlined in the previous chapters, undermine Paul's ability to function as a man and role model for his audience. If the Corinthians assess Paul and other apostles according to the standards applied to other prominent men in Corinth who jockey for status and power, then they will fail to understand the nature of Paul's ministry and the shape of the kingdom of God as embodied by Paul. Paul goes on to indicate that it is the means of assessment, not assessment in general, that needs to be adjusted by warning that he judges the Corinthians (1 Cor 5:3), that they should be able to make judgments regarding disputes within their community (1 Cor 5:12; 6:1–3), and that they should judge Paul's words (1 Cor 10:15; 11:13).

Paul uses the ensuing description of the Corinthians as kings and the apostles as the scum of the earth to recalibrate their means of judging individuals (1 Cor 4:7, 13; respectively). Paul's statement that he wishes that they had become kings so that he could reign with them indicates that his description of the Corinthians as wealthy, satisfied kings does not exactly represent their present condition. Rather, it indicates the types of superior positions at the top of the socio-economic ladder that some Corinthians were adopting in order to distinguish themselves from lower-class members of the community, superior positions that resemble the groups whom Paul earlier describes as rejecting the gospel (1 Cor 1:21–22; 2:8).[58] This continues through direct comparison where the Corinthians are said to be wise, strong, and honored (1 Cor 4:10), all terms that fit into the model of hegemonic masculinity that typified Roman ideals for men. In distinction from the positioning of the Corinthians, Paul launches into a description of the social, economic, and political positioning of the apostles. The fact that these are the terms used by Paul to frame apostolic weakness is just one more indication that some of the Corinthians were using these metrics to support their superiority over other members of the community. Paul's description of the apostolic office provides a litany of descriptors that would fundamentally undermine a person's masculinity. First, the apostles are displayed last like the rulers of a conquered nation being led in a Roman parade (1 Cor 4:9; 2 Cor 2:14). They are the quintessential example of men whose masculinity has utterly failed and who now stand ready to die in the arena, to receive a final penetrating blow as Rome reasserts its hegemonic dominance. Next, Paul goes on to to describe the apostles as fools, weak, and dishonored (1 Cor 4:10). The final description is redundant in light of the first two and reinforces the point from the previous verse. Third, Paul then appears to describe apostles as hungry, thirsty, wandering, poorly dressed, mistreated, homeless, manual laborers for their livelihood, and abused and slandered (1 Cor 4:11–12). Analyzing each of these terms on its own, although helpful, misses their collective force as Paul effectively casts the apostles in terms of the quintessential failed man. Not only do they fail to lead their households properly, they do not even have households to lead and are forced to work as manual laborers. They cannot protect or provide for their own bodies. And, maybe worst of all, when attacked they not only fail to answer the charges but they bestow blessing and tolerate their accusers (1 Cor 4:12–13). Although Quintilian can approve of an otherwise manly orator applying self-effacing rhetoric (Quintilian, *Inst.* 6.3.24–25), Paul's presentation surpasses anything Quintilian indicates as acceptable. Returning to the cosmic framework at the beginning of his description, Paul concludes with the apostles as the refuse of the cosmos and scum of all things and emphasizes the present nature of these descriptors (1 Cor 4:13).

Reading this passage in light of the earlier discussion regarding the real-world consequences for an author whose *persona* was deemed as insufficiently masculine forces us to wonder what Paul is doing by humiliating and so thoroughly removing himself and the other apostles from hegemonic positions of power. By reiterating this cosmic framework, Paul underscores the point that such judgments are not determined by God's metrics but those of the world. Although the world might view them as failed men, God places them in positions of oversight and power in the church. This discontinuity also explains Paul's reassurance about not writing "these things" to shame the Corinthians but to correct them as children (4:14). But why would Paul, after degrading himself, need to address shame felt by the Corinthians? Some commentators take Paul's comments as indicating that his treatment of the factionalism in the first four chapters is not meant to shame the Corinthians.[59]

The problem with this line of interpretation is that Paul will address some of the specific issues that underlie their factionalism and tell the Corinthians that they should feel shame over them (1 Cor 6:5; 15:34). It is possible that the shame that Paul refers to here, in chapter 4, is the shame the Corinthians would experience from the leader and founder of their community failing so spectacularly as a man, much as the Corinthians' shame might have motivated them to disassociate from Favorinus. As their father, his shame becomes their shame. It is the shame that would restrict their access to public, social, and civil positions because they, by association with the head of their community, would also be deemed as lacking the requisite masculine characteristics. They would, in other words, have to take subordinate positions within the patriarchal structure that ordered urban Roman settings like Corinth.

Paul's self-identification as the Corinthians' shameful father concludes with a call to imitate him and a warning about his eventual arrival in the city, including an apparent threat of violence (1 Cor 4:16–21). The warning centers on the unstated premise that if the Corinthian believers fail to imitate Paul, then he will come "with a rod" to discipline whereas if they succeed in imitating him then he will come "with love and spirit of gentleness" (1 Cor 4:21).[60] The threat of violence, whether as physical violence or as metaphor for being harsh, emphasizes the seriousness of the factionalism that Paul confronts and his authority.[61] While Mitchell demonstrates that censure, even strong censure that needed some level of apology, was widely used in deliberative rhetoric,[62] there is still the issue of whether the image of Paul as a censuring father is so hegemonic that it problematizes my argument about Paul's subordinate masculinity. Indeed, Jodamus concludes that Paul's reference to physical punishment "serves inadvertently as a call for the re-enactment of the *hegemonic masculinity(ies)* and in so doing upholds the *normative gendered hierarchy from the secular society* as a standard for the Corinthian community."[63] The problem with Jodamus's conclusion is that, as I have and will continue to demonstrate, Paul consistently fails to "uphold the normative gendered hierarchy." Remember that Paul has just failed so spectacularly to embody the normative gendered discourses of fatherhood that he addresses the shame that he knows his audience will feel if they judge him by those standard discourses (cf. 1 Cor 4:14).

To determine how the threat of a rod fits into Paul's self-portrayal as father, it is vital to more fully understand the corporal punishment of children in Paul's context. First, in Roman families, the father was not the only one who had the ability to physically discipline a child. Cicero, in the midst of discussing a family's obligation to mourn the loss of one of its members, says that, "indeed mothers and teachers are even accustomed to punish children, if in the midst of family sorrow they show any undue cheerfulness in act or speech, and not merely with words but even with the whip force them to shed tears" (Cicero, *Tusc.* 3.64). Cicero's comments also indicate that conforming children to group expectations was a family affair.[64] In the same treatise Cicero commends Spartan boys who conform to the famed toughness of their people through being beaten without even uttering a single whimper (cf. Cicero, *Tusc.* 2.34). Martial provides insight into the use of corporal punishment outside the house when he jokes that a downside of living close to a school is being woken from sleep by the sound of students being beaten (Martial, 7.210). So people like mothers and teachers could carry out corporal punishment without violating their subordinate roles in the family. Second, such punishment was executed with a concern to not overly punish the child because such punishment could permanently feminize the child's body, making it more like a slave's body which would be incapable of assuming the role of a citizen.[65] Paul's mention of the rod (ῥάβδος), as opposed to Cicero's mention of a whip (*verberibus*), fits this model since a whip carried increased shame because of its connection to slaves. Furthermore, the corporal punishment of children was understood as proper, necessary, to conform the child to the expectations of the family and society. This understanding is even applied to the gods, similar to parents, ruling over people, similar to children. Such a view is found in both the Hebrew Bible and New Testament (e.g., Prov 3:11–12 and Heb 12:6, respectively). In short, the corporal punishment of children was not meant to oppress or permanently subordinate the bodies on which it was carried out. It was, however, seen as a good and sometimes necessary course of action to bring about necessary and proper behavior, which is exactly how Paul uses it in his argument. However problematic such a reference might sound to contemporary ears, it does not require understanding Paul presenting himself as a hegemonic father over his children.

As I argued above regarding Paul's self-portrayal as a failed orator, Paul does not abandon problematic models that promote harmful hierarchies within the Corinthians. Rather, Paul adopts the rules of the model and emphasizes how he, because of and in connection with the message of a crucified lord, moves to the bottom of such models. Paul's embodiment of the role as a father continues in his deployment of the vice lists in 1 Cor 5:10–11 and 6:9–10 as he puts the paternal imagery to work in order to frame the Corinthians as undeveloped, feminine children.[66] Like the earlier usage of milk as teaching in rhetorical arguments to encourage people to mature and develop, such vice lists portray the audience as unruly youths who need to listen to their father in order to correct their behavior and act like men. Paul is a father figure for the Corinthians, and they should listen to him as such, even if it causes them great shame.

PAUL AS A CELIBATE

And, now, concerning the things about which you wrote; it is good for a man not to touch a woman. On account of sexual immoralities, each man should have his own wife and each wife should have her own husband. A husband should pay his obligation to his wife, and, likewise, the wife should pay her obligation to her husband. The wife does not have authority over her own body, but the husband. And, likewise, the husband does not have authority over his own body, but the wife. Do not defraud one another, except if decided upon in harmony for a short time, in order that you can devote yourselves to prayer. Then, again, you should be as you were, so that Satan cannot tempt both of you on account your lack of self-control. I say this as a concession not as a command. I wish that everyone was as I am, but each one has their own gift from God. One person in this way, another in that way.

—1 Cor 7:1–7

Paul's self-revelation about his celibacy offers another jarring moment in his self-presentation. The difficulty of Paul's comments, as well as his commands for the Corinthian congregation, have long troubled readers, both ancient and modern, who find it difficult to accept that Paul could speak of marriage and sex in less than positive terms or that he could do so without mentioning children.[67] Indeed, Paul's comment that "it is better not to touch a woman" is often assumed to be so far out of pace with Paul's own thinking that it is attributed to his opponents. Understanding the statement this way not only takes it out of Paul's argument but makes it a point that he counters. Yet Paul argues the superiority of celibacy at numerous points in the chapter. Beyond that, Paul's own celibacy and its role as a model for others has long been explained away rather than set within the discourses of passion and sex which make sense of it. Although there is an intimate (pun intended) connection between Paul's celibacy and his exhortations regarding sex, I explore the ramifications of Paul's celibacy in this section before I address its influences on his commands for the Corinthian congregation for the next chapter. Given the critical assessment of people's sexual proclivities that pervades the texts surveyed in the current volume, Paul's celibacy could not remain a private affair but is critical in understanding his self-presentation. As I will demonstrate below, Paul's celibacy must be understood as the intersection of several discourses. First, Paul advocates avoiding marriage because of how the institution entangles a person in social and civil concerns, thereby requiring certain levels of conformity to the patterns of the current age. Such an approach to the avoidance of marriage has similarities to the Therapeutae and more austere Cynics. Second, like the Therapeutae and Cynics, Paul realizes that accommodations must be made for such a counter-cultural lifestyle. The Cynics do not restrict sexual activity and can imagine a world in which marriage is possible while the Therapeutae are careful to show that their celibacy is not a threat to the social order. Paul's allowances, however, concern sexual immorality and resonate with certain first-century medical approaches to the human body. Ultimately, Paul's wish for people to remain unmarried stems from his apocalyptic expectations while his concessions to marriage and sex arise from his understanding of the human body. As Mitchell argues, such a concession is part of Paul's rhetorical strategy of exemplifying the type "concord" that the Corinthians desperately need.[68]

Paul's statement about his celibacy and directives for marriage come in the midst of his broader discussion of sexual immorality (πορνεία) which began in his discussion of having inappropriate sexual contact (cf. 1 Cor 6:15). Even though in 7:1 Paul uses the phrase περὶ δὲ, which can be understood as introducing a new topic for discussion, the focus of chapter seven continues Paul's discussion on πορνεία from the previous chapter. In 6:12, Paul introduces the subject of πορνεία with a statement about not being controlled by anything and, then, goes on to discuss a man having sex with a πόρνη. In light of what he will say in chapter 7, Paul's usage of πόρνη appears to refer to any woman with whom a man should not have sexual contact and vice versa; this usage is far broader than the standard Greek usage that focuses on prostitutes.[69] When Paul talks about sex within marriage, it is only as a prophylactic against temptation, and the decision to marry hinges on whether his readers can control their passion (1 Cor 7:5, 9). In other words, it seems as if Paul only addresses marriage because he sees it as the only appropriate protection against passion turning into sexual immorality.

Dale Martin demonstrates the importance of setting Paul's comments on sexual immorality within a first-century context. According to Martin, a failure to do so allows the various cultural biases of Paul's interpreters to override Paul's difficult statements about celibacy, marriage, and passion.

> Since the inception of Protestantism, there has been a broad, concerted attempt to package Paul as a promoter of sex and marriage, in spite of (and in reaction to) most of Christian history, which has taken Paul to be an advocate of sexual asceticism, allowing marriage only for those too weak for celibacy. Particularly in recent times, biblical scholars . . . have argued that Paul does not advocate celibacy in 1 Corinthians 7 but rather endorses the goodness of human sexuality, at least within the confines of the marriage bed.[70]

Martin correctly balances his assault on the pro-marriage construction of Paul by pointing out that Paul does not think that those who marry "sin" but enter a less than ideal position (cf. 1 Cor 7:36–38). The fact that Paul argues that celibacy is the better choice for both men and women, a point to which I will return, should create enough dissonance with modern conceptions of sexuality and marriage to cause contemporary readers to search for a more appropriate context in which to set Paul's commands.

The three main backgrounds typically referenced to help understand Paul's statements regarding sex and passion are philosophical, medical, and Hellenistic Jewish.[71] Martin and David Fredrickson each argue that Paul advocates for sex without passion. The basis for such a claim comes from reading Paul's negative understanding of sexual immorality in light of his statements about burning or self-control and setting this discussion in conversation with ancient texts that speak negatively of passion's ability to get out of control. Philosophical texts evidence a similar concern about passion's ability to become too great and harm a person, often using the imagery of burning. A text attributed to Ocellus that dates to the middle of the first century B.C.E. states that, "In the first place . . . [men] should not be connected with women for the sake of pleasure, but for the begetting of children. . . . [C]opulation should not be undertaken for the sake of voluptuous delight" (Ocellus, *On the Nature of the Universe* IV).[72] After discussing the danger of men losing control over themselves in terms of the breakdown of society, part of which will be seen in men marrying women who will dominate them in "wealth, birth, and friends" (Ocellus, *On the Nature of the Universe* IV), the text emphasizes "that the mind, in the act of copulation, should be in a tranquil state: for from depraved, discordant, and turbulent habits, bad seed is produced" (Ocellus, *On the Nature of the Universe* IV). Note that the text emphasizes control and the avoidance of *unrestrained* passion, not passion in general. Lucretius offers a more explicit positive appraisal of passion while retaining the critique of unrestrained passion.[73] Musonius Rufus also places limits on sex by advocating for sex within the context of marriage *and* only so far as it is for the purpose of having children (12.5–6). Musonius goes so far as to label marital sex that does not seek to produce children both unlawful and unjust (12.6–8), calling people who indulge in such sexual relationships "sinners" (12.24–25). Unlike Lucretius and Ocellus, Musonius never gives a positive assessment of passion and so might offer an example of the type of approach to sex and passion that Martin and Fredrickson describe, though that is tenuous since Musonius never makes such a statement and the emphasis on procreation would, in first-century medical understanding, require some level of passion for conception.

Turning to the medical texts, the general sense is that passion is a form of heat and, therefore, can be accommodated in moderation but has the potential to disrupt the natural balance of the body. Galen is representative of the view that the body's natural balances are disrupted through excessive passion or a sudden abstinence from sex.[74] He reports that a man who suddenly ceased sexual activity would experience nausea and depression because of a buildup of semen in his body (Galen, *On the Affected Parts* 6.5). The medical texts show less agreement over questions regarding virginity and the introduction of sex. Soranus argues against the position of other doctors who prescribe sex for young virgins as a cure for excessive passion since it will arouse in them "premature desires" and could lead to uncontrolled passion (Soranus, *Gynecology* 8). Apparently, some doctors, partially paralleling Paul's argument, prescribe sex as a means of alleviating passion or protecting against its damaging effects. Soranus offers a nuanced position to virginity, arguing that it neither alleviates nor abolishes passion but that perpetual virginity in men and women is beneficial, at least in certain religious vocations (Soranus, *Gynecology* 7.14). Unfortunately, Soranus does not elaborate on who should take on celibacy, whether that celibacy requires renunciation of all sexual activity, or the circumstances that lead a person to take on celibacy. What is clear in Soranus's writing is that virginity remains the exception while a natural level of passion and sex is mirrored in the behavior of animals, appropriate for bringing people together for the production of children, and plays a crucial role in promoting social stability.

Jewish texts from the period reflect a similar understanding as that seen above regarding the dangers of passion that could lead people into actions that undermine appropriate behavior and society. These Jewish texts do not, however, provide an explicitly positive assessment of passion within marriage as seen in some of the other texts surveyed in this chapter. *Susanna*, the Greek extension to Daniel, provides a helpful entry into the view of passion found in Jewish texts. It contains a story about two elders of Israel who look upon Susanna's beauty and are consequently overcome by their desire for Susanna.

> Every day the two elders used to see [Susanna], going in and walking about, and they grew in desire (ἐπιθυμία) for her. They suppressed their consciences and turned away their eyes from looking to Heaven or remembering their duty to administer justice. Both were overwhelmed with passion for her. (Susanna 1:8–10)[75]

The ability of a woman's beauty to kindle desire occurs in numerous other texts that deal with desire and appears to be a common theme across genres of Jewish literature (e.g., *T. Reub.* 3.10–4.1; *T. Jud.* 2.1–3; Prov. 6:25).[76] Proverbs addresses the dangers of beauty ("do not be overcome by desire (ἐπιθυμία) for her beauty") and goes onto discuss passion as fire and hot coals that burn the person who touches them (Prov. 6:25–29).[77] The portrayal of desire's corrupting influence on people, seen above in the elders "suppressing their consciences and turning their eyes from heaven" is reminiscent of the warnings found elsewhere about the consequences of allowing such desire to be kindled within a person. The critique here is particularly poignant since these men are elders and judges and their desire causes them to turn away from administering justice for Israel. Despite the numerous and widespread condemnations of inappropriate desire, there is little explicit discussion of desire within marriage. The closest the extant Hellenistic Jewish literature comes to offering a positive assessment of desire in marriage comes in relation to conception, but, even when desire produces children, desire is negative if the union is not licit; such negative desire is invariably traced to Adam's transgression or sin in general (2 Bar 56:6–7 and *T. Reub.* 2.8, respectively). So although there is incontestable evidence that Hellenistic Judaism affirmed sex within marriage,[78] it is uncertain what if any positive role desire played.[79] J. Edward Ellis takes this silence to mean that Hellenistic Judaism must have found an appropriate place for desire within marriage because desire outside of marriage receives such stringent attacks,[80] but such silence is hardly proof for a positive assessment.

As Ellis correctly points out, Martin and Fredrickson focus on excessive passion rather than passion in general, with many of the texts that they cite explicitly carving out an appropriate place for passion's preservation of society by leading people to produce children.[81] The problem with Ellis's argument is that Paul, unlike other ancient authors, never speaks of an appropriate level of passion that leads to the making of children. In 1 Cor 7:9 Paul says that passion is dangerous and needs to be mitigated. Martin uses the idea of a contagion to capture Paul's view of passion as a disease that threatens to infect and destabilize the balance within an individual and, therefore, within the community. If Ellis is correct that Paul does allow for some appropriate amount of passion, then that passion would have to serve some specific purpose like begetting children or holding the family and society together. But Paul never makes such a positive assessment of the result of passion. For example, when Paul does talk about family obligations he sounds more like the Cynic philosophers who advocate a lifestyle, including casual sexual liaisons and frequent masturbation, that kept familial and civic obligations to a bare minimum (e.g., *The Epistle of Diogenes* 44 and 47). But Paul's similarity with the Cynic view of marriage breaks down because Cynics do hold out the possibility, even if it is just hypothetical, of a beneficial marriage so long as the spouse, household, and city follow Cynic principles (Epictetus, *Disc.* 3.22.68–76). Paul never offers such hope for Christian marriages. Also, while Paul encourages Christians to marry other Christians (1 Cor 7:39), a point that has some resonance with the Cynic view of marriage in Epictetus discussed above, his allowance for nonbelieving spouses would be out of pace with the Cynic (1 Cor 7:13–16). When Paul does speak of allowing marriage, it is a choice a person should make in order to protect themselves from being overcome by passion (e.g., 1 Cor 7:9). If passion is a disease, then marriage is a treatment but with negative side-effects.

Although some ancient authors agree with Paul's statements in 1 Cor 7:7, 7:25–28, and 7:32–40 about the benefits of avoiding marriage, they do not teach that this meant total renunciation of sex or sexual activity. Cynic philosophers are the most outspoken proponents of rejecting marriage, but they never advocate giving up sex. Diogenes, according to Dio Chyrsostom, "did not need to go anywhere to find sexual pleasure, but jokingly said that he found the delights of Aphrodite everywhere and free of charge" (Dio Chyrsostom, *Tyr.* 6.18). Some Cynics do advocate avoiding sex because it is too time consuming; instead, the philosopher should just masturbate to alleviate desire (Laertius, *Lives and Opinions* VI.46, 69). These views see marriage and escalating levels of passion as the problem, not sexual acts per se. But this has more to do with understanding that marriage entangled a person in the life of the family which was itself bound up with the life of the city. Epictetus writes that the ideal Cynic could marry as long as the city was entirely comprised of like-minded Cynics (Epictetus, *Diss.* 3.22.67–82). Cynics do not avoid marriage because of the physiological impact but because it would entangle them in concerns that force them to live in "unnatural" ways. Yet, as seen above, these negative views of marriage as entangling a person in affairs that distract them from other pursuits do not require sexual celibacy. However, the idea that refraining from marriage allows one to avoid entanglement in civic obligations does cohere with Paul's reason for advocating celibacy.

While short-term periods of sexual celibacy appear in various religious contexts like Israelite and Egyptian worship,[82] the only clear case of a human character advocating for a perpetual state of complete sexual abstinence is Apollonius of Tyana.[83]

> Now Pythagoras was praised for saying that a man should not approach any woman except his wife, but according to Apollonius, Pythagoras had prescribed that for others, but he himself was not going to marry or even have sexual intercourse. . . . Thanks to his virtue and self-mastery, Apollonius was not subject to it even as an adolescent, but despite his youth and physical strength he overcame and "mastered" its rage. (Philostratus, *Vit. Apoll.* 1.13, trans. Jones)[84]

Note that Apollonius's strict sexual asceticism was never framed as something to be imitated, even by his students, and was possible only because of his extreme self-mastery.[85] Although Philostratus domesticates Apollonius's sexual celibacy, the fact that such a practice receives such attention and requires explanation indicates its subversive nature during Apollonius's life. Other well-known, long-term human celibates in Rome were the vestal virgins who had to maintain a state of sexual celibacy but were free to marry after concluding their service. Like other priestesses who undertook periods of sexual celibacy as part of their religious vocation, the initiation of a vestal virgin was seen as a fictitious marriage that applied the process of *captio*, the ritual that transferred a bride from the family of her parents to her husband's family. In the case of the vestal virgins, they moved out of their parent's family and became part of Rome's civic institution but not under a specific family.[86] The consequence was that their virginity became a symbol of Rome's virginity (i.e., not being penetrated/conquered by a foreign power) and so the virgins' lack of sexual activity was just as important to safeguarding Rome's identity as was the common citizens' mandate to engage in legal sexual activity for the production of citizens.

Paul's own celibacy and his encouragement for others to imitate his celibacy, therefore, contain some parallels to Greek and Roman authors but diverge in that none of the extant Stoic, Cynic, or medical texts advocate permanent sexual celibacy in the way that Paul does. For example, Paul's comments on how marriage forces a person to be concerned with the needs of their spouse coheres with the predominant view of marriage as obligation to family and society. Also, Paul's view that someone in the community who needs to marry should select someone who is also in the community parallels the Cynic view of marriage. Unlike the Cynics, however, Paul never speaks of a context in which marriage becomes the ideal state. If he did have such a vision, not only is it never expressed, but such a vision would be a departure from other visions for marriage in early Christian literature (e.g., 1 Tim 3:2; Tit 1:6). Furthermore, unlike the Stoics, Paul never sees marriage as an institution that protects the community. The only possible exception is Paul's view that married couples should engage in periodic sexual activity in order to prevent Satan from tempting them, which demonstrates concord with the view that appropriate sexual activity can act as a prophylactic against the dangers of passion leading to sexual immorality (1 Cor 7:5). Although some medical texts prescribe limited amounts of sex to alleviate passion, this pertains mostly to young, unmarried people and not to adult, married couples where sexual activity with the spouse is less regulated.[87]

Paul's view of long-term celibacy for both men and women does, however, find a striking, though not complete, parallel in the Therapeutae, a group of monastic Jews who lived outside Alexandria during the first century (cf. Philo, *Contempl.* 21–22).[88] The group engaged in long-term ascetic practices and appears to have been drawn primarily from Alexandrian Jews who were already acquainted with the types of allegorical exegesis for which the city was known. Philo, apparently needing to address the fact that long-term ascetic practices were almost always viewed with suspicion, frames the members of the community as not threatening the social order, going to far as to castigate Greek ascetics whose actions led to the destruction of ancestral land (Philo, *Contempl.* 14). The male members are those who "supposing their mortal lives have come to an end" distribute their money and fulfill their social obligations before leaving society (Philo, *Contempl.* 13–14). The female members, who could be liable for abandoning the traditional spheres for women, are described as older and mostly virgins (Philo, *Contempl.* 68). Though Philo's precise meaning is unclear, he seems to make the point that these women have passed the point of fulfilling their main social obligation of bearing children.[89] So both the male and female members of the community carefully disengage from their social obligations and leave society without threatening the society's stability. Furthermore, the women maintain their subordinate position within the social order of the community by exuding modesty and maternal characteristics.[90] The perennial fear seen in texts that address women taking traditionally male roles or attributes such as self-control and exemplified by the Therapeutrides' celibacy and other ascetic practices, therefore, is still subordinated under male authority and so poses no threat to patriarchy or social stability. With this in mind, Philo's positive framing of these women as philosophers and full participants in the revelatory experiences of the community retains his general unease about the feminine and need to keep the Therapeutrides from being perceived as threats to the male domination that structures the social order.[91]

The key to understanding Paul's relationship with the ideas from the sources surveyed above is that he does not see marriage and sexual activity as the most natural and desirable state for community members.[92] Sexual activity is only beneficial "on account of sexual immorality" and "lack of self-control" (1 Cor 7:2, 5, respectively). Paul returns to this idea to make a similar point when discussing whether widows should remarry when he says, "But if they do not have self-control, let them marry. For it is better to marry than to burn" (1 Cor 7:8–9). This is the third time that the problem of uncontrolled passions arises, but this time Paul adds that if a person has self-control they will not be in danger of succumbing to sexual immorality, apparently because having self-control would mean that passion does not pose a threat. If a person lacks self-control, then refraining from sexual activity will cause a person to burn; the connection between excessive or uncontrolled passion and burning is a common trope in ancient discourses on the subject (e.g., Ovid, *Fasti* 3.545–46 and Catullus 45.16). Also, Paul's admonition in 1 Cor 7:9 that the unmarried and widows refrain from marrying if they have the requisite self-control assigns a higher level of agency to women than is commonly seen in ancient texts dealing with sexuality. Paul indicates that he has the necessary level of self-control in order to enter into a state of perpetual sexual celibacy and thinks that other members of the Corinthian community, both men and women with the appropriate gifting from God, have the potential to do the same. This unexpected concession will be discussed in the following chapter as indicating the type of masculinity Paul wants his readers to embody.

Although the celibacy of the Therapeutae strongly resembles that put forward by Paul, he never advocates a careful or necessary retreat from society so as to assuage the suspicion of outsiders. Though Philo was careful to show that such radical celibacy does not pose a threat, Paul never makes such an argument. Paul's apocalyptic eschatology, present in such comments as the clash of cosmic powers and the transition from one epoch to another (1 Cor 2:6–8 and 7:31, 10:11; respectively), appears to provide an explanation for Paul's advocacy of celibacy and its ability to help maintain freedom from social obligations; in other words, "the time is short" (1 Cor 7:29).[93] The point is that participation in the institution of marriage entangles a person in the care and maintenance of a family which requires more participation in the affairs of society than is required of those people who are not married. As I will discuss in the next paragraph, this is precisely why Augustus instituted legislation designed to promote marriage, children, and enduring households. To refrain from participation in the institution of marriage and the production of children was viewed as a threat to social and political stability. Since Paul envisions the present age, along with its social and political institutions, as passing away, participating in it is, to a significant extant, superfluous for people who await the coming age. Paul's celibacy, therefore, makes sense within his expectation of the full inauguration of the next age, but just because apocalyptic eschatology helps explain Paul's reasoning for advocating celibacy does not mean that Paul is not also aware that such action will be understood as shameful and deviant in the present because it violates both the social and legal encouragement to form families and bear children.[94] In fact, this is precisely the type of logic that guides his use of the antitheses of strong/weak, wise/foolish, and human/divine power in 1 Cor 1:18–2:5.[95] As Gail Streete puts it, Paul's emphasis on ascetic and deviant practices "are in fact both training for living 'out of the world' (1 Cor 5:9–10) and also a means of resisting and overcoming the evil powers of this one."[96]

Paul's disclosure of his own celibate status, therefore, should be read as legally and socially transgressive, given the significance of celibacy in a context that puts a person at a legally inscribed socio-economic disadvantage.[97] Even before Augustus's legislation, Cicero indicates that Rome had institutional mechanisms for prohibiting and punishing celibacy (Cicero, *Leg.* 3.1.7), but these were revived and strengthened by Augustus. The reforms under the *Lex Iulia de maritandis ordinibus*, which were later strengthened under the *Lex papia poppaea*, penalized citizens for celibacy and failing to produce legitimate children.[98] A man, therefore, who could not name legitimate heirs during a census would suffer legal and social penalties and was restricted from holding key, public offices such as that of the *quaestor* and limiting the amount he could inherit.[99] The justification for such penalties is that such a man would have failed to fulfill his duties as, or act like, a man, and has weakened his society. Indeed, Augustus confronts a group of upper class bachelors with the words, "What am I to call you? Men? You have not yet proved yourselves to be men" and goes onto point to their refusal to have legitimate, Roman children despite the fact that "not one of [them] eats or sleeps alone" (Dio Cassius, *Roman History* 56.4–6, Foster). Juvenal relates a similar sentiment in referring to children as "the proofs of your manhood" (Juvenal, *Sat.* 9.85). Fear of the penalties associated with the law and failing to embody the status of man appears to have driven some men to leave detailed accounts of their infertility or their wife's miscarriages.[100] Women, likewise, reportedly sought to evade the legal penalties for failing to fulfill their social responsibility of marrying and bearing children by hiring lower-class men to pretend to be their husbands. The scope, penalties, and social significance of this system can be seen in Tacitus's comments, "From [the *lex Papia-Poppaea*], the chains became more bitter, guards were established and encouraged by rewards . . . so that if a person should be resistant to the rewards of parenthood, the populace, as though it were a parent to everyone, should step in to occupy the empty places" (Tacitus, *Ann.* 3.28, Moore).[101] Paul not only places himself outside the standard social model, thereby restricting his ability to be recognized and function as a full man, he also becomes a deviant to be monitored by society.

SYNTHESIS

My analysis of key instances of Paul's self-presentation reveals several vital aspects of how Paul's self-presentation intersects conventions of gender and the power associated with them. Paul's engagement with discourses associated with masculinity predominantly emphasizes Paul's failure to properly embody masculine roles and, therefore, depicts him as a failed man. Paul's self-presentation as an orator in 1 Cor 1:17 and 2:1–5 hinges on his inability to present and declaim like a real man. Instead, he depicts himself as weak, fearful, and trembling. The Corinthians would be sorely disappointed if they had hoped to align with Paul for social advancement as was common to do with other public orators, as the conflict between Favorinus and Polemo demonstrates. The same is true of Paul's self-presentation as their father. Instead of the proud, commanding, virile *paterfamilias*, Paul is a naked, beaten, starved criminal who is led to his death in a procession as a spectacle for the cosmos. The shame of having such a father is so great that Paul has to address it directly in the text. In both instances, Paul embodies masculine roles in ways that disqualify him from functioning as a hegemonic or complicit man. Rather, he would be forced to relinquish social and civil authority to others and take the position of a subordinate man.

Paul's application of feminine roles in his self-presentation has a similar effect. It scarcely matters which feminine role Paul would have selected because it is unheard of for a male author to appropriate feminine roles in their self-presentation. As noted above, one notable exception to this occurs in Roman love elegy; a form of erotic poetry that intentionally subverts gender roles as part of a broader critique of culture. However, even these erotic poems retain an awareness that the authors bring shame upon themselves because of their feminine behavior and evidence a struggle to recapture their lost masculinity. Paul, on the other hand, embraces the feminine with the abandon of a man who has gazed at the emptiness, or more accurately the antithetical nature, of his context's way of organizing people through gender based hierarchies. The abandonment of these systems is perhaps seen most clearly in his embrace of a feminine, or possibly an enslaved male, persona as he talks about feeding the Corinthians milk, but it appears throughout Paul's self-presentation.

As I have noted throughout the chapter, other scholars have pointed to the social impact of Paul's self-presentation, yet none has sought to offer a coherent explanation for the pattern that emerges from them. The two notable exceptions are Welborn, who takes Paul as embodying the role of a buffoon and Gorman who understands Paul as taking on a cruciform identity. While I find Welborn's treatment of the shame and scandal of Paul's self-presentation helpful, by focusing so specifically on the image of the mime he cannot account for instances of self-presentation that fall outside of this model. For example, Welborn can account for Paul's use of paternal imagery because it exists within the image of the buffoon,[102] but he offers no comment on Paul's presentation as a mother or wet nurse even though he is aware of Gaventa's treatment of milk.[103] Gorman's concept of cruciformity is less tied to a specific contextual image and, as a result, can better account for the variety of characters that Paul invokes in his self-presentation.[104] Although he notes the shame attached to the cross, his treatment leaves the social shame of adopting such an identity largely unexplored.[105] Furthermore, because Gorman does not engage the inextricable bond between gender and power that pervades the Greek and Roman worlds, he cannot integrate instances of femininity nor fully account for the repercussions for a failure of masculinity into his understanding of Paul's cruciform identity. Ultimately, accounting for gendered discourses in Paul's self-presentation helps elucidate the tangible legal and social implications of taking on a cruciform identity.

Taken together, Paul's instances of self-presentation reviewed in this chapter indicate that being a subordinate man was a key aspect of his identity. Such an individual would, supposedly by their very nature, be restricted from accessing the spheres of power and influence reserved for hegemonic and complicit men. If one cannot declaim, then one has little hope of defending one's self in court and, therefore, have no recourse to ward off legal attacks. It is possible that such a person's persona is problematic to the point that others would be reluctant to come to their defense for fear of guilt or feminization by association. If such a person was a father or the head of a household they would bring shame upon those under their control and struggle to represent the family in public. Mitchell is correct that a significant part of Paul's method to correct factionalism is the political trope of sacrificing one's rights and privileges for the common good, but the vehicle which Paul supplies the Corinthians to carry out such a radical command is a subordinate persona that lacks attachment to the trappings of power because it has surrendered the ability to access them.

NOTES

1. My approach will be similar to that used by Margaret M. Mitchell in *Paul and the Rhetoric of Reconciliation: An Exegetical Investigation of the Language and Composition of 1 Corinthians* (Louisville, Ky.: Westminster John Knox, 1993). Mitchell argues that 1 Corinthians should be read as a piece of deliberative rhetoric set within an epistolary framework. To substantiate her claim, since none of the rhetorical handbooks discuss deliberative arguments applied as letters, Mitchell first highlights places in 1 Corinthians that adopt the language and tropes of deliberative rhetoric and, then, looks at the overall effect of approaching 1 Corinthians through the lens of deliberative rhetoric.

2. Brendon Reay develops Cato's use of agricultural imagery within *De Agri Cultura* as well as in other works thought to be written by Cato to Cato's reshaping of elite masculine identity; "Agriculture, Writing, and Cato's Aristocratic Self-Fashioning," *CA* 24 (2005): 331–61.

3. Reay, Ibid., 333–34.

4. Jay Shanor, "Paul as Master Builder: Construction Terms in First Corinthians," *NTS* 34 (1988): 461–471.

5. Shanor, "Paul as Master Builder," 465–66.

6. J. Duncan M. Derrett, "Paul as Master-Builder," *EQ* 69 (1988): 129–37.

7. Even John Goodrich's limiting Paul's reference to either commercial agency or private administration does not help more specifically identify how such a usage

could impact Paul's presentation of his masculinity; *Paul as Administrator of God in 1 Corinthians* (Cambridge: Cambridge University Press, 2012), 25–102, 106.

8. Richard Duncan-Jones, *Power and Privilege in Roman Society* (Cambridge: Cambridge University Press, 2016), 142–53.

9. See the discussion in Jason König's "Conventions of Prefatory Self-presentation in Galen's *On the Order of My Own Books*," in *Galen and the World of Knowledge* (ed. Christopher Gill, Tim Whitmarsh, and John Wilkins; Cambridge: Cambridge University Press, 2009), 35–58. König compares the function of tropes in writing for friends in Nicomachus Gerasenus's *Introduction to Music*, Quintilian's the *Orator's Education*, and Galen's *On the Order of My Own Books*. Even a cursory reading of these texts demonstrates the application of a common trope across a range of genres bolster an author's argument by ingratiating the author to the audience.

10. Maud Gleason, *Making Men: Sophists and Self-Presentation in Ancient Rome* (Princeton: Princeton University Press, 1995), 55–130.

11. See Barbara K. Gold, "Introduction," in *A Companion to Roman Love Elegy* (ed. Barbary K. Gold; Oxford: Wiley-Blackwell, 2012), 1–7. Konstantinos P. Nikoloutsos analyzes Tibullus through the lens of a crisis in masculinity and argues for a reconstruction of masculine identity that overcomes apparent feminization; "From Tomb to Womb: Tibullus 1.1 and the Discourse of Masculinity in Post–Civil War Rome," *Sch* 20 (2011): 52–71. For a more optimistic reading for the portrayal of women in Latin love elegy, see Judith P. Hallett, "The Role of Women in Roman Elegy: Counter-Cultural Feminism," *Ar* 6 (1973): 329–47.

12. Ellen Greene, "Gender and Elegy," in *A Companion to Roman Love Elegy* (ed. Barbary K. Gold; Oxford: Wiley-Blackwell, 2012), 358. See Marilyn B. Skinner, "*Ego Mulier*: The Construction of Male Sexuality in Catullus," in *Roman Sexualities* (ed. Judith P. Halllett and Marilyn B. Skinner; Princeton: Princeton University Press, 1997), 129–50.

13. Kevin Ronald Scull, "Authority and Persuasion: Self-Presentation in Paul's Letters" (Ph.D. diss., The University of California Los Angeles, 2012). Although Scull offers a helpful argument regarding Paul's self-presentation and its function in the broader purposes of the letter, he does not integrate the details Paul presents so as to show that Paul presents a coherent identity commensurate with these goals.

14. Ibid., 18–24.

15. See Joseph B. Fitzmyer, *First Corinthians: A New Translation with Commentary* (ABC vol 32; New Haven: Yale University Press, 2009), 218–19. For comparison of Paul's self-description and other authors, see the discussion, below, and Peter Marshall, *Enmity in Corinth: Social Conventions in Paul's Relations with the Corinthians* [Tübingen: J. C. B. Mohr (Paul Siebeck), 1987], 356–64.

16. Marshall, *Enmity in Corinth*, 358–59.

17. Johannes Weiss, *Der erste Korintherbreif* (Göttingen: Vandenhoeck & Ruprecht, 1910), xli. Later, Weiss changed his position to allow for a third letter. See the discussion in Raymond F. Collins, *First Corinthians* (SP; Collegeville; MN: The Liturgical Press, 1999), 11–12. L. L. Welborn represents a continuation of Weiss's argument that changes in tone, train of thought, and apparently contradictory judgments

indicate the presence of multiple letters; see *Paul, the Fool of Christ: A Study of 1 Corinthians 1–4 in the Comic-Philosopher Tradition* (London: T&T Clark, 2005), 13. Welborn, like Weiss, understands 1 Cor 1–4 as a single text; see "On the Discord in Corinth: 1 Corinthians 1–4 and Ancient Politics," *JBL* 106 (1987): 85–111. Adam G. White provides a helpful overview of the main arguments for taking these chapters as a coherent text; *Where is the Wise Man?: Greco-Roman Education as a Background to the Divisions in 1 Corinthians 1–4* (London: Bloomsbury T&T Clark, 2015). Roy E. Ciampa and Brian S. Rosner disagree with the majority of scholars by arguing that 4:18 introduces a new section that transitions into discussion of specific issues in the community; they do not, however, suggest that it signals a redactional seam that indicates the presence of a separate letter; *The First Letter to the Corinthians* (Grand Rapids: Eerdmans, 2010), 23, 189–90.

18. Weiss argues that 1:10–3:23 outline Paul's approach to "das Verhältnis des Evangeliums zur "Weisheit" before returning to address the issues that have arisen between him and the factional parties in 4:1–13; *Korinthbrief*, 12.

19. Ibid., 15–20.

20. The fact that Paul emphasizes unity and harmony among the apostles and between him and Apollos provides a strong indication that the factionalism he addresses stems from the Corinthians aligning with various leaders as opposed to arising from Gnostic influences. Mitchell discusses Paul's use of "slogans" in 1 Cor 1:12 to describe the factions as borrowing political language which Paul will then counter by emphasizing the unity of these figures; *Rhetoric of Reconciliation*, 82–86, 201. Stephen M. Pologoloff offers a similar analysis and shows that Paul's focus is not on countering the teaching of these other figures, though he might have reason to do so, but to address the way the Corinthians divide over allegiances to these figures which resembles the way students in first-century urban environments would align with teachers and orators; see *Logos and Sophia: The Rhetorical Situation of 1 Corinthians* (Atlanta: Scholars Press, 1992), 99–104. Indicative of the persuasiveness of such an approach to the issues affecting the Corinthian congregation is the work of Nils A. Dahl who shows the weaknesses of Baur's theory and those who build upon it that Paul was primarily concerned with false teaching; most recently in *Studies in Paul: Theology for the Early Church* (Eugene; OR: Wipf & Stock, 2002), 41–42.

21. Bruce W. Winter, *Paul and Philo among the Sophists: Alexandrian and Corinthian Responses to a Julio-Claudian Moment* (2nd ed.; Grand Rapids: Eerdmans, 2002), 129–40.

22. Ben Witherington III offers a helpful discussion of such competitions between the various teachers and their disciples and situates the problems in Corinth within such a context; *Conflict and Community in Corinth: A Socio-Rhetorical Commentary on 1 and 2 Corinthians* (Grand Rapids: Eerdmans, 1995), 100–101. Witherington notes that such a context also helps to make sense of Paul's different calls for the Corinthians to imitate him and how he situates such a call within his own imitation of Christ. Pogoloff's analysis of the distinction between the use of the label of "wise" in philosophical or rhetorical circles is helpful and points to its broader appropriation in the first century where the goal was to be seen as a "competent public figure," or wise person, regardless of the circumstances; *Logos and Sophia*, 121–27. As noted in

the previous chapters, such assessments of public performances and competencies are closely linked to perceptions of masculinity.

23. Pologoloff, *Logos and Sophia*, 108–27. Pogoloff's work informs that of White, mentioned above, who argues that Paul intentionally presents himself in distinction to the stereotypical wise man; *Where is the Wise Man?*, 102–105. Winter also includes a helpful analysis of the phrase, translating it as "rhetorical skill;" see *Philo and Paul*, 187–88.

24. Johnathan Jodamus also presents a gender critical examination of Paul's use of masculinity in 1 Corinthians but concludes that Paul embodies a hegemonic masculinity. Despite this, Jodamus still acknowledges that Paul's depiction of his oratorical skill "impinges greatly on his masculinity;" "An Investigation into the Construction(s) and Representation(s) of Masculinity(ies) and Feminity(ies) in 1 Corinthians" (Ph.D. diss., University of Cape Town, 2015), 99.

25. See L. L. Welborn's treatment of the issue in *Paul, the Fool of Christ: A Study of 1 Corinthians 1–4 in the Comic-Philosophic Tradition* (New York: T&T Clark International, 2005), 15–48. Stanley Stowers offers one of the more helpful expositions of Paul's use of μωρία in terms of an antithetical approach to conventional approaches to wisdom; "Paul on the Use and Abuse of Reason" in *Greeks, Romans, and Christians: Essays in Honor of Abraham J. Malherbe* (ed. D. Balch, E. Ferguson, and W. Meeks; Minneapolis: Fortress Press, 1990), 253–86. Justin Martyr's comments on 1 Cor 1–2 come in *Apol.*, I, 13.4.

26. Welborn, *Fool of Christ*, 25–33. Welborn reviews the subtle difference between meanings of μωρία stemming from philosophical, rhetorical, political, and literary provenances with ample primary source evidence to substantiate each use.

27. Martin Hengel's pioneering work not only made the connection between the cross and public humiliation but also how this impacts how one should read Paul's framing of the gospel; see *Crucifixion in the Ancient World and the Folly of the Message of the Cross* (Philadelphia: Fortress, 1977), esp. 62 and 90; and Jerome H. Neyrey, "Despising the Shame of the Cross: Honor and Shame in the Johannine Passion Narrative" *Semia* 68 (1994): 113–138. Richard A. Horsley is one of the first to bring insights about the social stigma and shame of the cross into conversation with postcolonial interpretation; see "Introduction" in *Paul and Empire: Religion and Power in Roman Imperial Society* (ed. Richard A. Horsley; Philadelphia: Trinity, 1997), 10–24. More recently, Sean A. Adams provides a helpful update to the argument that applies advances in postcolonial theory to understanding the cross as imperial propaganda in his chapter, "Crucifixion in the Ancient World: A Response to L.L. Welborn" in *Paul's World* (ed. Stanley E. Porter; Leiden: Brill 2008), 111–30. Maybe more so than any other modern scholar, Michael Gorman has offered an insightful and pedagogically useful articulation about what it means for Paul to have integrated such a scandalous image into his proclamation about Christ in terms of cruciformity; see *Cruciformity: Paul's Narrative Spirituality of the Cross* (Grand Rapids: Eerdmans, 2001); *Apostle of the Crucified Lord: A Theological Introduction to Paul and His Letters* (Grand Rapids: Eerdmans, 2004); and *Inhabiting the Cruciform God: Kenosis, Justification, and Theosis in Paul's Narrative Soteriology* (Grand Rapids: Eerdmans, 2009).

28. David Tombs begins to explore this question but with a focus on the possibility of explicit sexual assault rather than the more discursive variety to which I allude; see "Crucifixion, State Terror, and Sexual Abuse," *USQR* 53 (1999): 89–100.

29. Adams, "Crucifixion," 113.

30. Welborn argues that such language function as quasi-technical terminology in the rhetorical tradition that indicates an insufficiency of rhetorical training and embodiment. Welborn further develops this into indicating that Paul invokes the image of the mime; 90–99. Although Welborn is correct that the figure of the mime included such characteristics, I do not find it necessary to look beyond the characterization of the failed orator for understanding Paul's language. See Winter, *Paul and Philo*, 157–58. Also, White, *Where is the Wise Man?*, 103-04.

31. Despite applying slightly different models or nuances to their readings of Paul's language in 1 Cor 1–4, Mitchell, White, Welborn, and Dutch all understand Paul as intentionally rejecting elevated social status and associating himself with those at the bottom of the social hierarchy.

32. It is not surprising that Diogenes comes to represent a similar rejection of the world's system for assessing value that becomes a hallmark of the Cynic tradition.

33. Margaret M. Mitchell, *The Rhetoric of Reconciliation*, 200–201.

34. Although Paul's usage would technically qualify as a simile because of the use of ὡς, ancient rhetoric did not draw a sharp distinction between the function of metaphor and simile within an argument. Aristotle says that, "The simile also is a metaphor" (*Rhet.*, 3.4.1). The main difference discussed by ancient grammarians and rhetoricians is that a metaphor is more pleasing because it is shorter and makes a more direct appeal to sensory input, particularly sight (e.g., Cicero, *De or.*, 3.158–160). See Collins's discussion of the use of metaphor in simile in Aristotle and Seneca; *1 Corinthians*, 140–45. White, *The Wise Man*, 125–27.

35. It should be noted that, in light of Greek and Roman medical texts, it is possible that ancients would have heard Paul as having actually nursed the adult members of the Corinthian congregation. Aristotle alludes to a Syrian man who breastfed a child (*Hist. an.*, 3.20.522). Galen describes the benefits of adults drinking breast milk, admitting that few are willing to do it so the milk should be removed from the breast and put into a cup (7.701).

36. Abraham Malherbe, "'Gentle as a Nurse': The Cynic Background to 1 Thess ii," *NovT* 12 (1970): 203–17.

37. Ibid., 204.

38. Gaventa, *Mother*, 22.

39. Gaventa arrives at a similar conclusion but without directly stating why; *Mother*, 24.

40. Philo equates the state of women with that of children in *Opif.* 132.

41. Even though Epictetus does not use milk (γάλα) in this text, the reference to weaning would have to mean milk or a mixture containing milk.

42. Valerie A. Fildes, *Breasts, Bottles, and Babies: A History of Infant Feeding* (Edinburgh: Edinburgh University Press, 1986); 8–12, 17–36.

43. Soranus, *Gynaecology* (Translated by Owessi Temkin; Baltimore; MD: The Johns Hopkins Press, 1956), 17[86].

44. Soranus advocating for a period of twenty days before the mother nurses is based on the "great change" experience by her body, *Gynaecology*, 2.18[87]. Soranus then discusses at great length how to select an appropriate, or even the best, wet nurse; *Gynaecology*, 2.18[87]–19[88]. Soranus goes on to give instructions about how to regulate the diet, sexual activities, and physical movements of the wet nurse so as to maintain a supply of good milk for an infant; *Gnyaecology*, 2.24[93]–27[96]. Soranus's extensive advice is often taken as an indication of the widespread use of wet nurses in Roman urban centers during the Empire.

45. Brown says that Paul's language in 3:1–3 would make "the message of the cross" that Paul first proclaimed to them tantamount to "baby food," *First Corinthians*, 187–88; Collins understands Paul's point somewhat more generally as "pastoral care" and notes that Paul is not giving a two-stage model for Christian maturity, *First Corinthians*, 142–45. It is unclear, however, what Collins thinks Paul means by "solid food." C. K. Barrett argues that Paul's use of νηποόις ἐν Χρίσοτῳ as indicating a status between being "heathen" and fully developed; *The First Epistle to the Corinthians* (New York: Harper and Row Publishers, 1968), 79–81. Hans Conzelmann reaches a similar conclusion about the status of Paul's audience; *1 Corinthians: A Commentary on the First Epistle to the Corinthians* (Philadelphia: Fortress Press, 1975), 71–72. Dieter Zeller provides a helpful review that balances Philo's usage of milk as teaching with the usage of milk as imagery for knowledge given to initiates as part of the induction into mystery cults; see *Der erste Brief an der Korinther* (Göttingen: Vandenhoek & Ruprecht, 2011), 151–52, esp. fn385.

46. Helmut Merklein, after reviewing the option that Paul contrasts two forms of teaching, concludes that Paul does not address their lack of progress (Fortschritt) but their lack of basic understanding (Grundverständnisses); *Der erste Brief an die Korinther: Kapitel 1–4* (Vol 1; Gütersloh: Gütersloher Verlagshaus Gerd Mohn; Würzburg: Echter Verlag, 1992), 250–51. Merklein's comments are indicative of a broader move away from reading 1 Corinthians against a backdrop of Gnostic influence which has resulted in a second form of the gospel which Paul must address. Zeller reviews the history of such approaches and points out the problem of reading the factionalism of 1 Corinthians in light of the issues that arise later and are the focus of 2 Corinthians; *Der erste Brief an der Korinther*, 40–45.

47. Hooker picks up on this idea that the Corinthians had not ingested the milk that Paul gave them when she argues that Paul's point is not between "two quite different diets which [Paul] has to offer, but between the true food of the Gospel which he has fed them . . . and the synthetic substitute which the Corinthians have preferred"; "Hard Sayings: 1 Cor 3:2," *Th* 69 (1966): 21. Fitzmyer develops this point further by arguing that Paul uses the imagery of milk refutes their claim to "advanced knowledge" when they are still babes in need of milk; *First Corinthians*, 187. Thiselton integrates this point with the rest of letter, "If Paul meant that even now you still cannot manage something more complex than the milk of proclamation, it is difficult to see what he expects them to make of his rigorous arguments about ethical conduct, marriage and celibacy, the nature of freedom in relation to food offered to idols, the eucharist, spiritual gifts or person in a corporate setting, and the resurrection"; *First Corinthians*, 292.

48. This line of thinking requires some form of two-stage teaching and, as I argue, does not fit the broader rhetorical purpose of the passage; see Gillis Gerleman, *Der Heidenapostel. Ketzerische Erwägungen zur Predigt des Paulus zugleich ein Streifzug in der griechischen Mythologie* (Stockholm: Almqvist & Wiksell, 1989) and Walter Grundmann, "Die νήπιοι in der urchristlichen Paränesis," *NTS* 5 (1958–59): 188–205.

49. Hooker, "Hard Sayings," 19–22. Collins, *First Corinthians*, 143.

50. Zeller argues, contra Lindemann, that Paul connects his message of the cross with solid food; *Der erste brief Korinther*, 151. The point, then, is not a two-stage process of Christian of development but a correct, cross-shaped understanding of the Christian life in contrast with an understanding of the Christian life that embodies the social structures and practices of the broader culture. Andreas Lindemann, as with others who see Paul's focus on the stages of Christian development, sees the beginning stage of Christian development in Paul's use of νήπιοι and γάλα in contrast to the mature stage of Christian development which is characterized as τέλειοι and can handle βρῶμα; see *Der Erste Korintherbrief* (Tübingen: Mohr Siebeck, 2000), 78.

51. Gaventa, *Mother*, 41–50.

52. Although, as evident in Tacitus's reference to a male helper for the wet nurse, men could be used in the care for infants, it is untenable to see Paul as adopting this "male" role for the sake of his argument. These men ranked so low within the social and family structure that they are essentially servants to "the most worthless member of the household" (*Dial.*, 29). They would not, therefore, qualify as "real men." Furthermore, male nurses would have to use milk from an animal, which would not fit with Paul's use of the imagery of milk for moral formation.

53. Gaventa, *Mother*, 48; emphasis added. Susan Eastman makes a suggestion similar to Gaventa's but leaves the comment as speculation without fleshing out the details; Susan Eastman, "Imagery, Gendered: Pauline Literature," in *The Oxford Encyclopedia of the Bible and Gender Studies: Vol 1* (ed. Julia M. O'Brien; Oxford: Oxford University Press, 2014), 379–80.

54. Fitzmyer, *First Corinthians*, 222. Eva Maria Lassen provides a helpful overview of the development and use of paternal imagery in Roman discourses and suggests that Paul applies such familial language in order to place himself in a position of authority over the Corinthian community; "The Use of the Father Image in Imperial Propaganda and 1 Corinthians 4:14–21," *TynBul* 42 (1991): 127–36. Although Lassen correctly understands the trope of the *paterfamilias*, by separating the image from the preceding description in 1 Cor 4:9–13 she misses Paul's ironic twist which I will outline, below.

55. John Byron offers a helpful treatment of Paul's use of the titles of servant and steward in 1 Corinthians, concluding that Paul did not use the these titles to communicate his slavery to Christ but his placement within in a position of subordinate authority within God's ordering of the universe; see "Slave of Christ or Willing Servant?: Paul's Self-Description in 1 Corinthians 4:1–2 and 9:16–18," *Neot* 37 (2003): 178–98. Byron counters Dale Martin's argument that Paul's use of servant and steward are meant to give the impression that Paul is Christ's slave; see *Slavery as Salvation: The Metaphor of Slavery in Pauline Christianity* (New Haven: Yale University Press, 1990).

56. I understand Paul's use of κρίνω in 1 Cor 4:5, and ἀνακρίνω in 4:3–4, as an initial critique of the type of judgements that the Corinthians have already passed on lower-class members of the community. Paul needs to address these standards of judging before moving to the later comments on judging where he chastises the Corinthians for not judging the actions of community members (e.g., 1 Cor 6:1–3). As Mitchell points out, the factionalism in Corinth stems from incorrect judgments about status and behavior; *Rhetoric of Reconciliation*, 218–21. Before Paul can offer the correct perspective that the Corinthians should use to judge one another, he first needs to do away with their current way of judging that mirrors that of the broader society and is promoting division within the community.

57. Byron, "Paul's Self-Description," 185.

58. Lassen, "The Use of the Father Image," 135.

59. Fitzmyer clearly takes this position; see *First Corinthians*, 211. Thiselton provides a lengthy and somewhat obscure argument based on speech-act theory that indicates the harsh things that Paul says about the Corinthians in 1 Cor 1–4 is in view; *First Corinthians*, 368–69.

60. Glancy's assessment of Paul's threat of violence, though focusing on 2 Corinthians, reaches similar conclusions to those I offer here; see *Corporal Knowledge*, 44–45.

61. The severity of the issue carries into Paul's other correspondence with the Corinthian believers in 2 Cor 13:10.

62. Mitchell, *Rhetoric of Reconciliation*, 222–25.

63. Jodamus, *An Investigation*, 111; emphasis added.

64. Richard Saller offers a helpful overview of the function of physical violence in Greek and Roman families; see "Corporal Punishment, Authority, and Obedience in the Roman Household," in *Marriage, Divorce, and Children in Ancient Rome* (ed. Beryl Rawson; New York: Oxford University Press, 1996), 144–165. As Saller's investigation makes clear, there were conflicting approaches to the proper use of the corporal punishment of children in Greek and Roman authors, but it was a broadly accepted part of parenting.

65. Ibid., 163–64.

66. For more on the paternal imagery at work in Paul's use of vice lists, see Fredrik Ivarsson, "Vice Lists and Deviant Masculinity: The Rhetorical Function of 1 Corinthians 5:10–11 and 6:9–10," in *Mapping Gender in Ancient Religious Discourses* (ed. Todd Penner and Caroline Vander Stichele; Leiden: Brill, 2007), 172.

67. Ancient views on marriage, especially those influenced by Christian writings, are almost unanimous in arguing that sex must have procreative intent to be valid. For a discussion of the prevalence of this view and Christianity's influence upon it, see Martin's comments in "Familiar Idolatry and the Christian Case against Marriage," in *Sex and the Single Savior: Gender and Sexuality in Biblical Interpretation* (Louisville: Westminster John Knox, 2006), 103–24. Protestant interpreters and their heirs find it almost impossible to imagine that Paul would have a negative view of sex within the context of marriage.

68. Mitchell identifies concord as a specific focus of deliberative rhetoric, the form of argumentation found in 1 Corinthians, and argues that the call for adaptability on

behalf of those with more power or control both fits Paul's usage and is found in other Greek and Latin texts; *Rhetoric of Reconciliation*, 60–64

69. Loader, *Sexuality in the New Testament*, 168–69; Gaca, *Making of Fornication*, 171–72.

70. Martin, *Corinthian Body*, 209. Martin goes on to argue that the view that reading Paul as supporting marriage and sex stem from modern constructions of sexuality and marriage.

71. Martin's work was one of the first to offer an in-depth engagement of Paul's discussion of sex and passion in light of Stoic, Cynic, and medical texts and concludes that Paul advocated avoidance of passion, even when having sex within a marital context; *Corinthian Body*, 212–17. Fredrickson broadly agrees with Martin's assessment that Paul has a consistently negative view of passion and also argues that Paul thinks that passion, even within marriage, should be avoided, *Passionless Sex*, 26–30. Against this view, J. Edward Ellis argues that Paul takes issue with excessive passion, not passion in general; *Paul and Ancient Views of Sexual Desire: Paul's Sexual Ethics in 1 Thessalonians 4, 1 Corinthians 7, and Romans 1* (London: T&T Clark, 2007), 146; William Loader takes a middling position and argues that Paul, "to some degree," sees marriage as a "necessary evil" but this is balanced by his understanding of marriage and sex as originating in God's creation of Adam and Eve; *Sexuality in the New Testament: Understanding the Key Texts* (Louisville: Westminster John Knox, 2010), 46–47.

72. For a discussion of the text and its attribution to Ocellus, see Deming, *Paul on Marriage*, 67, 231.

73. Pamela Gordon offers a helpful overview of the two portraits of "Venus" as human sexuality that appears in Lucretius's work; "Some Unseen Monster: Rereading Lucretius and Sex," in *The Roman Gaze: Vision, Power, and the Body* (ed. David Fredrick; Baltimore; Md.: Johns Hopkins Press, 2002), 94–99. The first portrait of sexuality comes in the first book of *On the Nature of Things* and shows sexuality as a benevolent force that brings animals, including people, together for the benefit of their species and the world (1.1–32). In the final book, however, sexuality has overtaken Rome's young men to the point that they transform the riches of their ancestors into gifts for their lovers, bring their family names to ruin, and destabilize society (4.1121–1130). Gordon offers a more balanced approach than that of Robert D. Brown, who influences Frederick's reading of Lucretius; see *Lucretius on Love and Sex: A Commentary on "De Rerum Natura" IV, with Prolegomena, Text, and Translation* (Leiden: Brill, 1987), 100–143.

74. Galen, *Hygiene* 3.4. See the discussion in Martin, *Corinthian Body*, 198–229.

75. The text of *Susanna* survives in two close but distinct recensions. The shorter version is contained in Alexandrinus while the longer is contained in Sinaiticus. Each version describes the result of the elders watching Susanna in terms of kindling ἐπιθυμία even though the word occurs in different forms. For a description of the text in each manuscript see D. M. Kay, "Susanna" in *The Apocrypha and Pseudepigrapha of the Old Testament Volume One: Apocrypha* (ed. R. H. Charles and D. Litt; Oxford: Clarendon Press, 1913), 638–40.

76. The problem is not beauty per se, but the danger that an inappropriate engagement with beauty poses for kindling desire. Raphael, the angel who guides Tobias on his journey, praises beauty as one of Sarah's endearing traits (Tobit 6:12).

77. The MT also contains the respective term for desire (גמה).

78. Gary Anderson offers a wide-ranging survey of Hellenistic Jewish and Rabbinic literature that demonstrates that Jewish tradition both affirms the goodness of sex within marriage and could not have started as a response to Christian sexual asceticism; see "Celibacy or Consummation in the Garden? Reflection on Early Jewish and Christian Interpretations of the Garden of Eden," *HTR* 28 (1989): 121–48.

79. *T. Ab.* contains a story that portrays this dynamic of a clear condemnation of sexual violation with a silent nod of approval to sex within marriage. In the story, Abraham sees a couple on their way to the bridal chamber to consummate their marriage and says nothing about it but, later, sees a different couple engaged in sexual immorality and requests divine intervention to stop them (10.2–11).

80. Ellis, *Paul and Ancient Views*, 40–91.

81. Ibid., 3–5, 167–68.

82. It is never framed as an activity that would be beneficial for people in general, even if they could undertake such a course of action.

83. Deming makes the point that no extant Cynic or Stoic text argues for the type of perpetual sexual celibacy seen advocated by Paul in 1 Cor 7; *Paul on Marriage and Celibacy*, 61n38. It seems unusual that Deming places such a comment in a footnote since his book seeks to elucidate the background for Paul's approach to marriage and sex.

84. It should be noted that Pythagoras, though held up in this text as a model of sexual celibacy, was widely held to have at least one daughter, Damo, whom he trained as a philosopher (cf., Diogenes Laertius, *Lives* 8.42–43). It would appear that even for Pythagoras, then, sexual celibacy was only periodic.

85. James A. Francis, *Subversive Virtue: Asceticism and Authority in the Second-Century Pagan World* (University Park; Pa.; University of Pennsylvania Press, 1995), 101–02. It is interesting to note that Philostratus will later frame Apollonius's asceticism as physiological preparation of the body for divine revelation (II.35–37). Aside from not being distracted from devotion to the Lord, Paul never indicates what other positive outcomes his sexual celibacy produces.

86. Robin Lorsch Wildfang, *Rome's Vestal Virgins: A Study of Rome's Vestal Priestesses in the Late Empire and Early Republic* (New York: Routledge, 2006), 51–63.

87. The fact that a behavior is less regulated, commented upon, or held in suspicion is a key indicator that the activity falls within the bounds of accepted behavior. Foucault makes this point in seeking to understand why certain behaviors, or objects as Foucault would describe them, become the center of attention at different points in time; see *The Archeology of Knowledge and the Discourse of Language* (trans. A. M. Sheridan Smith; New York: Random House, 1972), 31–49. This is one reason why studying sexual activity of married couples poses such a challenge.

88. Philo's *On the Contemplative Life* provides our only source for the Therapeutae and Therapeutrides, male and female members of the monastic Jewish community which existed on near Lake Mareotis outside of Alexandria. Eusebius makes mention of Philo's work and appreciation for the Therapeutae and appears to appropriate them as part of the Christian tradition (*Hist. eccl.* 2.15.2; see the discussion in G. Peter Richardson, "Philo and Eusebius on Monasteries and Monasticism—The Therapeutae and Kellia," in *Origins and Method: Towards a New Understanding of Judaism and Early Christianity: Essays in Honour of John C. Hurd* (ed. Bardley H.

McLean; Sheffield: JSOT Press, 1993], 344–59.) Joan E. Taylor has recently offered an insightful analysis of Philo's portrait of this group, focusing particularly on the women members of the community, that incorporates insights into the construction of gender in the Hellenistic and Roman worlds; *Jewish Women Philosophers of First-Century Alexandria: Philo's 'Therapeutae' Reconsidered* (Oxford: Oxford University Press, 2003). Ross Sheppard Kraemer emphasizes that, despite indications of unease about the presence of the women in the community, Philo treats these women as fully trained philosophers and participants in the community; "Women's Judaisms at the Beginning of Christianity," in *Women and Christian Origins* (ed. Mary Rose D'Angelo; Oxford: Oxford University Press, 1999), 50–79.

89. See Taylor's discussion of the various renderings of the Greek and what each means for the community; *Jewish Women Philosophers*, 252–54.

90. Philo appears to be modeling the Therapeutrides after female Pythagorean philosophers whose philosophical training is literally made safe through domestication. These women do not learn at a public school but at home from a man in position of authority over them and they apply their philosophical training to be better wives and caretakers of the home; Taylor, *Jewish Women Philosophers*, 241–47. The emphasis on teaching women some philosophy in order to more fully equip them to fulfill their female tasks traces back to Pythagoras, who taught his daughter in order to promote domestic harmony; see Barnes, *Philosophically Educated Women*, 224–28.

91. Taylor, *Jewish Women Philosophers*, 227–64.

92. Paul's statements about the "impending crisis" and that "the present form of the world is passing away" are indications that Paul's instructions should be set within an apocalyptic framework that expects the imminent end of the present age and the inauguration of the next age (1 Cor 7:21 and 31; respectively). First Corinthians contains several striking images related to the apocalyptic, Hellenistic Jewish expectations such as when Paul refers to the "rulers of the present age" and the "ends of the ages" (1 Cor 2:6, 8 and 10:11; respectively). One key issue raised by understanding the presence of Paul's framework is whether Paul would offer different advice if he had known that the church would continue to exist for at least the next two millennia. Unfortunately, such questions require speculation and cannot be answered with any critical certainty.

93. See Alexandra R. Brown, *The Cross and Human Transformation: Paul's Apocalyptic Word in 1 Corinthians* (Minneapolis: Fortress, 1995). Martinus C. de Boer's work on apocalypticism in 1 Corinthians focuses on the imagery of resurrection in chapter 15, but has a helpful discussion of apocalyptic as a category and its usefulness in understanding Paul's thought in 1 Corinthians; *The Defeat of Death: Apocalyptic Eschatology in 1 Corinthians 15 and Romans 5* (Sheffield: Sheffield Academic, 1988). John. J. Collins, *The Apocalyptic Imagination: An Introduction to Jewish Apocalyptic Literature* (Grand Rapids: Eerdmans, 2016), 331–34.

94. Fitzmyer, *First Corinthians*, 276–77.

95. Ibid., 65–104.

96. Gail Corrington Streete, "Discipline and Discourse," in *Vision and Persuasion: Rhetorical Dimensions of Apocalyptic Discourse* (ed. Greg Carey and L. Gregory Bloomquist; St. Louis, Mo.: Chalice, 1999), 82.

97. Michelle J. Morris makes a similar argument concerning Paul's rhetoric in Romans; see "The Fruits of Infertility: Paul and the Rhetoric of a Fertile Empire," *WTJ* 47 (2012): 107–15.

98. The *Lex papia poppaea* (9 C.E.) adjusted many of Augustus's earlier reforms from 29, 19 and 18 B.C.E. pertaining to the penalties for remaining unmarried after a certain age or after the death of a spouse and for failing to produce children. It also closed a loophole that allowed a betrothal to protect people from the monetary fines associated with remaining unmarried. See the discussion in Thomas A. McGinn, *Prostitution, Sexuality, and the Law in Ancient Rome* (Oxford: Oxford University Press, 1998), 70–84, 99. The lack of specific examples from Augustus's earlier legislation makes it difficult to determine whether certain areas were strengthened or relaxed; see Adam M. Kemezis, "Augustus the Ironic Paradigm: Cassius Dio's Portrayal of the *Lex Julia* and *Lex Papia Poppaea*," *Phoenix* 61 (2007): 274–75. Richard I. Frank outlines the socio-economic scope and goals of Augustus's laws; "Augustus' Legislation on Marriage and Children," *CSCA* 8 (1975): 41–52. Determining the law's efficacy proves difficult aside from evidence of a notable population increase, especially among the upper class, following Augustus's reforms; whether this indicates causation or merely correlation, however, cannot be determined. See Kristina Milnor, "Augustus, History, and the Landscape of the Law," *Ar* 40 (2007): 7–23.

99. Suetonius relates an account of a man whom Tiberius removes from the office after only one day because he divorced his wife immediately after receiving the position (Suetonius, *Tib.*, 35).

100. Judith Evans Grubbs offers such an interpretation of Pliny's account of his wife's infertility; see "The Roman Family," *A Companion to the Roman Empire* (ed. David S. Potter; Oxford: Blackwell, 2009), 314–16, 320.

101. It should be noted that just prior to this comment, Tacitus downplays the law's efficacy when he states that it "failed to make marriage and the family popular—childlessness remained the vogue. On the other hand, there was an ever-increasing multitude of persons liable to prosecution" (Tacitus, *Ann.*, 3.25). See the discussion in James A. Field, Jr., "The Purpose of the *Lex Iulia* et *Papia Poppaea*," *CJ* 40 (1945): 389–416.

102. Welborn, *Paul, the Fool*, 86–90.

103. Ibid., 88, 115, 265.

104. Though this is clearest in Gorman's discussion of cruciformity as seen in the Kenosis hymn of Philippians 2, it shows up elsewhere in his treatment of how conforming to the likeness of the crucified Christ means accounting for the implications of crucifixion; see *Apostle to the Crucified Lord: A Theological Introduction to Paul and His Letters* (Grand Rapids: Eerdmans, 2004).

105. A review of Gorman's major treatments on Paul's cruciform identity reveals only a handful of instances when Gorman outlines the actual connection between shame and identifying with a crucified person without the full implications ever being spelled out. The closest Gorman comes is in his discussion of 1 Cor 1:18–2:5 where he mentions the "oxymoron . . . of a crucified Messiah" and how this emphasizes God's "'preferential option' for the poor, the bottom rung of society, and is again in the business of subverting the status quo by making somebodies out of nobodies—and vice versa (1:28)"; *Apostle of the Crucified Lord*, 241.

Chapter Five

Manifestations of Subordinate Masculinity in Paraenesis

The current chapter will demonstrate that Paul's commands to male members of his audience require the men in the community to embody a subordinate masculinity similar to that present in Paul's self-presentation. As discussed in the previous chapter, Paul's subordinate masculinity is one key aspect of his persona that influences his use of power by informing which roles he adopts and how he performs them. Requiring that men in the community adopt similar masculinities should come as no surprise since the letter contains two explicit commands to imitate Paul (1 Cor 4:16 and 11:1). Paul's masculinity, then, becomes a key part of the identity which he expects all men in the community to embody. I will begin by discussing the socio-political context of first-century Roman Corinth in terms of broad patterns and correlations, rather than narrowly focusing on specific groups or individuals. This discussion demonstrates the presence and influence of a social hierarchy, including discourses of gender, that place hegemonic men over other men and women. The idea that the men and women in the audience, even those of low status, would be cognizant of the implications of Paul's commands for gender and status is sustained by the use of such gendered discourses for comedic effect in plays that were performed for a common audience and for political propaganda reliefs and statues that were intended for public display.[1] I will then discuss the role of hegemonic and subordinate masculinity in this evidence in order to show that the frameworks of masculinity presented in my second and third chapters are relevant for understanding the socio-political dynamics in the city. I will then demonstrate that Paul's commands to men would restrict their ability to embody hegemonic or complicit masculinities in such a socio-political context.

This last point is of critical importance in understanding 1 Corinthians as a whole. As discussed in the introduction, Paul's stated objective in 1

Corinthians is to end the factionalism that threatens the unity of the believing community (1 Cor 1:10). By undermining the hegemonic or complicit masculinities requisite for public oratory (1 Cor 3:18), success in court (1 Cor 6:1–8), or at a public banquet (1 Cor 8:1–11:1), Paul prevents the manipulation of such institutions as vehicles for taking advantage of or separating from other members of the believing community. I select these particular texts because, as I will discuss in relation to each section, the institutions in view would be reserved almost exclusively for men, so any command concerning them would almost exclusively pertain to male members of the community. Women would certainly have heard such commands since the letter indicates that they are prominent members of the believing communities (e.g., women praying and prophesying in 1 Cor 11:5, Chloe's household in 1 Cor 1:11, and Prisca in 1 Cor 16:19) and Paul does address women when articulating a vision for their proper behavior in the community (e.g., 1 Cor 7:3–5).[2] Yet, I will demonstrate that when Paul addresses both men and women in the community, such as in his commands regarding the mutual submission and divorce in marriage (1 Cor 7:1–11), the men are still called to embody a subordinate masculinity. We will see that Paul does not, however, require that women make a corresponding adjustment to their status the way that he does for the men because the women already occupy a position that restricts their access to the institutions and mechanisms of power addressed by Paul. This creates a significant degree of equality within the community because men and women now occupy similar social positions. Furthermore, these commands support Paul's goal of eliminating factionalism because these commands require the community to conduct itself in ways that limit the ability of some higher-status male members to use and abuse positions of power to dominate women and lower-status men.[3]

WHO WERE THE CORINTHIANS DURING THE FIRST CENTURY C.E.?

The search for the identity and beliefs of Paul's audience and possible opponents in 1 Corinthians has a long and variegated history. Scholars have cast Paul's opposition and impetus for composing 1 Corinthians as stemming from issues ranging from Gnostics, proto-Gnostics, overly realized eschatology, or even an out-of-control group of female prophets.[4] Although each approach might resonate with part of the letter, seeking to determine Paul's opponents from his writing elevates speculative historical reconstructions over the integrity of Paul's argument as a whole. This mirror reading has been sufficiently critiqued, and I do not wish to follow the mistakes of such readings even while I seek to capitalize upon their insights. The problem is not the use of background information, but the overly zealous application of such information beyond what is clearly demonstrable in the text. More recent approaches to 1 Corinthians seek to maintain the integrity of Paul's argument by applying a more focused approach that explores broad and widely accepted cultural patterns rather than specific groups. For example, rather than situating Paul in discussion with Gnostic or proto-Gnostic antagonists as in some previous studies,[5] Paul's language and argument can be situated within the broader cultural phenomenon of rhetoric and oratorical education and public competitions.[6] Since such education and competitions are attested in Corinth and throughout the Roman Empire, it is likely that there would be at least some in Paul's audience who would be familiar with such issues and understand Paul's self-description as a failed orator within such a context. This type of approach begins with broadly attested discourses and then examines evidence for their presence in Roman Corinth with the aim of informing a reading of the text without restricting the text's meaning to a single, hypothetical historical or cultural phenomenon. Regarding this study, such an approach required a sustained description of the pervasiveness and importance of gender in relation to the body, public presentation, and power as found in chapters 2 and 3, above. I argue that it is also why Paul can make the specific commands that he does regarding wisdom, lawsuits, sex, and dining practices as part of an argument that has the overall aim of combatting factionalism.

So what can be said about the people who lived in Corinth during the first century and how will this inform my reading of Paul's command to a small subset of them? Broadly speaking, the men of first-century Corinth were freedmen, *negotiatores*,[7] and a sizable population that had continued to inhabit Corinth after its destruction by the Roman general Mummius in 146 B.C.E. The epigraphic or archeological evidence does not support previous interpretations that assume that Corinth was refounded by Rome in 44 B.C.E. as a veterans' colony with a significant influx of Roman soldiers.[8] Arguments that frame Roman Corinth as a veterans' colony draw most of their evidence from conflating accounts of the refounding of Corinth with that of Carthage.[9] Rather, the evidence points to a cosmopolitan city comprised largely of individuals of lower status who were drawn to an environment that provided opportunities for social and economic advancement in ways that were not as readily accessible in more established Roman cities. This connection between identity and opportunity serves as a key point in my argument about Paul's use of subordinate masculinity in 1 Corinthians since calling his audience to behave in such subordinate ways would restrict their access to such opportunities for power and advancement. Paul's command to imitate him as he imitates Christ (1 Cor 11:1), one whose crucifixion is a scandal to all (1 Cor 1:23), would necessarily require his audience to abandon attempts to increase power and status.[10]

Yet the population was broader than just those male bodies that are best remembered because of their building projects or positions of political power. The population included women, children, slaves, and other men whose lower status prevented them from playing a significant role on Roman Corinth. As discussed in my development of gender criticism, these lower-status bodies are often pushed aside and only made visible when used to support the prevailing systems of power. Such is the case with Junia Theodora, a Roman woman who lived in Corinth during the first century and who achieved significant honor and status.[11] She is described as noble (καλή) and displaying benefaction (εὐεργεσία) (l. $_2$ and $_{26}$; respectively).[12] She is also described as the patron of the Lycian Federation, a collection of some 36 cities.[13] Such evidence indicates Junia Theodora's wealth and status, but there is no indication of her holding an official political office. Indeed, our only evidence for her existence comes from a single text that was later reused as a door for a tomb. Although she, along with about a dozen other women from the first-century Roman world, are attested with significant status in inscriptions found in various Roman cities, their positions never include political office and they are consistently portrayed as working to maintain Roman domination and the patriarchy that went with it.[14] They were held up as ideal subjects whose status reinforced the broader social structures. As Steven Friesen notes, "Junia negotiated the complex structural parameters set by gender, wealth, family, marriage, ethnicity, inheritance, and religion, and fashioned a subject position that extended Roman domination.... [H]er achievements as a woman were a victory for patriarchy."[15] The population certainly included women, children, and lower-status men, but they play an insignificant role in wielding the power that guided and shaped Roman Corinth. The discussion of the population, then, will be skewed to focus on those male bodies that could participate in the public competition of status through displays of masculinity.

Epigraphic evidence from dedications, tombstones, and graffiti provides another important witness to the population and social institutions of Roman Corinth.[16] Although there are limits to what can be deduced from the form of a name, the patterns and regional differences included in names can indicate status and origin.[17] The names from the first two centuries of Roman Corinth follow the traditional Roman *tria nomina* which consists of a *praenomen*, *nomen*, *cognomen*, and occasionally a filiation to show relation or belonging. Latin honorary inscriptions include a patronymic indicated by a *f*, for *filius* (son), combined with the first letter of the father's praenomen, and inserted between the person's *nomen* and *cognomen*. A freedman would be indicated by a *l*, for *libertus* (freedman of), with the initial of their former owner. Such identity markers could be used strategically in order to display one's status, such as for freedman of the emperor's household whose ongoing association with the emperor gave them unique advantages. Inscriptions lacking either indicator, especially with the presence of a Greek cognomen, could indicate a freedman who was attempting to hide his status as an ex-slave. For example, Cn. Babbius Philinus is a widely accepted example of a powerful freedman in Corinth attempting to erase the marks of his former slavery.[18] On the other hand, if a man was one of Caesar's freedmen, the benefits of associating with Caesar could outweigh the costs of being an ex-slave, making it more beneficial to include such a marking in your name. For example, at least some of Mark Antony's freedmen, such as M. Antonius Theophilus, adopted his name by including *Antonius* in their own and passed it on to their sons as a sign of high status (cf., Plutarch, *Ant.* 67).[19] Another aspect of epigraphic evidence of Roman Corinth is the hybridity evident in the negotiation between Greek and Roman identities based on names and titles and the construction projects with which they are associated.[20] The onomastic evidence, then, shows both the upward mobility of some freedman and the manipulation of one's public identity to secure or help facilitate these identities. Greek *negotiatores* made similar alterations to their names as they settled in Roman colonies and attempted to translate money into Roman citizenship and political power.[21]

These names also provide evidence of freedmen participating in positions of power and benefaction at significantly higher rates than in other Roman cities. Roman cities typically restricted freedmen from positions of political authority and so forced them to express their status through public benefaction, as will be discussed in the next paragraph in terms of the *Augustales*. This is not the case in Julian colonies that inscribe the ability of freedmen to hold political office in their founding charters.[22] This made Julian colonies attractive locations for wealthy freedmen who wished to take on significant, public roles instead of just working to secure the political futures of their sons who would not bear the legally restrictive identity of being a former slave. The most important and powerful office was that of the *duoviri*, which was an appointment lasting for one year and gave the person administrative control of the city and the ability to represent the city before the emperor.[23] Three of the earliest *duoviri* in Corinth were freedmen associated with Antony;[24] this trend appears to have continued, since at least 19 percent of the known *duoviri* in Corinth are freedmen, a remarkable accomplishment for people who were former slaves.[25] The second most significant political appointment was that of *aedile*. Like the *duoviri*, the *aedile* was a temporary appointment that typically excluded freedmen and required significant financial contributions by the appointee.[26] Part of the prestige associated with the position of *aedile* was the ability to wear the *toga praetexta,* which was reserved for Roman magistrates and was a clear sign of authority and status.²⁷ Roman Corinth, then, was a place where those who were not well-born, or εὐγενής to borrow Paul's language (1 Cor 1:26), could rise above the circumstances of their birth to achieve significant positions of power and influence.

The names found in connection with the *Augustales* offer another concrete example of the social and economic opportunities afforded to freedmen in Roman Corinth.²⁸ The *Augustales* is an association primarily composed of freedmen and freeborn members who are wealthy but otherwise prevented from greater participation in the political life of their city;²⁹ this made the group an attractive avenue for people who desired to show benefaction or court the emperor's favor through service in the imperial cult and general acts of benefaction.³⁰ Although evidence from Roman Corinth shows the presence of freedmen among the *Augustales*, the percentage of freedmen is less than in other Roman cities. This makes sense if freedmen in these other cities were restricted from other political appointments, essentially funneling them toward participation in the *Augustales* as one of the only outlets for displaying public benefaction.

The importance of the *Augustales* along with the number of names associated with freedmen and their positions of power in Roman Corinth indicate that the city's unique administrative allowances provided a form of upward mobility for some residents that are not present in most other urban Roman settings. This evidence, however, must be balanced by the socio-economic disparity evident amongst the population in Roman Corinth. As Friesen convincingly demonstrates, the language of upward mobility must be significantly tempered to match the "ideology of inequality" that pervades Roman Corinth and much of the Roman Empire.³¹ In this article, Friesen draws on his earlier work that shows the distorting effects of transposing modern socio-economic terminology onto evidence from the first-century Roman empire.³² Rather than understanding Roman Corinth's initial allowances for freedmen participation in higher-status positions as the beginning of a more equitable distribution of resources, the evidence indicates that the same socio-economic disparity evident in other Roman cities is also present in Roman Corinth. Paul reprimands the Corinthians' conduct at the Lord's Table because it reflects this same disparity where people who had attained a higher economic position in terms of procuring more than enough food and wine did not distribute these resources to those in need but segregated the community along economic lines (1 Cor 11:17–34). What makes Roman Corinth noteworthy is that it provided more opportunities for men to construct masculine personas that had the potential of placing them in positions of social or political power.

The numismatic evidence of coins minted in Roman Corinth manifests similar patterns of hybridity as the onomastic evidence discussed above and gives further support for understanding Roman Corinth as a prominent context for the construction of new identity. The coins can be broadly categorized into two groups. The first group contains those coins produced from the city's refounding to Vespasian's edict rescinding the city's authorization to mint coins. The second group contains those coins minted under Domitian and has a terminus of 205 C.E.[33] The coins of the first group bear the names of the *duoviri* who were in office when the coin was minted, mention of the Julio-Claudian line, and either conventional Roman images or Greek images that were especially important in Corinth's history.[34] The fact that local elites and magistrates selected the coin's designs, which intertwine political and religious history and concerns, make them a key public expression of local concerns.[35] For example, a coin dating from 44–43 B.C.E. has Julius's head on one side and Bellerophon riding Pegasus on the reverse. The use of Julius's bust represents an obvious deference and an attempt to court favor. The use of Bellerophon, the son of one of Corinth's great kings, involves recasting a favorite myth in order to weave together Corinth's past with its present.[36] The coin blends Corinth's past and present by juxtaposing Julius with this ancient myth that recalls a hero from Corinth's glorious Greek past. As opposed to other Julian colonies that positioned their place in the empire by minting coins that celebrate their new beginning as a Roman colony, Corinth's coins create a hybrid fiction. This appropriation of important symbols within a new context so as to understand the present parallels what Paul does in 1 Corinthians as he reworks the concepts of wisdom, strength, the cross, and masculine behavior in light of the calling of the God.

The fiction that attempts to forge continuity with Corinth's Greek past in order to legitimate its Roman present can also be seen in architecture and cultic activity. Although the social and political implications of these changes is not as directly pertinent to individual families as the manipulation of names or availability of civic positions, they still demonstrate the same ability to adopt and adapt the past in light of Rome's power. Roman Corinth witnessed the renewal of the Temple of Apollo, the Sanctuary of Demeter and Kore, the Sanctuary of Aphrodite, and the Sanctuary of Asklepios.[37] Although tracking alterations to the buildings and matching those changes to specific cultural causes is tenuous at best, Wickkiser has offered a careful analysis of changes to the Sanctuary of Askelpios in the first century C.E. that correspond to form and specific function of Asklepios in Rome.[38] One of the most noticeable changes made during the restoration following 44 C.E. is the construction of a small building that restricts direct access between the upper and lower courts.[39] This change corresponds with the sudden absence of votives and the conversion of parts of the sanctuary that facilitated incubation, the practice of sleeping in the sanctuary in order to affect healing, which was not a part of the worship of Asklepios in Rome.[40] Another prime example of the blending of Greek past and Roman present comes from the design of a monument that was erected before the end of the first century C.E.[41] The monument is the work of the *Augustales* and pays homage to the Caesar while incorporating architectural elements; the sloped edge of the bench incorporates a particularly Greek architectural style. As Laird puts it, "If the monument of the *Augustales* expressed the empire-wide language of emperor worship, it did so within a particularly Corinthian and Achaian framework."[42] The city itself manifests a cultural moment of transformation that sought to rebuild and hybridize identity as expediently as possible given the current socio-political moment in the Principate. Yet the increased fluidity of identities and the expanded access to status and power afforded by them did not alter the basic shape of the social structure and the discourses that support it.

The influence on social space meant that the patterns for organizing bodies and assigning power evident in Rome and other Roman colonies also appear in Corinth. The importance of the intersection of public space, civic institutions, and status means that the conceptions of masculinity that I discuss in the second chapter are just as tangible and impactful in Roman Corinth. Although we do not have Corinth's charter, we have the charter of Urso, another Julian colony which was also founded in 44 C.E. the same year as Corinth, as well as other urban Roman centers that show substantial overlap with Roman Corinth.[43] Urso's charter, and others like it, shows that even newly founded colonies were subject to the same types of social and political jockeying found in more established cities and that Roman officials sought to limit these behaviors to a certain extent.[44] The importance of this for my study of Paul's commands is that Paul is seeking to set similar kinds of limitations on members of the community. The difference is that Paul cannot legally restrict behavior but seeks to have the Corinthians embody identities which would necessarily make them ineligible to manipulate such positions. Of particular interest to my study will be connecting Paul's discussion of behavior at dinner parties with the way these charters circumscribe the use of dinner parties and other meals for social and political gain.

The patterns that emerge from comparing the different evidence indicate that most of Corinth's population hails from humble beginnings, either because of their servile or foreign origins. Although some of these people achieve positions of significant status, Roman Corinth's social dynamics broadly reflect the inequalities evident in other urban Roman settings. This means that whatever upward mobility was attainable for some freedmen like Babbius or the *negotiatores*, such people were embedded in a society that manifested the type of social stratification evident elsewhere in urban Roman contexts. Beyond the standard gifts of euergetism, the successful freedmen do not appear to have leveraged success to help other freedmen or people of lower status, at least at any level that is evident in the archeological records. The evidence that we have indicates that whatever upward mobility individuals were able to achieve served to reinscribe Roman patterns of broad separation between socio-economic groups.

The pattern of social competition for status and the manipulation of that status within institutions appears to be the dynamic that sits at the heart of the factionalism that is threatening the unity of the Corinthian community. Paul's reference to not many of them being well-born (οὐ πολλοὶ εὐγενεῖς) indicates a category that includes slaves, freedman, and foreigners (1 Cor 1:26). At the same time, Paul rebukes some of his audience over their manipulation of the courts and access to food (1 Cor 6:1–8 and 11:17–22; respectively), both of which are strong indications of status. The rest of the chapter will highlight instances where Paul's critique and commands address how some men manipulate institutions and practices in ways that take advantage of their positions of power to reinscribe the types of hierarchies that exist in the broader culture. Paul does not ignore the presence of such systems or hierarchies in the broader culture but prevents their manipulation in the community of believers by requiring that believers take on identities that would prevent them from accessing and abusing such systems. Theissen's work on the social character of the divisions within the community at Corinth is correct. Paul's answer to such divisions is to encourage the men to whom he writes to adopt identities that would prevent such division by making them subordinate men and, thereby, restrict them to identities that could not manipulate status in the oppression of others.

SPECIFIC EXAMPLES OF PAUL EXHORTING SUBORDINATE MASCULINITY IN HIS PARAENESIS TO THE CORINTHIANS

Becoming Fools (1 Cor 1–4)

The opening four chapters of 1 Corinthians contain several exhortations which undermine conventions of wisdom and status and culminate with the necessity for the Corinthians to become imitators of Paul (1 Cor 4:16). The fact that Paul sends Timothy to facilitate this imitation and, later, repeats this call to imitate him and extends this imitation to include Christ further supports taking this imitation as a significant aspect of Paul's argument (1 Cor 4:18–21 and 11:1). Mitchell's examination situates the call for imitation within deliberative rhetoric by showing that the imitation of a notable figure's behavior functions as a solution for communal discord and is a commonly used example (παραδείγματα) in deliberative rhetoric.[45]

When taken together with the thesis of 1 Corinthians that the community should move beyond factionalism toward unity (1 Cor 1:10), Paul's use of himself as a model for the Corinthians to imitate becomes a significant rhetorical point in accomplishing this goal. Furthermore, as Adam White demonstrates, 1 Corinthians 1–4 engages the language of public oratory and discourses of the "wise man" in order to undermine the use of wisdom and status as identity markers that were directly tied to masculinity.[46] I will build on White's argument to show how reversing typical approaches to wisdom and status corresponds with the type of subordinate masculinity that I discuss in the previous chapter. Paul's call to imitation, then, can be seen as a specific call to imitate his subordinate masculinity.

To demonstrate the function of Paul's subordinate masculinity as an appropriate ideal for the community to imitate, I will examine the various commands given in the first four chapters through the use of exhortation language (παρακαλέω) and the imperative mood and show how imitating Paul addresses the factionalism that threatens the community's unity.[47] As I work through the various commands, it will be important to keep in mind the discussion from the previous chapters about the public and widespread nature of displaying masculinity; Paul's audience would be familiar with the way manipulating behavior and aspects of identity would affect a man's standing in the community.[48] As such, Paul's commands force his audience to come to a new understanding of what high status and power (i.e., masculinity) look like in the cruciform community. Ultimately, Paul asks the men in the audience to act as subordinate men in order to protect the community. Although these commands do not address the behavior of the women in the community, these commands do provide the groundwork for Paul giving them authority over their husbands' bodies (1 Cor 7:3–5). The social consequences of such unmanly behavior are clearly seen in a passage from Dio Chrysostom who, like Paul, advocates that a group of men willingly abrogate their rights for the sake of communal unity: "For the unwillingness ever to yield or make concession to our neighbor—that is, without a feeling of humiliation—or while receiving some things ourselves, to concede some to the other, is not *manly* (ἀνδρεῖον), as *some imagine*, but, to the contrary, senseless and stupid" (*Or.* 40.34; emphasis added).[49] Dio Chrysostom must redefine masculinity since some people will assess the behavior that he advocates as unmanly even though, as he argues, that behavior is the best course of action for the protection of the community, which is one of the main points of masculinity in Greek and Roman contexts. Likewise, Paul advocates unmanly behavior as the way to imitate him and Christ and, therefore, to be men as is appropriate according to the standards of this community (cf., ἀνδρίζεσθε 1 Cor 16:13).[50]

Paul's commands and statements about wisdom, power, and the means of assessment sit at the center of these four chapters and serve both to undermine the Corinthians' attempt to construct identities of high status and to critique their use of society's means of assessing status. Four of the imperatives that Paul uses in the section directly address issues of assessment.[51] In two places, Paul says that they are to consider (βλεπέτω) a person's status or course of action (1 Cor 1:26, 3:10; respectively): the former commands them to consider the lower status of many in the community at the time of their calling by God, the latter is a direct appeal to adjust their means of assessing Paul's ministry. The need for the Corinthians to adjust their means of assessing Paul is part of the broader appeal to adjust their understanding of wisdom and status. This adjustment requires them to reckon (λογίζομαι) Paul as a servant and a steward (1 Cor 4:1), positions which would be associated with lowliness and humility. This corresponds with Paul's earlier point that the Corinthians were primarily of lower status when they were called by God and is part of Paul's point that God intentionally chooses those things, both people and symbols, that the world's wisdom finds foolish (1 Cor 1:27–28).[52] Paul continues that not only do they need to adjust their means of assessment, but they should refrain from certain aspects of judging (κρίνω) since some of what needs to be considered in their judgment is currently hidden and will not be revealed until "the Lord comes" (1 Cor 4:5).

The Corinthians' need to recalibrate their means of assessment arises from the converse relationship between the way that the world and God assess status. Paul uses the Corinthians as evidence of this because many of them are, or at least were at the time that God called them, people of low status. Yet Paul's point is not primarily to criticize his audience but to show how their low status corresponds to the shape of God's kingdom. Their low status, then, is an asset since God has chosen things of low status in order to shame the things of the world. This is clearly the point when Paul draws a direct comparison between the wisdom of the world and wisdom of God by saying, "For since in the *wisdom* (σοφίᾳ) of God the world by its *wisdom* (σοφίας) did not know God, God was pleased to save those who believe by the *foolishness* (μωρίας) the proclamation" (1:21). In fact, the contrast between wisdom and foolishness runs throughout 1:18–31 and shows that Paul is not setting up a competition between the world's way of achieving status and God's, but showing that excelling in the world's system means failure in God's and vice versa.[53] In order to demonstrate this, Paul applies a means of assessment using two contrasting images, the wise man (σοφός) and the fool (μωρός).[54] As White and Welborn demonstrate, the wise man represented an ideal figure to which young men would aspire in their education and training as a means to achieve higher levels of social status while the fool represented the antithesis.⁵⁵ When read against my analysis of gender and status from the second chapter of the current work, the image of a wise man represents one hegemonic masculine identity and the fool as a failed and, therefore, subordinate masculine identity. The wise man wields wisdom and rhetoric to display mastery and dominate any challenger. The fool is an image that even women and children mock (cf., Athenaeus, *Deip.* 15.698c–f; *POxy* 413 188–208). Paul develops the contrast through three sets of triads.⁵⁶ The first triad addresses the identities of the wise man (σοφός), the scribe (γραμματεύς), and the debater (συζητητής) (1 Cor 1:20). Although there is no consensus on the specific vocations behind each identity,⁵⁷ the fields described would almost exclusively be the domain of men, as women were thought incapable of mastering their bodies and the knowledge necessary to succeed in them.⁵⁸ The contrast that Paul draws between them and God making foolish the wisdom of this age indicates that Paul deploys these categories as exemplars of worldly wisdom.⁵⁹ The second triad addresses the characteristics of wise according to human standards (σοφός κατὰ σάρκα), powerful (δυνατός), and well-born (εὐγενής) (1 Cor 1:26). These characteristics often function as key markers of masculine identity, and further, Paul stating that not many of the Corinthians could claim such characteristics at the time of their calling is clear indication of their lower-status origins.⁶⁰ Again, Paul's point is not to shame his audience but to show how their lower status was not incidental to but actually corresponds to the shape of God's kingdom. The third triad provides a series of direct comparisons that explain that God's counterintuitive selections are for the purposes of shaming and bringing to nothing the things that the world holds in high esteem (1 Cor 1:27–28). The comparisons that Paul use applies the categories from the earlier two triads through juxtaposition: the things the world considers foolish (μωρὰ) in order to shame the wise men (σοφούς), the things the world considers weak to shame the strong, and the things that the world considers nothing (τὰ μὴ) to shame the things that are (τὰ ὄντα).⁶¹ Theissen notes that this triad concludes with a clear social comparison because of the use of the verb εξουτενέω and the phrase τὰ μὴ ὄντα and their applications in philosophical texts to describe the way that different behaviors and philosophies affect the social standing of the practitioner (e.g., Plato, *Phaedr.* 234).⁶² Both the terms and their clustering together leave little doubt that "behind the Corinthian idea of σοφία is a comparison to an elite, educated ideal in the culture . . . by elite, educated members of the Christian community."⁶³ Placing such a move in the patriarchal connections between gender, body, and power as outlined in chapter 2 makes it clear that Paul's command is both a change in understanding wisdom and the masculinity that went along with it.

The purpose of these reversals becomes clear as Paul engages in a sustained critique of this gender and social hierarchy which culminates in a command to become foolish according to the standards of the world (1 Cor 3:18). The consequence of becoming foolish is to nullify the influence of marks of high social status along with the systems they sustain. Paul begins by addressing how God has silenced any boasting of status on the basis of such worldly standards and so people can only boast of those characteristics that God deems commendable (1 Cor 1:29, 31; 3:21). With the old system critiqued, it is no wonder, then, that the scandalous, counterintuitive symbol of the cross and the crucified king serve as the centerpiece of Paul's message (1 Cor 2:2). Richard Hays puts it well, "Paul has taken the central event at the heart of the Christian story—the death of Jesus—and used it as the lens through which all human experience must be projected and thereby seen afresh. The cross becomes the starting point for an epistemological revolution, a *conversion of the imagination*."[64] This is why Paul commands them to not be deceived and to move away from being considered a wise man in order to be considered a fool (1 Cor 3:18). He uses the symbols of the world in order to demonstrate advancement in the kingdom of God. Calling to mind the earlier comments on gender and social status shows that Paul is attempting to convert the imaginations of his community so that they seek to embody a subordinate masculinity as opposed to the hegemonic masculinity that is threatening the unity and peace of the community. Recalling the earlier discussion on Quintilian and the necessity to embody masculinity through public displays of oratorical skill and dominance, becoming a fool would thus correspond to a loss of masculinity and the status that corresponds to it (cf. *Inst.* 12.1.4). This command to become fools would require the men of the community to abandon their attempts to be a *vir bonus* and, instead, take on dominated, or subordinate identities and the social positions that accompany them.

The effects of such a public failure of masculinity would touch on every aspect of the man's life and require a new means of adjudicating his place in the social order. Paul, therefore, stands as a quintessential representation of such an identity because of the way that he moves toward the subordinate end of the spectrum with each position that he fills. He is a failed orator, a fool, and not the wise man. He is a breastfeeding woman. He is a shameful father. Paul has already taken on the subordinate masculinity that he commands the Corinthian men to adopt, he understands the shame that will accompany such a move (1 Cor 4:14), but he understands such a change as necessary to function appropriately within the kingdom of God. These are the connections that allow and sustain Paul's command that the Corinthians must imitate him as he resists positions of power and superiority and identifies with those bodies that the world deems weak and worthless (1 Cor 4:16). This is the power of the cross that Paul fears the Corinthians' pursuit of hegemonic ideals will empty (1 Cor 1:17).

Not Going to Court (1 Cor 6:1–8)

Paul's discussion of the Corinthians taking one another to court provides another example of Paul commanding men to embody a subordinate masculinity as a means to overcome the manipulation of status that is contributing to the community's factionalism. In order to substantiate this point, I will first review the judicial context of Paul's comments in order to demonstrate the influence of status and the ramifications for unity. Roman courts were well-established "instruments of social control . . . in which superior social status was displayed and maintained."[65] This connection will be demonstrated in terms of the language of status, competition, and power dynamics that appear to be at work as some in the Corinthian community take other members to court. As we shall see, the fact that some in Paul's audience manipulate such a system to gain or secure status parallels the discussion of status in relation to public oratory as discussed in 1 Cor 1–4. Next, I will address the use of καθίζω in 1 Cor 6:4 to show that Paul does, in fact, have a command within this section and that this command reverses the conventional function of status in Roman courts. Finally, I will show how appointing "those who are despised" as judges within the community fits the pattern of Paul's own self-presentation and of the Corinthians appropriating a subordinate masculinity as part of their identity (1 Cor 6:4). The intersection of public display and status within the Roman judicial system made it a prime location for the construction and display of hegemonic masculinity. It is this impulse that Paul undermines in this section of his argument as he, again, seeks to overcome issues that contribute to the current factionalism of the Corinthian believers.

The most important factor for understanding Roman justice and judicial procedures is that social status, not guilt or innocence, is the most determinative factor in the outcome of a civil case.[66] J. M. Kelly was one of the first to clearly trace the significant disadvantages that a person of lower status faced in Rome's judicial system.[67] Not only did members of the upper classes (e.g., senators, decurions, etc.) receive lighter penalties than humiliores, but they could circumvent prosecution altogether, either through the use of "friendships" or by simply ignoring the charges and never having to stand trial.[68] In fact, social standing played such a vital role in legal proceedings that great care was taken to assess whether a litigant's social standing even allowed the possibility of prosecution before initiating a trial (cf. *Digest* 4.3.2.1).[69] Although there are examples that laud the impartiality (*fides*) of a judge in deciding a case, even from Cicero who is not naïve about the shape of Roman justice (Cicero, *Caecin*. 43), the reality is that assumptions of value and honesty which were correlated with social status, so predetermine the assumptions of guilt and innocence that bribery was superfluous since simply possessing wealth was often enough to secure a judgment.[70] The system's goal was the maintenance and reinforcement of the established social hierarchy rather than what might be referred to as a justice in any sort of a modern sense. For a city such as Roman Corinth, which provided a striking opportunity for the construction and display of social status, the use of the courts provided another mechanism for wealthy freedmen and others who were looking to establish or display their masculinity. Just as with other displays of masculinity, a man could establish dominance over other men but also women and children, and the courts are no different (cf. Tacitus, *Ann*. 2.34). The context suggests that men in Paul's audience who are the ones dragging their fellow community members, both men and women,[71] into court would only take such action if they knew such a system, along with its bias toward social status, would benefit them.

The basic judicial procedures also embody the type of social bias and control discussed in the previous paragraph.[72] In Roman Corinth, a civil case was initiated through either the *aedile* or one of the *duoviri*, positions that drew exclusively from the top echelon of society and would have been uniquely available to some freemen in Corinth.[73] If there were sufficient grounds for a case, the officer would contact the accused and request his appearance. As described above, the case would only proceed if the person bringing the charges had sufficient status in general and with relation to the accused in particular; in fact, the law prevented certain classes of people or people in certain subordinate positions such as children or slaves from bringing charges.[74] Seneca includes a story of a poor man who finds other means of exacting justice on a wealthy man who killed the poor man's father (Seneca the Elder, *Controv*. 10.1.2). The poor man knows he would lose any court case because of the disparity of status and so seeks other avenues for justice. Such restrictions extended to other subordinate men whose masculinity was so problematized that they ceased to function as men in the public sphere and so take on a social and legal standing comparable to that of children and slaves. If a plaintiff lacked the requisite status, the accused could simply refuse to appear in court. If both parties did appear, the case could be heard by a group of jurors or a single judge, all of whom were drawn from the wealthiest Roman citizens in the city.[75] Even the ability to prosecute a case required substantial rhetorical training that was only available to a select few citizens.[76] This process was only interrupted if the charges involved the commerce or political stability of the city, at which point a governor or other regional official who was appointed by Rome would typically intervene.[77] The resulting judicial system placed those with status and wealth at a significant advantage and became a key venue for the display and construction of masculinity. Bruce Winter summarizes the results as, "Generally, lawsuits were conducted between social equals who were from the powerful (οἱ δυνατοί) of the city, or by a plaintiff of superior social status and power against an inferior."[78]

Before moving to outline some of the key features of Roman courts that relate to masculinity, I need to more fully address the presence of some women in Roman courts. Although women do appear as litigants and defendants in courts during the early Principate, they appear at far smaller rates than do men and, when they do appear, are always reliant on the power of men to function in the judicial system. In fact, women were restricted from bringing a suit and had to rely on their husband, father, or guardian unless they were *sui iuris*, free from *potestas* of a father or husband (e.g., *Dig.* 47.10.18.2, 48.2.1–2). During the early Principate there is no evidence for women representing themselves in court.[79] Although there is some evidence of women representing themselves during the Republic (cf. Valerius Maximus 8.3),[80] these women were lampooned as monsters who transgressed nature by entering the traditionally male environment of the court.[81] Valerius Maximus records the death of Gaia Afrania, one such woman, and notes that "it is better to record when such a monster has died than when it is born" (8.3).[82] When women are mentioned in connection with Roman courts, they almost always appear as part of the audience and are often strategically used to elicit pity or anger depending on the needs of the trial. The restrictions placed on women's use of and appearance in Roman courts makes it difficult if not impossible to imagine Paul's restrictions on the abuse of Roman courts being directed to the women in the community. Rather, it would be men who had significant enough status to assert their dominance in a public setting.

When taking into account the importance of masculinity for a person's status and the way that people of inferior status were associated with failed masculinity, it is no wonder that legal proceedings involve direct attacks that seek to undermine an opponent's masculinity. Part of Favorinus's self-defense of his own masculinity relies on the efficacy of just such an examination of a body within a judicial setting (*Cor. orat.* 22). Cicero notes that the bodies of orators were exposed to more criticism than actors (Cicero, *De or.* 1.113–36)! Cicero also places such an examination of an orator within the court when he comments that Crassus, a famous orator, embodied such masculinity that he could persuade a judge by simply wiggling his finger (*De or.* 2.188; cf. *De or.* 1.59).[83] Cicero's anecdote predicates success in court on the successful demonstration of masculinity. It is also evident that a jurist's performance should be determined by the social status of their client; higher-status clients receive a more robust performance while lower-status clients receive a more reserved one.[84] The Roman courtroom, then, was a place where men competed to demonstrate their masculinity and to leverage that masculinity as a means to dominate others of lower status.

While the system created a legal gulf between people of higher and lower status, it also created animosity between people of similar social positions or who belonged to the same associations or families. Mitchell discusses Greek and Latin authors who attempt to ease friction caused by such lawsuits by minimizing the importance of trivial matters and by subordinating personal status to that of the community.[85] Although not specifically addressing legal disputes, Plutarch compares the way that communities divide over trivial matters to the way that great fires often begin from insignificant sources such as a single lamp rather than a large flame (*Mor.* 825A). Edsall examines Cicero's *Pro caelio* to demonstrate that Cicero can use the shame of intragroup litigation being judged by those outside the group metonymically as part of his defense of his friend, Maruc Caelius Rufus.[86] Cicero conjures the images of a barbaric tribe in which members take each other to judges outside the community to dismiss the need to mount a defense against such charges. Cicero's point is that such behavior befits barbarians, those whose bodies cannot measure up to Roman standards of decorum and masculinity, and, therefore the charges against his friend should be dropped lest the accuser be thought of as barbaric. In short, even if the accuser succeeds in the prosecution, he will reap his own judgment in the form of lost status. The fact that Cicero won the case indicates that such repercussions for taking intragroup litigation to outsiders was understood even without Cicero needing to state so explicitly. Edsall and David Horrell each provide examples from various civic groups that inscribe such punishments for members who won or even just took a fellow member to judgment before an outsider.[87] One of the key features of such attempts to quell public litigation is to keep the dispute within the group by having fellow members, especially people in positions of authority like priests, judge the dispute (e.g., Cicero, *Phil.* 2.85). The animosity generated by public litigation was, therefore, seen as a necessary consequence, one that organizations sought to avoid through keeping litigation within the group.

As the above discussion of Roman courts make clear, hegemonic masculinity or access to a man who has such a masculinity was broadly understood as necessary for successfully litigating a dispute. Yet hegemonic masculinity was not only an issue for pursuing litigation. A man's masculinity could be jeopardized if he lost or was otherwise undermined in court.[88] Paul's question of, "wouldn't it be better to be wronged/defrauded?" would receive a resounding "no!" from any men in the audience who valued their own masculinity over the harmony of the group (1 Cor 6:7), and surrendering their masculinity is exactly what Paul asks the men in his audience to do by making such a counterintuitive decision to be wronged rather than to take the issue to court.

Paul's critique opens with the issue that some members of the Corinthian believers are taking intragroup conflicts to non–group members (1 Cor 6:1). He strengthens the charges by describing the situation as "brother takes brother to judgement, and that before unbelievers" and then describes such actions as wronging and defrauding (1 Cor 6:6, 8; respectively).[89] Paul's charge and the language with which he describes it fit the above discussion about the negative views of such action in the Greek and Roman organizations. The main issue is that such disputes should be handled within the community and that the concord of the community should take precedent over complaints regarding the type of ordinary matters (κριτηρίον ἐλάσσων in 6:2 and βιωτικός in 6:4). In fact, Plutarch compares these types of divisions between members of a community to divisions between different parts of the same body, an image that Paul conjures in 1 Cor 12:12–26. Minimizing the cause of intragroup legal conflicts due to the importance of communal concord became a common trope in urging communities to overlook such insignificant grievances to preserve unity.[90] Isocrates comments that such actions cause the community to "risk our lives fighting as we do over trifles" (*Or.* 4.11). Philo says that a community fighting over trivial matters is like dividing over a mere shadow (*Post.* 119). Paul's command to reassess what is better, then, fits within the framework of valuing the unity of the community over an individual's complaint.

Strikingly, Paul's response to the Corinthian believers' litigiousness goes further to undermine the function of social status in judicial proceedings by commanding that they should appoint members of low status to be judges of such disputes. If Paul had simply insisted on judgment within the community, there is no reason to think that the Corinthian believers would not simply replicate the same power dynamics as found outside the community.[91] "Therefore, if you have civil lawsuits, appoint from within the church those who are of low standing to judge!" (1 Cor 6:4). Although most modern translations and commentaries take Paul's use of καθίζετε in the indicative mood and functioning as an interrogative or statement of present circumstances, there is compelling grammatical, historical, and rhetorical evidence to read it as a command in the imperative mood.[92] The ambiguity arises because καθίζετε is second-person-plural active but in either indicative or imperative moods.[93] Since parsing cannot decide the issue, some scholars take the verb's placement at the end of the sentence as indicating an interrogative use.[94] This does not account for the fact that Paul uses imperatives at the end of sentences throughout his writings, with seven occurrences just in 1

Corinthians (1 Cor 4:16; 7:21; 10:31; 11:33; 14:20; 16:1, 13).[95] Philippians 4:4 is of particular importance since, like 1 Cor 6:4, the imperative at the end of a sentence is preceded by a demonstrative pronoun. Therefore, arguments on morphology and syntax cannot settle the matter since they allow either possibility.[96] In terms of historical context, Brent Kinman points out that the Corinthian community was in no position to appoint judges in the courts of Roman Corinth.[97] Yet, the idea that Paul could command the community to appoint its own judges, essentially handling civil lawsuits as a *de facto* legal system, has precedent in both Jewish and Roman sources.[98] Mitchell shows that such advice was used within deliberative rhetoric to reconcile communities that were experiencing division.[99] So the idea that Paul could command the Corinthians to appoint judges from within the community to handle civil complaints is plausible, while the idea that Paul tells them to appoint people from outside the community requires understanding the idea as ironic.

Although some scholars who comment on the punctuation of the verse appeal to the above information, the deciding factor appears to be their understanding of how such a command would fit into the rhetoric of Paul's argument. Edsall comments that referring to some members as reviled (τοὺς ἐξουθενημένους) "would work against [Paul's] reconciliatory rhetoric in 1 Corinthians" and uses such a rationale to explain why καθίζετε should be read in the indicative mood.[100] Such reasoning, however, misses the importance of humility and reversal in Paul's argument and brings me to the function of Paul reversing the social dynamics of the Corinthian believers by appointing those with low status to the position of judges. First, Paul has already used the language of humiliation to summarize elements that indicate a low social status (1 Cor 28): not wise/foolish, nor powerful (weak), and not well born (1 Cor 1:26–27). Although such terms would normally be used to shame the person to whom they are applied, Paul reframes this terminology as positive since they are precisely the characteristics that God uses to defeat the world. For Paul, such terms are not shameful but indicative of the type of people whom God chooses, thereby transforming otherwise shameful attributes into positive ones. This is why Paul can say that they should not be ashamed to have such a failed and disgraceful father figure (cf. 1 Cor 4:14). Interpreting Paul as referring to those outside the community as despised undermines his earlier usage and assumptions about status within the community. So not only would the audience hear the language of low social status as referring to many within the community, but they would know that this was the type of social status that God uses to demonstrate the superiority and shape of God's kingdom. Again, the transformation of what the world deems shameful is why the cross functions as the symbol *par excellence* of God's victory over the kingdom of the world.

But the most crucial change of reading καθίζετε as a command is that it provides Paul's solution to the community's litigiousness by undermining their attempts to manipulate high status as a means to dominate members of lower status. By restricting access to Roman courts, Paul denies "the higher status members . . . one of the most important means by which they defended and promoted their prestige and status."[101] Without Paul commanding the appointment of lower-status community members as judges, his solution must otherwise be inferred from some combination of the rhetorical questions throughout this passage. It would be somewhat strange for Paul to not offer a precise course of action since he offers just such commands elsewhere (e.g., 1 Cor 6:18 and 7:2). More important, however, is the way that such a command coheres with other commands, such as the need for the Corinthian believers to become fools as discussed in the previous section of this chapter. Paul's point in both commands is to reverse the logic of masculine hegemony by elevating those subordinate men, read in these texts as the foolish and those of low status, respectively. The figure of the judge not only wielded power but symbolized the ideals of the community, and judges who failed to embody such ideals were subject to ridicule (e.g., Claudius in Suetonius, *Claud.* 15.4).[102] By appointing lower-status members of the community to the positions of judges, Paul provides both a mechanism for preventing the use of high status to oppress people of lower status and a shameful symbol for the community to emulate, which is precisely his point when outlining his own shameful behavior as their father and the shame of the crucified Jesus.

Paul brings his argument in 6:1–4 together by labeling his audience's behavior as shameful (1 Cor 6:5a). As Horrell notes, the connection between shame and Paul's previous comment about appointing despised judges would apply whether 6:4 is read as an imperative or an interrogative: either the Corinthian believers should feel shame because they have violated commonly understood practices that maintain group concord (indicative) or they must allow low-status members of the community to judge them (imperative).[103] Although both make sense within Paul's argument, I take the latter as more persuasive since it follows the same pattern used earlier by Paul when he describes how God uses people of low status to shame people of high status (1 Cor 1:28). This unexpected elevation of those that society deems less valuable is exactly what happens in this text as Paul elevates lower-status members of the community to positions of power in order to bring shame on those men who had been using their higher status for power and control. By taking their disputes into a judicial setting that maintains a clear bias for those of higher status, Paul's audience fails to embody this reversal of status. It is the failure to embody this dynamic of reversal that Paul says is shameful. The Corinthians' use of the courts appears to cohere with Roman standards and so would not be shameful from a Roman perspective. In other words, Paul's audience should be ashamed because they replicate the patterns of institutionalized power and oppression that their society deems natural. This point is reinforced by comparison with Paul's earlier statement that they are not to feel shame by acknowledging him as their father, despite his apparently shameful behavior (1 Cor 4:14). In that text, Paul describes himself in ways that evidence a failure to perform a hegemonic masculinity; thus, making him a subordinate man and, as a shameful father figure, a disgrace to the members of his family. The Corinthians, however, are not to feel shame at having such a father because those failures of masculinity are precisely the marks of obedience to and conformity with God's standards of behavior and assessment where the low and despised are valued. Paul continues to apply this shame by saying that it would be better for the Corinthian believers to be wronged and defrauded than to settle such disputes in public courts (1 Cor 6:7). Again, Paul calls shameful the very behavior that was deemed proper and codified within the Roman law. As discussed above, it would be shameful to shrink back from legal action against someone who wronged you.

The focus on shame highlights the implications of Paul's commands regarding litigation for the men in the believing community. They are to shun institutions that favor hegemonic masculinity because such masculinity is inconsistent with the values of this community. In fact, they should find it shameful to attempt to assert such an identity or exert the power that comes with it. As noted in the discussion of masculinity in the second chapter, a Roman man who was wronged, slighted, or in any way had his masculinity challenged was required to respond or suffer the social and legal consequences of feminized identity. Most men in Roman Corinth would respond to Paul's question as to whether or not it is better to go to court or be wronged with a clear affirmation of the former. Paul requires the men in the believing community to remove themselves from such systems and to submit to the authority of people of low status. Such action would preclude hegemonic or subordinate masculine identities but would correspond to a subordinate masculinity.

Adopting the Diets of the Weak (1 Cor 8:1–11:1)

Paul's comments on eating food sacrificed to idols cover over a fifth of the total text of his letter and include discussions on the nature of demons (1 Cor 8:4–6), Paul's own divestiture of apostolic rights (1 Cor 9:1–23), athletic training (1 Cor 9:24–27), the experiences of the wilderness generation as examples for his audience (1 Cor 10:1–13), eating practices with outsiders (1 Cor 10:23–30) and, finally, Jesus (11:1).[104] The length and complexity of the argument highlights the importance of this issue as Paul addresses yet another apparent cause of the factionalism affecting the Corinthian believers. Although the convergence of such varied images in a single line of thought makes it difficult to understand fully each aspect of Paul's argument,[105] Paul's basic commands and their impetus are clear: the Corinthian believers who consider themselves "strong" because of their knowledge should not knowingly eat food associated with an idol on account of people who would perceive such action as participating in idolatry.[106] Why should they be willing to abrogate their own rights as they take such action for the sake of others? Paul says that this action is loving, strengthens the community (1 Cor 8:1, 13), and avoids idolatry (1 Cor 10:21), but ultimately it is because such action imitates Jesus (1 Cor 11:1). Part of the reason that Paul uses such a complex argument to accomplish this is because he has to reframe strength in terms of the ability to sacrifice one's rights for the sake of someone else rather than associating strength with knowledge. My focus in this section will be on the social effects of such adaptability to the diets of others considering the public and social nature of food, and exploration of issues of adaptability as a sign of femininity.

In this section, it is difficult to isolate commands that would only apply to men. Although eating in a temple, buying food in the marketplace, or dining at the home of another could apply equally to women and men in Roman Corinth,[107] the social consequences of Paul's commands regarding refusing food is likely to have greater consequence for the male Corinthian believers because it associates them with weakness whereas women were presumed to already hold such a position. The tension is aptly demonstrated by Cicero's portrayal of a dinner party between Philodamus as host and Rubrius as his guest (Cicero, *Verr*. 2.1.66). Philodamus keeps the women separate because he wishes to spare his daughter the indignity of the apparently inevitable sexual advances of men at a dinner party. Rubrius, however, asks for his daughter to join them, justifying such a request by indicating that having women at a dinner party was common practice among the Greeks. Again, even if women were to be present, the juxtaposition of strength and weakness in connection to diet would be more directly applicable to men because of the correlation between strength and masculinity which has been a hallmark of the texts examined in the present volume (e.g., Quintilian, *Inst*. 6.11; Demosthenes, *Andr*. 26).

One of the main points of confusion in reading 1 Cor 8:1–11:1 is the idea that Paul offers a systematic treatment of idolatry, idols, or demons rather than focusing on issues of factionalism. Statements such as "an idol in this world is nothing" and "I do not want you to be partners with demons" can be held together by understanding that for Paul, and Hellenistic Jews more broadly, the idols created by Gentiles are not representative of other gods but are the result of overly elevating demons (1 Cor 8:4 and 10:20; respectively).[108] Paul agrees with the basic point under discussion but not with the application of that point. So, although there is a logically consistent view of idols and demons behind Paul's argument, the focus, as it is throughout the rest of the letter, commands specific actions that address the factionalism that threatens the community. This is why of the fifteen uses of the imperative in 1 Cor 8:1–11:1, only two directly address idolatry: "Do not be (γίνεσθε) idolaters, as some of them were" and "flee (φεύγετε) idolatry" (10:7 and 14; respectively). These commands fall within Paul's discussion of the wilderness generation which is an example that resonates with the issue of factionalism (cf. Exod 32; Num 11, 14, 25). As Mitchell demonstrates, each aspect of the wilderness generation that Paul references in this section was related to factionalism and revolt against God's call to unity.[109] The other commands that possibly related to idolatry can all be understood within the broader heading of not acting in ways that harm other members of the community. This makes sense of why Paul's first command is that they are to "watch out (βλέπετε) that your authority does not hinder others" and his later statement "do not seek (ζητείτω) your own good but the good of the other" (8:9 and 10:24; respectively). It is important to note that Paul uses the idea of a weak conscience to describe those who are scandalized by eating food sacrificed to idols but *never* applies the corresponding idea of strength to describe those whose consciences allow them to eat such food (1 Cor 8:1–13). Although the connection of food and idolatry is the issue under discussion, Paul's concern is not to offer a systematic treatment of idols but to grant as much ground as possible to each side, those who abstain from food sacrificed to idols and those who partake, in order to promote the concord of the community through focus on the benefit of those who are more susceptible to suffer on account of such actions (i.e., the weak).

The focus on the common good and the benefit of others explain Paul's use of his own renunciation of his rights as an example in the section and his discussion about renouncing personal freedom for the benefit of others (1 Cor 9:1–23 and 10:23–11:1). Paul uses his rights to take along a believing wife and to receive compensation for his work as examples of instances where he demonstrates the renunciation of personal rights because that course of action is of greater benefit to the community. Paul's reasons for not taking along, or even having, a wife are obvious in light of his discussion of the benefits of celibacy as outlined in 1 Cor 7:7, 7:25–28, and 7:32–40 and discussed in the current and previous chapters of this volume, but his reasoning for not accepting compensation requires setting such statements within a historical context where public oratory and rhetorical instruction could allow a person to attract students and earn income from their tuition. Paul's self-description in the first four chapters has already rejected using such a lens to understand his own ministry so it comes as no surprise to see him refusing further financial entanglement.[110] Paul shifts the discussion away from compensation to responsibility by noting that he is compelled, and is not a voluntary participant, in the expansion of the kingdom of God (1 Cor 9:17). Rather than money, Paul sees his reward as the freedom to adapt to the needs of any group or, in Paul's words, becoming "a slave to all" (1 Cor 9:19).[111] Not only does Paul reject the use of his position for economic or social gain, he makes his reward the scandalous act of conforming to the needs of others, using the language of slavery to emphasize his point (1 Cor 9:19). As in his discussion from 1 Cor 8, Paul mentions conforming to the weakness of the weak (1 Cor 9:22), but he never mentions the corollary group of the strong or the idea of adapting to their needs.[112] This lacuna is key to understanding how Paul redefines his audience's understanding of strength in terms of one's ability to conform to the needs of others, which is why Paul finishes this section by pointing to himself and, ultimately, to Jesus (1 Cor 11:1).[113]

Paul's statements about conforming to the needs of others as a strategy for overcoming factionalism resonate with political discussions of how to achieve concord but, ultimately, require a level of accommodation that would be detrimental to the masculinity of one's persona.[114] Mitchell argues that authors often counsel more powerful groups to protect or bear with weaker or less respected groups in order to achieve and maintain social and political harmony, frequently applying the labels of the strong to the group that is being asked to conform to the needs of the weak.[115] She offers Plutarch as a prime example:

> The Greek states which were weak would be preserved by mutual support when once they had been bound as it were by the common interest and that just as the members of the body have a common life and breath because they cleave together in a common growth, but when they are drawn apart and become separate they wither away and decay.... (Plutarch, *Arat.* 24.5, trans. Perrin)[116]

While Plutarch does use the language of weakness within a discussion promoting mutual support, nowhere does Plutarch use the idea that the strong need to adapt to the needs of those who are weak. Another of Mitchell's key examples comes from Dionysius of Halicarnassus, who includes an argument for the renunciation of some rights and privileges by stronger members for the sake of weaker ones in order to prevent conquest by barbarians.

> After he had taken this resolution he called together the most important men of every city . . . and made a long speech exhorting them to concord, pointing out what a fine thing it is when a number of states agree together and what a

disgraceful sight when kinsmen are at variance and declaring that concord is a source of strength to weak states while mutual slaughter reduces and weakens even the strongest. (Dion Hal., *Ant. rom.* 4.26.2, Cary)

Although the speech does juxtapose different actions for the strong and the weak as a means of achieving concord, the strong, in this case Rome, must make relatively few concessions to the weak, the other Latin and Greek peoples. Most importantly, the strong are never asked to conform their behavior to that of the weak. Rather, it is the weak, the Latin and Greek peoples, who make the greatest concessions by conforming to Roman laws (i.e., practice) and submitting to Roman rule. They are promised a degree of self-governance,[117] but it is set within subordination to Rome. The closest any of Mitchell's examples come to encouraging the type of renunciation of rights advocated by Paul is when those with power are asked to defer some of that power to those below them.

> For enmity can not only expose and humiliate the weak, to say nothing of the hardships they have already, but also annoy those who are prosperous and distress their spirits. Therefore sensible persons prefer to submit to defeat in ordinary matters to be not too precise in defending their rights rather than, by quarrelling over every matter and never making any concessions to any one, always to have persons plotting against them and making war on them, persons feel resentment at their good fortune and, so far as they are able, try to stand in the way of it, and who, on the other hand, if any reverse should take place—and many are the reverses which do occur—rejoice and seize the opportunity to display his malice and hatred. (Dio Chry., *Or.* 40.20–21, trans. Crosby)

This advice comes closer to Paul's commands, but further examination shows that this concession has clear limits that safeguard the strong from compromising their superiority.

> And let no one imagine that I mean we should be wholly submissive, and that when they are not at all just or fair in their policies we should beg and entreat them; nay, but when they choose friendship and display an eagerness for it, to show ourselves more favourable to this policy. (Dio Chry., *Or.* 40.20–21, trans. Crosby)

Whatever rights the stronger members concede should not jeopardize their dominance by making them appear wholly submissive. Rather, the goal is to ameliorate the resentment of weaker or lower-status groups by acquiescing on matters that do threaten the dominance of the strong. Such gendered logic where the stronger (i.e., more masculine) partner should bear with shortcomings of the weaker (i.e., more feminine) partner parallels that found in discussions of the proper relationship between a husband and wife.[118] Even Plutarch, who represents a more progressive picture of marriage by advocating for husbands to keep in mind the feelings, responses, and education of their wives so as to help them live peaceably, maintains a gendered hierarchy that gives more rights and privileges to the husband because of his stronger nature.[119] The husband, like the stronger group or city in the texts discussed above, is cautioned against ruling too severely but never asked to subordinate himself to the weaker party or adopt the weaker party's behavior. This type of condescension that asks the stronger part to bear with the weaknesses of others without jeopardizing their own positions is almost exactly like Theissen's love-patriarchy but fails to take account of the full impact of Paul's commands.[120]

If Paul were going to follow such advice and create a system where the strong could exercise their strength without damaging or provoking the weak, then he would need to create a space where idol food could knowingly be consumed. But the only time that Paul allows for the possibility of consuming idol food is when the person does not know that it is idol food. His commands about eating whatever is served at a meal hosted by nonbelievers allows the possibility that you could eat idol food *as long as you do not know that it is* (1 Cor 10:27). The rub is that Paul says that as soon as the person knows it is idol food they are to refuse to eat it (1 Cor 10:28). In other words, Paul never allows a person to eat idol food *knowingly*. Recalling the above discussion about Dionysius's advice to the strong, a strong person should only curtail some actions so that they can exercise their strength when needed or desired (i.e., the Rome should allow Greek cities some freedoms but force them to conform in areas like governance and law), but Paul never allows people to exercise the strength of knowing "that an idol in this world is nothing" (quoted by Paul in 1 Cor 8:4). Using Dio Chyrsostum's terminology from *Or.* 40.20–21 above, Paul commands that those with knowledge should become "wholly submissive" to the needs of the weak (cf. *Ant. rom.* 40.23), which is the very thing that Dionysius said would jeopardize a person's or a nation's masculinity. This means that Paul, as I have shown in terms of his own identity and the commands examined above, does not secure masculine identity but abrogates it by embodying subordinate behavior.

Rather than safeguarding the superiority of those who might refer to themselves as strong because of their boldness in eating food associated with idols, Paul calls people to take whatever action is necessary for the sake of others. The focus on the needs or views of other people manifests throughout the discussion, but becomes particularly sharp when Paul references the person reporting the status of the food and conscience of the weak (1 Cor 10:28). In the process, Paul redefines strength in terms of adaptability regardless of the consequences. In distinction from the authors above who advise groups to adapt only as long as it does not threaten their superiority (i.e., political or marital hegemony), Paul repeats that the ultimate consideration is the effect of one's actions on another. Yes, they are free, but that freedom must be exercised by enslaving oneself to the needs of another. This level of adaptability is what the rhetoricians degrade as the behavior of an actor, those feminized individuals who would abandon their own personae to scandalous degrees in order to win the favor a crowd. Such men were not masculine enough to function publicly as men but could only imitate others. Quintilian denigrates actors as those "people whose entire art consists of imitation" because they lose themselves in their imitation of characters instead of, like a proper orator, mastering those characters whom they imitate (*Inst.* 11.3.91; cf. 2.5.10–12, 4.2.39).[121] In fact, Quintilian evidences a deep and pervasive suspicion of anything that even hints at *actio* (*Inst.* 11.3.28–32, 76). The actor raises another point that illuminates the social consequences for Paul's audience in following his commands since the actor jeopardizes his masculinity by imitating women, boys, and slaves. Imitation of the wrong type of people, such as those considered weak, would be disastrous for the masculinity of Paul's audience since this behavior would make them susceptible to charges of femininity.

Degrading a person because of their diet is broadly attested in Greek and Latin literature. Seneca reports that he gave up a vegetarian diet at the request of his father so that he would not appear to participate in "certain foreign rites . . . [that required] abstinence from eating certain animals" (Seneca, *Ep.* 108.98.22). Seneca changes his diet specifically because of the negative associations that others would make about his diet and group associations. A similar connection can be seen regarding the lavish diets on display in Rome. Polybius, writing in the second century B.C.E., can already detect a feminizing of the Roman young men because of their consumption of foreign food and the extravagant price paid for it (31.25.4–5). Juvenal, writing almost three hundred years later, makes a similar critique of spending 6,000 sesterces on mullet, connecting such unnatural expenditures to the moral degradation of Roman society (Juvenal, *Sat.* 4). Juvenal's point is that such expenditures evidence a lack of self-control and moderation, key marks of masculinity, and, therefore, represent a loss of masculinity. Sallust complains that the Roman army's corruption by foreign foods is evidenced by their willingness to go to unnatural lengths to acquire such delicacies (Sallust, *Bell. Cat.* 13.3). Although Greek and Latin authors often critiqued gluttony, as the above sources show, the very types of food could also make a person, especially men, liable to charges of femininity.[122] Although women's gluttony or taste for foreign food is mentioned, it does not draw the same level of ire because women are thought to naturally desire such extravagance (Seneca, *Ben.* 7.9). When men seek such extravagance they act like women, becoming soft and unable to exhibit hegemonic masculinity.[123]

> Lucius Sulla, in order to make loyal to him the army he had brought into Asia, had allowed his soldiers luxury and license foreign to the ways of our ancestors and, in their leisure hours, the warlike spirits of those men were easily softened by the charms and pleasures of those places. (Sall. *Cat.* 11.5, Ramsey; cf. Seneca, *Ep.* 114, 122; Cicero, *In Verr.* 5.81)

Paul asking his audience, especially the men, to adopt diets that they associate with the weak makes them liable to charges of femininity. This is yet another example of Paul encouraging behavior that requires the men in his audience to embody a subordinate masculinity.

Husbands Submitting to Their Wives and Wives Submitting to Their Husbands (1 Cor 7:1–6)

Paul's commands on the mutual submission of bodies within a marriage provide an interesting test case since he addresses both men and women. I will show that not only does Paul continue to command that men embody a subordinate masculinity by submitting their bodies to their wives (1 Cor 7:3–4), he also commands the empowerment of the party that is most liable to the abuse of power in this institution by providing women the power to divorce but not the men (1 Cor 7:10–11). This strategy rhetorically parallels his commands that restrict the use of the Roman courts and require appointing low-status members of the community as judges over any disputes that arise.

Much of the background for understanding Paul's commands on celibacy and marriage is covered in the previous chapter's discussion of Paul's status as a celibate man. The key points concern the fact that all people, men in particular, are expected to participate in the system of patriarchy that emphasizes men as dominant (i.e., penetrating) members of society and fulfill corresponding roles in society's understanding of sexuality. Men who fail to embody this ideal are subject to legal and social repercussions associated with being a subordinate, or failed, man. The antidote to such failures of masculinity are for the men to reassert their masculinity through displays of domination or penetration. One example of such requirements pertains to laws governing adultery (e.g., *Dig.* 48.5.2.2, 48.5.2.6). First, laws that punish sex with a person's spouse focus almost exclusively on regulating the behavior of the wife. A husband could only be brought up on such charges if his extramarital sexual relationships hinder his ability to fulfill his marital duties to his wife, duties that are primarily geared toward producing legitimate children. Second, such laws often focus on the feminizing implications for the status of the husband and the threat such feminization poses to the society. A wife who asserted control or domination through sex subverted the social order and restoration required her husband to assert control over her. The point was to return her to her proper, subordinate position. A cuckolded husband or father could restore his masculinity either by dominating (i.e., beating his wife and/or her lover) or by sexually penetrating his wife's lover (*Dig.* 47.5.24–35; 48.5.2.2; 48.5.2.6). The fact that a cuckolded husband could be required by law to restore his masculinity by taking the active sexual role with the man who had slept with his wife shows just how seriously the Romans took their understanding of the gender hierarchy and the lengths to which sexuality reinforces it.

Although the commands that Paul gives in 1 Cor 7:2–3 introduce a new set of questions, they continue the line of thinking from 1 Cor 6 on the avoidance of sexual immorality (πορνεία). While the same principle applies in each category (e.g., self-control as the key to avoiding sexual immorality), understanding the distinction that Paul draws between the married and unmarried and the agency allowed to people in either situation is critical in understanding the way such commands would be understood by the Corinthian believers. For the unmarried, avoiding sexual immorality means abstaining from all sexual contact through celibacy and assumes the person, male or female, has the requisite self-control. For the married, avoiding sexual immorality means a person keeps all sexual activity within the marriage *and* in mutual submission to his or her spouse. I will highlight the assumptions and function of these commands and how they require the more powerful members of the community to embody a subordinate position within the community of believers.

The commands that Paul gives regarding marriage and sex can be grouped in two main categories: commands to the married and commands to the unmarried. The first set of commands address the benefits of marriage as a safeguard against sexual immorality and proper conduct within marriage (1 Cor 7:2–5; 10–11).[124] These commands contain symmetrical and asymmetrical rights that highlight the ways that Paul wants the Corinthian believers to use and relate to power. First, Paul commands a symmetrical, mutual submission of bodies within marriage (1 Cor 7:2–5). While a husband's control over his wife's body would be a given, the idea that a wife could have such authority over her husband's body would have shocked Paul's audience because of the way it would disrupt the assumed patriarchy of the household. Even Plutarch, who is rather progressive concerning women in the context of first-century Rome, cautions a wife not to seek to control but to tolerate her husband's extramarital sexual encounters (*Conj. praec.* 16). Furthermore, Plutarch's discussion of the use of sexuality puts far more emphasis on the wife as a submissive object of desire who should behave according to the husband's desires (e.g., *Conj. praec.* 46).[125] Paul, however, commands the husband to submit his body, along with its rights to seek sex outside of marriage (cf. 1 Cor 5:9–13), to his wife. Although the husband is given the same right over his wife's body, a man who submitted to his wife's desires and wishes was lambasted as a subordinate, feminine man who were not fit for positions of authority (i.e., hegemony) such as those of the *aedile* or *duoviri*.[126] This is all the more striking when set within the broader context as sex within marriage as an outlet for sexual desire and thus guarding against sexual immorality. The sexual desire of women, unchecked by male domination, was seen as an existential threat to society and required her husband to control her. Messalina is one of the most well-known examples of this as her unrestrained sexuality feminizes Claudius, making him unable to function as a man, thereby making him unfit to rule Rome (Tacitus, *Ann.* 11; Suetonius, *Claud.* 26, 29).[127] For the men in Paul's audience, submitting their bodies to their wives would make them liable to such charges of femininity. Paul's command for mutual submission, then, should be read as asking the husband to engage in a type of submission of his body that would jeopardize his status.

Paul's instructions on divorce follow a similar reversal of power dynamics within the marriage by giving asymmetrical instructions regarding the ability to enact a divorce. At the center of Paul's commands are the ideas that husbands and wives should not divorce as seen in the parallel statements that "a wife should not separate (χωρισθῆναι) from her husband" and "a husband should not divorce (ἀφιέναι) his wife" (1 Cor 7:10–11).[128] Between the two commands, however, Paul introduces the caveat that "if [the wife] separates (χωρισθῇ) [from her husband], let her remain unmarried or be reconciled to her husband" (1 Cor 7:11a). Paul provides a caveat that allows for the wife to take the very action that he just cited Jesus as commanding couples not to take. Although women were sometimes allowed to take legal action against their husband, divorce was typically initiated by the husband.[129] There is no parallel command for men that allows for such separation nor an indication that this is an ellipsis where Paul expects his audience to supply such a command. Although Roman wives generally, and at least some Jewish wives judging from the evidence of Salome divorcing her husband (Josephus, *Ant.* 15.259), had the legal right to divorce, certain legal and social mechanisms made divorce a less appealing option for women since they had less access to public institutions, required the consent of their *paterfamilias* due to his ongoing *patria potestas*, and were almost guaranteed to lose any children (*Digest* 23.3.2 [Ulpian]; 24.2.2 [Gaius]).[130] Paul allowing women the right to divorce while restricting the husband's right, then, evidences a similar reversal of power as that discussed in relation to litigation where the assumed subordinate member in the relationship is given greater power while the assumed dominant member's power is restricted. Paul does not ignore differences between bodies but institutes systems that account for those differences while working toward a functional equality.[131]

Paul's positivity toward marriage, however, must be tempered by understanding that he advocates marriage only if necessary because the person lacks the sufficient self-control (1 Cor 7:6–9; 32–40).[132] As discussed in the previous chapter, advocating long-term celibacy was nearly unheard of and often categorized as socially subversive due to the way that it freed a person from the civic and social structures that maintained the stability of the city and nation. By framing such action under the heading of self-control, a description commonly used in association with masculinity, Paul normalizes and exalts an otherwise marginal and subversive activity.[133] The problem is that any man in Paul's audience who sought to embody Paul's approach to self-control would be seen as failing to fulfill the broader Greek and Roman ideals of masculinity and suffer a corresponding loss of status and privilege. Such men, like those who could not defend themselves in court, were guaranteed to be read as failed, subordinate men.

"Be [subordinate] men!" (1 Cor 16:13)

An ancient letter's closing, as Jeffery Weima demonstrates, provides a "hermeneutical spotlight, highlighting the central concerns of the Apostle,"[134] and Paul's concluding remarks in the final chapter of 1 Corinthians are no exception as he reinforces and recapitulates his main point and argument about the answer to factionalism.[135] Recalling Mitchell's rhetorical analysis and her argument about Paul's *propositio* on concord as a mechanism to overcome factionalism, means that a focus on concord should at least be evident, if not the main point, as Paul closes the letter.[136] Such a focus on concord is, in fact, evident in Paul's command to submit to people who, like the household of Stephanus, show a devotion to the service of those in the community, and the command to greet one another with a holy kiss (1 Cor 16:15–16, 20; respectively). As Paul argues throughout the letter, the ability to submit to the needs of another is a key marker of maturity, is an imitation of both Paul and Jesus, and helps overcome the factionalism that threatens the community. Although scholars debate the exact significance of the holy kiss, it clearly indicates communal harmony and affection, behaviors that would ameliorate factionalism.[137] Once again the rhetorical situation that motivates Paul's argument is addressed directly in statements and also obliquely in the strategies and methods he employs.[138]

The function of the five imperatives in 16:13–14 in summarizing Paul's argument is less clear, especially the command to be men (ἀνδρίζεσθε) which is my present focus. Thiselton notes the gendered ideology of the terms but argues that such a focus is "unnecessarily sensitive" and that it is better to understand Paul as commanding maturity rather than something specifically connected to gender.[139] While Thiselton is correct that this command carries with it the goal of maturity, he misses the importance of connecting this maturity to the gendered logic that runs throughout Paul's argument. What Thiselton and others who eschew the gendered nature of the term fail to understand is that, as I have demonstrated throughout the present work, such discourses on maturity function within a gendered logic where the body was to advance from an immature, feminine state to a mature, masculine one.[140] Paul has carefully and consistently applied this gendered logic throughout 1 Corinthians, and it would be unwise to think he would deviate from this practice at such a crucial point in his argument and letter.

Although the gendered logic of a term such as Ἀνδρίζομαι, containing as it does the Greek stem ἀνδρ- which relates to that associated with the actions of men,[141] might appear obvious, it is important to trace the connections through actual usage, especially in the imperative mood, in the extant literature. The vast majority of the occurrences of Ἀνδρίζομαι are directed to men and pertain to performing bravely in battle or to conforming to the various social expectations of men (e.g., Aristotle, *Eth. nic.* 3.6.8–12; Lucian, *Anach.* 15; Plutarch, *Stoic. rep.* 27; Xenophon, *Anab.* 3.3.34, 5.8.15; *Oec.* 5.4). Lucian describes the way that Bagaos, a lawyer, "acts manly (ἀνδρίζεται) by keeping his case in hand and, in hoping to win each case, show that he is not a bit inferior to any man in service" (Lucian, *Eunuch.* 13). Here, masculinity is expressed in that quintessential characteristic of dominating others while retaining self-control. Josephus has Titus use the term to encourage his men that "to show themselves to be truly manly men (ἀνδρίζεσθαι) requires that when they fought their enemies they received no harm from them at the same time" (Josephus, *J.W.* 5.316). Titus's statement captures the gendered logic of Ἀνδρίζομαι by emphasizing the connection between masculinity, dominating your opponent, and maintaining total control over your own body.

In the three uses that are directed to women, one compliments women for fighting like men in fierce battle (Appian, *Hist. rom.* 7.5.29) while two use the term ironically for women who masquerade and act like men and thereby destabilize the social order (Philostratus, *Imag.* 1.2.10; Julian, *Orat. 3* 127B). Appian's positive assessment of "women acting no less manly (ἀνδριζομένον) than the men" fits the pattern described by Barry Williams whereby women and other nonmen can be praised for fighting as long as they do so in defense of the home (Appian, *Hist. rom.* 7.5.29).[142] These instances are deemed appropriate because the women act to protect the space for which they are primarily responsible, the domestic space. In contrast, Julian's use highlights the problems that arise when women act like men outside of the domestic space. Julian gives examples of the fantastic and incredible where he describes "a crowd of women who act like men (ἀνδριζομένον) in not very decent ways . . . and were the causes of dissension and long wars among countless nations" (Julian, *Orat. 3* 127B). This use follows the more common usage whereby gender transgression destabilizes the social order and leads to a lack of harmony.

Of the fifty-four total occurrences of Ἀνδρίζομαι, thirty are in the imperative mood as is the case in 1 Cor 16:13 (e.g., Deut 31:6; Josh 1:6; 2 Sam 10:12; Herm. *Vis.* 1.4.3), and all but one of these thirty occur in Jewish or Christian literature. This single exception comes from Dio Cassius, who uses the verb in dialogue between two soldiers as one commands the other act like a man and fight (Dio Cassius, *Rom. hist.* 7.26). As noted above, this evokes the connection between acting like a man and military dominance. Jewish literature primarily relies on this connection with 60 percent (12/20) of the uses referring to military action (e.g., Josh 1:9; 1 Chron 32:7). With this in mind, The Song of Deborah condemns the men of Israel for hiding from battle while Deborah and Jael defeat Israel's enemies (Judges 5:7–8, 24–30); the point is that the men failed to do what men should do and the men's failure, here, serves to reinforce the descent-into-chaos motif of the broader narrative of Judges. Although not using Ἀνδρίζομαι, Judges emphasizes the failure of the military power and will of the men of Israel to conquer their enemies. The other main use in Jewish literature, in 25 percent (5/20) of the occurrences, is to command a man to adhere to Torah (e.g., Josh 1:7; 1 Chron 22:13). The only use in Jewish literature of Ἀνδρίζομαι in connection with a woman comes in Micah, where it is used for Jerusalem, personified as a woman, in labor (Micah 4:10). In Jewish literature, Ἀνδρίζομαι in the imperative mood is often paired with other terms associated with masculinity, usually Ἰσχύω in the imperative (e.g., Duet 31:7; 1 Macc 2:64). There are three instances where it is paired with the imperative of κραταιόομαι as Paul does in 1 Cor 16:13 (2 Sam 10:12; Pss 26:14, 30:25); although, the usages in the Psalms specifically mention strengthening the heart. Sirach uses Ἀνδρίζομαι in the imperative mood in reference to maintaining self-control when drinking wine and remaining decorous at dinner parties (Sir 31:25). One last notable usage in Jewish literature comes in 2 Maccabees, where a mother encourages her sons to suffer brutal torture and execution rather than transgress Torah; the mother is said to have "stirring up her female reasoning with a man's courage" (2 Macc 7:21). Again, although not using Ἀνδρίζομαι, the text understands the mother's ability to remain faithful to Torah despite her horrific circumstances as masculine behavior and describes it as such.

Broadly speaking, the evidence indicates that ἀνδρίζομαι is, with four exceptions, used to encourage men or boys to conform to expectations of masculinity within a specific context. It is used with a specific set of gendered discourses in mind and is used to command or express conformity to that which is associated with masculinity. In those few instances where it is used to describe women, two of those cases disdain such actions and view them as threatening the order of the community and only one provides clear praise for an exceptional case where women fight like men. As these instances demonstrate, telling someone to "grow up" with such a gender-specific term would carry the inherent charge that they are currently feminine and need to become masculine through development.[143]

Paul's usage is no different and serves as a rhetorically powerful ending to his argument and use of gender throughout. Earlier in the letter, he comments on the Corinthians' immaturity and their need to listen to Paul as their father (1 Cor 4:15–17).[144] This gendered dynamic is an important part of Paul's self-presentation as the community's father as he scolds them as immature youths and commands them to show maturity by imitating him (cf. 1 Cor 4:15–16). The command to be men, then, serves as a return to and culmination of the gendered discourse that formed a key part of Paul's self-presentation and argument at the beginning of the letter. The women of the community would certainly have heard this command and understood its importance within an argument that deals extensively with behavior. There is even a slight possibility that the women could, as evidenced by Appian's use (*Rom. hist.*7.5.29), understand that in extreme cases they must act in manly ways to safeguard the community. The women could, as in Paul's discussion of mutual submission (1 Cor 7:2–4), understand that they have their own role to play in seeking the advantage of others, but, throughout 1 Corinthians, Paul has not asked the women to subordinate themselves in the same way that he has asked the men to take such action. The reason would most likely be that the patriarchal social structure of first-century Corinth would not present as many opportunities for women to gain the type of social status that would afford the opportunity to oppress others. As would be consistent with the majority of extant uses of ἀνδρίζομαι in Greek, Roman, and Jewish literature, Paul appears to use the term to tell the men in the community to conform to the ideal patterns of masculinity set forth by their respective community.

But what type of men did Paul command his audience to become? This is a world where men were supposed to be wise and dominant in public displays of oratory, but Paul has told his audience not to become wise but to become fools. In a world where wisdom and the ability to display mastery or wisdom was a key aspect of masculinity, conforming to the image a fool would mean that Paul's audience would not be able to take full advantage of the positions and privileges available to those who men who adequately demonstrated their masculinity. This is a world where men were meant to maintain their dominance using relationships and courts that codified patriarchal and classist hierarchies in order to secure a class structure that favored the elite and the male, but Paul has told them not to take advantage of such a court system. Instead, they are to be wronged by allowing themselves to be defeated. This is also a world where a man was supposed to model the impenetrability of Roman dominance through his command over his household, but Paul has also commanded the men in his audience to submit their bodies to their wives. Men were never supposed to submit their bodies to others, especially to a woman. For the men in Paul's audience, having to submit to a woman would also impugn their masculinity. This is a world where one's freedoms and abilities constitute a major aspect of distinguishing those who were strong from those who were weak, but Paul tells the strong to conform to the practices of the weak. The results will be that everyone will be seen as weak.

Taken together, Paul's commands require his audience to misperform discourses of masculinity in ways that would prevent them from taking either hegemonic or complicit positions in the patriarchal institutions that comprise a Roman city. The only remaining option is that these men become subordinate men who conform to the social position of those people whose bodies and identities keep them at the bottom of Roman society. Such a command would appear ludicrous from the perspective of the broader society, and that is one reason why Paul has had to repeatedly engage and renegotiate his audience's conceptions of gender. In his conclusion, Paul now commands them to embody a type of masculinity that imitates his own and will address the factionalism of the community by creating a system that resists oppression and encourages equality.

Paul does not try to defend his actions as the truly masculine (i.e., hegemonic), as does Favorinus, or adequately masculine (i.e., complicit), as do Philo and Josephus. Rather, Paul takes hold of the patriarchal systems and consciously embodies behaviors and roles that force him to the bottom of such a system. His repeated call for his audience to imitate him means that they cannot be men in ways that correspond to the systems of oppression and power that reinforce such patriarchal systems. His argument throughout the letter systematically disqualifies the types of behavior typically associated with such a call to manhood. Rather, the Corinthians must follow Paul in taking subordinate positions that prevent them from participating in the oppression that results from such a system. They are to take on subordinate positions that would place them on equal footing with women, slaves, and other men whose bodies prevent them from ascending to lofty social positions. Embodying a subordinate masculinity addresses the community's factionalism by subverting the system and goals that motivate such factionalism in the first place, thus making such a subversive masculinity a crucial tool for addressing the issue of factionalism that sits at the heart of 1 Corinthians.

NOTES

1. For the use of gender, specifically the use of the buffoon as a failed man, for comedic effect, see L. L. Welborn, *Paul, the Fool of Christ: A Study of 1 Corinthians 1–4 in the Comic-Philosophic Tradition* (JSNTSup 293; New York: T&T Clark International, 2005), 25–48. For the use of gendered discourses for the purpose of political propaganda in reliefs produced during the Principate and present in Roman Colonies, see Davina Lopez, *Apostle to the Conquered: Reimagining Paul's Mission* (Minneapolis: Fortress Press, 2008), 22–55.

2. Antoinette Clark Wire persuasively argues for the presence of some women who Paul thinks disrupt the concord of the community by asserting too much authority; *The Corinthian Women Prophets: A Reconstruction through Paul's Rhetoric* (Minneapolis: Fortress Press, 1991). Although there are points of interpretation on which we differ, I do not see my basic thesis in conflict with Wire's argument that Paul attempts to restrain the abuse of power by certain groups. We do, however, disagree on the group that Paul attempts to constrain. As I argue, the institutions of public oratory, the courts, and certain behavior at public meals would be understood to pertain almost exclusively to men, which is why I read Paul's commands regarding such institutions as articulating a vision for a subordinate masculinity. Another point to keep in mind is that, aside from the command to avoid divorce in 1 Cor 7:10 and the order of nature discussed in 1 Cor 11, Paul's commands are based on the structure of those institutions within that context rather than an abstract, theological necessity. In other words, Paul's commands would look substantially different if issued in contexts which did not share the patriarchal structure of the first-century Principate.

3. As Friesen's work on economics in the Roman Empire makes clear, the distinction between high and low status does not adequately address the structure of Roman society or the various statuses that are evident in Paul's writings. The main target of Friesen's work is the way that scholars like Theissen and Meeks utilize a variety of factors in determining a person's status but fail to explain how these factors coalesce in determining that status. Friesen does not argue with the idea that social identity is important or that it is comprised of a variety of factors but how it is comprised by those factors. Friesen does not, however, abandon the concept of status, social or otherwise, or the idea that communities create hierarchical arrangements of status. In fact, Friesen focuses on economics because it offers one of the clearest indications of a person's position within society. See, Steven J. Friesen, "Poverty in Pauline Studies: Beyond the So-Called New Consensus," *JSNT* 26 (2004): 323–61; "The Wrong Erastus: Ideology, Archeology, and Exegesis," in *Corinth in Context: Comparative Studies in Religion and Society* (ed. Steven J. Friesen, Daniel N. Schowalter, and James C. Walters; Leiden: Brill, 2010), 231–57. In his more recent work, Friesen applies the

concept of intersectionality in an effort to more carefully integrate the various factors that determine a person's status; see "Junia Theodora of Corinth: Gendered Inequalities in the Early Empire," in *Corinth in Contrast: Studies in Inequality* (ed. Steven J. Friessen, Sarah A. James, and Daniel N. Schowalter; Leiden: Brill, 2014), 203–26.

4. Edward Adams and David G. Horrell edited an invaluable resource for surveying the history of scholarship on the Corinthian correspondence; see *Christianity at Corinth: The Quest for the Pauline Church* (Louisville; KY: Westminster John Know, 2004). This collection of key texts in the study of 1 Corinthians, along with their introductory essay, provides a helpful guide for anyone seeking to make sense of the different stages of scholarship on the Corinthians. Walter Schmithals is one of the more vigorous and widely known proponents of understanding gnostic or protognostic influences as the main impetus for the issues that Paul addresses; see *Gnosticism in Corinth: An Investigation of the Letters to the Corinthians* (trans. J. E. Steely; Nashville: Abingdon, 1971); *Paul and the Gnostics* (Nashville: Abingdon,1972). Ulrich Wilckens is another key figure in the application of Gnosticism in reading 1 Corinthians; *Weisheit and Torheit* (Tübingen: Mohr, 1959).

Gerd Theissen's publications throughout the 1970s played a significant role in shifting the scholarly discussion of Paul's opponents in Corinth away from focusing on purely theological issues (e.g., Gnosticism or overly realized eschatology) by demonstrating the influence of social contexts and conflict over social standing; 'Soziale Schichtung in der korinthischen Gemeinde: Ein Beitrag zur Soziologie des hellenistischen Urchristentums,' *ZNW* 65 (1974): 232–72; 'Soziale Integration und sakramentales Handeln: Eine Analyse von 1 Cor. XI 17–34,' *NovT* 16 (1974): 179–206; 'Legitimation und Lebensunterhalt: Ein Beitrag zur Soziologie urchristlicher Missionaire,' *NTS* 21(1975): 192–221; 'Die Starken und Schwachen in Korinth: Soziologische Analyse eines theologischen Streites,' *EvT* 35 (1975): 155–72; "Die soziologische Auswertun reliogiöser Überlieferungen: Ihre methodologischen Probleme am Beispel des Urchristentums," *Kairos* 17 (1975): 284–99. Theissen's arguments for the importance of social settings in the conflicts addressed in 1 Corinthians provided the groundwork for studies focusing on social status and rhetoric, many of which I discuss in the introduction, including: Dale B. Martin, *The Corinthian Body* (New Haven: Yale University Press, 1995); David G. Horrell, *The Social Ethos of the Corinthian Correspondence* (Edinburgh: T&T Clark, 1996); P. Marshall, *Enmity in Corinth: Social Conventions in Paul's Relations with the Corinthians* (WUNT, 2.23; Tübingen: Mohr, 1987); Wayne A. Meeks, *The First Urban Christians: The Social World of the Apostle Paul* (New Haven: Yale University Press, 1983); Bruce Winter, *Philo and Paul among the Sophists* (SNTSMS, 96; Cambridge: Cambridge University Press, 1997); L. L. Welborn, *Politics and Rhetorician the Corinthian Epistles* (Macon, GA: Mercer University Press, 1997); Margaret M. Mitchell, *Paul and the Rhetoric of Reconciliation: An Exegetical Investigation of the Language and Composition of 1 Corinthians* (Louisville, Ky.: Westminster John Knox Press, 1993); Andrew D. Clarke, *Secular and Christian Leadership in Corinth: A Socio-Historical and Exegetical Study of 1 Corinthians 7–6* (AGJU, 18; Leiden: E.J. Brill, 1993). Although most readings of 1 Corinthians favor Paul's perspective, feminist scholars have reversed this assumption by privileging the Corinthians as more progressive in their understanding of the gospel than Paul; see Antoinette Clark Wire's argument that Paul corrects a group of female prophets whom he thinks disrupts the communal harmony by asserting too much authority; *The Corinthian Women Prophets* and Elisabeth Schüssler Fiorenza, "Rhetorical Situation and Historical Reconstruction in 1 Corinthians," *NTS* 33 (1987): 386–403. The work of Johannes Munck should also be mentioned in connection with Theissen's work. Although predating Theissen, Munck's work provided a key point of departure for studies like Theissen's since it convincingly argued that the issues involving disputes over wisdom that run throughout 1 Corinthians do not address theological conflicts but differences between Paul's wisdom and the wisdom of the Greeks; see *Paul and the Salvation of Mankind* (London: SCM, 1951), 136, 152. The shift from theological divisions represented a major departure from the view first made famous by Baur that the theological issue related to a conflict between Pauline and Petrine churches and centered over what has come to be called Judaizing.

A collection of essays from a recent SBL seminar group on Ancient Myths and Modern Theories of Christian Origins shows how previous assumptions of a stable and cohesive "Christian" identity centered on Paul's gospel for Paul's audience misunderstands the textual evidence, especially in 1 Corinthians, and imports later understandings of Christian identity into Corinth; *Redescribing Paul and the Corinthians* (ed. Ron Cameron and Merrill P. Miller; ECIL 5; Atlanta; GA: Society of Biblical Literature, 2011). The work produced by this group demonstrates that the factionalism at the center of 1 Corinthians can best be explained by competing identities and social identities that were already present before Paul arrived in Corinth and not just to factions that appear after Paul left Corinth, a clear reference to Winter's work; *Redescribing*, 4–5.

5. E.g., Schmithals, *Gnosticism in Corinth*, 198–206.

6. See my discussion in the second chapter of the present work.

7. A. J. Spawforth, "Roman Corinth: The Formation of a Colonial Elite," in *Roman Onomastics in the Greek East: Social and Political Aspects* (ed. A. D. Rizakis; Athens: Research Center for Greek and Roman Antiquity, 1996), 167–82.

8. Spawforth offers one of the earlier examination of tombstones which shows the paucity of evidence for veterans amongst Roman Corinth's earliest settlers; "Roman Corinth: The Formation of a Colonial Elite," 167–82.

9. For a refutation of Roman Corinth as a veterans' colony; see Benjamin W. Willis, "The Social and Ethnic Origins of the Colonists in Early Roman Corinth," in *Corinth in Context: Comparative Studies on Religion and Society* (ed. Steven J. Friesen, Daniel N. Schowalter, and James C. Walters; Leiden: Brill, 2010), 17–21. Sarah A. James agrees and also discusses the conflation of the destruction and rebuilding of Corinth and Carthage and issues related to taking accounts of either one at face value; see "The Last of the Corinthians? Society and Settlement from 146 to 44 B.C.E.," in *Corinth in Contrast: Studies in Inequality* (ed. Steven J. Friessen, Sarah A. James, and Daniel N. Schowalter; Leiden: Brill, 2014), 21–37.

10. Concannon makes a similar point in his examination of Paul's manipulation of identity; *"When You Were Gentiles": Specters of Ethnicity in Roman Corinth and Paul's Corinthian Correspondence* (New Haven: Yale University Press, 2014), 79.

11. Friesen, "Junia Theodora of Corinth," 203–4. Hans Joseph Klauch, "Junia Theodora und die Gemeinde von Korinth," in *Kirche und Volk Gottes: Festschrift für Jürgen Roloff* (ed. Martin Karrer, et al.; Neukirchen-Vluyn: Neukirchen Verlag, 2000), 42–57. Bruce W. Winter, *Roman Wives, Roman Widows: The Appearance of New Women and the Pauline Communities* (Grand Rapids: Eerdmans, 2003), 183–91. The inscription itself is catalogued as Corinth Inventory No. 2486 and all references are to this text.

12. Our only knowledge of Junia Theodora comes from a single Greek inscription that combines five different texts. See Friesen's discussion, "Junia Theodora of Corinth," 204.

13. Pliny, *Nat.* 5.101. See, Winter, *Roman Wives, Roman Widows*, 192.

14. The more negative assessment of the role these women played in supporting Roman domination of others, notably the vast majority of women, is found in Friesen, "Junia Theodora of Corinth," and Judith Evans Grubbs, *Women and the Law in the Roman Empire: A Sourcebook on Marriage, Divorce, and Widowhood*," (London: Routledge, 2002), 71–72. Winter takes a more optimistic position on the freedom and power of such women; *Roman Wives, Roman Widows*, 181–93. Although Winter is correct that the titles and descriptions associated with these women, most notably Junia, are those that often signal high status and political influence, there is no indication that these women ever occupied the types of political offices that would have been available for men of similar status.

15. Friesen, "Junia Theodora of Corinth," 223.

16. The seminal treatment of names found at Corinth comes from the work of A. D. Rizakēs and S. Zoumbaki, *Roman Pelopennese: Roman Personal Names in Their Social Context*, vol. 1 (Athens: Research Centre for Greek and Roman Antiquity National Hellenic Research Foundation, 2001). For some of their examples of onomastic evidence of freedmen and their descendants in Corinthian epigraphic evidence, see nos. 8, 63, 68, 76, 90, 111, 119, 181, 193, and 200.

17. For a helpful introduction to the intersection of onomastic patterns and identity, see Christoph Schuler, "Local Elites in the Greek East," in *The Oxford Handbook of Roman Epigraphy* (ed. Christer Bruun and Jonathan Edmondson; Oxford: Oxford University Press, 2015), 264–68.

18. Millis, "The Local Magistrates," 39–41. Spawforth, "Roman Corinth," 169. Concannon, *Gentiles*, 59–60. Williams, "Corinth, 1987," 162.

19. Spawforth, "Roman Corinth," 170.

20. Christine M. Thomas, "Greek Heritage in Roman Corinth and Ephesos: Hybrid Identities and Strategies of Display in the Material Record of Traditional Mediterranean Religions," in *Corinth in Context: Comparative Studies on Religion and Society* (ed. Steven J. Friesen, Daniel N. Schowalter, and James C. Walters; Leiden: Brill, 2010), 136–41. Thomas's examination does make some use of evidence from other Julian colonies that show significant overlap with Roman Corinth, but her conclusions on the use of both Greek and Roman aspects of identity helpfully describes the blending of cultures that is evident in the material record. Katy Valentine discusses the fluidity between Greek and Roman cultures in terms of "cultural bilingualism"; see "'For You Were Bought With a Price': Slaves, Sex, and Self-control in

a Pauline Community" (Ph.D. diss., Graduate Theological Union, 2014). Valentine builds her understanding of cultural bilingualism on the work of Andrew Wallace-Hadrill, who uses it to explain the way cities throughout the Roman Empire coped with Romanization while still being able to conjure or incorporate elements of their original identities when necessary; see *Rome's Cultural Revolution* (Cambridge: Cambridge University Press, 2008). It is important to note that Wallace-Hadrill does not apply the term Romanization to his understanding of the cultural hybridity of first-century Roman cities because he argues that it fails to recognize the diversity in how Roman and local cultures mixed and the ability of local people's to switch between identities when necessary.

21. J.-S. Balzat and A. J. S. Spawforth, "'Becoming Roman': À Propos de Deux Générations Parentes de Néo-Citoyens Romains À Sparte et À Athènes," in *Onomatologos: Studies in Greek Personal Names Presented to Elaine Matthews* (ed. R. W. V. Catling and F. Marchland; Oxford: Oxford Books, 2010), 183–94; Spawforth, "Roman Corinth," 171–73.

22. Susan Treggiari, *Roman Freedmen during the Late Republic* (Oxford: Oxford University Press, 200), 63–64. More recently, Henrik Mouritsen argues that the allowance for freedman to hold political offices in Julian colonies was not part of a broader shift in Rome but specific allowances as part of resettlement strategies; *The Freedman in the Roman World* (Cambridge: Cambridge University Press, 2011), 74–75.

23. Christian Gizewski, "Duoviri, Duumviri," *Brill's New Pauly: Encyclopedia of the Ancient World* (vol 4; Hubert Cancik and Helmuth Schneider, eds; Leiden: Brill, 2004), 740. The New Testament uses the Greek equivalent στρατηγός for the Latin *duoviri* as seen in Acts 16:22; see BDAG, 947–948.

24. Spawforth, "Roman Corinth," 170.
25. Concannon, *Gentiles*, 56.
26. Clarke, *Secular and Christian Leadership*, 14–16.
27. L. Bonfante Warren, "Roman Costumes: A Glossary and Some Etruscan Derivations," *ANRW* 1 (1973): 390–92; Kelly Olson, "Toga and *pallium*: Status, Sexuality, Identity," in *Sex in Antiquity: Exploring Gender and Sexuality in the Ancient World* (ed. Mark Masterson, Nancy Sorkin Rabinowitz, James Robison; London: Routledge, 2015), 435; Alice T. Christ, "The Masculine Ideal of 'The Race that Wears the Toga,'" *Art* 52 (1997): 24–30. Vergil's comment that the Romans are the "toga-wearing race" hints at the toga's importance for distinguishing Romans from outsiders (*Aen.* 1.282), but variations of the toga also communicated a social grammar that distinguished classes and advertised legal rights and protection. The social grammar communicated by the different colors, stripes, and layering of togas was one of the most public ways for a Roman citizen to display rank. The coordination between toga and rank can be seen in Dio's discussion of the change in togas following the death of Octavia and, later, Augustus as every senator and magistrate donned a toga of their social inferiors (Dio, *Roman History* 56.31.2). Jonathan Edmondson discusses such uses of the toga and the significance for representing the socio-political hierarchy and the meaning of a person changing their dress; "Public Dress and Social Control in Late Republican and Early Imperial Rome," in *Roman Dress and the Fabrics*

of Roman Culture (ed. Jonathan Edmondson and Alison Keith; Toronto: University of Toronto Press, 2008), 21–46.

28. John H. D'Arms, *Commerce and Social Standing in Ancient Rome* (Cambridge; MA: Harvard University Press, 1981). Mouritsen cautions against assigning the label "middle class" to people who participate in the *Augustales* because such people were just as wealthy as those who participated in public offices but lacked some other form of identity necessary to do so; see, *The Freedmen in the Roman World*, 252.

29. Benedikt Eckhardt demonstrates that the evidence from Roman Corinth, like Urso and other Julian colonies, shows Rome placing a significant restriction on voluntary associations, usually referring to Greek *thiasoi* or Roman *collegia*, that do not directly support the civic order; "The Eighteen Associations of Corinth," *GRBS* 56 (2016): 646–62. The *Augustales* are given as an example of the type of association that could thrive in such an environment because of its overt support for the Empire.

30. Laird, "The Emperor in a Roman Town," 72. Larid's analysis strikes a much-needed balance between arguments between the group's cultic and social functions by showing that the group's emphasis varied from city to city and, overall, is more prominent in the western part of the empire. Also see Lily Ross Taylor, "Augustales, Seviri Augustales, and Seviri: A Chronological Study," *TPAPA* 45 (1914): 231–53.

31. Friesen, "The Wrong Erastus," 235.

32. Friesen, "Poverty in Pauline Studies," 323–61.

33. Mary E. Hoskins Walbank, "Image and Cult: The Coinage of Roman Corinth," in *Corinth in Context: Comparative Studies in Religion and Society* (ed. Steven J. Friesen, Daniel N. Schowalter, and James C. Walters; Leiden: Brill, 2010), 154–55.

34. M. Amandry, *Le Monnayage des Duovirs Corinthiens* (Paris: de Boccard, 1988).

35. Walbank, "Image and Cult," esp. 195–97.

36. Angela Ziskowski, "The Bellerophon Myth in Early Corinthian History and Art," *Hesp.* 83 (2014): 81–102. This is all the more surprising since the Bellerophon myth had been surpassed by the monster-killer Herakles.

37. For an overview of the renewal, architectural changes, and cultic activity in Roman Corinth, see Daniel N. Schowalter and Steven J. Friesen, eds., *Urban Religion in Roman Corinth: Interdisciplinary Approaches* (Cambridge; Mass: Harvard University Press, 2005).

38. Wickkiser, "Asklepios in Greek and Roman Corinth," 39–61.

39. Carl Roebuck, *The Asklepieion and Lerna Based on the Excavations and Preliminary Studies of F. J. de Wade* (Princeton: Princeton University Press, 1951), 78–90.

40. Wicckiser, "Asklepios in Greek and Roman Corinth," 52–53.

41. For the reconstruction, positioning, and dating of the monument, see R. L. Scranton, *Medieval Architecture in the Central Area of Corinth* (Princeton: The American School of Classical Studies at Athens, 1957), 148–49. For a discussion of the intersection of the monument's design with the ideology of emperor worship, see Laird, "The Emperor in a Roman Town," 70–71. Greg Woolf, "Becoming Roman, Staying Greek: Culture, Identity, and the Civilizing Process in the Roman East," *PCPS* 40 (1994): 116–43.

42. Laird, "The Emperor in a Roman Town," 93.

43. Friesen and Walters each utilize Urso's charter in their comparative work on Corinth's social and political structures; see Friesen, "The Wrong Erastus," 245–47; James C. Walters, "Paul and the Politics of Meals in Roman Corinth," in *Corinth in Context: Comparative Studies in Religion and Society* (ed. Steven J. Friesen, Daniel N. Schowalter, and James C. Walters; Leiden: Brill, 2010), 343–64. Michael H. Crawford provides the text of the available sections of the charter along with comments on their significance, see *Roman Statutes* (2 vols.; London: Institute of Classical Studies, 1996), 393–454.

44. Walters, "Paul and the Politics of Meals," 348.

45. As discussed in the introduction, Mitchell argues that 1 Corinthians is a piece of deliberative rhetoric with the purpose of overcoming community division and achieving concord. Mitchell's discussion of examples, or παραδείγματα as referenced in the rhetorical handbooks, shows that the use of a notable of figure or leader as an example for the audience to imitate is a commonly used trope in deliberative rhetoric; see *Rhetoric*, 41. For a discussion of Paul's role as that exemplar and its function in 1 Corinthians, see *Rhetoric*, 49–50, 209.

46. Adam G. White, *Where is the Wise Man?: Graeco-Roman Education as a Background to the Division in 1 Corinthians 1–4* (LNTS 536; London: Bloomsbury T&T Clark, 2015). White's work builds on that of Welborn and argues that Paul systematically misperforms the role of the wise man in order to intentionally play the part of a fool; see, *Paul, the Fool of Christ*.

47. 1 Corinthians 1–4 contains eight uses of the imperative mood (1:26, 31; 3:10, 21; 4:1, 5, 16) and two uses of παρακαλέω (1:10, 4:13).

48. As Foucault demonstrates throughout his archaeological investigations, cultural discourses create power and are effective because they are widely accepted and recognizable in a variety of acts. This is part of the rationale behind the power of the panopticon; see *Discipline and Punish: The Birth of the Prison* (trans. Alan Sheridan; 2nd ed.; New York: Vintage Books, 1995), 195–230. The relevant point for the present study as evidenced in the sources reviewed in chapter 2, is that the importance of discourses regulating gender and power might be at the disposal of people of higher status but they are effective because everyone, including people whose lower status prevents their benefiting from such discourses, assumes their veracity. Quintilian's commands on the control of a man's eyebrows, head, shoulders, and voice when he declaims would only be directly applicable to men of status and means who could attempt such an act (*Inst.* 11.3.76–129), but the reason the man would need to take care with his voice is because the audience, including those of lower status, would know if he misperformed (cf., Quintillian's comment on the struggles of performing in the glare of the public). This means that the effects of commands infringing on masculinity and masculine behavior would still be evident even to women, who undoubtedly were in the audience, even though they did not directly pertain to them. The same can be argued for distinctions in class. As discussed above, slaves who would not be able to put the letter "l" on their tombstones would still recognize the significance of such a marking on the tombstone of another.

49. Dio Chrysostom's point is that the type of concessive and reconciliatory behavior he exhorts in order to overcome the στάσις of the community might seem to some to be a feminine course of action, but it is actually the correct way to maintain order and stability in the community, which are essentially masculine categories.

50. In fact, the parallel between Paul and Dio Chyrsostom continues in how both authors question the sufficiency of oratorical training for leadership of a community. This is particularly evident in *Or.* 13, 17–19; see the discussion in White, *Where is the Wise Man?*, 113–15.

51. Βλέπω in 1:26 and 3:10, λογίζομι in 4:1, and κρίνω in 4:5.

52. Theissen is representative of scholars who emphasize that Paul's statement that "not many" of the Corinthians were of high status at the time of their calling to indicate that some must have been of high status; see *The Social Setting of Pauline Christianity*, 70–72. As Friesen notes, such assumptions must still account for the reality of the actual social hierarchy in the Empire, which would have put individuals like Erastus well beyond the sphere of the community; "The Wrong Erastus," 235–36; Joseph L Rife, "Religion and Society at Roman Kenchreai," in *Corinth in Context: Comparative Studies in Religion and Society* (ed. Steven J. Friesen, Daniel N. Schowalter, and James C. Walters; Leiden: Brill, 2010), 424.

53. White, *Where is the Wise Man?*, 71–72.

54. Welborn demonstrates that the language of foolishness is never associated with the cross, as Paul does in 1 Cor 1:18, in earlier Greek literature or the rest of the New Testament; "*Μωρός γένεσθω*: Paul's Appropriation of the Role of the Fool in 1 Corinthians 1–4," *BI* 10 (2002): 420–22.

55. White, *Where is the Wise Man?*, 83–102. Welborn, *Paul, the Fool of Christ*, 34–48, 102–16. Stanley Stowers argues that Paul would have specifically avoided the types of public speaking that might entangle him in such a display of social status; "Social Status, Public Speaking, and Private Teaching: The Circumstances of Paul's Preaching Activity," *NT* 26 (1984): 59–82.

56. White, *Where is the Wise Man?*, 72–76.

57. Roy E. Ciampa and Brian S. Rosner provide a helpful overview of the possibilities for the imagery behind these three vocations; see *The First Letter to the Corinthians* (PNTS; Grand Rapids: Eerdmans, 2010), 94–95. Horsley represents a minority position in resisting the identification of a specific referent behind each vocation; *1 Corinthians*, 48–49. Welborn identifies specific vocations and argues for a particular importance for each within Paul's argument; *Paul, the Fool of Christ*, 177–78.

58. See the overview by Emily A. Hemelrijk which demonstrates that the material evidence indicates some women did receive an education comparable to that of the men who occupy public roles such as the *grammaticus*, but these women were liable to accusations of transgressing the proper role of women if they ever tried to function in such a role. The only widely accepted way for woman to publicly display her education was as an actress, but actresses were already deeply suspect on a number of levels and so could not operate in other public roles; see, "The Education of Women in Ancient Rome," in *A Companion to Ancient Education* (ed. W. Martin Bloomer; Walden, Mass.: Wiley-Blackwell, 2015), 292–305. Rebecca Flemming

reaches a similar conclusion but has a narrower focus on medicine; "Writing and Medicine in the Classical World," *CQ* 57 (2007): 257–79. Nathan J. Barnes argues for a greater number of educated women philosophers in the Roman world than is evident from the extant sources; *Reading 1 Corinthians with Philosophically Educated Women* (Eugene, Or.; Penwick, 2014), 37–121. Barnes's main evidence is that some philosophical schools granted women greater access to education and positions than was traditionally allowed. While the similarity between Paul and some of the philosophical schools means that such could be the case within the Pauline communities, it should be noted that Paul frames the Corinthians' positions against those of the broader culture which would not have allowed women to operate in such positions.

59. Conzelmann, *1 Corinthians*, 43.

60. Welborn, *Paul, the Fool of Christ*, 125. White sees Paul's terminology drawing a clear parallel to Stoic descriptions of the wise man. White surveys evidence from Psuedo-Plutarch, Cassius Dio, and Theon to demonstrate the way that these characteristics function to determine a person's status; *Where is the Wise Man?*, 72–72.

61. Thiselton offers a helpful overview of the comparison between the two lists and emphasizes that the slight change from well-born to the things that are contains a clear connection to high social position; *First Corinthians*, 178–83.

62. Theissen, "Soziale Schichtung in der korinthischen Gemeinde," 233–35.

63. White, *Where is the Wise Man?*, 76.

64. Richard Hays, "Wisdom according to Paul," in *Where Shall Wisdom Be Found?: Wisdom in the Bible, the Church and the Contemporary World* (ed. Stephen C. Barton; Edinburgh: T&T Clark, 1999), 113. The connection between the shame of the cross and its consequences for the bodies associated with it is the focus of Wenhua Shi's *Paul's Message of the Cross as Body Language* (WUNT 254; Tübingen: Mohr Siebeck, 2008).

65. John S. Kloppenborg, "Egalitarianism in the Myth and Rhetoric of Pauline Churches," in *Reimagining Christian Origins: A Colloquium Honouring Burton L. Mack*, (ed. Elizabeth A. Castelli and Hal Taussig; Valley Forge, PA: Trinity Press International, 1996), 255.

66. Emphasis on the importance of social status in Roman legal proceedings can be traced back to J. A. Crook, *Law and Life in Rome: 90 B.C.–A.D. 212* (Ithaca; NY: Cornell University Press, 1967); P. Garnsey, *Social Status and Legal Privilege* (Oxford: Clarendon, 1970); J. M. Kelly, *Roman Litigation* (Oxford: Clarendon, 1966). More recently, Andrew M. Riggsby, *Roman Law and the Legal World of the Romans* (Cambridge: Cambridge University Press, 2010). This work has had a noticeable effect on scholarship on 1 Corinthians by emphasizing the importance of social status and the use of the courts as instruments of social control. Erik explores how the exploitation of such social discrepancies pervade declamations, which were means of practicing oratory and court performances, as Roman men "play and parody . . . the syntax and grammar of Roman identity"; *Declamation, Paternity, and Roman Identity: Authority and the Rhetorical Self* (Cambridge: Cambridge University Press, 2003), 18. Andrew D. Clarke provides a helpful overview and analysis in *Secular and Christian Leadership in Corinth: A Socio-Historical and Exegetical Study of 1 Corinthians 1–6* (New York: Brill, 1993). Bruce W. Winter's "Civil Litigation in Secular Corinth and the Church:

The Forensic Background to 1 Corinthians 6:1–8" (*NTS* 37 [1991]: 559–72) forms a key part of his sociological approach to 1 Corinthians and the problems Paul faced in *After Paul Left Corinth: The Influence of Secular Ethics and Social Change* (Grand Rapids: Eerdmans, 2001), 58–75. Also see John K. Chow, *Patronage and Power: A Study in the Social Networks in Corinth* (JSNTSup 75; Sheffield: JSOT Press, 1992), 123–30; Alan C. Mitchell, "Rich and Poor in the Courts of Corinth: Litigiousness and Status in 1 Corinthians 6.1–11," *NTS* 39 (1993): 562–86; Brent Kinman, "'Appoint the Despised Judges!' (1 Corinthians 6:4)" *TynBul* 48 (1997): 345–54. The distinction between criminal and civil cases runs throughout the aforementioned works but is helpfully applied to the issues in 1 Corinthians by Thiselton, *First Corinthians*, 419–21.

67. Kelly, *Roman Litigation*; 33, 52–61.
68. Garnsey, *Legal Privilege*; 4, 217–34.
69. Clarke, *Secular and Christian Leadership*, 62–63.
70. See the discussion in Bruce W. Frier's *The Rise of the Roman Jurists: Studies in Cicero's "Pro Caecina"* (Princeton: Princeton University Press, 1985), 57–78. Frier shows that legal systems codify the assumptions and practices of a society by passing them through a "screen of legal culture" that determines how such assumptions should be accepted or repudiated within a legal system; *Roman Jurists*, 77. Roman judicial systems were designed to reify the prejudices that reinforced the social hierarchy. So Cicero could simultaneously speak of a judge's faithfulness and impartiality and the need to account for a litigant's social status in rendering a verdict because that was how Roman society organized itself more broadly. Clark, *Secular and Christian Leadership*, 63–64.
71. Michael Peppard argues that fraternal lawsuits and inheritance disputes in Roman legal documents provide a key background for 1 Cor 6:1–11 because of the familial language of ἀδελφός and Paul's fictive kinship where the believing community becomes a family; "Brother against Brother: *Contraversiae* about Inheritance Disputes and 1 Corinthians 6:1–11," *JBL* 133 (2014): 179–92. Peppard's point that such lawsuits almost always involve disputes over inheritance helpfully explains Paul's discussion of inheritance in 1 Cor 6:9–11 that follows the discussion of lawsuits in 1 Cor 6:1–8 as well as the importance of familial bonds in mitigating such disputes. Peppard's examination focuses on brothers in Roman declamation, but he argues that Paul clearly has both men and women of the community in view. Although Peppard does not address the importance of social status in Roman courts or in the passage (cf. 1 Cor 6:4), our examinations each highlight unity as Paul's rhetorical goal.
72. Winter, *After Paul Left Corinth*, 58–64.
73. Clarke, *Secular and Christian Leadership*, 60–62.
74. Garnsey, *Social Status and Legal Privilege*, 182.
75. Crook, *Roman Life and Law*, 90.
76. During the Republic, the role of advocate fell under the patronal obligations an elite citizen owed to those under his care. Starting in the second century B.C.E. and then developing more quickly during the Principate, a professional legal class of jurists developed which did not necessarily require the practitioner to hail from a high status and provided an opportunity for those with rhetorical ability to advance their status; see Riggsby, *Roman Law*, 51–54.

77. Crook, *Roman Life and Law*, 79.

78. Winter, *After Paul Left Corinth*, 60.

79. Leanna Bablitz, *Actors and Audience in the Roman Courtroom* (London and New York: Routledge, 2007), 82.

80. One of the most notable instances of a women speaking publicly in an official capacity is Hortensia, who represented a group of elite women against taxation following Caesar's death. Quintilian remarks that her performance of such eloquence that it was written down and preserved for others to imitate (*Inst.* 1.1.6). As remarkable as this example is, Hortensia was not acting within an official court proceeding and so does not show a favorable assessment of a woman function in a Roman court.

81. Matthew J. Perry, "Defining Gender" in *The Oxford Handbook of Roman Law and Society* (ed. Paul J. Du Plessis, Clifford Ando, Kaius Tuori; Oxford: Oxford University Press, 2016), 432–42.

82. Jane F. Gardner, *Women in Roman Law and Society* (Bloomington, Ind.: Indiana University Press, 1986), 263–64.

83. See the discussion in Anthony Corbeill, *Nature Embodied: Gesture in Ancient Rome* (Princeton: Princeton University Press, 2004), 116–17. Crassus further exhibits the potency of his masculinity by gaining self-control and mastery over those aspects of his identity, such as his passion, that could potentially undermine his masculinity (Cicero, *De. or.* 1.58–60).

84. Jon Hall notes that the intersection of masculinity and public performance, especially in oratorical displays such as those of a court room, manifest "[c]oncerns with masculinity [as part of] a wider concern with the orator's ability to function as a leading member of the civic community"; "Oratorical Delivery and the Emotions: Theory and Practice," in *A Companion to Roman Rhetoric* (ed. William Dominik and Jon Hall; Malden; MA: Blackwell, 2007), 228–30.

85. Mitchell, *Rhetoric of Reconciliation*; 25–38, 117–18.

86. Benjamin Edsall, "When Cicero and St Paul Agree," 30–34. David G. Horrell, *The Social Ethos of the Corinthian Correspondence: Interests and Ideology from 1 Corinthians to 1 Clement* (Edinburgh: T&T Clark International, 1996), 110.

87. Ibid., 31–34; Horrell, *Social Ethos of the Corinthian Correspondence*, 141.

88. Catherine Edwards, "Unspeakable Professions: Public Performance and Prostitution in Ancient Rome," *Roman Sexualities* (ed. Judith P. Hallett and Marilyn B. Skinner; Princeton: Princeton University Press, 1997), 74–75.

89. Paul also notes that the mere fact that there are disputes within the community already indicates a serious problem (1 Cor 6:7), but that is a slight at their lack of unity without a specified course of action. This disunity, then, fits broadly under the critique and solutions for factious behavior found throughout the letter and discussed above in relation to 1 Cor 1–4.

90. Mitchell, *Rhetoric Reconciliation*, 60–64.

91. The replication of Roman social patterns and the power dynamics they create seems to have happened in Corinth in the celebration of the Lord's Table; see, Rachel M. McRae, "Eating with Honor: The Corinthian Lord's Supper in Light of Voluntary Associations Meal Practices," *JBL* 130 (2011): 165–81. Richard S. Ascough, "What Are They *Now* Saying about Christ Groups and Associations," *CBR* 13 (2014): 207–44.

92. My work on καθίζω is indebted to Brent Kinman's article "'Appoint the Despised as Judges!' (1 Corinthians 6:4)," *TB* 48 (1997): 345–54. J. D. M. Derret makes a similar argument for the reading καθίζετε in the imperative rather than the indicative mood, but offers less detail than Kinman. In my opinion, Kinman's argument, especially in light of the more recent work on the social context of the letter, has not been given sufficient attention. Recent commentaries often note the strengths of Kinman's argument but ultimately rule against it in favor of reading καθίζετε as an interrogative because they assume Paul would not refer to believers as those despised persons (τοὺς ἐξουθενημένους); see Thiselton; *First Corinthians*, 431–33; Craig S. Keener, *1–2 Corinthians*, 51–54; Fitzmyer, *First Corinthians*, 252–53; Fee, *First Epistle to the Corinthians*, 258–60. On the other hand, Ciampa and Rosner appear to be persuaded by Kinman and so read it as a command but take it as ironic because of improbability of actually meaning such as pejorative description to refer to believers; *First Letter to the Corinthians*, 229–30. David E. Garland follows Kinman's argument and emphasizes how it addresses the social factionalism affecting the Corinthians; *First Corinthians* (PNTC; Grand Rapids: Baker Academic, 2003), 204–08. Dutch's work on the influence of elite social status in creating factions in the in community also follows Kinman; *Educated Elite*, 32–33. Horrell, drawing on Derret's work, notes that such an interpretation has important parallel with the "implied reversal of social roles and resonance of God's choice of τὰ ἐξουθενημένα" but concludes that such an interpretation is not "entirely convincing;" *Social Ethos of the Corinthian Correspondence*, 139. Kinman points to the review of sources from the second through the sixteenth century as found in H.A.W. Meyer's *Handbuch über den ersten Brief an die Korinther* (KEKNT; 6th ed.; Göttingen: Vandenhoeck und Ruprecht, 1881), 150–51.

93. The lack of punctuation in the earliest Greek manuscripts of 1 Corinthians means that the semicolon indicating an interrogative as found in NA28 and UBS5 are part of the scholarly interpretation of the passage. The lack of grammatical marking and ambiguous morphology also produces ambiguity in verses 6 and 8. The structure appears to indicate a parallelism, but NA28 and punctuates verse 6 as a question and verse 8 as a statement. See the discussion in Edsall, "When Cicero and St. Paul Agree: Intra-Group Litigation among the *Luperci* and the Corinthian Believers," *JTS* 46 (2013): 28.

94. For example, Fee, *First Corinthians*, 225.

95. Examples in the rest of the Pauline corpus can be found in: Rom 12:14; Gal 5:1; Phil 4:4; 1 Thess 5:22; Phlm 8.

96. Kinman, "'Appoint the Despised as Judges!'" 348–50. Fee also appeals to the fact that the introduction of an imperative would interrupt the rhetorical flow of the what has been a series of rhetorical questions that began in 6:1 but cites no evidence for what constitutes a style or a pattern other than his own opinion; *First Corinthians*, 258–59. Edsall's work does not bother to engage morphology or syntax but moves directly to the rhetorical impact of either reading; "When Cicero and St Paul Agree."

97. Ibid., 350–51. This point is held by almost all commentators regardless of their treatment of καθίζετε, which requires them to treat it as an interrogative with an ironic sense; see footnote 69 in the current chapter.

98. Thiselton outlines the Jewish background for establishing a means of administering judgment in civil matters that extends from the wilderness generations in Exod 18:13–26 through the first century as seen in institutions like the Sanhedrin; see Hugo Mantel, *Studies in the History of the Sanhedrin* (Cambridge: Harvard University Press, 1961), 54–101. Greek and Roman sources also advise groups to handle civil matters internally without going to those outside the community. Philostratus reports that this is Polemo's advice for handling matters related to money and certain other infractions; *Vit. soph.* 532.

99. Mitchell, *Rhetoric of Reconciliation*, 118–21.

100. Edsall, "When Cicero and Paul Agree," 28.

101. Horrell, *Social Ethos of the Corinthian Correspondence*, 141.

102. Catherine Edwards argues that the true test of a judge is that he adheres to the rules and precedents by which he judges others; *The Politics of Immorality in Ancient Rome* (Cambridge: Cambridge University Press, 1993), 164–65. Welborn's discussion of the image of the fool in political invective discusses such charges; *Paul, The Fool of Christ*, 34–47.

103. Horrell, *Social Ethos of the Corinthian Correspondence*, 140.

104. Thiselton offers a helpful overview of the issues surrounding the translation of εἰδωλόθυτος, ultimately demonstrating that while a focus on food in general is possible Paul's focus is on meat involved in cultic activities; *First Corinthians*, 617–20.

105. Derek Newton, *Deity and Diet: The Dilemma of Sacrificial Food at Corinth* (JSNTSup., 169; Sheffield: Sheffield Academic Press, 1998).

106. Alex T. Cheung, *Idol Food in Corinth: Jewish Background and Pauline Legacy* (JSNTSup., 176; Sheffield: Sheffield Academic Press, 1999). Thiselton agrees that 8:1–11:1 form a cohesive argument built around the need to forgo personal rights for the sake of others in the community; *First Corinthians*, 607–12. Thiselton's work builds upon that of Mitchell, who shows that many of the images and examples that Paul offers are often associated with deliberative rhetoric that aims to promote concord within a community; *The Rhetoric of Reconciliation*, 126–49. Eriksson demonstrates that the use of traditions such as that seen in Paul's use of the wilderness generation fit such a rhetorical pattern; *Traditions as Rhetorical Proof: Paul's Argumentation in 1 Cor* (ConBNT; Stockholm: Almqvist & Wiksell, 1998). Such nuanced understandings of the complex use of rhetoric and imagery within a single type of rhetoric further support the work of Schrage who argues that Paul's personal example of the renunciation of his rights for the sake of others provides the background to understand what Paul has in mind when he commands his audience to imitate him (1 Cor 11:1) and how such a command functions as an antidote for factionalism; *Der erste Breif an die Korinther* (EKKNT 7/2; Neukirchen-Vluyn: Neukirchener, 1995), 211–486. Although much of this work confirms Theissen's sociological approach to the issues affecting the Corinthian believers, more specifically anchoring the argument in the dynamics of that society will undermine Theissen's argument for a Liebspatriachalismus; *Social Setting*, 107–10. This critique of Theissen's more conservative approach to Paul's commands and social critique follows that of scholars like Horrell who emphasizes the "strenuous demands upon the socially prominent members of the churches, urging them to imitate him in costly self-lowering for the

sake of others, so that the community may be united"; *An Introduction to the Study of Paul* (2nd ed; London: T&T Clark, 2006), 111. Elsewhere, Horrell argues that Theissen's model does fit later writings like 1 Clement which leaves the social structure of patriarchy intact while seeking to soften the discord between groups; *The Social Ethos of the Corinthian Correspondence*, 261–65. Although I think that Horrell correctly articulates the social and class issues that are at stake, his comments on the accessibility of meat reflect scholarly assumptions that have since been corrected; For Horrell's perspective on the scarcity of meat see, *Corinthian Correspondance*, 105-06. J. J. Meggitt, *Paul, Poverty and Survival* (Edinburgh: T&T Clark, 1998). For Theissen's response, "Social Conflicts in the Corinthian Community: Further Remarks on J. J. Meggitt's *Paul, Poverty, and Survival*," *JSNT* 25 (2003): 371–91. I address the issues of food, social hierarchy, and Paul's commands to conform in further detail, below.

107. Kathleen Corley demonstrates how women and meals presented in the New Testament, primarily in the Synoptic Gospels, reflect the changing social customs of the first century where women, especially those of higher status, were becoming more acceptable in public spaces (e.g., at meals served in the homes besides one's own); see, *Private Women, Public Meals: Social Conflict in the Synoptic Tradition* (Peabody; Mass.: Hendrickson, 1993). Although women begin to appear in public spaces like dinner parties (e.g., Horace *Odes* 3.6; Cicero *Att.* 2.3, 12; and Suet. *Aug.* 69.1), there are still limits on their behavior, such as displays of knowledge in literature and culture which were traditionally reserved for men (Juvenal, *Sat.* 6; Sallust, *Cat.* 24.3–25.5; Tacitus, *Ann.* 13.45; such behavior was in contrast to the reserved learning that supported the husband which is praised by Pliny in *Ep.* 4.19).

108. See the discussion in Kathy Ehrensperger, "To Eat or Not to Eat—Is This the Question? Table Disputes in Corinth," in *Decisive Meals: Table Politics in Biblical Literature* (*LNTS* 449; ed. Nathan MacDonald, Kathy Ehrensperger, Luzia Sutter Rehmann; New York: T&T Clark, 2012), 114–33.

109. Mitchell, *Rhetoric of Reconciliation*, 138–40.

110. David J. Downs offers a helpful analysis of the possible financial entanglements that arise because of Paul's collection for Jerusalem and the possibility of his own financial payments from his churches raising the suspicion of patronage; see *The Offering of the Gentiles: Paul's Collection for Jerusalem in Its Chronological, Cultural, and Cultic Contexts* (WUNT 2/248; Tübingen: Mohr Siebeck, 2008), 42–52. Peter Marshall also understands Paul's apparent inconsistency in accepting money from his communities arising from the possible manipulation of such financial gifts; see *Enmity in Corinth: Social Conventions in Paul's Relationship with the Corinthians* (WUNT 2/23; Tübingen: Mohr Siebeck, 1987), 214.

111. Paul's use of the imagery of slavery is often noted but, likely because of its recurrence throughout his writings and the spiritualizing of such language by commentators, their radical meaning is seldom understood. For example, Martial transforms the toga into a symbol of slavery in order to highlight the shameful and humiliating service required by the wearer (e.g., Martial, *Ep.* 3.46.1), and Juvenal describes a removal from this social enslavement as being able to "escape the toga" (*Sat.* 11.200–204); see Michele George, "The 'Dark Side' of the Toga," in *Roman Dress and the Fabrics of Roman Culture* (ed. Jonathan Edmondson and Alison Keith; Toronto: Toronto

University Press, 2008), 94–112. Such a connection between slavery, servitude, and humiliation should not be overlooked in Paul's language as he transforms the image of the figure whom the community should imitate into that of a slave.

112. Horrell notes the absence of the corresponding term of strength or strong; *The Social Ethos of the Corinthian Correspondence*, 209. Although the discussions are not exactly parallel, the discourse about food and special days in Romans 14–15 makes a similar use of weakness associated with a particular set of beliefs without a corresponding discussion of strength as the opposite of such beliefs. In that discussion, Paul seems to more clearly argue that strength is adaptability to the needs of others not holding a particular set of beliefs. Gaventa argues for this reading of Romans 14:1–15:6; see "Reading for the Subject: The Paradox of Power in Romans 14:1–15:6," in *JTI* 5 (2011): 1–12.

113. Thiselton, *First Corinthians*, 795–97.

114. Horrell makes a similar point about the detrimental effects of Paul's commands on those who consider themselves strong but does not trace this through the language of masculinity or gender; *The Social Ethos of the Corinthian Correspondence*, 208.

115. Mitchell, *Rhetoric of Reconciliation*, 145.

116. It is important to note that Plutarch does not leave this advice in the abstract but demonstrates that when these states begin to seek their own advantage rather than remain as a unified whole they eventually succumb and lose their independence. The inclusion of the imagery of different parts of a body and growth lends credence to Mitchell's argument about such imagery functioning as stock language within homonoia speeches helps explain the convergence and purpose of such imagery in 1 Corinthians, lending support to the necessity to understand Paul's discussion as a means to achieve unity rather than an exposition on the topic of idols or food sacrificed to them.

117. Ibid., 4.26.2–3.

118. This relationship is codified in Roman law by protecting the wife from too much abuse by her husband but also punishes a husband for failing to keep his wife in her proper place; Grubbs, *Women and the Law in the Roman Empire*, 24–59.

119. At times Plutarch cautions both husbands and wives to take equal care so as not to provoke their spouse; *Conj. praec.* 44–45. Overall, however, Plutarch's commands evidence the type of patriarchal system found throughout Greek and Roman cultures and discussed throughout the present volume that assumes that women cannot be expected to exercise self-control and so need to be controlled by men (e.g., *Conj. praec.* 48). This analysis follows that of Pieter J. J. Botha, who cautions against reading comments, like those of Plutarch's, that could indicate equality between the sexes outside of the broader patriarchal systems that are still evident in such texts; see, "Submission and Violence: Exploring Gender Relations in the First-century World," *Neot* 34 (2000): 1–38.

120. Originally expressed as Liebespatriarchalismus and incorporated throughout Theissen's later work. Theissen first used the term in "Wanderradikalismus. Literatursoziologische Aspekte der Überlieferung von Worten Jesu im Urchristentum," in *ZTK* 70 (1973): 269. Theissen cites Ernst Troeltsch, who made a broader argument

that the Christian tradition broadly expresses a patriarchy which is for the benefit and protection of the community; see *Die Soziallehren der christlichen Kirchen und Gruppen* (Tübingen: Mohr, 1912), 67–83.

121. Erik Gunderson, *Staging Masculinity: The Rhetoric of Performance in the Roman World* (Ann Arbor: University of Michigan Press, 2000), 117–35. Amy Richlin, "Gender and Rhetoric: Producing Manhood in the Schools," in *Roman Eloquence: Rhetoric in Society and Literature* (ed. William J. Dominik; London: Routledge, 1997), 90–110.

122. Anthony Corbeill, "Dining Deviants in Roman Political Invective," in *Roman Sexualities* (ed. Judith P. Hallett and Marilyn B. Skinner; Princeton: Princeton University Press, 1997), 99–128.

123. Catherine Edwards, *The Politics of Immorality*, 80–81.

124. It is important to note that these commands appear to assume that husband and wife are both part of the believing community. Such a conclusion is reasonable based on the otherwise inconsistent commands that Paul gives when either the husband or wife is not part of the community (cf. 1 Cor 7:12–16). See the discussion in Fee, *First Corinthians*, 297.

125. Although assigning more agency to women than many of his contemporaries, Plutarch still assumes that the husband, through his behavior and status, will set the tone that others in the household will follow. For example, Plutarch cautions the husband that his wife will not "refrain from immoderate display and extravagance if she sees that you do not despise these things" (*Conj. praec.* 48). Suzanne Dixon correctly cautions against anachronistic or reductionist reading of Greek and Roman marriages that paint the wife as either sexual feminist or victim, depending on which modern assumptions and ancient background are used; "Sex and the Married Woman in Ancient Rome," in *Early Christian Families in Context: An Interdisciplinary Dialogue* (ed. David L. Balch and Carolyn Osiek; Grand Rapids: Eerdmans, 2003), 111–15.

126. Tacitus's depiction of Messalina is a prominent account of the use of sexual domination of a husband by his wife as an indication of or reason for the husband's loss of masculinity (*Ann.* 11). Juvenal makes a broader charge regarding the degrading of Roman morality and society connected with the sexual domination of women over men (*Sat.* 2, 6).

127. Sandra R. Joshel, "Female Desire and the Discourse of Empire: Tacitus's Messalina," *Signs* 21 (1995): 50–82.

128. For a discussion of Paul's reference to the command as a saying from Jesus, see Fee, *First Corinthians*, 323–24. The use of two distinct words for the action of divorce appears to simply be alteration for style rather than any specific meaning; see Valentine, *For You Were Bought with a Price*, 233–34.

129. Treatments of Paul's argument here tend to favor either a Jewish or Roman background for the commands on divorce. For a helpful overview of the secondary literature, see Raymond F. Collins, "Divorce in the New Testament," *Bib* 75 (1994): 590–93. For a treatment that deals with Paul's and Jesus's commands on divorce almost exclusively from a Jewish perspective, see David Instone-Brewer, *Divorce and Remarriage in the Bible: The Social and Literary Context* (Grand Rapids: Eerdmans, 2002). More recently, scholars have noted that the distinctiveness of Jewish marriage

that marks the *halakha* of the Rabbinic texts is far less pronounced in first-century and earlier Jewish texts; see Susan Marks, *First Came Marriage: The Rabbinic Appropriation of Early Jewish Wedding Ritual* (Princeton: Gorgias Press, 2013); Ross S. Kraemer demonstrates that the Rabbinic scorn on the divorce of these Herodian women does not indicate that their divorce shows they were operating outside of Judaism but that some streams within the Judaism of the first century allowed divorce, "Typical and Atypical Jewish Family Dynamics: The Cases of Babatha and Berenice," in *Early Christian Families in Context* (ed. David Balch and Carolyn Osiek; Grand Rapids: Eerdmans, 2003). The result has been for scholars to emphasize the similarities in Jewish and Roman marriages, especially in regulating the wife's body and sexuality; see Michael Satlow, *Jewish Marriage in Antiquity* (Princeton: Princeton University Press, 2001).

130. Susan Treggiari, *Roman Marriage: Iusti Coniugus from the Time of Cicero to the Time of Ulpian* (Oxford: Clarendon Press, 1991), 441–46; Judith Evans Grubbs, *Women and the Law in the Roman Empire: A Sourcebook on Marriage, Divorce, and Widowhood* (London: Routledge, 2002), 195–210. Grubbs notes that the regulations of divorce became more restrictive during the Principate except in matters of consensual divorce, which was not regulated until the sixth century; *Woman and the Law*, 202-03.

131. In the conclusion to this volume I will show that this line of thinking is the same trajectory that is at work in Paul's commands regarding head coverings in 1 Cor 11:2–16.

132. Although some scholars point to Paul's reference of the "coming distress" as the reason for his commands regarding marriage, the primary concern is avoiding sexual immorality through the exercise of self-control. Winter argues that the grain famines which struck Corinth and much of the Empire around 51 C.E. is the referent behind Paul's warning; *After Paul Left Corinth*, 215–25. Winter's presentation is persuasive on many points, especially that of the timing of a devastating grain famine, the literary evidence for how such a famine plunged a city into riots and chaos, and the epigraphic evidence for how Corinth handled such famines. My issue with Winter's approach is that he takes what is a secondary point and makes it Paul's main motivation. The effect is that, while acknowledging the radical nature of Paul assigning sexual agency and control to women, Winter misses the way that such a command would reshape the community's social and political experiences in the present so as to create the type of social harmony and care that are the goals of the argument of 1 Corinthians.

133. Valentine, *'For You Were Bought with a Price,'* 124–37.

134. Weima, *Neglected Endings*, 238.

135. I agree with Jeffery A. D. Weima that the epistolary closing begins at 16:13 because of the final use of περί δὲ in 16:12 and the fact that the material in 16:13–24 summarizes the main argument of 1 Corinthians and includes salutations reminiscent of other endings in Paul's letters; see, *Neglected Endings: The Significance of the Pauline Letter Closings* (*JSNT* 101; Sheffield: JSOT Press, 1994), 201–2.

136. Mitchell, *Rhetoric of Reconciliation*, 179. Mitchell is followed by Eriksson, who further nuances her argument, especially showing the function of Paul's final salutation in 16:21–24; see, *Traditions as Rhetorical Proof*, 279–98.

137. William Klassen, "The Sacred Kiss in the New Testament: An Example of Social Boundary Lines," *NTS* 39 (1993): 122–35. Michael Philip Penn further develops Klassen's analysis and also provides a helpful discussion that dispels the often-repeated assertion that such kissing was often seen by outsiders as sexually licentious; *Kissing Christians: Ritual and Community in Late Antiquity* (Philadelphia: University of Philadelphia Press, 2005), 26–56, 104–7.

138. Elizabeth Schüssler Fiorenza argues a similar point about 1 Corinthians and the way that the rhetorical situation in Corinth shapes Paul's response both in terms of content and form; "Rhetorical Situation and Historical Reconstruction in 1 Corinthians," *NTS* 33 (1987): 386–403. A main difference between my analysis and that of Schüssler Fiorenza is that, while we agree that Paul argues for subordination, I have shown that Paul's commands more narrowly focus on the subordination of some men to others in the community rather than establishing the type of patriarchal model that Schüssler Fiorenza argues is Paul's goal. It is interesting that we agree that Paul's gospel required those of higher social status to relinquish power and privilege and to embrace powerlessness; "Rhetorical Situation," 399–400.

139. Thiselton, *First Corinthians*, 1336.

140. For example, see my discussion of infants and milk in chapter 4.

141. BDAG lists several words where the ἀνδρ- stem appears to result from crasis and elision between ἀνήρ (man) and another word, e.g., ἀνήρ + φόνος = ἀνδροφόνος (man killer or murderer). See BDAG 76.

142. William D. Barry, "Roof Tiles and Urban Violence in the Ancient World" *GRBS* 37 (1996): 55–75.

143. Such a use of ἀνδρίζομαι is seen in Dio Cassius's account of Marcus developing (ἀνδρίζεσθαι) from a weak body to powerful one (*Rom. Hist.* 72.2). Later, Dio Cassius will use it in connection with ruling over the Gauls (*Rom. Hist.* 7.26). Lucian uses it in connection with a powerful display of oratorical skill (*Eunuch.* 13). Plutarch uses it to describe a display of character that evidences masculinity even if a person otherwise appears weak (*Stoic. rep.* 27). Josephus uses it to describe Tacitus's men proving their masculinity in battle (*J.W.* 5.3). As discussed in the previous note, each case under discussion has a direct relationship to the construction of masculinity that I have demonstrated throughout this volume. To grow up, develop the body, evidence oratorical skill, virtue, and courage in battle were all hallmarks of what it meant to be masculine.

144. Frederick Ivarsson, "Vice Lists and Deviant Masculinity: The Rhetorical Function of 1 Corinthians 5:10–11 and 6:9–10)," in *Mapping Gender in Ancient Religious Discourse* (ed. Todd Penner and Caroline Vander Stichele; Leiden: Brill, 2007), 171–72.

Chapter Six

Summary and Test of the Argument

This final chapter will serve two functions. First, I will offer a summary of the argument. Since the project covers a wide range of texts, theories, and addresses a selection of passages from 1 Corinthians, it is helpful to step back and review the project as a whole so as to remember how and why those passages were selected and how gender and power intersect within them. Second, I will then offer an interpretive test of Paul's commands regarding head coverings in 1 Cor 11:2–16. I refer to this as an interpretive test because I assume that Paul argues for a subordinate masculinity. Under the guidance of this assumption, I examine key texts that inform an understanding of the use of head coverings in an urban Roman environment during the first century. The result is a reading of one of most beguiling passages in the Pauline corpus that counters the use of this passage to dominate women and that coheres with Paul's empowerment of women as seen in 1 Cor 7:2–11. It is my hope that such an interpretive test serves not as a conclusion but as an invitation to see the potential of subordinate masculinity to confront kyriarchal readings of Pauline literature, both in 1 Corinthians and beyond.[1]

SUMMARY OF THE ARGUMENT

In the first chapter, I propose an excavation of Paul's body and its function in 1 Corinthians with specific attention to the connection between power and gender. As the length and breadth of the current volume attest, such an excavation is no easy task. It first requires asking about the study of bodies, specifically their gender and how that gender is perceived and functions within a specific context. In the second chapter, I trace the development of masculinity studies and how it makes visible the all-too-often-invisible patriarchal norms that structure many societies, both ancient and modern. My work in that chapter then applies this gender critical lens to demonstrate the connections among gender, power, and the body in the late Roman Republic and early Principate. The texts surveyed demonstrate the clear and inextricable linkage of masculinity and power. Questions about one's masculinity were also questions about one's power and status, and people developed precise rubrics for analyzing one's masculinity. How a man walked or scratched his head, conducted himself in public debate, or exercised could determine whether he was masculine enough to be recognized, both socially and legally, as a man. Masculinity was not connected to everything, but it was connected to most things. As a result, understanding the social effects of Paul's commands requires accounting for their intersection with the norms of masculine identity by which the men in his audience would be judged.

The third chapter develops a more nuanced approach to the relationship of masculinity and power by distinguishing hegemonic, complicit, and subordinate masculinity as three distinct types of masculinity. Hegemonic masculinity refers to those ideal men who best embody the discourses of masculinity and, consequently, have more access to power. Complicit masculinity refers to those men who fail to embody the ideal but, nevertheless, still benefit from the patriarchal power structure. Subordinate masculinity refers to those men who not only fail to embody masculine discourses, but also violate those discourses to the point of problematizing their status as men. Finally, I use a gender critical analysis to demonstrate the application of such categories in the writings of Favorinus, Philo, and Josephus. Each author struggles to address aspects of their own or their community's identity that could problematize their masculinity. These authors show an awareness of the importance of masculinity for social status, the connection between gender and power that I outline in the second chapter, and the rhetorical flexibility of gendered discourses within a specific text. Favorinus addresses what should be a fatal flaw in his masculinity, the fact that he is a congenital eunuch, and positions himself as a truly hegemonic man whom the Corinthians should imitate and honor. In contrast, Josephus and Philo each argue that the majority of Jewish men should be understood as complicit men, not so masculine as to challenge Roman control but not so unmanly as to require oppressive rule. This chapter further develops the connection between gender, power, and the body in texts written by authors who are near contemporaries to Paul and demonstrates the viability of my proposal on the use of masculinity for rhetorical effect within a text.

In the next two chapters, I apply my gender critical analysis to 1 Corinthians. In chapter 4 I demonstrate that Greek and Latin authors not only took great care in crafting their authorial personas, but that these constructions often intersect with concerns about masculinity as the author seeks to wield authority over an audience. I then argue that Paul's self-presentation throughout 1 Corinthians evidences the same concern as Paul constructs his authorial persona and repeatedly presents himself as a figure to be imitated. The surprising part of Paul's self-presentation is not that it engages discourses of masculinity but that it consistently fails to embody the ideal position in these discourses. He is a man who cannot speak well, a woman who nurses a child, a father who brings shame on his children, and a celibate man. Such a man would necessarily take a subordinate position and, as a result, be excluded from institutions and positions that were reserved for men. Such a failure, I argue, is not a mistake by or shortcoming of Paul but a direct result of his understanding of the gospel and his own imitation of Christ. From Paul's perspective, institutions of patriarchy represent oppressive structures of the present age and not representative of the way the people of God are to live.

Chapter 5 analyzes commands in Paul's paraenesis that have a clear or implicit relation to gender. In these commands, in continuity with Paul's self-presentation, Paul directs the men in his audience to misperform discourses of masculinity. They are to be fools not dominant orators, not to take advantage of status in Roman courts but appoint lower-status men to arbitrate disputes, to submit their bodies to their wives, and to conform to the dining practices of the weak. The point of such practices is to prevent the factionalism that threatens to tear apart Paul's audience by ending practices that create and sustain the competition for power and status that were rampant in Roman Corinth. Paul crafts a specific masculine identity that he knows will subvert the type of status and power games that were the norm in urban Roman contexts. Paul's goal is the unity of the believing community. In order to achieve this unity, Paul directly challenges systems that value some members of the community over others by calling those members of the community that could benefit from such systems to intentionally embody identities that identify them with lower-status members of the community. Because of the pervasive linkage of power and masculinity, addressing such discrepancies in power requires Paul to address the masculinity to which the men in the community aspire.

The implications of my research and argument are far reaching. To understand Paul's writing not only requires setting the language within its socio-linguistic context but understanding the social effects of his rhetoric and argument. This means that to understand what Paul says to or about men and women must be understood within the cultural discourses that inform not only how Paul understands those bodies but how such actions could be understood by others. As I demonstrate, focusing on the effects of Paul's commands evidences a consistent understanding of the type of community he wants his audience to create. His goal is not to stop the Corinthian men from using public oratory to compete with each other or abusing the judicial system. Rather, his goal is to create a community where those with power do not abuse and, in fact, willingly abnegate such power for the sake of those that their society oppresses. Public oratory and the use of the judicial system are simply means to that end. Such a community imitates, or takes the cruciform shape of, Christ whose weakness is a display of strength and whose apparent defeat on the cross is actually his victory over the rulers of this world. The commands, images, and argument are all in service of shaping a cruciform community that lives in the light of such a victory. To understand Paul's discussion of wisdom, the use of the judicial system, marriage, dining practices, and any other detail within his writing requires attending to the way it facilities this goal. Said more bluntly, there are no discrete theological statements in Paul's writing, only contextual arguments that serve a theological goal.

INTERPRETIVE EXPLORATION: UNDERSTANDING PAUL'S COMMANDS ON HEAD COVERINGS IN LIGHT OF THE CURRENT PROJECT

Some readers might wonder how an examination on gender and power in 1 Corinthians could fail to engage Paul's discussion of head coverings found in 1 Cor 11:2–16. I have thus far avoided commenting on the passage because, as stated by Jouette M. Bassler, "Paul's comments in these verses are as obscure as any he makes, though his basic point is clear: women who prophesy and pray during congregational meetings must wear veils."[2] Although Paul's commands to men and women appear obvious enough, the lack of clarity about what practices or context Paul has in view makes the interpretation of these commands dependent on the reader's broader understanding of 1 Corinthians. What I propose here is to analyze the commands regarding head coverings in light of my broader argument to see what interpretive possibilities emerge. I will not attempt to solve every textual or logical puzzle in the text or discuss them in detail,[3] but, by focusing on the Paul's desired outcome for which bodies wear what, I will argue that gender and power intersect in this passage in ways that limit the use and abuse of hierarchies by those who would most obviously benefit from such uneven distributions of power. As I have demonstrated, such a move would be consistent with Paul's commands elsewhere in 1 Corinthians and support my argument about the importance and function of subordinate masculinity in the rhetoric and function of 1 Corinthians. To accomplish this, I will review the possible settings which might help make sense of the Corinthian believers' use of veils, discuss the two main discourses that Paul applies to substantiate his commands, and show that the implications of the commands regarding head coverings are commensurate with Paul's emphasis on a subordinate masculinity demonstrated elsewhere in the argument.

The first and most important point that must be established before attempting to make sense of this passage is the function of veils in a first-century Roman context and what Paul's comments indicate about the setting for his commands.[4] Although most treatments of the passage make this point, few of these treatments acknowledge the semiotic potency of veils and the various ways they function depending on the context and the body who wore or abstained from wearing them.[5] Before addressing the changing meanings of a veil across different settings, it is first important to understand how important veils were for displaying identity. For example, in some Roman contexts, a woman wearing a veil could be associated with modesty (*pudicitia*), especially in public, where she might come under the gaze of men who were not part of her household.[6] Such modesty had specific legal and social ramifications for women and the people who interacted with them. Roman legislation understood a woman who wore a veil in public as a matron and, consequently, punished men who slept with or propositioned them more harshly than if the woman was not wearing a veil (*Digest* 47.10.15.15; cf. 9.9.20).[7] Lucian, writing to a second-century C.E. audience, explains the absence of a head covering on a statue of a woman, an artistic lacuna that would be a violation of social protocol at the time he writes, as resulting from the use of techniques and styles from the fifth century B.C.E. (*Imag.* 6). The veil, or lack thereof, communicated something about the status of the person that affected social and legal standing.

There is also evidence that Roman men could publicly wear their togas in a fashion that would be considered a veil or head covering. The shift to understand the importance of male behavior in relation to Paul's commands about veils has been noted by some, but has yet to be broadly incorporated into interpretations of the passage or how such a move supports Paul's argument for concord. Ben Witherington, building on the work of Richard Oster, argues that men's use of veils are just as much in Paul's view and concludes that Paul's commands on the use of veils produces equality between men and women.[8] Although I agree with much of Witherington's analysis, there is a lacuna in his argument because, as I will show, Paul cannot simply argue for equality between men and women in this particular setting because he gives the marker of authority, i.e., status, only to women. In other words, Paul intentionally creates an inequality where the women have more power than the men. But I am getting ahead of myself. Before more fully integrating Paul's commands into his argument for concord, I need to review the evidence for men wearing veils in both religious and public settings. Plutarch is worth quoting at length since he not only addresses the issue of male head covering but does so in a way that indicates the reasoning behind the practice.

> Why is it that when [men] worship the gods, they cover their heads, but when they meet any of their fellow-men worthy of honour, if they happen to have the toga over the head, they uncover? ... But if there is anything else to be said, consider whether it be not true that there is only one matter that needs investigation: why men cover their heads when they worship the gods; and the other follows from this. For they uncover their heads in the presence of men more influential than they: it is not to invest these men with additional honour, but rather to avert from them the jealousy of the gods, that these men may not seem to demand the same honours as the gods, nor to tolerate an attention like that bestowed on the gods, nor to rejoice therein. (Plutarch, *Quaest. rom.* 266, trans. Babbitt)

First, it appears that it is possible for men to appear in public with their heads covered, though not required. Second, Plutarch's comments indicate that the rules for covering and uncovering one's head are not determined by factors of honor and social status, although these issues are present, but by maintaining the appropriate hierarchy within the cosmic order. If a man meets another man who is his social superior and *keeps* his head covered, then he would signal his subordinate position to the other man in a way that Plutarch indicates was reserved specifically for the gods, a point to which I will return below. So even in a public setting, what men have or do not have on their head is determined by deference to the gods. Yet even though Plutarch focuses on the anger of the gods, he assumes that men will be able to assess each other's status and determine an appropriate course of action based on status differences. An onlooker who saw such a performance on the street would, therefore, be able to deduce the relative social positions of the men involved. Furthermore, in Roman Corinth during the time when Paul's audience would have read his letter, there was a statue of the emperor with a veiled head, symbolizing his authoritative position as *pontifex maximus*.[9] The statue stood in the Julian Basilica, and the portrayal of Julius with a covered head represented an important departure from his usual portrayal as the first among equals.[10] In other words, by wearing a veil, Julius demonstrated his superior status and power in this particular setting. The veil, therefore, can act as a public and political symbol of authority for the one wearing the veil.

The discussions of men and women wearing veils leads to the importance of veils in a religious setting, especially since the public wearing of veils by men is set within a religious discourse of the gods, which emphasizes the veil's protective function. Again, Plutarch's comments are helpful:

But [the men] thus worshipped the gods, either humbling themselves by concealing the head, or rather by pulling the toga over their ears as a precaution lest any ill-omened and baleful sound from without should reach them while they were praying. That they were mightily vigilant in this matter is obvious from the fact that when they went forth for purposes of divination, they surrounded themselves with the clashing of bronze. (Plutarch, *Quaest. rom.* 266, trans. Babbitt)

Unlike Plutarch's previous comments where men might happen to have their heads covered while in public, this religious setting seems to require some men to cover their heads either as a sign of subordination before the gods or as a means of protecting those who actively participate in the religious actions. Making loud noise using instruments, i.e., clashing bronze, appears to function as an extra precaution for safeguarding the men, and indicates that these religious rites were thought to involve acute danger. The portrayal of heightened danger during religious ceremonies is also evident when women are the main actors, such as with the depiction of the vestal virgins in the Ara Pacis Augustae, where the relief displays a religious ceremony where only the figures actively involved in the sacrifice, both vestal virgins and male priests, are veiled while the spectators, both women and men, are not.[11]

In religious ceremonies, women could wear or remove their veils depending on the setting and their role in the ceremony. Women who were spectators at religious ceremonies would remove their veils while the priests or priestesses would be veiled. Lucan provides an account of a priestess at Delphi whose covering is shaken loose and her life threatened as she is possessed by Apollo (cf., *De Bello Civili* 5.170). This evidence indicates that the danger posed by the gods in public settings, such as in Plutarch's description of men unveiling when in public, is heightened when approaching them in a religious ceremony. Although having some women and men veiled while others are not might appear to be a breakdown of the logic of the veil discussed at the opening of this section, recalling the reasons why women were thought to require head coverings while in public shows at least a similarity in the use of the head covering. The veil itself, and sometime even the removal of the veil, functions as a barrier that protects a vulnerable individual or community from an external threat. In each case, it is not simply gender that determines whether to veil or not but the body's status and role in that setting.[12]

Yet those men and women who wore veils in a religious setting would not just signal their heightened vulnerability but, also, their superior position within the ceremony. These individuals would almost exclusively hail from the elite classes, making a person's role as priest or priestess yet another public manifestation of status in a context rife with them. The use of a veil in a religious ceremony, therefore, would signal the superior status of those with a veil in distinction from those without.[13] The use of a veil to signal a distinct status is also evident in nonreligious settings. Lisa A. Hughes examines Italian funerary monuments from the late Republic and Principate in order to demonstrate the ways that veils could be used or not used in order to display ethno-racial and social differences.[14] Hughes rightly resists a unifying theory for the use of a veil and emphasizes the need to account for the specifics of the setting in order to understand how and what the veil signaled about the person in view.[15]

Although the exact details of what the Corinthian believers signaled through their use or neglect of veils is lost to history, Paul is clearly at pains to provide them a new framework within which to understand how to apply veils. Such a framework combined with the above discussion on the function of head coverings in a cultic setting helps to clarify the cohesion of Paul's commands within a letter that is more broadly concerned with undermining the manipulation of status and the factionalism that results from such practices. The connection to religious discourses also offers an important parallel since the setting for Paul's commands is not behavior or style in general but specifically in references to actions within a cultic setting.[16] This is evident from Paul's qualifications that a man or woman who "prays or prophesies" either with uncovered or covered heads, respectively, brings shame upon their "head" (1 Cor 11:4, 5; respectively).[17] Later, when Paul returns to the idea of prophesying, his commands clearly set prophecy within a communal, religious ceremony (especially 1 Cor 14:24, 31). The religious discourse is also evident when Paul tells his audience to judge for themselves whether it is proper for a woman to pray to God with an uncovered head (1 Cor 11:13). Although Paul uses general examples within the argument, such as his statements that it is "natural" for men to have short hair and women to have long hair (1 Cor 11:14–15), these examples are applied specifically to a religious setting for the community with no indication that these commands are to be applied to other settings.

Furthermore, as discussed above, the use of veils during religious ceremonies served a dual function of protecting the men or women performing in the ceremony as well as signaling their superior status.[18] At one level, then, Paul's command that during these gatherings any man and any woman should follow the custom appropriate for their respective gender neutralizes the use of head coverings as a sign of status and distinction from other men and women within the community (cf. 1 Cor 11:4–5). In fact, given the evidence above that head coverings in cultic settings signaled superior status, Paul's commands would place women in a more honorable position than men. This line of thinking is close to Martin's interpretation that Paul's use of veils functions as a prophylactic for the female body, which is weaker, more porous, and thereby more susceptible to invasion from outside forces.[19] The veil, therefore, provides the necessary protection so that women can function alongside men in religious activity, an action that Martin refers to "boundary-breaking" because of how it elevates women's status in the community.[20] This act coheres with my argument that a theme throughout Paul's commands is his desire for the men in the community to avoid manipulating markers of identity that would elevate them above other members of the community. In other words, the same dynamics of limiting the abuse of power by those with greater access to it and of empowering those community members in more precarious positions appear to be at work in Paul's commands regarding head coverings. In regards to head coverings, all the men are to perform a subordinate masculinity while giving the symbol of authority, i.e., hegemony, to the women of the community.

Before I can declare my interpretive exercise a success, I need to address Paul's statements about women being shamed (1 Cor 11:5–6) and the two discourses on image, glory, and creation (1 Cor 11:7–9 and 11–12; respectively) because these texts are potentially liable to be used in arguments for Paul's subordination of women to men. First, it is important that Paul also raises the possibility of men bringing shame on their head if they pray or prophesy with their head covered (1 Cor 11:4). In line with Thiselton, I take the language of head as referring to both the physical head as well as the person as a whole.[21] In the immediate context of Paul's argument, the image of a man's head has already been expanded to refer to Christ, which means that a man wearing a veil while praying or prophesying shames Christ (cf. 1 Cor 11:3). Keeping in mind the discussion from above, Paul could be arguing that any man who attempts to don a symbol of authority in a religious setting, i.e., take a hegemonic position, shames Christ. At the outset, this should caution against using Paul's discussion of shame to focus too narrowly on controlling women. Second, Paul mentions shame for women as the consequence for violating his commands that are meant to move the community closer to a functional equality (1 Cor 11:5–6). In other words, women who fail to embody the equality that Paul desires are just as liable to shame as men who fail to follow Paul's instructions. Although women cutting their hair short or shaving their heads could signal the completion of a religious rite or vow (e.g., Lucian, *De syria dea* 6; Plutarch, *Quaest. rom.* 267B; Josephus, *J.W.* 2.313), most discussions of female hair cutting and head shaving associate the act with shame or punishment.[22] Tacitus writes of a German man who shaves his wife's head to punish her for committing adultery (Tacitus, *Germ.* 19). Dio Chrysostom reports a similar practice of shaving a woman's head as part of the punishment for adultery (Dio Chrysostom, *Or.* 62.2–4). Achilles Tatius, likely writing in the early second century C.E., wrote a romance novel which made numerous references to cutting and/or shaving hair of

Luecippe, one of the story's star-crossed protagonists. Luecippe cuts her hair short, maybe shaving it, in order to look like a man (e.g., *Leuc. Clit.* 5.19.3 and 7.12.1). Even more interesting is a reference to Luecippe's shaved head as indicating a shameful past and being "robbed of the crowning glory of her hair" (*Leucippe and Clitophon* 7.5.4). These texts clearly indicate the semiotic possibility of associating a woman's lack of hair with shame, a possibility that Paul applies to support his command for women to cover their heads while praying or prophesying (1 Cor 11:5–6). But, as I show above, this is a shame that comes from not donning a symbol of authority. Paul commands them to perform a more authoritative role in the community and only invokes the specter of shame if they fail to do so. In the same way, men will experience shame if they fail to remain in the subordinate role of not wearing a veil in a religious setting.

A careful examination of the two discourses that Paul applies to substantiate his commands regarding head coverings further supports the idea that they are functions to promote equality within the community.[23] The first discourse which runs from 1 Cor 11:3–12 involves a clear hierarchical ordering: God is the head of Christ, Christ is the head of every man, and the man is the head of a woman (1 Cor 11:3).[24] Paul substantiates this hierarchy through the use of the concepts of glory, image, and origin as found within the creation accounts of Genesis 1 and 2–3. In the first case, Paul uses the idea of man, not woman, being in the image *and* glory (εἰκὼν κάι δόξα) of God to show man's position beneath God (1 Cor 11:7). Although man has a subordinate position in this pairing, it is one that is *immediately* subordinate to God. Woman's position is subordinate to man because she is the glory (δόξα) of man, but note the absence of the corresponding term image (1 Cor 11:8). Here, Paul uses the language of glory (δόξα) to link the pairs of God/man and man/woman in subordinate relationships. Paul then appears to confirm women's position by stating, "For man did not come from (ἐκ) woman, but woman from (ἐκ) man. Indeed, man was not created on account of woman but woman on account of man" (1 Cor 11:8–9), apparently referencing the story of Eve's being fashioned from part of Adam (cf. Gen 2:21–23).

Paul's logic in this first discourse might be treacherous, but his point that male and female bodies are distinct is easy enough to understand. The question, though, is what effect such distinction will have in the ordering of the community. Will such distinction result in a patriarchy similar to that found in Greek and Roman contexts? As I demonstrate in chapter 5, Paul recognizes distinctions based on status and gender elsewhere in 1 Corinthians and requires behavior that prevents those of higher status from manipulating their positions in order to exercise power over those members of lower status. In this interpretive test, is it possible to understand Paul's distinctions in the created order as having a similar effect? In order to answer this question, I will first address the second discourse that Paul uses to address the distinction and/or equality between men and women before returning to how the use of veils fits into Paul's goal of men performing a subordinate masculinity and preventing factionalism.

Paul's second discourse, like the first, affirms distinction between male and female while resisting any sense of patriarchy that might result (1 Cor 11:11–12). This second discourse begins by qualifying his statements from 11:8–9, which rely on the relationship established through the use of ἐκ, with the idea that "woman is not independent of man, nor is man independent of woman. Because just as woman came from (ἐκ) man, so man comes through (διά) woman. But all things come from God" (1 Cor 11:11–12). Paul's introduction of the idea that man comes through woman is an addition to the logic from the first discourse and leads to a climax where Paul can say that all things, that is men as well as women, come from God. The construction using ἐκ/διά to differentiate seemingly parallel phrases mirrors Paul's earlier statement about God and Jesus (1 Cor 8:6). "But for us there is one God, the Father, from (ἐξ) whom are all things and for whom we live, and one Lord, Jesus Christ, through (δι') whom are all things and through whom we live" (1 Cor 8:6).[25] In this verse, Paul adapts the language of God's oneness that traces back to the Shema.[26] Although it is difficult to understand why exactly Paul uses the ἐκ/διά variance, his basic point appears to be the expression of distinction within a statement about singularity; in other words, distinction without subordination.[27] Paul's use of the ἐκ/διά construction in the discussion of men and women appears to function in the same way by allowing him to assert a clear distinction without allowing such a distinction to devolve into patriarchy. Again, the point of this otherwise enigmatic construction comes at the end of the verse where Paul groups men and women together as both originating from God. Paul's use of creational language in 1 Cor 11:8–9 and 11–12, then, culminates in a statement of equality where all things are from God.[28]

In fact, Paul appears to elevate the woman by giving her control and making her an active agent over the sign of authority.[29] Such actions maintain the appropriate created order and protects the women, as well as the rest of the community, from external threats (i.e., the angels mentioned in 1 Cor 11:10).[30] As with the commands regarding marriage and divorce, Paul acknowledges and accounts for the differences between male and female bodies by commanding behavior that reverses expectations of power. This is a more optimistic reading than Penner and Vander Stichele who emphasize the inherent androcentrism and kyriarchy within Paul's logic as a permanent blockade to any gender equality within the community.[31] While Penner and Vander

Stichele are correct that Paul retains an inherent difference between male and female that requires some accommodation in the present (i.e., veils),[32] Paul tempers the force of the hierarchy so that it does not produce the functional subordination of women to men.

Paul's second line of justification appears not to derive from Jewish tradition per se but from generally accepted rules governing what is "appropriate" for men and women in terms of hair (1 Cor 11:13):[33] "Does not nature (φύσις) itself teach you that if a man has long hair, it is a disgrace for him, but if a woman has long hair, it is her glory? Because her hair is given to her for a covering" (1 Cor 11:14–15). Although Paul has already alluded to what can be thought of as generally accepted rules governing hair in his reference to it being shameful for a woman to cut her hair or have her head shaved (1 Cor 11:5–6), his reference to what is taught by nature strengthens the point by giving the origin of the logic.[34] By pointing to what is appropriate for each person based on their gender, Paul restricts a person's ability to veil or not based on his or her social position. Gender, not class or status, is what should determine a person's attire during worship.

Paul's commands regarding the use of veils, however perplexing they may be in their details, clearly establish appropriate patterns of behavior corresponding to gender: men do not cover their head whereas women cover their head. That much is clear. What is less clear but still apparent in the above discussion is that these behaviors conform to the pattern of commanding men to embody a subordinate masculinity by intentionally behaving in ways that would limit their power over the bodies of others. By giving the symbol of authority, a head covering, to someone else, they are limiting their own access to that authority. Paul's commands regarding veils not only do not impinge on the functional equality of women but give women control over a symbol of authority (1 Cor 11:10). From the above discussion, such a symbol, especially within a religious context, would indicate that women take prominent roles in the community's gatherings. If the religious setting of Paul's commands is read in connection with the use of veils in such depictions as the Ara Pacis Augustae, then Paul's commands could be taken as giving a prominent symbol of authority to the women while restricting its use by men. This would prevent the manipulation of veils as a source of distinction from and domination over lower-status members in the community. The dynamic created by obedience to these commands fits the pattern I have demonstrated throughout the rest of the letter as Paul appropriates symbols and discourses from the broader culture and repurposes them to create a cruciform community which supports and empowers the lower-status members of the community rather than abusing and further subordinating them.

NOTES

1. The assumption of patriarchy and the subordination of women that is a necessary component of such a system has a long and problematic place within Pauline studies. Dale Martin offers a helpful overview of the way that such assumptions can guide interpretation of a passage, specifically Gal 3:28, and the effects of a non-patriarchal approach on reading the passage; see *Sex and the Single Savior*, 77–90. Such an approach would also aid feminist readings such as those given by Clark (*The Corinthian Women Prophets*) and Elaine H. Pagels ("Paul and Women: A Response to Recent Discussion," *JAAR* 42 (1974): 538–49) who each detect liberating elements in the gospel that are undermined as Paul inscribes gender differences in such a way as to produce patriarchy within the believing community. Rather than using these gender differences to inscribe patriarchy, Paul articulates a system that accounts for them as he moves the believing community toward relationships of equality.

2. Jouette M. Bassler, "1 Corinthians," in *The Women's Bible Commentary: Revised and Updated* (3rd ed.; ed. Carol A. Newsom, Sharon H. Ringe, and Jacqueline E. Lapsley; Louisville: Westminster John Knox, 2012), 562. Scholars divide at every point in this brief bit of text. Fee, for example, takes Paul's reference to men who pray or prophesy with their heads uncovered as a hypothetical, making Paul's inclusion of it more rhetorical; *First Corinthians*, 507–8. The current section understands the main issue that Paul confronts, as Bassler indicates, as the use of veils not hairstyles. While hairstyles are addressed in 1 Cor 11:14–15, the main issue is veils. The scholarly consensus is that Paul's main focus is women who wear inappropriate hairstyles. Preston T. Massey traces the main push for reading ἀκατακάλυπτος in 1 Cor 11:5 and 13 as referencing hair to the work of Abel Isaksson (*Marriage and Ministry in the New Temple: A Study with Special Reference to Mt. 19.13 and 1 Cor 11:3–16*, [ASNU 24; Lund: Gleerup, 1965].) and James B. Hurley ("Did Paul Require Veils or the Silence of Women? A Consideration of 1 Cor 11.2–16 and 1 Cor 14.33b–36" *WThJ* 35 (1972): 190–220.]; "The Meaning of κατακαλύπτω and κατὰ κεφαλῆς ἔχων in 1 Corinthians 11.2–16," *NTS* 53 (2007): 502-05. Massey offers a compelling counterargument to the focus on hairstyles, arguing that the terminology most naturally indicates veils. Richard Oster reaches a similar conclusion regarding the main issues at stake in Paul's discussion; "When Men Wore Veils to Worship: The Historical Context of 1 Corinthians 11.4," *NTS* 34 (1988): 481–505. This dual shift that both focuses more directly on veils and attends to the fact that Paul's commands have as much to do with men as with women is represented forcefully in Gillian Townsley's published dissertation *The Straight Mind in Corinth: Queer Readings across 1 Corinthians 11:2–16* (SemiaSt 88; Atlanta: Scholars Press, 2017).

3. Townsley offers a helpful overview of the arguments concerning possibilities for Paul's argument about the created order in 1 Cor 11:3–10 and the tensions created by Paul's apparent contradiction in 1 Cor 11:11–15; *The Straight Mind*; 139–53, 259–67.

4. Although Paul does address hair and various hairstyles that he deems appropriate for men and women, the commands regard covering and not covering the head and

hair rather than the hairstyle itself. Massey offers one of the most important critiques of the interpretation that Paul's main concern is with hairstyles rather than veils; see "The Meaning of κατακαλύπτω and κατὰ κεφαλῆς ἔχων in 1 Corinthians 11.2–16," *NTS* 53 (2007): 502–23. Although Townsley focuses more on the distortions caused by the heteronormative bias of modern scholars in focusing on hairstyles and homosexuality, she provides a helpful review of the scholarship that points to the use of veils as Paul's concern; see *The Straight Mind*, 261–63.

5. This is a main conclusion of Elizabeth Smith's thesis, *Female Head Covering in the Early Imperial Period: Questions of the Covered 'Other' and the Ideal of Augustan Womanhood* (Master's Thesis; Macquarie University, 2014), 95–96. Smith's survey brings together the work of scholars like Richard Oster and Mary Rose D'Angelo, whom I will discuss, in order to show that any treatment of veils must carefully attend to how the veils function in that specific presentation as opposed to putting forward a single explanation for their form and function. Mark Finney makes a similar point about shaved heads as a polyvalent symbol, the precise meaning of which can only be understood after accounting for the specifics of the situation; D'Angelo, "Honour, Head-coverings and Headship: 1 Corinthians 11.2–16 in its Social Context," *JSNT* 33 (2010): 37; Richard E. Oster, "When Men Wore Veils to Worship: The Historical Context of 1 Corinthians 11.4," *NTS* 34 (1988): 481–505.

6. Although Roman women had more license to enter public spaces than their Greek counterparts, how they presented themselves in public was still governed by feminine standards; see Bruce W. Winter, *Roman Wives, Roman Widows: The Appearance of New Women in the Pauline Communities* (Grand Rapids: Eerdmans, 2003), 81–86.

7. Winter discusses the issue of head coverings and hairstyles as part of Rome's focus on so called "new women" who were challenging traditional decorum and roles for women; *Roman Wives, Roman Widows*, 17–31.

8. Ben Witherington, *Conflict and Community in Corinth: A Socio-Rhetorical Commentary on 1 and 2 Corinthians* (Grand Rapids: Eerdmans, 1995), 232–40; Oster, "When Men Wore Veils to Worship," 481–505.

9. Janelle Peters, "Leveling the Playing Field: Egalitarian Veils and the Athletic Metaphors in 1 Corinthians" (Ph.D. diss., Emory University), 282. The examination of the statue is found in F. P. Johnson, *Corinth IX, 1. The Sculpture* (Cambridge; Mass.: The American School of Classical Studies at Athens, 1931), 70–72.

10. Cynthia L. Thompson, "Hairstyles, Head-coverings, and St. Paul: Portraits from Roman Corinth," *BA* 51 (1988): 101–2.

11. See the discussion in Gill, "Head-coverings 1 Corinthians 11:2–16," 245–52. Finney offers a similar assessment; "Honour, Head-covering and Headship," 37. Although scholars must take a chastened approach to reading paintings, frescos, reliefs, vases, and other pieces of art as if they offer a realistic depiction of a point in time, the fact that a picture depicts veils and the type of social and functional differentiation evident in other texts lends credibility to this use of the Ara Pacis Augustae. David W. J. Gill, "The Importance of Roman Portraiture for Head-coverings in 1 Corinthians 11:2–16," *TynBul* 41 (1990): 252–53.

12. The issue with head coverings is protection, not gender roles per se. Such can be seen by the way that authors addressed priests and priestesses whom were perceived as violating the gender structure in what might be referred to as transvestitism; see Nicole Loraux, "Herakles: The Super-Male and the Feminine," in *Before Sexuality: The Construction of the Erotic Experience in the Ancient Greek World* (ed. David M. Halperin and John J. Winkler; Princeton: Princeton University Press, 1990), 21–52. This is an important point because some understand Paul as addressing homosexual activity. Jerome Murphy O'Connor is a notable example of such a reading since he offers a helpful discussion of Paul's issues with soft (i.e., femininized) men but overlooks the cultic context of Paul's commands regarding head coverings; see *Keys to First Corinthians: Revisiting the Major Issues* (Oxford: Oxford University Press, 2009), 30–31, 138–39. O'Connor's reading not only overlooks Paul's focus on veils, not hair, but also overly determines the semiotic fluidity of head coverings. One example of this fluidity is that, when mourning a father, men would wear veils and women would not; see Plutarch's discussion in *Mor.* 267. Plutarch does not see these actions as problematizing gender boundaries but appropriate actions that symbolize how each gender responds to this particular experience. Again, the action must be understood within its specific context.

13. Gill, "The Importance of Roman Portraiture," 245–60.

14. Lisa A. Hughes, "Unveiling the Veil: Cultic, Status, and Ethnic Representations of Early Imperial Freedwomen," *MaterRelig* 3 (2007): 218–41.

15. One of the main weaknesses with Hughes's otherwise useful and insightful works is that she does not account for the fact that the mourning period was a liminal experience that allowed for the inversion of customary behavior.

16. Fee, *First Corinthians*, 558. Although projecting a clear distinction between religious and secular is anachronistic, the texts surveyed above understand differences in behavior and danger when in a cultic space as opposed to a non-cultic space.

17. Oster argues that commentators treating Paul's statements regarding the behavior of some men in this passage as addressing a hypothetical situation stems from their focus on disorderly women; see, "Use, Misuse and Neglect of Archeological Evidence in Some Modern Works on 1 Corinthians (1 Cor 7, 1–5; 8, 10; 11, 2–16; 12, 14–26)," *ZNW* 83 (1992): 67–68. Fee is an example of such an approach to Paul's reference to men covering their heads since he sees no reference to male head covering except in Jewish settings; see, *First Corinthians*, 559–60.

18. Gill reaches a similar conclusion in stating, "the social elite within the church . . . were adopting a form of dress during worship which drew attention to their status in society"; "The Importance of Roman Portraiture," 250.

19. Martin, *The Corinthian Body*, 229–49.

20. Ibid., 249.

21. Thiselton, *First Corinthians*, 826–28.

22. Plutarch's discussion of the discussion of a cutting a wife's hair short and dressing her like a man on her wedding night is part of complicated marriage practices that are beyond the scope of this discussion; see *Lyc.* 48.

23. The literature on key terminology used within this section (e.g., κεφαλή, ἀνδρός/ἀνήρ, γυνή) is voluminous. I will follow Thiselton's conclusions regarding

Paul's combination of metaphorical and literal meanings for κεφαλή; see, *First Corinthians*, 802–803, 812–823.

24. I do not take Paul's alteration of ἀνδρός to ἀνήρ in 11:3 to signal a switch from men in general to a husband because the entire discussion of order and authority is grounded in creation, not marriage. The term γυνή could refer to either a wife or a woman of marriageable age and requires further evidence to decide which is intended. Winter is surely incorrect in arguing that "[t]he very mention of the word 'veil' by Paul would automatically indicate to the Corinthians that the females under discussion in this passage were married"; *After Paul Left Corinth*, 127. In some settings, a veil would signal marriage, but, as the above discussion shows, it did not necessarily signal marriage.

25. The crasis of ἐκ to ἐξ and διά to δι' should not obscure the syntactical parallel with 1 Cor 11:12.

26. Mark D. Nanos, "Paul and the Jewish Tradition: The Ideology of the Shema" (paper presented at Villanova University, Villanova, Pa., October 23, 2008).

27. See the discussion in Thiselton, *First Corinthians*, 636–38. As Thiselton demonstrates, although a diverse group of scholars agree that Paul adapts the Shema, there is little consensus on why he does so.

28. As important as the readings of Wire, Schüssler-Fiorenza, and other feminist scholars are in combatting sexist readings of the text, Paul's presentation does not require nor support the subordination of women nor the restriction of their activity. My reading, therefore, supports the general thrust of Wire's assertion that part of the issue Paul addresses is women functioning in powerful and typically masculine ways; *The Corinthian Women Prophets*, 62–71. I disagree with Wire that Paul's commands about head coverings support the restriction of these women. Instead, Paul accounts for the argument against their ability to function as prophets without ever calling for them to cease such activity. He essentially silences any objections against these women.

29. This line of treatment comes from Morna D. Hooker, "Authority on Her Head: An Examination of 1 Cor 11:10," *NTS* 10 (1964): 410–16. Thiselton shows how such a line of thinking undermines uses of this passage that seek to silence women, *First Corinthians*, 838–39.

30. The presence of external threats that have the potential to disrupt the community is about all one can say confidently about Paul's reference to angels (1 Cor 11:10). Martin refers to the term as a "pregnant ambiguity" that holds together the issues of gender, authority, and vulnerability in a way that encourages obedience to Paul's commands on the use of veils; see, *The Corinthian Body*, 245. Some scholars note the similarity to how certain texts form the Dead Sea Scrolls envision angels present amongst the community when it worships, thus requiring a heightened state of purity; for example, Joseph A. Firtzmyer, "A Feature of Qumran Angelogy and the Angels in 1 Cor 11:10," in *Paul and Qumran* (ed. J. Murphy O'Connor; London: Chapman, 1968), 31–48. But the mention of angels and the dangers posed by the inappropriate use of veils has also been shown to appear in Roman contexts, both public and cultic. Other scholars note that Paul references angels and other

divine forces earlier in the letter as aligned with the world in opposing the kingdom and people of God (cf., 1 Cor 2:8, 4:9).

31. Penner and Vander Stichele, "Unveiling Paul," 14.

32. Martin's work is another example of how the ongoing differences between male and female bodies that remain in the present age can be accommodated to allow a functional equality within the believing community, *The Corinthian Body*, 229–33. Martin correctly critiques the work of Wayne Meeks, who argues that Paul adopts the image of the androgynous human as the ideal to which members of the believing community could aspire; *The Corinthian Body*, 229–30. Martin rightly points out the androgynous ideal embodied masculine ideals and that conformity was always masculinization and never feminization (e.g., women were shown to become men, not vice-versa); *The Corinthian Body*, 231–32.

33. For the translation of πρέπον as appropriate instead of the more common proper, see Thiselton, *First Corinthians*, 843.

34. The connection between nature and what is appropriate for each gender has already been thoroughly addressed in the second chapter of the present volume.

Bibliography

Abbott, Elizabeth. *A History of Celibacy: From Athena to Elizabeth I, Leonardo da Vinci, Florence Nightingale, Gandhi, & Cher.* New York: Scribner, 1999.

Adams, Edward, and David G. Horrell, eds. *Christianity at Corinth: The Quest for the Pauline Church.* Louisville; KY: Westminster John Know, 2004.

Adler, Eve. *Vergil's Empire: Political Thought in the Aeneid.* New York: Rowman & Littlefield, 2003.

Alston, Richard. "Arms and the Man: Soldiers, Masculinity and Power in Republican and Imperial Rome." Pages 205–23 in *When Men Were Men: Masculinity, Power and Identity in Classical Antiquity.* Edited by Lin Foxhall and John Salmon. New York: Routledge, 1998.

Amandry, M. *Le monnayage des duovirs corinthiens.* Paris: de Boccard, 1988.

Anderson, Gary. "Celibacy or Consummation in the Garden? Reflection on Early Jewish and Christian Interpretations of the Garden of Eden." *Harvard Theological Review* 28 (1989): 121–48.

Anderson, Janice Capel, and Stephen D. Moore, "Matthew and Masculinity." Pages 67–92 in *New Testament Masculinities.* Edited by Stephen D. Moore and Janice Capel Anderson. Atlanta: Society of Biblical Literature, 2003.

Anderson, Karrin Vasby. "'Rhymes with Rich': 'Bitch' as a Tool of Containment in Contemporary American Politics." *Rhetoric and Public Affairs* 2 (1999): 599–623.

Asikainen, Susanna. "'Eunuchs for the Kingdom of Heaven': Matthew and Subordinate Masculinities." Pages 156–88 in *Biblical Masculinities Foregrounded.* Edited by Ovidiu Creangă and Peter-Ben Smit. Sheffield: Sheffield Phoenix Press, 2014.

Aymer, Margaret. "'Mother Knows Best': The Story of Mother Paul Revisited." Pages 187–98 in *Mother Goose, Mother Jones, Mommie Dearest: Biblical Mothers and Their Children.* Edited by Cheryl A. Kirk-Duggan and Tina Pippin. Atlanta: Society of Biblical Literature, 2009.

Bablitz, Leanna. *Actors and Audience in the Roman Courtroom.* London and New York: Routledge, 2007.

Baer, Richard Arthur. *Philo's Use of the Categories Male and Female*. Leiden: Brill, 1970.
Balzat, J. S. and A. J. Spawforth. "'Becoming Roman': À Propos de Deux Générations Parentes de Néo-Citoyens Romains À Sparte et À Athènes." Pages 183–94 in *Onomatologos: Studies in Greek Personal Names Presented to Elaine Matthews*. Edited by R. W. V. Catling and F. Marchland. Oxford: Oxford Books, 2010.
Barclay, John M. *Jews in the Mediterranean Diaspora: From Alexander to Trajan (323 B.C.E.–117 C.E.)*. Edinburgh: T&T Clark, 1996.
Barigazzi, Adelmo. *Favorini di Arelate Opere*. Florence, 1966.
Barnes, Nathan J. *Reading 1 Corinthians with Philosophically Educated Women*. Eugene, Or.; Penwick, 2014.
Barrett, C. K. *The First Epistle to the Corinthians*. Blacks New Testament Commentary. New York: Harper and Row Publishers, 1968.
Barry, William D. "Roof Tiles and Urban Violence in the Ancient World." *Greek, Roman, and Byzantium Studies* 37 (1996): 55–75.
Baynes, Leslie. "Philo, Personification and the Transformation of Grammatical Gender." *Studia Philonica Annual* 14 (2002): 31–47.
Beasley, Christine. "Re-Thinking Hegemonic Masculinity in a Globalizing World," *Men and Masculinities* 11 (2008): 86–103.
———. "Problematizing Current Men/Masculinities Theorizing: The Contribution of Raewyn Connell and Conceptual-Terminological Tensions Today," *The British Journal of Sociology* 63 (2012): 747–65.
———. "Mind the Gap? Masculinity Studies and Contemporary Gender/Sexuality Thinking," *Australian Feminist Studies* 28 (2013): 108–24.
Blayney, Jan, "Theories of Conception in the Ancient Roman World." Pages 230–236 in *The Family in Ancient Rome: New Perspectives*. Edited by Beryl Rawson. Ithaca, NY: Cornell University Press, 1987.
Bloomer, W. Martin. "Schooling in Persona: Imagination and Subordination in Roman Education." *Classical Antiquity* 16 (1996): 57–78.
Botha, Pieter J. J. "Submission and Violence: Exploring Gender Relations in the First-century World." *Neotestamentic* 34 (2000): 1–38.
Bowersock, G. W. *Greek Sophists in the Roman Empire*. Oxford: Clarendon, 1969.
Bowie, Ewen. "The Greeks and their Past in the Second Sophistic." *Political Psychology* 46 (1970): 3–41
Boyarin, Daniel. "Paul and the Genealogy of Gender." *Representations* 41 (1993): 1–33.
———. *Carnal Israel: Reading Sex in Talmudic Culture*. Berkeley: University of California Press, 1993.
———. *Unheroic Conduct: The Rise of Heterosexuality and the Invention of the Jewish Man*. Berkeley: University of California Press, 1997.
Brown, Alexandra R. *The Cross and Human Transformation: Paul's Apocalyptic Word in 1 Corinthians*. Minneapolis: Fortress, 1995.
Brown, Peter. *The Body and Society: Men, Women, and Sexual Renunciation in Early Christianity*. New York: Columbia University Press, 1988.

———. *Power and Persuasion in Late Antiquity: Towards a Christian Empire*. Madison; Wis: University of Wisconsin Press, 1992.
Brown, Robert D. *Lucretius on Love and Sex: A Commentary on "De Rerum Natura" IV, with Prolegomena, Text, and Translation*. Leiden: Brill, 1987.
Burrus, Virginia. "Mapping as Metamorphosis: Initial Reflections on Gender and Ancient Religious Discourses." Pages 1–10 in *Mapping Gender in Ancient Religious Discourses*. Edited by Todd Penner and Caroline Vander Stichele. Leiden: Brill, 2007.
Butler, Judith. "Foucault and the Paradox of Bodily Inscriptions." *The Journal of Philosphy* 86 (1989): 601–7.
———. *Gender Trouble: Feminism and the Subversion of Identity*. New York: Routledge, 1990.
———. *Bodies that Matter: On the Discursive Limits of 'Sex.'* New York: Routledge, 1993.
Bynum, Caroline Walker. *Jesus as Mother: Studies in the Spirituality of the High Middle Ages*. Berkeley: University of California Press, 1982.
Byron, John. "Slave of Christ or Willing Servant?: Paul's Self-Description in 1 Corinthians 4:1–2 and 9:16–18." *Neotestamentica* 37 (2003): 178–98.
Cameron, Ron. Merrill P. Miller. *Redescribing Paul and the Corinthians*. Atlanta: Society of Biblical Literature, 2011.
Carrigan, Tim, R. W. Connell, and John Lee. "Toward a New Sociology of Masculinity." *Theory and Society* 14 (1985): 551–604.
Carson, Anne. "Putting Her in Her Place: Women, Dirt, Desire." Pages 135–69 in *When Men Were Men: Masculinity, Power and Identity in Classical Antiquity*. Edited by Lin Foxhall and John Salmon. New York: Routledge, 1998.
Castelli, Elizabeth Anne. *Imitating Paul: A Discourse of Power*. Louisville, Ky.: Westminster/John Knox Press, 1991.
———. "The *Ekklēsia* of Women and/as Utopian Space: Locating the Work of Elisabeth Schüssler Fiorenza in Feminist Utopian Thought." Pages 36–52 in *On the Cutting Edge: The Study of Women in the Biblical World: Essays in Honor of Elisabeth Schüssler Fiorenza*. Edited by Jane Schaberg, Alice Bach, and Esther Fuchs; New York: Continuum Press, 2004.
Cherian, Jacob. "The Moses at Qumran: The מורה הצדק as the Nursing-Father of the יחד." Pages 351–62 in *The Bible and the Dead Sea Scrolls: The Second Princeton Symposium on Judaism and Christian Origins*. Edited by James H. Charlesworth. Waco: Baylor University Press, 2006.
Cheung, Alex T. *Idol Food in Corinth: Jewish Background and Pauline Legacy*. Journal for the Study of the New Testament: Supplement Series 176. Sheffield: Sheffield Academic Press, 1999.
Chow, John K. *Patronage and Power: A Study in the Social Networks in Corinth*. Journal for the Study of the New Testament: Supplement Series 75. Sheffield: JSOT Press, 1992.
Christ, Alice T. "The Masculine Ideal of 'The Race that Wears the Toga.'" *Art Journal* 52 (1997): 24–30.

Ciampa, Roy E., and Brian S. Rosner. *The First Letter to the Corinthians*. Grand Rapids: Eerdmans, 2010.
Clarke, Andrew D. *Secular and Christian Leadership in Corinth: A Socio-Historical and Exegetical Study of 1 Corinthians 7–6*. Arbeiten zur Geschichte des antiken Judentums und des Urchristentums 18. Leiden: E.J. Brill, 1993.
Clay, Diskin. "The Theory of the Literary Persona in Antiquity." *Materiali e discussioni per l'analisi dei testi classici* 40 (1998): 9–40.
Clines, David J. A. "David the Man: The Construction of Masculinity in the Hebrew Bible." Pages 212–43 in *Interested Parties: The Ideology of Writers and Readers of the Hebrew Bible. Journal for the Study of the Old Testament* Supplement 205. Edited by David J. A. Clines. Sheffield: Sheffield Academic Press, 1995.
———. "Paul, the Invisible Man." Pages 181–92 in *New Testament Masculinities*. Edited by Stephen D. Moore and Janice Capel Anderson. Semeia Studies 45. Atlanta: Society of Biblical Literature, 2003.
Collins, John Joseph. *Jewish Cult and Hellenistic Culture: Essays on the Jewish Encounter with Hellenism and Roman Rule*. Supplements to the *Journal for the Study of Judaism* 100. Leiden: Brill, 2005.
———. "Apocalyptic Eschatology in Philosophical Dress in the Wisdom of Solomon." Pages 93–107 in *Shem in the Tents of Japheth*. Edited by James L. Kugel. Leiden: Brill, 2002.
———. *The Apocalyptic Imagination: An Introduction to Jewish Apocalyptic Literature*. Grand Rapids: Eerdmans, 2016.
Collins, Raymond F. "Divorce in the New Testament." *Biblica* 75 (1994): 590–93.
———. *First Corinthians*. Sacra Pagna 7. Collegeville; MN: The Liturgical Press, 1999.
Connell, R. W. *Masculinities*. 2nd ed. Berkeley: University of California Press, 2005.
———. *Gender in World Perspective*. 2nd ed. Cambridge: Polity, 2009.
Connell, R. W., and James W. Messerschmidt, "Hegemonic Masculinity: Rethinking the Concept." *Gender and Society* 19 (2005): 829–59.
Conway, Colleen. "Gender and Divine Relativity in Philo of Alexandria." *Journal for the Study of Judaism in the Persian, Hellenistic, and Roman Periods* 34 (2003): 471–91.
———. *Behold the Man: Jesus and Greco-Roman Masculinity*. Oxford: Oxford University Press, 2008.
Conzelmann, Hans. *1 Corinthians: A Commentary on the First Epistle to the Corinthians*. Hermeneia. Philadelphia: Fortress Press, 1975.
Corbeill, Anthony. "Dining Deviants in Roman Political Invective." Pages 99–128 in *Roman Sexualities*. Edited by Judith P. Hallett and Marilyn B. Skinner. Princeton: Princeton University Press, 1997.
———. *Nature Embodied: Gesture in Ancient Rome*. Princeton: Princeton University Press, 2004.
Corley, Kathleen. *Private Women, Public Meals: Social Conflict in the Synoptic Tradition*. Peabody; Mass.: Hendrickson, 1993.
Countryman, L. William. *Dirt, Greed, & Sex: Sexual Ethics in the New Testament and Their Implications for Today*. Philadelphia: Fortress, 1988.

Craig, Christopher P. "Cato's Stoicism and the Understanding of Cicero's Speech for Murena," *Transactions of the American Philological Association* 116 (1986): 229–39.
Crawford, Michael H. *Roman Statutes*. 2 volumes. London: Institute of Classical Studies, 1996.
Creangă, Ovidiu ed., *Men and Masculinity in the Hebrew Bible and Beyond*. Sheffield: Sheffield Phoenix Press, 2010.
Crook, J. A. *Law and Life in Rome: 90 B.C.–A.D. 212*. Ithaca; NY: Cornell University Press, 1967.
D'Angelo, Mary Rose. "Women Partners in the New Testament." *Journal of Feminist Studies of Religion* 6 (1990): 65–86.
———. "Gender and the Geopolitics in the Work of Philo of Alexandria: Jewish Piety and Imperial Family Values." Pages 63–88 in *Mapping Gender in Ancient Religious Discourse*. Edited by Todd Penner and Caroline Vander Stichele. Leiden: Brill, 2007.
D'Arms, John H. *Commerce and Social Standing in Ancient Rome*. Cambridge; Mass.: Harvard University Press, 1981.
Davidson, James. "Dover, Foucault, and Greek Homosexuality: Penetration and the Truth of Sex." *Past and Present* 170 (2001): 3–51.
de Beauvoir, Simone. *Le deuxième sexe*. Paris: Gallimard, 1949. Reprint of *The Second Sex*. Translated by Constance Borde and Sheila Malovany-Chevallier. New York: Alfred A. Knopf, 2010.
de Boer, Martinus C. *The Defeat of Death: Apocalyptic Eschatology in 1 Corinthians 15 and Romans 5*. Sheffield: Sheffield Academic, 1988.
Deissmann, Adolf. *Light from the Ancient East: The New Testament Illustrated by Newly Discovered Texts of the Graeco-Roman World*. Translated by Lionel R. M. Strachan. 4th ed. London: Harper & Brothers, 1927.
Dench, Emma. "Austerity, Excess, Success, and Failure in Hellenistic and Early Imperial Italy." Pages 121–46 in *Parchments of Gender: Deciphering the Bodies of Antiquity*. Edited by Maria Wyke. Oxford: Clarendon Press, 1998.
Derrett, J. Duncan M. "Paul as Master-Builder." *Evangelical Quarterly* 69 (1988): 129–137.
deVega, Jessica Lyn Tinklenberg. *"A Man Who Fears God": Constructions of Masculinity in Hellenistic Jewish Interpretations of the Story of Joseph*. Ph.D. diss., Florida State University, 2006.
Dixon, Suzanne. "Sex and the Married Woman in Ancient Rome." Pages 111–29 in *Early Christian Families in Context: An Interdisciplinary Dialogue* (ed. David L. Balch and Carolyn Osiek; Grand Rapids: Eerdmans, 2003.
Donaldson, Mike. "What is Hegemonic Masculinity?" *Theory and Society* 22 (1993): 643–57.
———. "Studying Up: The Masculinity of the Hegemonic." Pages 156–79 in *Male Trouble: Studying Australian Masculinities*. Edited by Stephen Tomsen and Mike Donaldson. Melbourne: Pluto Press, 2003.
Dover, Kenneth J. *Greek Homosexuality*. 2nd ed. Cambridge; Mass: Harvard University Press, 1989, 1978.

———. "Eros and nomos (Plato, *Symposium* 182A–185C)." *Bulletin of the Institute of Classical Studies* 11 (1964): 31–42.

Downs, David J. *The Offering of the Gentiles: Paul's Collection for Jerusalem in Its Chronological, Cultural, and Cultic Contexts*. Wissenschaftliche Untersuchungen zum Neuen Testament 2/248. Tübingen: Mohr Siebeck, 2008.

Drake, Susanna. *Slandering the Jew: Sexuality and Difference in Early Christian Texts*. Philadelphia: University of Pennsylvania Press, 2013.

Duncan-Jones, Richard. *Power and Privilege in Roman Society*. Cambridge: Cambridge University Press, 2016.

Dunning, Benjamin H. *Specters of Paul: Sexual Difference in Early Christian Thought*. Philadelphia: University of Pennsylvania, 2011.

Eastman, Susan G. *Recovering Paul's Mother Tongue: Language and Theology in Galatians*. Grand Rapids: Eerdmans, 2007.

———. "Imagery, Gendered: Pauline Literature." Pages 378–83 in *The Oxford Encyclopedia of the Bible and Gender Studies: Vol 1*. Edited by Julia M. O'Brien. Oxford: Oxford University Press, 2014.

Eckhardt, Benedikt. "The Eighteen Associations of Corinth." *Greek, Roman, and Byzantine Studies* 56 (2016): 646–62.

Edmondson, Jonathan. "Public Dress and Social Control in Late Republican and Early Imperial Rome." Pages 21–46 in *Roman Dress and the Fabrics of Roman Culture*. Edited by Jonathan Edmondson and Alison Keith. Toronto: University of Toronto Press, 2008.

Edsall, Benjamin. "When Cicero and St. Paul Agree: Intra-Group Litigation among the *Luperci* and the Corinthian Believers," *Journal of Theological Studies* 46 (2013): 25–36.

Edwards, Catherine. *The Politics of Immorality in Ancient Rome*. Cambridge: Cambridge University Press, 2002.

Edwards, Tim. *Cultures of Masculinity*. London; New York: Routledge, 2006.

Ehrensperger, Kathy. *Paul and the Dynamics of Power: Communication and Interaction in the Early Christ-Movement*. London; New York: T & T Clark, 2007.

———. *That We May Be Mutually Encouraged: Feminism and the New Perspective in Pauline Studies*. London; New York: T & T Clark International, 2004.

———. "To Eat or Not to Eat—Is This the Question? Table Disputes in Corinth." Pages 114–33 in *Decisive Meals: Table Politics in Biblical Literature*. Library of New Testament 449. Edited by Nathan MacDonald, Kathy Ehrensperger, Luzia Sutter Rehmann. New York: T&T Clark, 2012.

Ehrlich, Susan, Miriam Meyerhoff, and Janet Holmes, eds. *The Handbook of Language, Gender, and Sexuality*. 2nd ed. Oxford: John Wiley & Sons, 2014.

Eilberg-Shwartz, Howard. *God's Phallus and Other Problems for Men and Monotheism*. Boston: Beacon Press, 1994.

———. "Unmanning Israel." Pages 167–83 in *Men and Masculinities in Christianity and Judaism: A Critical Reader*. Edited by Björn Krondorfer. London: SCM, 2009.

Elliott, John. *Social-Scientific Criticism of the New Testament: An Introduction*. London: SPCK, 1995.

———. "From Social Description to Social-Science Criticism." *Biblical Theologicy Bulletin* 38 (2008): 26–36.
Ellis, J. Edward. *Paul and Ancient Views of Sexual Desire: Paul's Sexual Ethics in 1 Thessalonians 4, 1 Corinthians 7, and Romans 1.* London: T&T Clark, 2007.
Eriksson, Anders. *Traditions as Rhetorical Proof: Paul's Argumentation in 1 Cor.* Coniectanea neotestamentica or Coniectanea biblica: New Testament Series 29. Stockholm: Almqvist & Wiksell, 1998.
Essed, Philomena, D. H. Goldberg, and A. Kobayshi. "Introduction: A Curriculum Vitae for Gender Studies." Pages 1–28 in *A Companion to Gender Studies*. Edited Philomena Essed, D. H. Goldberg, and A. Kobayshi. Oxford: Blackwell, 2005.
Fatum, Lone. "Image of God and Glory of Man: Women in the Pauline Congregations." Pages 50–133 in *The Image of God: Gender Models in Judaeo-Christian Tradition*. Edited by Kari Elisabeth Børresen; Minneapolis: Fortress Press, 1995.
Field, James A., Jr. "The Purpose of the *Lex Iulia* et *Papia Poppaea*." *Classical Journal* 40 (1945): 389–416.
Fildes, Valerie A. *Breasts, Bottles, and Babies: A History of Infant Feeding.* Edinburgh: Edinburgh University Press, 1986.
Filene, Peter. *Him/Her/Self: Sex Roles in Modern America*. 2nd ed. Baltimore: Johns Hopkins University Press, 1986.
Fischler, Susan. "Imperial Cult: Engendering the Cosmos." Pages 165–83 in *When Men Were Men: Masculinity, Power and Identity in Classical Antiquity*. Edited by Lin Foxhall and John Salmon. New York: Routledge, 1998.
Fitzmyer, Joseph B. *First Corinthians: A New Translation with Commentary*. Anchor Bible Commentary vol 32. New Haven: Yale University Press, 2009.
Flemming, Rebecca. "Writing and Medicine in the Classical World." *Church Quarterly* 57 (2007): 257–79.
Foucault, Michel. *The Archeology of Knowledge and the Discourse of Language.* Translated by A. M. Sheridan Smith. New York: Random House, 1972.
———. *History of Sexuality*. 3 vols. New York: Pantheon, 1978–1988.
———. *Discipline and Punish: The Birth of the Prison*. Translated by Alan Sheridan. New York: Vintage Books, 1995.
Francis, James A. *Subversive Virtue: Asceticism and Authority in the Second-Century Pagan World*. University Park; Pa.: University of Pennsylvania Press, 1995.
Frank, Richard I. "Augustus' Legislation on Marriage and Children." *California Studies in Classical Antiquity* 8 (1975): 41–52.
Fredrickson, David E. "Natural and Unnatural Use in Romans 1:24–27: Paul and the Philosophical Critique of Eros." Pages 197–222 in *Homosexuality, Science, and the "Plain Sense" of Scripture*. Edited by David L. Balch. Grand Rapids: Eerdmans, 2000.
———. "Passionless Sex in 1 Thessalonians 4:4–5." *Word & World* 23 (2003): 23–30.
Frier, W. *The Rise of the Roman Jurists: Studies in Cicero's "Pro Caecina."* Princeton: Princeton University Press, 1985.
Friesen, Steven J. "Poverty in Pauline Studies: Beyond the So-Called New Consensus." *Journal for the Study of the New Testament* 26 (2004): 323–61.

———. "The Wrong Erastus: Ideology, Archeology, and Exegesis." Pages 231–57 in *Corinth in Context: Comparative Studies in Religion and Society*. Edited by Steven J. Friesen, Daniel N. Schowalter, and James C. Walters. Leiden: Brill, 2010.

———. "Junia Theodora of Corinth: Gendered Inequalities in the Early Empire." Pages 203–26 in *Corinth in Contrast: Studies in Inequality*. Edited by Steven J. Friessen, Sarah A. James, and Daniel N. Schowalter. Leiden: Brill, 2014.

Furnish, Victor Paul. *Theology and Ethics in Paul*. Louisville: Westminster John Knox, 2009.

Galinsky, Karl. *Augustan Culture: An Interpretive Introduction*. Princeton: Princeton University Press, 1996.

Gardiner, Judith Kegan. "Introduction." Pages 1–30 in *Masculinity and Feminist Theory: New Directions*. New York: Columbia University Press, 2002.

———. "Men, Masculinity, and Feminist Theory." Pages 35–50 in *Handbook of Studies on Men and Masculinities*. Edited by Michael S. Kimmel, Jeff Hearn, and R. W. Connell. Thousand Oaks; CA: Sage Publications, 2005.

Gardner, Jane F. *Women in Roman Law and Society*. Bloomington, Ind.: Indiana University Press, 1986.

———. "Sexing a Roman: Imperfect Men in Roman Law." Pages 136–52 in *When Men Were Men: Masculinity, Power and Identity in Classical Antiquity*. Edited by Lin Foxhall and John Salmon. New York: Routledge, 1998.

Garnsey, P. *Social Status and Legal Privilege*. Oxford: Clarendon, 1970.

Gaventa, Beverly Roberts. "The Maternity of Paul: An Exegetical Study of Galatians 4:9." Pages 189–201 in *The Conversation Continues: Studies in Paul and John in Honor of J. Louis Martyn*. Edited by Robert T. Fortna and Beverly Roberts Gaventa; Nashville: Abingdon, 1990.

———. "Our Mother St. Paul: Toward the Recovery of a Neglected Theme," *Princeton Seminary Bulletin* 17 (1996): 29–44

———. "Mother's Milk and Ministry in 1 Corinthians 3." Pages 101–13 in *Theology and Ethics in Paul and His Interpreters: Essays in Honor of Victor Furnish*. Edited by Eugene H. Lovering, Jr. and Jerry L. Sumney. Nashville: Abingdon, 1996.

———. *Our Mother Saint Paul*. Louisville: Westminster John Know, 2007.

George, Michele. "The 'Dark Side' of the Toga." Pages 94–112 in *Roman Dress and the Fabrics of Roman Culture*. Edited by Jonathan Edmondson and Alison Keith; Toronto: Toronto University Press, 2008.

Gerleman, Gillis. *Der Heidenapostel. Ketzerische Erwägungen zur Predigt des Paulus zugleich ein Streifzug in der griechischen Mythologie*. Stockholm: Almqvist & Wiksell, 1989.

Glancy, Jennifer A. "Protocols of Masculinity in the Pastoral Epistles." Pages 235–64 in *New Testament Masculinities*. Edited by Stephen D. Moore and Janice Capel Anderson. Atlanta: Society of Biblical Literature, 2003.

———. *Corporal Knowledge: Early Christian Bodies*. Oxford: Oxford University Press, 2010.

Glazebrook, Allison. "Sexual Rhetoric: From Athens to Rome." Pages 431–45 in *A Companion to Greek and Roman Sexualities*. Edited by Thomas K. Hubbard. Oxford: Blackwell, 2005.

Gleason, Maud W. "The Semiotics of Gender: Physiognomy and Self-Fashioning in the Second Century C.E." Pages 389–416 in *Before Sexuality: The Construction of Erotic Experience in the Ancient Greek World*. Edited by Daivd M. Halperin, John J. Winkler, and Froma I. Zeitlin. Princeton; NJ: Princeton University Press, 1990.

———. *Making Men: Sophists and Self-Presentation in Ancient Rome*. Princeton: Princeton University Press, 1995.

Gold, Barbara K. "'Vested Interests' in Plautus's *Casina*: Cross-Dressing in Comedy," *Helios* 25 (1998): 17–30.

———. "Introduction." Pages 1–7 in *A Companion to Roman Love Elegy*. Edited by Barbary K. Gold. Oxford: Wiley-Blackwell, 2012.

Golden, Mark, and Peter Toohey. *Sex and Difference in Ancient Greece and Rome*. Edinburgh: Edinburgh Univ. Press, 2008.

Goldhill, Simon. *Being Greek under Rome: Cultural Identity, The Second Sophistic and the Development of Empire*. Cambridge: Cambridge University Press, 2001.

Goodrich, John. *Paul as Administrator of God in 1 Corinthians*. Cambridge: Cambridge University Press, 2012.

Goold, G. P. "The Cause of Ovid's Exile." *Illinois Classical Studies* 8 (1983): 94–107.

Gordon, Pamela. "Some Unseen Monster: Rereading Lucretius and Sex." Pages 86–109 in *The Roman Gaze: Vision, Power, and the Body*. Edited by David Fredrick. Baltimore; Md.: Johns Hopkins Press, 2002.

Gramsci, Antonio. *Prison Notebooks, Volume 1*. Translated Joseph A. Buttigieg. New York: Columbia University Press, 1992.

Greene, Ellen. "Gender and Elegy." Pages 357–71 in *A Companion to Roman Love Elegy*. Edited by Barbary K. Gold. Oxford: Wiley-Blackwell, 2012.

Grimaldi, William M. A. *Aristotle, Rhetoric II: A Commentary*. New York: Fordham University Press, 1988.

Grubbs, Judith Evans. *Women and the Law in the Roman Empire: A Sourcebook on Marriage, Divorce, and Widowhood*. London: Routledge, 2002.

———. "The Family." Pages 312–26 in *A Companion to the Roman Empire*. Edited by David S. Potter. Oxford: Blackwell, 2009.

Gruen, Erich S. "Cicero and the Alien." Pages 13–27 in *Roman Literature, Gender and Reception: Domina Illustris*. Edited by Donald Lateiner, Barbara K. Gold, and Judith Perkins. New York: Routledge, 2013.

Grundmann, Walter. "Die νήπιοι in der urchristlichen Paränesis." *New Testament Studies* 5 (1958–59): 188–205.

Guest, Deryn. *Beyond Feminist Biblical Studies*. Sheffield: Sheffield Phoenix Press, 2012.

Gunderson, Erik. "Discovering the Body in Roman Oratory." Pages 169–89 in *Parchments of Gender: Deciphering the Bodies of Antiquity*. Edited by Maria Wyke. Oxford: Clarendon, 1998.

———. *Staging Masculinity: The Rhetoric of Performance in the Roman World*. Ann Arbor; Mich.: University of Michigan Press, 2000.

———. *Declamation, Paternity, and Roman Identity: Authority and the Rhetorical Self*. Cambridge: Cambridge University Press, 2003.

Haddox, Susan E. "Favored Sons and Subordinate Masculinities." Pages 2–19 in *Men and Masculinity in the Hebrew Bible and Beyond*. Edited by Ovidiu Creangă. Sheffield: Sheffield Phoenix Press, 2010.

Hall, Jon. "Oratorical Delivery and the Emotions: Theory and Practice." Pages 218–34 in *A Companion to Roman Rhetoric*. Edited by William Dominik and Jon Hall. Malden; Mass.: Blackwell, 2007.

Hallett, Judith. "The Role of Women in Roman Elegy: Counter-Cultural Feminism." *Arethusa* 6 (1973): 329–47.

———. "Perusinae Glandes and the Changing image of Augustus." *American Journal of Ancient History* 2 (1977): 151–71.

Halperin, David M. *One Hundred Years of Homosexuality: And Other Essays on Greek Love*. New York: Routledge, 1990.

———. "Why Is Diotima a Woman? Platonic *ERŌS* and the Figuration of Gender." Pages 257–308 in *Before Sexuality: The Construction of Erotic Experience in the Ancient Greek World*. Edited by David M. Halperin, John J. Winkler, and Froma I. Zeitlin. Princeton: Princeton University Press, 1990.

———. "Forgetting Foucault: Acts, Identities, and the History of Sexuality." *Representations* 63 (1998): 93–120.

Halperin, David M., John J. Winkler, and Froma I. Zeitlin, eds. *Before Sexuality: The Construction of Erotic Experience in the Ancient Greek World*. Princeton: Princeton University Press, 1990.

Harper, Kyle. *From Shame to Sin: The Christian Transformation of Sexual Morality in Late Antiquity*. Cambridge: Harvard University Press, 2013.

———. "Porneia: The Making of a Christian Sexual Norm." *Journal of Biblical Literature* 131 (2012): 363–83.

———. "Culture, Nature, and History: The Case of Ancient Sexuality." *Comparative Studies in Society and History* 55 (2013): 986–1016.

Harris, William V. "The Roman Father's Power of Life and Death." Pages 81–96 in *Studies of Roman Law in Memory of A. Arthur Schiller*. Edited by Roger S. Bagnall and William V. Harris. Leiden: Brill, 1986.

Hawking, Stephen W. *A Brief History of Time: From the Big Bang to Black Holes*. Toronto: Bantam Books, 1988.

Hays, Richard. "Wisdom According to Paul." Pages 111–23 in *Where Shall Wisdom Be Found?: Wisdom in the Bible, the Church and the Contemporary World*. Edited by Stephen C. Barton; Edinburgh: T&T Clark, 1999.

Hemelrijk, Emily A. "The Education of Women in Ancient Rome." Pages 292–304 in *A Companion to Ancient Education*. Edited by W. Martin Bloomer. Walden, Mass.: Wiley-Blackwell, 2015.

Holford-Strevens, Leofranc. *Aulus Gellius*. Chapel Hill: University of North Carolina Press, 1988.

Holmes, Brooke. *Gender: Antiquity and Its Legacy*. Oxford: Oxford University Press, 2012.

Hooker, Morna D., "Authority on Her Head: An Examination of 1 Cor 11:10." *New Testament Studies* 10 (1964): 410–16.

———. "Hard Sayings: 1 Cor 3:2." *Theology* 69 (1966): 19–22.
———. "A Partner in the Gospel: Paul's Understanding of His Ministry." Pages 83–100 in *Theology and Ethics in Paul and His Interpreters: Essays in Honor of Victor Furnish*. Edited by Eugene H. Lovering, Jr. and Jerry L. Sumney. Nashville: Abingdon, 1996.
Hornsby, Teresa J., and Ken Stone. *Bible Trouble: Queer Reading at the Boundaries of Biblical Scholarship*. Atlanta: Society of Biblical Literature, 2011.
Horrell, David G. *The Social Ethos of the Corinthian Correspondence*. Edinburgh: T&T Clark, 1996.
———. *An Introduction to the Study of Paul*. 2nd ed; London: T&T Clark, 2006.
Howson, Richard. *Challenging Hegemonic Masculinity*. New York: Routledge, 2006.
———. "Hegemonic Masculinity in the Theory of Hegemony: A Brief Response to Christine Beasley's 'Rethinking Hegemonic Masculinity in a Globalizing World.'" *Men and Masculinities* 11 (2008): 109–13.
Hoyland, Robert. "A New Edition and Translation of the Leiden Polemon." Pages 239–464 in *Seeing the Face, Seeing the Soul: Polemo's Physiognomy from Classical Antiquity to Medieval Islam*. Edited by Simon Swain. Oxford: Oxford University Press, 2007.
Instone-Brewer, David. *Divorce and Remarriage in the Bible: The Social and Literary Context*. Grand Rapids: Eerdmans, 2002.
Isaac, Benjamin H. *The Invention of Racism in Classical Antiquity*. Princeton: Princeton University Press, 2004.
Ivarsson, Fredrik. "Vice Lists and Deviant Masculinity: The Rhetorical Function of 1 Corinthians 5:10–11 and 6:9–10." Pages 163–84 in *Mapping Gender in Ancient Religious Discourses*. Edited by Todd Penner and Caroline Vander Stichele. Leiden: Brill, 2007.
Jacobs, Sandra. "Divine Virility in Priestly Representations: Its Memory and Consummation in Rabbinic Midrash." Pages 146–70 in *Men and Masculinity in the Hebrew Bible and Beyond*. Edited by Ovidiu Creangă. Sheffield: Sheffield Phoenix Press, 2010.
James, Sarah A. "The Last of the Corinthians? Society and Settlement from 146 to 44 B.C.E." Pages 17–37 in *Corinth in Contrast: Studies in Inequality*. Edited by Steven J. Friessen, Sarah A. James, and Daniel N. Schowalter. Leiden: Brill, 2014.
Jeffreys, Sheila. *Beauty and Misogyny: Harmful Cultural Practices in the West*. 2nd ed. New York: Routledge, 2015.
Jodamus, Johnathan. "An Investigation into the Construction(s) and Representation(s) of Masculinity(ies) and Feminity(ies) in 1 Corinthians." Ph.D. diss., University of Cape Town, 2015.
Jones, C. P. "The Reliability of Philostratus," Pages 11–16 in *Approaches to the Second Sophistic*. Edited by G.W. Bowersock. University Park, Pa: American Philological Association, 1974.
Joshel, Sandra R. "Female Desire and the Discourse of Empire: Tacitus' Mesalina." Pages 221–54 in *Roman Sexualities*. Edited by Judith P. Hallett and Marilyn B. Skinner. Princeton: Princeton University Press, 1997.

Kasher, Aryeh. "Polemic and Apologetic Methods of Writing in *Contra Apionem*." Pages 143–86 in *Josephus' Contra Apionem: Studies in Its Character and Context with a Latin Concordance to the Portion Missing in Greek*. Edited by Louis H. Feldman and John R. Levinson. Leiden: Brill, 1996.

Kay, D. M. "Susanna." Pages 638–40 in *The Apocrypha and Pseudepigrapha of the Old Testament Volume One: Apocrypha*. Edited by R. H. Charles and D. Litt. Oxford: Clarendon Press, 1913.

Kelly, J. M. *Roman Litigation*. Oxford: Clarendon, 1966.

Kemezis, Adam M. "Augustus the Ironic Paradigm: Cassius Dio's Portrayal of the *Lex Julia* and *Lex Papia Poppaea*." *Phoenix* 61 (2007): 270–85.

Kennedy, G. A. *New Testament Interpretation through Rhetorical Criticism*. Chapel Hill; N.C.: University of North Carolina Press, 1984.

Kimmel, Michael S., Jeff Hearn, and Raewyn Connell. *Handbook of Studies on Men & Masculinities*. Thousand Oaks, Calif.: Sage Publications, 2005.

King, Karen L. "Comparative Study of Gendered Strategies to Represent the Sacrality of the Group: Philo of Alexander and a Korean-American Presbyterian Church." Pages 3–21 in *Bodies, Borders, Believers: Ancient Texts and Present Conversations*. Edited by Anne Hege Grung, Marianne Bjelland Kartzow, Anna Rebecca Solevåg. Eugene, Oreg.: Penwick, 2015.

Kinman, Brent. "'Appoint the Despised Judges!' (1 Corinthians 6:4)." *Tyndale Bulletin* 48 (1997): 345–54.

Kittredge, Cynthia Briggs. *Community and Authority: The Rhetoric of Obedience in the Pauline Tradition*. Harrisburg: Trinity Press International, 1998.

Klassen, William. "The Sacred Kiss in the New Testament: An Example of Social Boundary Lines." *New Testament Studies* 39 (1993): 122–35.

Klauch, Hans Joseph. "Junia Theodora und die Gemeinde von Korinth." Pages 42–57 in *Kirche und Volk Gottes: Festschrift für Jürgen Roloff*. Edited by Martin Karrer, et al. Neukirchen-Vluyn: Neukirchen Verlag, 2000.

Kloppenburg, John S. "Egalitarianism in the Myth and Rhetoric of Pauline Churches." Pages 247–63 in *Reimagining Christian Origins: A Colloquium Honouring Burton L. Mack*. Edited by Elizabeth A. Castelli and Hal Taussig. Valley Forge, Pa.: Trinity Press International, 1996.

König, Jason. "Favorinus's *Corinthian Oration* in Its Corinthian Context." *Cambridge Classical Journal* 47 (2001): 141–71.

———. König, Jason. "Conventions of Prefatory Self-presentation in Galen's *On the Order of My Own Books*." Pages 35–58 in *Galen and the World of Knowledge*. Edited by Christopher Gill, Tim Whitmarsh, and John Wilkins. Cambridge: Cambridge University Press, 2009.

Konstan, David, and Martha C. Nussbaum. *Sexuality in Greek and Roman Society*. Providence: Brown University Press, 1990.

Kraemer, Ross A. "Monastic Jewish Women in Greco-Roman Egypt: Philo Judaeus on the Therapeutrides." *Signs* 14 (1989): 342–70.

———. "The Other as Woman: An Aspect of Polemic among Pagans, Jews, and Christians in the Greco-Roman World." Pages 121–44 in *The Other in Jewish*

Thought: Constructions of Jewish Culture and Identity. Edited by Laurence J. Silberstein and Robert L. Cohn. New York: New York University Press, 1994.

———. "Typical and Atypical Jewish Family Dynamics: The Cases of Babatha and Berenice." Pages 130–56 in *Early Christian Families in Context*. Edited by David Balch and Carolyn Osiek; Grand Rapids: Eerdmans, 2003.

———. *Unreliable Witnesses: Religion, Gender, and History in Greco-Roman Mediterranean*. Oxford: Oxford University Press, 2011.

Kraemer, Ross Sheppard. "Women's Judaisms at the Beginning of Christianity." Pages 50–79 in *Women and Christian Origins*. Edited by Mary Rose D'Angelo. Oxford: Oxford University Press, 1999.

Krondorfer, Bjorn, ed. *Men and Masculinities in Christianity and Judaism: A Critical Reader*. London: SCM Press, 2009.

Kuefler, Matthew. *The Manly Eunuch: Masculinity, Gender Ambivalence, and Christian Ideology in Late Antiquity*. Chicago: Chicago University Press, 2001.

L'Hoir, Francesco Santoro. *The Rhetoric of Gender Terms: 'Man,' 'Woman,' and the Portrayal of Character in Latin Prose*. Leiden: Brill, 1992.

Laqueur, Thomas Walter. *Making Sex: Body and Gender from the Greeks to Freud*. Cambridge: Harvard University Press, 1990.

Larmour, David H. J., Paul Allen Miller, and Charles Platter. *Rethinking Sexuality: Foucault and Classical Antiquity*. Princeton: Princeton University Press, 1998.

Larson, Jennifer. "Paul's Masculinity." *Journal of Biblical Literature* 123 (2004): 85–97.

Lassen, Eva Maria. "The Use of the Father Image in Imperial Propaganda and 1 Corinthians 4:14–21," *Tyndale Bulletin* 42 (1991): 127–36.

Lazarewica-Wyrzykowska, Ela. "Samson: Masculinity Lost (and Regained?)." Pages 171–88 in *Men and Masculinity in the Hebrew Bible and Beyond*. Edited by Ovidiu Creangă. Sheffield: Sheffield Phoenix Press, 2010.

Leach, Eleanor Winsor. "Horace Carmen 1.8: Achilles, the Campus Martius, and the Articulation of Gender Roles in Augustan Rome." *Classical Philology* 89 (1994): 334–43.

Levine, Amy-Jill. *Women like This: New Perspectives on Jewish Women in the Greco-Roman World*. Atlanta: Scholars Press, 1991.

Levine, Molly Myerowitz. "The Gendered Grammar of Ancient Mediterranean Hair." Pages 76–130 in *Off with Her Head!: The Denial of Women's Identity in Myth, Religion, and Culture*. Edited by Howard Eilberg-Schwartz and Wendy Doniger. Berkeley: University of California Press, 1995.

Lewis, Naphtali. *Life in Egypt under Roman Rule*. Oxford: Clarendon, 1983.

Lincicum, David. "Philo and the Physiognomic Tradition." *Journal for the Study of Judaism in the Persian, Hellenistic, and Roman Periods* 44 (2013), 57–86.

Lindemann, Andreas. *Der Erste Korintherbrief*. Tübingen: Mohr Siebeck, 2000.

Littlewood, Cedric. "Seneca's *Thysetes*: The Tragedy with No Women?" *Materiali e discussioni per l'analisi dei testi classici* 38 (1997): 57–86

Loader, William R. G. *The Dead Sea Scrolls on Sexuality: Attitudes towards Sexuality in Sectarian and Related Literature at Qumran*. Grand Rapids: Eerdmans, 2009.

———. *Sexuality in the New Testament: Understanding the Key Texts*. Louisville: Westminster John Knox, 2010.

———. *The Pseudepigrapha on Sexuality: Attitudes towards Sexuality in Apocalypses, Testaments, Legends, Wisdom, and Related Literature*. Grand Rapids: Eerdmans, 2011.

———. *Philo, Josephus, and the Testaments on Sexuality: Attitudes towards Sexuality in the Writings of Philo and Josephus and in the Testaments of the Twelve Patriarchs*. Grand Rapids: Eerdmans, 2011.

———. *The New Testament on Sexuality*. Grand Rapids: Eerdmans, 2012.

———. *Making Sense of Sex: Attitudes towards Sexuality in Early Jewish and Christian Literature*. Grand Rapids: Eerdmans, 2013.

Lopez, Davina C. *Apostle to the Conquered: Reimagining Paul's Mission*. Minneapolis: Fortress, 2008.

Maier, Harry O. "A Sly Civility: Colossians and Empire," *Journal for the Study of the New Testament* 27 (2005): 323–49.

Malherbe, Abraham. "'Gentle as a Nurse': The Cynic Background to 1 Thess ii." *Novum Testamentum* 12 (1970): 203–17.

Mantel, Hugo. *Studies in the History of the Sanhedrin*. Cambridge; Mass.: Harvard University Press, 1961.

Marks, Susan. *First Came Marriage: The Rabbinic Appropriation of Early Jewish Wedding Ritual*. Princeton: Gorgias Press, 2013.

Marshall, Peter. *Enmity in Corinth: Social Conventions in Paul's Relations with the Corinthians*. Wissenschaftliche Untersuchungen zum Neuen Testament 2/23 Tübingen: J. C. B. Mohr Siebeck, 1987.

Martin, Dale B. *Slavery as Salvation: The Metaphor of Slavery in Pauline Christianity*. New Haven: Yale University Press, 1990.

———. *The Corinthian Body*. New Haven: Yale University Press, 1995.

———. *Sex and the Single Savior: Gender and Sexuality in Biblical Interpretation*. Louisville: Westminster: John Knox Press, 2006.

Matilla, Sharon Lea. "Wisdom, Sense Perception, Nature, and Philo's Gender Gradient." *Harvard Theological Review* 89 (1996): 103–30.

Mauss, M. "Une catégorie de l'esprit humain: La notion de personnne, celle de 'moi.'" *Journal of the Royal Anthropological Institute of Great Britain and Ireland* 68 (1938): 263–81.

May, Alistair. *The Body for the Lord: Sex and Identity in 1 Corinthians 5–7*. A & C Black, 2004.

Mayer, Ronald G. "Persona Problems: The Literary Persona in Antiquity Revisited." *Materiali e discussioni per l'analisi dei testi classici* 50 (2003): 55–80.

Mayordomo, Moisés. "'Act like men!' (1 Cor 16:13): Paul's Exhortation in Different Historical Contexts." *Cross Currents* 61 (2011): 515–28.

McCullough, Anna. "Gender and Public Image in Imperial Rome." Ph.D. diss., University of St. Andrews, 2007.

McDonnell, Myles. *Roman Manliness: Virtus and the Roman Republic*. Cambridge: Cambridge University Press, 2006.

McGinn, Thomas A. *Prostitution, Sexuality, and the Law in Ancient Rome*. Oxford: Oxford University Press, 1998.

McInerney, Jeremy. "Plutarch's Manly Women." Pages 319–44 in *Andreia: Studies in Manliness and Courage in Classical Antiquity*. Edited by Ralph Mark Rosen and Ineke Sluiter. Leiden: Brill, 2003.

McIntosh, Mary. "The Homosexual Role." *Social Problems* 16 (1968): 182–92.

McLaren, James S. "The *Jewish War* as a Response to the Crisis of Flavian Propaganda." Pages 9–28 in *Ancient Jewish and Christian Texts as Crisis Management Literature: Thematic Studies from the Centre of Early Christian Studies*. Edited by David C. Sim and Pauline Allen. London: T&T Clark, 2012.

McNeel, Jennifer Houston. *Paul as Infant and Nursing Mother: Metaphor, Rhetoric, and Identity in 1 Thessalonians 2:5–8*, 2014. Early Christianity and Its Literature 12. Atlanta: Society of Biblical Literature, 2014.

McRae, Rachel M. "Eating with Honor: The Corinthian Lord's Supper in Light of Voluntary Associations Meal Practices." *Journal for Biblical Literature* 130 (2011): 165–81.

Meeks, Chet, and Arlene Stein, "Refiguring the Family: Towards a Post-Queer Politics of Gay and Lesbian Marriage." Pages 136–55 in *Intersections between Feminist and Queer Theory*. Edited by Diane Richardson, Janice McLaughlin, and Mark E. Casey. New York: Palgrave MacMillan, 2006.

Meeks, Wayne A. *The First Urban Christians: The Social World of the Apostle Paul*. New Haven: Yale University Press, 1983.

Meggitt, J. J. *Paul, Poverty and Survival*. Edinburgh: T&T Clark, 1998.

Mensching, E. *Favorin von Arelate: Der erste Teil der Fragmente*. Berlin: Walter de Gruyter, 1963.

Merklein, Helmut. *Der erste Brief an die Korinther: Kapitel 1–4*. Volume 1. Gütersloh: Gütersloher Verlagshaus Gerd Mohn. Würzburg: Echter Verlag, 1992.

Messerschmidt, James W. "And Now the Rest of the Story: A Commentary on Christine Beasley's 'Rethinking Hegemonic Masculinity in a Globalizing World.'" *Men and Masculinities* 11 (2008): 104-08

———. *Hegemonic Masculinities and Camouflaged Politics*. Boulder; Colo.: Paradigm, 2010.

———. "Engendering Gender Knowledge: Assessing the Academic Appropriation of Hegemonic Masculinity." *Men and Masculinities* 15 (2012): 56–76.

Meyer, H. A. W. *Handbuch über den ersten Brief an die Korinther*. Kritischexegetischer Kommenatar über das Neue Testament; 6th ed.; Göttingen: Vandenhoeck und Ruprecht, 1881.

Meyers, Carol L. "Was Ancient Israel a Patriarchal Society?" *Journal of Biblical Literature* 133 (2014): 8–27.

Milnor, Kristina. "Augustus, History, and the Landscape of the Law." *Arethusa* 40 (2007): 7–23.

———. *Graffiti and the Literary Landscape of Roman Pomepeii*. Oxford: Oxford University Press, 2014.

Mitchell, Alan C. "Rich and Poor in the Courts of Corinth: Litigiousness and Status in 1 Corinthians 6.1–11." *New Testament Studies* 39 (1993): 562–86.
Mitchell, Margaret M. *The Rhetoric of Reconciliation: An Exegetical Investigation of the Language and Composition of 1 Corinthians.* Louisville, Ky.: Westminster/ John Knox, 1993.
Moore, Stephen D. *God's Gym: Divine Male Bodies of the Bible.* New York: Routledge, 1996.
———. *God's Beauty Parlor: And Other Queer Spaces in and Around the Bible.* Stanford: Stanford University Press, 2001.
———. "'O Man, Who Art Thou . . .?': Masculinity Studies and New Testament Studies." Pages 1–22 in *New Testament Masculinities.* Edited by Stephen D. Moore and Janice Capel Anderson. Atlanta: Society of Biblical Literature, 2003.
———. *The Bible in Theory: Critical and Postcritical Essays.* Atlanta: Society of Biblical Literature, 2010.
Moore, Stephen D., and Janice Capel Anderson. "Taking It Like a Man: Masculinity in 4 Maccabees." *Journal of Biblical Literature* 117 (1998): 249–74.
———. *New Testament Masculnities.* Atlanta: Society of Biblical Literature, 2003.
Morris, Michelle J. "The Fruits of Infertility: Paul and the Rhetoric of a Fertile Empire." *Westminster Theological Journal* 47 (2012): 107–15.
Munck, Johannes. *Paul and the Salvation of Mankind.* London: SCM, 1951.
Murphy, Peter Francis. *Feminism and Masculinities.* Oxford; New York: Oxford University Press, 2004.
Newton, Derek. *Deity and Diet: The Dilemma of Sacrificial Food at Corinth. Journal for the Study of the New Testament*: Supplement Series 169. Sheffield: Sheffield Academic Press, 1998.
Nguyen, V. Henry T. *Christian Identity in Corinth: A Comparative Study of 2 Corinthians, Epictetus, and Valerius Maximus.* Tübingen: Mohr Siebeck, 2008.
Nikoloutsos, Konstantinos P. "From Tomb to Womb: Tibullus 1.1 and the Discourse of Masculinity in Post-Civil War Rome." *Scholia: Studies in Classical Antiquity* 20 (2011): 52–71.
Nissinen, Martti. *Homoeroticism in the Biblical World: A Historical Perspective.* Minneapolis: Fortress Press, 1998.
Nussbaum, Martha C. "The Incomplete Feminism of Musonius Rufus, Platonist, Stoic, and Roman." Pages 283–326 in *The Sleep of Reason: Erotic Experience and Sexual Ethics in Ancient Greece and Rome.* Edited by Martha C. Nussbaum and Juha Sihvola. Chicago: University of Chicago Press, 2002.
Økland, Jorunn. "Feminist Reception of the New Testament: A Critical Reception." Pages 131–56 in *The New Testament as Reception.* Edited by Mogens Müller and Henrik Tronier. *Journal for the Study of the New Testament* Supplement 269. London: Sheffield Academic, 2002.
———. *Women in Their Place: Paul and the Corinthian Discourse of Gender and Sanctuary Space. Journal for the Study of the New Testament*: Supplement Series 269. New York: T&T Clark International, 2004.

Olson, Kelly. "Toga and *pallium*: Status, Sexuality, Identity." Pages 422–448 in *Sex in Antiquity: Exploring Gender and Sexuality in the Ancient World*. Edited by Mark Masterson, Nancy Sorkin Rabinowitz, and James Robison. London: Routledge, 2015.

Oster, Richard E. "When Men Wore Veils to Worship: The Historical Context of 1 Corinthians 11.4." *New Testament Studies* 34 (1988): 481–505.

Pagels, Elaine H., "Paul and Women: A Response to Recent Discussion." *Journal of the American Academy of Religion* 42 (1974): 538–49.

Parchami, Ali. *Hegemonic Peace and Empire: The Pax Romana, Britannica, and Americana*. New York: Routledge, 2009.

Penn, Michael Philip. *Kissing Christians: Ritual and Community in Late Antiquity*. Philadelphia: University of Philadelphia Press, 2005.

Penner, Todd, and Caroline Vander Stichele. *Mapping Gender in Ancient Religious Discourses*. Leiden: Brill, 2007.

Peppard, Michael. "Brother against Brother: *Contraversiae* about Inheritance Disputes and 1 Corinthians 6:1–11." *Journal of Biblical Literature* 133 (2014): 179–92.

Perry, Matthew J. "Defining Gender." Pages 432–42 in *The Oxford Handbook of Roman Law and Society*. Edited by Paul J. Du Plessis, Clifford Ando, and Kaius Tuori. Oxford: Oxford University Press, 2016.

Pogoloff, S. M. *Logos and Sophia: The Rhetorical Situation of 1 Corinthians*. Atlanta: Scholars Press, 1992.

Polaski, Sandra Hack. *A Feminist Introduction to Paul*. St. Louis: Chalice Press, 2005.

Preston, Rebecca. "Roman Questions, Greek Answers: Plutarch and the Construction of Identity." Pages 86–119 in *Being Greek Under Roman Rule: The Second Sophistic and the Development of Empire*. Edited by Simon Goldhill. Cambridge: Cambridge University Press, 2001.

Reay, Brendon. "Agriculture, Writing, and Cato's Aristocratic Self-Fashioning." *Classical Antiquity* 24 (2005): 331–61

Reeder, Caryn A. "Gender, War, and Josephus." *Journal for the Study of Judaism in the Persian, Hellenistic, and Roman Periods* 46 (2015): 65–85.

Reeser, Todd W. *Masculinities in Theory: An Introduction*. Chichester; Malden, MA: Wiley-Blackwell, 2010.

Repath, Ian. "Anonymous Latinus, *Book of Physiognomy*." Pages 549–636 in *Seeing the Face, Seeing the Soul: Polemo's Physiognomy from Classical Antiquity to Medieval Islam*. Edited by Simon Swain. Oxford: Oxford University Press, 2007.

Richardson, G. Peter. "Philo and Eusebius on Monasteries and Monasticism—The Therapeutae and Kellia." Pages 334–59 in *Origins and Method: Towards a New Understanding of Judaism and Early Christianity: Essays in Honour of John C. Hurd*. Edited by Bardley H. McLean. Sheffield: JSOT Press, 1993.

Richlin, Amy. "Approaches to the Sources on Adultery at Rome." *Women's Studies* 8 (1981): 225–50.

———. *The Garden of Priapus: Sexuality and Aggression in Roman Humor*. Oxford: Oxford University Press, 1992.

———. "Not before Homosexuality: The Materiality of the Cinaedus and the Roman Law against Love between Men." *Journal of the History of Sexuality* 3 (1993): 523–77.

———. "Gender and Rhetoric: Producing Manhood in the Schools." Pages 90–110 in *Roman Eloquence: Rhetoric in Society and Literature*. Edited by William J. Dominik; London: Routledge, 1997.

———. "Foucault's History of Sexuality: A Useful Theory for Women?" Pages 138–70 in *Rethinking Sexuality: Foucault and Classical Antiquity*. Edited by D. H. J. Larmour, P. A. Miller, and C. Platter. Princeton; Princeton: Princeton University Press, 1998.

———. "Slave-Woman Drag." Pages 37–67 in *Women in Roman Republican Drama*. Edited by Dorota Dutsch, et al. Madison: University of Wisconsin Press, 2015.

Rife, Joseph L. "Religion and Society at Roman Kenchreai." Pages 391–432 in *Corinth in Context: Comparative Studies in Religion and Society*. Edited by Steven J. Friesen, Daniel N. Schowalter, and James C. Walters. Leiden: Brill, 2010.

Riggsby, Andrew M. *Roman Law and the Legal World of the Romans*. Cambridge: Cambridge University Press, 2010.

Ritner, Robert K. "Egypt under Roman Rule: The Legacy of Ancient Egypt." Pages 1–33 in *The Cambridge History of Egypt: Vol 1*. Edited by Carl F. Petry. Cambridge: Cambridge University Press, 1998.

Rizakēs, A. D., and S. Zoumbaki. *Roman Pelopennese: Roman Personal Names in Their Social Context*. Volume 1. Athens: Research Centre for Greek and Roman Antiquity National Hellenic Research Foundation, 2001.

Roebuck, Carl. *The Asklepieion and Lerna Based on the Excavations and Preliminary Studies of F.J. de Wade*. Princeton: Princeton University Press, 1951.

Roetzel, Calvin. *Paul: A Jew on the Margins*. Louisville: Westminster John Knox, 2003.

Rosen, Ralph, and Mark Sluiter, I., eds. *Andreia: Studies in Manliness and Courage in Classical Antiquity*. Leiden: Brill 2003.

Rothenberg, Paula S. *Race, Class, and Gender in the United States: An Integrated Study*. 2nd ed. New York: St. Martin's, 1992.

Rubin, Mark, and Miles Hewstone. "Social Identity, System Justification, and Social Dominance: Commentary on Reicher, Jost et al., and Sidanius et al." *Political Psychology* 25 (2004): 823–844.

Saller, Richard P. "*Pietas*, Obligation and Authority in the Roman Family." Pages 393–410 in *Alte Geschichte und Wissenschaftsgeschichte: Festschrift fur K. Christ*. Edited by P. Kneissl and V. Losemann. Darmstadt, 1988.

———. *Patriarchy, Property, and Death in the Roman Family*. Cambridge: Cambridge University Press, 1994.

———. "Corporal Punishment, Authority, and Obedience in the Roman Household." Pages 144–165 in *Marriage, Divorce, and Children in Ancient Rome*. Edited by Beryl Rawson. New York: Oxford University Press, 1996.

Satlow, Michael. "'Try to Be a Man': The Rabbinic Construction of Masculinity." *Harvard Theological Review* 89 (1996): 19–40.

———. "Jewish Constructions of Nakedness in Late Antiquity." *Journal of Biblical Literature* 116 (1997): 429–54.

Schippers, Mimi. "Recovering the Feminine Other: Masculinity, Femininity, and Gender Hegemony," *Theory and Society* 36 (2007): 85–102.

Schlossmann, S. *Pernosa und ΠΡΟΣΩΠΟΝ im Recht und christlichen Dogma*. Kiliae: Lipsius and Tischer, 1906.

Schmithals, Walter. *Gnosticism in Corinth: An Investigation of the Letters to the Corinthians*. Translated by J. E. Steely. Nashville: Abingdon, 1971.

———. *Paul and the Gnostics*. Nashville: Abingdon, 1972.

Scholz, Susanne. "Second Wave Feminism." Pages 242–52 in *Oxford Encyclopedia of the Bible and Gender Studies* 1:242–251. Edited by Julia M. O'Brien, et al. Oxford: Oxford University Press, 2014.

Schowalter, Daniel N. and Steven J. Friesen, eds. *Urban Religion in Roman Corinth: Interdisciplinary Approaches*. Cambridge; Mass.: Harvard University Press, 2005.

Schuler, Christoph. "Local Elites in the Greek East." Pages 250–73 in *The Oxford Handbook of Roman Epigraphy*. Edited by Christer Bruun and Jonathan Edmondson. Oxford: Oxford University Press, 2015.

Schüssler Fiorenza, Elisabeth. *In Memory of Her: A Feminist Theological Reconstruction of Christian Origins*. New York: Crossroad, 1985.

———. "Remembering the Past in Creating the Future: Historical Critical Scholarship and Feminist Biblical Interpretation." Pages 55–63 in *Feminist Perspectives on Biblical Scholarship*. Edited by Y. A. Collins. Atlanta: Scholars Press, 1985.

———. "Rhetorical Situation and Historical Reconstruction in 1 Corinthians." *New Testament Studies* 33 (1987): 386–403.

———. *But She Said: Feminist Practices of Biblical Interpretation*. Boston: Beacon, 1992.

———. "Between Movement and Academy: Feminist Biblical Studies in the Twentieth Century." Pages 1–20 in *Feminist Biblical Studies in the Twentieth Century: Scholarship and Movement*. Edited by Elisabeth Schüssler Fiorenza. Atlanta: Society of Biblical Literature, 2014.

Scranton, R. L. *Medieval Architecture in the Central Area of Corinth*. Princeton: The American School of Classical Studies at Athens, 1957.

Scull, Kevin Ronald. "Authority and Persuasion: Self-Presentation in Paul's Letters." Ph.D. diss., The University of California Los Angeles, 2012.

Sebesta, Judith Lynn. "Women's Costume and Feminine Civic Morality in Augustan Rome." *Gender and History* vol. 9 (1997): 529–41

Sedgwick, Eve Kosofsky. *Between Men: English Literature and Male Homosocial Desire*. New York: Columbia University Press, 1985.

Seland, Torrey. "Philo as a Citizen: *Homo politicus*." Pages 47–74 in *Reading Philo: A Handbook on Philo of Alexandria*. Edited by Torrey Seland. Grand Rapids: Eerdmans, 2014.

Shanor, Jay. "Paul as Master Builder: Construction Terms in First Corinthians." *New Testament Studies* 34 (1988): 461–471.

Shapiro, Judith. "Cross-Cultural Perspectives on Sexual Differentiation." Pages 269–308 in *Human Sexuality: A Comparitive and Developmental Perspective*. Edited by Herant A. Katchadourian. Berkeley: University of California Press, 1979.

Shi, Wenhua. *Paul's Message of the Cross as Body Language*. Wissenschaftliche Untersuchungen zum Neuen Testament 254. Tübingen: Mohr Siebeck, 2008.

Sjörberg, Birgitta L. "More than Just Gender: The Classical *Oikos* as a Site of Intersectionality." Pages 48–59 in *Families in the Greco-Roman World*. Edited by Ray Laurence and Agneta Strömberg. New York: Continuum International, 2012.

Skinner, Marilyn B. "*Ego Mulier*: The Construction of Male Sexuality in Catullus." Pages 129–50 in *Roman Sexualities*. Edited by Judith P. Halllett and Marilyn B. Skinner. Princeton: Princeton University Press, 1997.

———. *Sexuality in Greek and Roman Culture*. Malden, Mass: Blackwell, 2005.

Sly, Dorothy. *Philo's Perception of Women*. Brown Judaica Series 209. Atlanta: Scholars Press, 1990.

Solevåg, Anna Rebecca. *Birth Salvation: Gender and Class in Early Christian Childbearing Discourse*. Leiden: Brill, 2013.

Spawforth, A. J. "Roman Corinth: The Formation of a Colonial Elite." Pages 167–82 in *Roman Onomastics in the Greek East: Social and Political Aspects*. Edited by A. D. Rizakis. Athens: Research Center for Greek and Roman Antiquity, 1996.

Stanley, Christopher D, ed. *The Colonized Apostle: Paul through Postcolonial Eyes*. Minneapolis: Fortress Press, 2011.

Stearns, Peter. *Be A Man! Males in Modern Society*. New York: Holmes and Meier, 1986.

Stichele, Caroline Vander, and Todd Penner. *Contextualizing Gender in Early Christian Discourse: Thinking Beyond Thecla*. London: T&T Clark, 2009.

———. *Her Master's Tools?: Feminist And Postcolonial Engagements of Historical-Critical Discourse*. Leiden: Brill, 2005.

Stone, Ken. "Gender Criticism: The Un-Manning of Abimelech." Pages 183–201 in *Judges and Method: New Approaches to Biblical Studies*. 2nd ed., edited by Gale A. Yee. Minneapolis: Fortress Press, 2007.

Streete, Gail Corrington. "Discipline and Discourse." Pages 81–94 in *Vision and Persuasion: Rhetorical Dimensions of Apocalyptic Discourse*. Edited by Greg Carey and L. Gregory Bloomquist. St. Louis, Mo.: Chalice, 1999.

Swancutt, Diana M. "Still before Sexuality: 'Greek' Androgyny, the Roman Imperial Politics of Masculinity and Roman Invention of the *Tribas*." Pages 11–62 in *Mapping Gender in Ancient Religious Discourses*. Edited by Todd Penner and Caroline Vander Stichele. Leiden: Brill, 2007.

Szesnat, Holger. "'Pretty Boys' in Philo's *De Vita Contemplativa*." *Studia Philonica* 10 (1998): 87–107.

Tajfel, H. "Social Categorization, Social Identity and Social Comparison." Pages 61–76 in *Differentiation Between Social Groups: Studies in the Social Psychology of Intergroup Relations*. Edited by H. Tajfel. London: Academic Press, 1978.

———. "Individuals and Groups in Social Psychology," *British Journal of Clinical Psychology* 18 (1979): 183–90.

Taylor, Joan E. *Jewish Women Philosophers of First-Century Alexandria: Philo's 'Therapeutae' Reconsidered*. Oxford: Oxford University Press, 2006.
Taylor, Lily Ross. "Augustales, Seviri Augustales, and Seviri: A Chronological Study." *Transactions and Proceedings of the American Philological Association* 45 (1914): 231–53.
Temkin, Owsei. *Soranus' Gynecology*. Baltimore, MD: Johns Hopkins Press, 1956.
Theissen Gerd. "Soziale Schichtung in der korinthischen Gemeinde: Ein Beitrag zur Soziologie des hellenistischen Urchristentums," *Zeitschrift für die neutestamentliche Wissenschaft und die Kunde der älteren Kirche* 65 (1974): 232–72.
———. "Soziale Integration und sakramentales Handeln: Eine Analyse von 1 Cor. XI 17–34," *Novum Testamentum* 16 (1974): 179–206.
———. "Legitimation und Lebensunterhalt: Ein Beitrag zur Soziologie urchristlicher Missionaire," *New Testament Studies* 21 (1975): 192–221.
———. "Die Starken und Schwachen in Korinth: Soziologische Analyse eines theologischen Streites," *Evangelische Theologie* 35 (1975): 155–72.
———. "Die soziologische Auswertun reliogiöser Überlieferungen: Ihre methodologischen Probleme am Beispel des Urchristentums," *Kairos* 17 (1975): 284–99.
———. "Social Conflicts in the Corinthian Community: Further Remarks on J.J. Meggitt's *Paul, Poverty, and Survival*." *Journal for the Study of the New Testament* 25 (2003): 371–91.
Thomas, Christine M. "Greek Heritage in Roman Corinth and Ephesos: Hybrid Identities and Strategies of Display in the Material Record of Traditional Mediterranean Religions." Pages 114–44 in *Corinth in Context: Comparative Studies on Religion and Society*. Edited by Steven J. Friesen, Daniel N. Schowalter, and James C. Walters. Leiden: Brill, 2010.
Townsley, Gillian. *The Straight Mind in Corinth: Queer Readings across 1 Corinthians 11:2–16*. Semeia Studies 88. Atlanta: Scholars Press, 2017.
Treggiari, Susan. *Roman Marriage: Iusti Coniugus from the Time of Cicero to the Time of Ulpian*. Oxford: Clarendon Press, 1991.
Valentine, Katy. "'For You Were Bough With a Price': Slaves, Sex, and Self-control in a Pauline Community." Ph.D. diss., Graduate Theological Union, 2014.
Valian, Virginia. *Why So Slow? The Advancement of Women*. Cambridge, Mass.: MIT Press, 1998.
Van den Hoek, Annawies. "Endowed with Reason or Glued to the Senses: Philo's Thoughts on Adam and Eve." Pages 63–75 in *The Creation of Man and Woman: Interpretations of the Biblical Narratives in Jewish and Christian Traditions*. Edited by G. P. Luttikhuizen. Themes in Biblical Narrative 3. Leiden: Brill, 2000.
Van der Horst, Pieter W. "Bitenosh's Orgasm (1QapGen 2:9–15)." *Journal for the Study of Judaism* 43 (2012): 613–28.
———. *Studies in Ancient Judaism and Christianity*. Leiden: Brill, 2014.
von Ehrenkrook, Jason. "Effeminacy in the Shadow of Empire: The Politics of Transgressive Gender in Josephus's *Bellum Judaicum*." *Jewish Quarterly* 101 (2011): 145–63.
Walbank, Mary E. Hoskins. "Image and Cult: The Coinage of Roman Corinth." Pages 151–98 in *Corinth in Context: Comparative Studies in Religion and*

Society. Edited by Steven J. Friesen, Daniel N. Schowalter, and James C. Walters. Leiden: Brill, 2010.

Wallace-Hadrill, Andrew. *Rome's Cultural Revolution*. Cambridge: Cambridge University Press, 2008.

Walters, James C. "Paul and the Politics of Meals in Roman Corinth." Pages 343–64 in *Corinth in Context: Comparative Studies in Religion and Society*. Edited by Steven J. Friesen, Daniel N. Schowalter, and James C. Walters. Leiden: Brill, 2010.

Walters, Jonathan. "Invading the Roman Body: Manliness and Impenetrability in Roman Thought." Pages 29–46 in *Roman Sexualities Roman Sexualities*. Edited by Judith P. Hallett and Marilyn B. Skinner. Princeton: Princeton University Press, 1997.

Warren, L. Bonfante. "Roman Costumes: A Glossary and Some Etruscan Derivations." *Aufstieg und Niedergang der römischen Welt: Geschichte und Kultur Roms im Spiegel der neueren Forschung* 1.4 (1973): 584–614.

Watson, Duane F. "The New Testament and Greco-Roman Rhetoric: A Bibliography." *Journal of the Evangelical Theological Society* 31 (1998): 465–72.

Wegner, Judith Romney. "Philo's Portrayal of Women: Hebraic or Hellenic?" Pages 41–66 in *"Women Like This": New Perspectives on Jewish Women in the Greco-Roman World*. Edited by A. J. Levine. Atlanta: Scholars Press, 1991.

Weima, Jeffery A. D. *Neglected Endings: The Significance of the Pauline Letter Closings*. Journal for the Study of the New Testament 101; Sheffield: JSOT Press, 1994.

Weiss, Johannes. *Der erste Korintherbreif*. Göttingen: Vandenhoeck & Ruprecht, 1910.

Weitzer, Ronald, and Charis Kubrin. "Misogyny in Rap Music: A Content Analysis of Prevalence and Meaning." *Men and Masculinities* 12 (2009): 3–29.

Welborn, L. L. "On the Discord in Corinth: 1 Corinthians 1–4 and Ancient Politics." *Journal of Biblical Literature* 106 (1987): 85–111.

———. *Politics and Rhetorician the Corinthian Epistles*. Macon, Ga: Mercer University Press, 1997.

———. "Μωρός γένεσθω: Paul's Appropriation of the Role of the Fool in 1 Corinthians 1–4," *Biblical Interpretation* 10 (2002): 421–35.

———. *Paul, the Fool of Christ: A Study of 1 Corinthians 1–4 in the Comic-Philosopher Tradition*. London: T&T Clark, 2005.

White, Adam G. *Where is the Wise Man?: Greco-Roman Education as a Background to the Divisions in 1 Corinthians 1–4*. London: Bloomsbury T&T Clark, 2015.

Whitmarsh, Tim. "Thinking Local." Pages 1–16 in *Local Knowledge and Microidentities in the Imperial Greek World*. Edited by Tim Whitmarsh. Cambridge: Cambridge University Press, 2010.

Wilckens, Ulrich. *Weisheit and Torheit*. Tübingen: Mohr, 1959.

Wildfang, Robin Lorsch. *Rome's Vestal Virgins: A Study of Rome's Vestal Priestesses in the Late Empire and Early Republic*. New York: Routledge, 2006.

Williams, Craig A. *Roman Homosexuality*. Oxford: Oxford University Press, 2010.

Willis, Benjamin W. "The Social and Ethnic Origins of the Colonists in Early Roman Corinth." Pages 13–36 in *Corinth in Context: Comparative Studies on Religion and*

Society. Edited by Steven J. Friesen, Daniel N. Schowalter, and James C. Walters. Leiden: Brill, 2010.

Wilson, Brittany E. *Unmanly Men: Refigurations of Masculinity in Luke-Acts*. Oxford: Oxford University Press, 2015.

Winkler, John J. *The Constraints of Desire: The Anthropology of Sex and Gender in Ancient Greece*. New York: Routledge, 1990.

Winter, Bruce W. *Philo and Paul among the Sophists: Alexandrian and Corinthian Responses to a Julio-Claudian Movement*. Grand Rapids: Eerdmans, 2002.

———. "The Toppling of Favorinus and Paul by the Corinthians." Pages 291–306 in *Early Christianity and Classical Culture: Comparative Studies in Honor of Abraham J. Malherbe*. Edited by John T. Fitzgerald, Thomas H. Olbricht, and L. Michael White. Leiden: Brill, 2003.

———. *Roman Wives, Roman Widows: The Appearance of New Women and the Pauline Communities*. Grand Rapids: Eerdmans, 2003.

———. "You Were What You Wore in Roman Law: Deciphering the Dress Codes of 1 Timothy 2:9–15." *Society of Biblical Literature Forum*. No Pages. Cited June 2015. Online: http://sbl-site.org/Article.aspx?ArticleID=277.

Wire, Antoinette Clark. *The Corinthian Women Prophets: A Reconstruction through Paul's Rhetoric*. Minneapolis: Fortress Press, 1991.

Witherington, Ben, III. *Conflict and Community in Corinth: A Socio-Rhetorical Commentary on 1 and 2 Corinthians*. Grand Rapids: Eerdmans, 1995.

Woolf, Greg. "Becoming Roman, Staying Greek: Culture, Identity, and the Civilizing Process in the Roman East." *Proceedings of the Cambridge Philological Society* 40 (1994): 116–43.

Wyke, Maria. *Parchments of Gender: Deciphering the Bodies of Antiquity*. Oxford: Clarendon, 1998.

Zeller, Dieter. *Der erste Brief an der Korinther*. Göttingen: Vandenhoek & Ruprecht, 2011.

Ziskowski, Angela. "The Bellerophon Myth in Early Corinthian History and Art." *Hesperia: Journal of the American School of Classical Studies at Athens* 83 (2014): 81–102.

Subject Index

1 Corinthians, unity of the text and argument, 2, 4–5, 11, 117, 121, 216–17

advantage (συμφέρει, συμφέρον), 6, 8, 13, 181–82, 192–93
active-passive (strong-weak) framework, 48, 53, 89–90, 121–22, 124–25, 143, 170–71, 180–84, 191
adaptability, 182–85, 189
Aristotle, 49, 70, 115, 126, 150n34
Augustus, 36, 47, 52–53, 89, 93, 98, 102, 143–44

the body:
    conception and maturation, 40–43, 48–49, 84–85, 122–29, 134
    diet, effect on, 123–29, 185
    ideology of. *See* physiognomy
    performance of, 7, 8, 10, 12, 24–25, 40, 42–43, 45–46, 48, 69, 75–79, 81, 98–99, 113, 159, 176, 179, 188–89, 216–24
    implication of. *See* social status

Catiline, 72, 96
celibacy, 9, 10–11, 12, 113, 135, 137–43, 189

concord, 1, 5–6, 8, 10, 12–13, 113–14, 121, 129, 136, 150, 167, 176, 181, 189, 193–94, 217
courage, 48, 99–100, 102–03
crucifixion (cross, crucified, cruciform), 9, 13, 117, 118, 120, 134, 145–56, 162, 171, 224

eunuch, 12, 27, 32–33, 44, 52, 76, 78, 81, 86, 95

factionalism, 1, 5, 8, 10, 13, 116–17, 121, 128, 132–33, 146, 150, 167, 172, 180–82, 189, 193–94
father (fatherhood), 12, 46–47, 93–94, 130–31, 133–34, 145
Favorinus, 12, 19–20, 37–38, 44, 51, 53, 65, 75–82, 88, 118, 120, 127, 129–30, 144–45, 174, 193
femininity (effeminacy), 2, 3, 11, 12, 19, 21–22, 23, 24, 25–27, 28–35, 38–39, 42–43, 44–46, 47–48, 49, 53, 68–69, 75, 78, 79, 83–86, 89–92, 94–96, 98–99, 102–3, 121, 124, 126, 129–30, 140–42, 160, 162, 186–88, 191–92, 217, 220–24
construction and use of. *See* gender
Flaccus, 87–92

255

foolishness, 4, 117, 119, 121–22, 124–26, 169–71, 177–79
freedman, 161–64, 167

gender (gendered discourses):
  construction and use of, 2–4, 7, 8, 12, 19, 23–26, 27, 28–30, 31–32, 33–34, 35–39, 40–48, 48–54, 65–69, 70–75, 78–82, 82–92, 93–95, 98–103, 113, 115–16, 119–25, 129–30, 132–33, 141–42, 172–73, 184–85, 190–91, 221–22
  legal consequences of, 51–52, 68–69, 75–76, 80, 120, 143–44, 169–70, 176–79, 192–94
  hierarchy of, 19–20, 27, 34–35, 40, 46–47, 48–54, 82–83, 85–87, 93–99, 102, 116–17, 120–22, 130, 141–42, 144–45, 161–62, 169–71, 173–75, 186–89, 213, 223–24
  manipulation of, 1, 9, 10–11, 12–13, 19–20, 22, 24–26, 31–32, 41, 45, 50–52, 84, 92–95, 102–3, 113, 116, 120, 121–22, 129–30, 173, 183–84, 190
  related to intercourse, 44–45, 50, 51, 85–86, 94, 98–99, 135, 137–44, 186–89
  See also conception and maturation; father; passion; self-control; slave; virtue; wisdom

head coverings. *See* veils
Homer, 39

idol (idolatry), 180–81, 184
imitation, 1, 5, 8, 9, 13, 80–82, 93, 113–14, 117, 128–29, 159, 168

Josephus, 12, 20, 30, 65, 75, 87, 92–103, 190, 193

lawsuit, 5, 39, 131, 172–79

marriage, 135–44, 186–89
masculinity:
  construction and use of. *See* gender
  complicit, 4, 20, 36, 66, 68, 71–71, 75, 88–90, 92, 101, 104, 160
  hegemonic, 4, 10, 12–13, 20, 22, 31, 32, 36, 39, 50, 54, 65–69, 71–72, 75, 76, 80, 81–82, 91, 93–96, 101, 104, 132–34, 145, 159–60, 169, 171–72, 175, 179, 186–88, 190–94
  subordinate (failed), 4, 10, 11, 12–13, 20, 22–23, 31, 36, 54, 65–69, 71–72, 75, 81–82, 92, 96, 104, 113, 116–17, 124–25, 129–34, 145, 159–60, 171, 179, 186, 189, 192–94, 221, 224
milk, 123–29, 145

obedience, 32, 89–90, 92, 93–95, 98–99, 104
orator (oratory, including the loss of or ability to speak), 9, 12, 34–35, 43, 76–77, 78, 81–82, 91, 100, 118–21, 134, 145, 161, 181

παιδεία, 38–39, 76, 80–81, 118
passion, 26, 37, 45, 71, 73, 83–86, 90, 99, 100–101, 135–42, 188
patriarchy. *See* gender, hierarchy of
persona, 8–9, 12, 65, 70–75, 79–81, 92, 103–4, 115-17, 129–30, 132
penetration, 26, 28, 35–36, 42, 45–46, 47, 51, 132, 187
  related to punishment, 134
  See also gender: related to intercourse
Philo, 12, 20, 30, 65, 75, 82–92, 98, 123–24, 141–43, 176, 193
physiognomy, 37–38, 39, 43–44, 48–50, 76–81, 116, 120
pietas. *See* virtue
Plato, 39, 170

Polemo, 37–38, 49, 76, 78–79, 99, 118, 144–45
πορνεία (sexual immorality), 136–40, 142, 187–88
πρόσωπον (face). See *persona*

self-control, 2, 23, 26, 27, 29, 36, 37, 41, 44–45, 49, 53, 74–75, 80, 84–85, 90, 93–94, 97–100, 124–25, 132, 187–89
self-presentation, 9, 12, 24–25, 48–49, 65, 72–75, 78–81, 101, 113, 115–16, 118, 120–21, 159, 161, 171, 181
shame, 9, 120, 129–30, 132–34, 144–45, 161, 170–71, 177–79, 189
slave (slavery), 47, 85, 113–15, 129, 134, 162–63, 167
social status, 6, 7–8, 10, 114–17, 119, 129, 134, 159, 161–64, 170, 172–75, 178, 190, 218, 220–21
   conflict over, 6, 7–8, 131–32, 146, 160–61, 164, 169, 175
   related to the body, 7, 8, 23–24, 39, 49, 51–52, 66–67, 69, 80, 85–86, 120, 141–42, 144, 161, 169–71, 174, 189, 193–94, 219–24
   related to social identity theory, 70–73, 161–67
sophist, 76–82, 118–22

Theodora, Junia, 162
Therapeutae, 135–36, 141–43

unity. See concord

veils, 5, 10–11, 13, 213, 216–24
virgin(s), 141
virtue, 3–4, 23, 37, 43, 46–47, 50, 84–86, 87–88, 93, 99–101, 123–25

wet nurse (nursing), 9, 12, 41–42, 121–30
wisdom (σοφία), 4, 11, 83–84, 86, 119–21, 124–25, 131, 169–70, 177

Author Index

Anderson, Janice Capel, 30–31

Baer, Richard A., 82–83
Bassler, Jouette M., 216
de Boer, Martinus C., 4–5
Boyarin, Daniel, 30
Butler, Judtih, 24, 25, 40

Carrigan, Tim, 66
Castelli, Elizabeth Anne, 9
Clines, David J. A., 29
Collins, Raymond, 128–29
Connell, R. W., 22, 31, 50, 65–66, 69
Conway, Colleen, 93–94
Creangă, Ovidiu, 31

D'Angelo, Mary Rose, 86–87
Donaldson, Mike, 67
Dover, Kenneth J., 26, 35

Eastman, Susan, 3
Edsall, Benjamin, 175, 177
Eilberg-Schwartz, Howard, 29, 30, 32
Ellis, J. Edward., 139

Filene, Peter, 21
Foucault, Michel, 9, 12, 19, 24, 27–28, 28–29

Fredrickson, David, 137, 139
Friesen, Steven, 162, 164, 194n3

Gardiner, Judith Kegan, 21
Gaventa, Beverly, 2, 3, 123, 129–30, 145
Glancy, Jennifer, 31
Gleason, 77
Gorman, Michael, 9, 145
Greene, Ellen, 116
Guest, Deryn, 23
Gunderson, Erik, 35

Haddox, Susan, 32
Halperin, David, 12, 25, 27
Hays, Richard, 171
Horrell, David G., 175, 178
Hughes, Lisa A., 219–20

Jodamus, Johnathan, 133, 149n24
Kelly, J. M., 172
Kinman, Brent, 177
König, Jason, 115–16
Kuefler, Matthew, 27

Lee, John, 65–66
Lopez, Davina, 35, 96

Malherbe, Abraham, 122–23
Martin, Dale, 7–8, 10, 41, 136–37, 139, 220–21
Mattila, Sharon, Lea, 82–83
Mayer, Ronald G., 73
Meeks, Chet, 25
Messerschmitt, James W., 67–69
Mitchell, Margaret, 1–2, 5–6, 8, 10, 122, 133, 136, 167, 175 ,176, 182–83, 189
Moore, Stephen J. 30–31

Nguyen, V. Henry T., 8–9, 70–71

Oster, Richard, 217–18

Penner, Todd, 223–24
Pogoloff, Stephen M., 119

Reeder, Caryn, 97
Reeser, Todd W., 21
Richlin, Amy, 12

Satlow, Michael, 29
Sebesta, Judith Lynn, 47

Sedgwick, Eve Kosofsky, 23, 24
Shapiro, Judith, 21
Schippers, Mimi, 67
Schüssler Fiorenza, Elizabeth, 10
Scull, Kevin Ronald, 116
Stearns, Peter, 21
Stein, Arlene, 25
Stone, Ken, 24
Streete, Gail, 143

Theissen, Gerd, 6, 7–8, 170, 184
Thiselton, Anothony, 6–7, 151n47
Townsley, Gillian, 11

Vander Stichele, Caroline, 223–24

Weima, Jeffery, 189
Weiss, Johannes, 4, 117
Welborn, L. L., 119–20, 145, 169
White, Adam, 168–69
Whitmarsh, Tim, 76
Wilson, Brittany, 54
Wire, Antoinette Clark, 10
Witherington, Ben, 217–18, 148n22

Ancient Sources

Hebrew Bible

Genesis
1, 222
2–3, 222
2:21–23
29:23, 85
29:32, 85
30:16, 85

Exodus
4:21–26, 29
32, 181

Numbers
11, 181
11:4–15, 29
14, 181
25, 181

Deuteronomy
24:1–4, 87
31:6, 191

Joshua
1:6, 191
1:7, 191
1:9, 191

Judges
5:7–8, 191
5:24–30, 191

2 Samuel
10:12, 191

1 Chronicles
32:7, 191

Psalms
26:14, 191
30:25, 191

Proverbs
3:11–12, 134
6:25–29, 138
6:25, 138

Isaiah
54:5, 32
61:10, 32

Ezekiel
16, 32

Hosea
2:16–20, 32

Micah
4:10, 191

New Testament

Matthew
19:27–29, 31

Acts
22:25–29, 51

1 Corinthians
1–4, 3, 4, 9, 117, 121
1:10, 5, 121, 160
1:12, 112
1:13, 118
1:17–18, 117
1:17, 144, 172
1:18–2:5, 143
1:18–31, 169
1:18, 121
1:20, 170
1:21–22, 131
1:21, 169
1:23, 162
1:26, 164, 167, 169–70, 177
1:27–28, 169–70
1:28, 178

Ancient Sources

1:29, 171
1:31, 171
2:1–5, 118–19, 120, 144
2:2, 171
2:3, 120
2:8, 131
2:6–8, 143
3:1–4, 121
3:1–3, 121, 126, 129
3:2, 2, 122, 128
3:4–9, 119
3:4, 128
3.5–6, 114
3:6–8, 114
3:6, 114
3:9, 114
3:10–13, 114
3:10, 114–15, 169
3:18, 4, 160, 171
3:21, 171
4:1–4, 114
4:1, 131, 169
4:5, 169
4:6, 131
4:7, 131
4:9–13, 131
4:9, 29, 116, 132,
4:10–16, 75
4:10, 131–32
4:11–12, 132
4:14–15, 130
4:14, 132, 171, 177–78
4:15–16, 192
4:16–21, 133
4:16, 128, 129, 159, 171–72
5, 7, 44, 47
5:3, 131
5:9–13, 188
5:9–10, 143
5:10–11, 134
5:12, 131
6, 7
6:1–8, 4, 160, 167

6:1–4, 178
6:1–3, 131
6:1, 176
6:2, 176
6:4, 172, 176
6:5, 133
6:6, 176
6:7, 175, 178
6:8, 176
6:9–10, 134
6:12–20, 4
6:12, 6
6:15, 136
6:18
7,7, 44, 140
7:1–11, 160
7:1–7, 135
7:1–4, 20
7:1, 136
7:2–11, 213
7:2–5, 187
7:2–4, 192
7:2, 142, 178
7:3–5, 4, 160
7:3–4, 186
7:5, 136, 141, 142
7:7, 181
7:8–9, 142
7:9, 136, 140, 142
7:10–11, 186–88
7:11, 188
7:13–16, 139
7:23, 187
7:25–28, 140, 181
7:29, 143
7:31, 143
7:32–40, 181
7:35, 6
7:36–38, 136–37
7:39, 139
8:1–11:1, 4, 160, 180–81
8–10, 7
8:1, 180
8:4–6, 179

8:4, 180–81
8:6, 223
8:9, 181
8:13, 180
9:1–23, 179, 181
9:17, 182
9:19, 182
9:22, 182
9:24–27, 179
10:1–22, 4
10:1–13, 179
10:7, 181
10:11, 143
10:14, 181
10:15, 131
10:20, 181
10:21, 180
10:23–30, 4, 179, 181
10:24, 181
10:27, 184
10:28, 184–85
11, 7
11:1, 8, 128, 129, 159, 161–62, 179–80, 182
11:2–24, 4
11:2–16, 11, 13, 20, 213
11:3–12, 222
11:3, 222
11:4–5, 220
11:4, 220–21
11:5–6, 221–22
11:5, 220
11:7–9, 221
11:8–9, 222–23
11:10, 223–24
11:11–12, 221–223
11:13, 131, 220, 224
11:14–15, 220
11:15, 160
11:17–34, 164
11:17–22, 167
12:12–26, 176
14:24, 220
14:31, 220

15:8, 113
16:13-14, 190-91
16:13, 114, 130-31, 168
16:19, 160

2 Corinthians
6:14–7:1, 4

1 Thessalonians
2:2, 123
2:8, 123

Philippians
4:4, 176

1 Timothy
3:2, 141

Titus
1:6, 141

Hebrews
12:6, 134

**Jewish and
Christian Sources**

1 Maccabees
2:64, 191

2 Maccabees
7:21, 191

Letter of Aristeas
144, 53
250–51, 53–54

Josephus
Against Apion, 92

Antiquities of the Jews, 92
1.162, 100
2.230–31, 100–01
3.58, 100
4.129, 100
4.290–91, 99
4.291, 101
6.160, 100
15.23, 100
15.259, 188

Wars of the Jews
1.1, 97
1.7, 97
1.8, 97
1.9, 97
1.10, 98
1.11, 98
1.24, 98
1.27, 98
1.197–99, 45
1.204–05, 100
1.283, 100
1.321–22, 99–100
1.328–29, 100
1.354–55, 100
1.386–90, 100
2.313, 221
2.356–88, 97
3.152–53, 101
3.204–6, 101–2
3.248, 103
3.263, 101
3.276, 102
3.303, 102
3.304, 102
3.347–48, 102
3.464, 101
4.9, 101
4.70–83, 103
4.107, 98
4.118, 98
4.230, 100
4.392, 100
4.624, 100
4.357–60, 98
4.561–62, 98–99
4.599–62, 98
5.72–74, 98
5.73–75, 101
5.81, 101
5.314, 100
5.316, 190
6.69–80, 101
6.152–55, 101

Philo
De agricultura
9, 123

De Abrahamo
101–2, 84
135–36, 86
136, 75
245–52

De cherubim
41, 85
49, 83
78, 124

*De congressu
    erditionis gratia*
19, 124

De decalogo
126–31, 87

*Quod Deus sit
    immutabilis*
1.111, 85

De ebrietate
30–31, 83

De fuga et invention
51–52, 83
51, 83
199–201, 90

In Flaccum
1–4, 90
2, 90
4, 89–90
8, 90

16, 90
17–21, 91
17, 92
23–24, 88
25, 88
27–29, 88
29, 92
33–34, 90–91
41, 91
43, 92
46–47, 88–89
48–49, 88
50, 89
74, 89
75–80, 46
89, 89
90, 89
91, 89–90
103, 88
125–26, 92
127, 91
137, 89
170–73, 87

Legat ad Gaium
143–47, 98

Legum allegoriae
3.2, 86
3.40, 87
3.88, 86
3.156, 85

De mutatione nominum
132–33, 85
254, 85

Quaestiones et solutiones in Exodum
1.8, 84
3.18, 85
4.167–68, 85

Quod omnis probus liber sit
1.124, 86

De opificio mundi
167, 87

De posteritae Caini
119, 176

Quis reruin divinarum heres sit
127, 83
160, 124

De sacrificiis Abelis et Caini
103, 82
80, 90

De somniis
1.22–23, 86
2.10, 124

De special legibus
1.201, 82
1.325, 86
2.19, 90
2.50, 86
3.30–31, 87
3.37–42, 86
3.199–200, 125
4.91, 90

De virtutibus
18–21. 86
130, 125

De vita contemplative
13–14, 142
21–22, 141
33, 87
60, 86

De vita Mosis
2.184, 90–91

Qumran
1QapGen^{ar} ii, 1–17, 41

Sirach
31:25, 191

Shepherd of Hermes
Vision
1.4.3, 191

Susanna
1.8–10, 138

Testament of Judah
2.1–3, 138

Testament of Rueben
2.8, 139
3.10–4.1, 138

Greco-Roman Literature
Achilles Tatius
Leucippe et Clitophon
5.19.3, 221–22
7.5.4, 222
7.12.1, 221–22

Appian
Historia roman
7.5.29, 190, 192

Aristotle
Ethica nichomachea
3.6.8–12, 190

De generatione ananamalium
727a32–35, 40
729a20–33, 40

Historia animalium
3.21.523a.9–13, 126
7.10.587b.18–19, 126

Politica
1.2.1254a, 115

Rhetorica
1356b30–34, 34

1369a13–19, 34
1388b12–1391b17, 34
1417a3–8, 34
1418b14–15, 34

Athenaeus
Deipnosophistae
15.698c–f, 170

Augustus
Res gestae divi augusti
3, 96
8, 94
13, 93
26–33, 93
26, 37
29, 96
32, 96

Catullus
Poems
16, 73–74
45.16, 142
63, 44, 67

Cato
De agricultura
1.1, 114
1.4, 114
2.1–2, 114

Cicero
Pro Caecina
43, 173

In Catalinam
2.7–11, 96

De legibus
3.1.7, 143

De officiis
1.105–25, 71
1.05, 71
1.07–08, 71
1.07, 71

1.09–10, 71
1.110–14, 71
1.115–16, 71
1.124–25, 71
1.128–32, 72
1.129, 50
3.43–44, 50–51

De oratore
1.113–36, 174
3.216, 42

In Verrem
2.1.66, 180
2.5.3, 46
2.5.33, 46
5.81, 186

Pro Murena
13–14, 39
15, 39

Orationes philippicae
2.85, 175

Pro Plancio
72, 52

Pro Rabirio
  Perduellionis Reo
16, 120

Pro Rabirio Postumo
26–27, 39

Pro Sestio
93, 50

Tusculanae
  disputationes
2.34, 134
2.47–48, 93
2.52, 95
3.1–2, 127
3.64, 133–34
4.71, 73

Demosthenes
Adversus Androtionem
26, 180

Digesta
2.9.5, 51
4.3.2, 172
9.9.20, 217
23.3.2, 188
24.2.2, 188
25.7.1, 51
47.5.24–35, 187
47.10.15, 51, 217
47.10.18, 174
48.2.1–2, 174
48.5.2.2, 186–87
48.5.2.6, 186–87
49.14.12, 51

Dio Cassius
Historia Romana
7.26, 191
56.4–6, 144
69.3.1–5, 77
69.3.4, 77

Dio Chrysostom
De concordia cum
  Apamensibus (Or. 40)
20–21, 183–84
34, 168

De regno iv (Or. 4)
74, 122–23

De regno et tyrannide
  (Or. 62)
2–4, 221

Tarsica prior (Or. 33), 3

De tyrannide (Or. 6)
18, 140

De virtute (Or. 8)
9–11, 118

Diodorus
Historical Library
5.32.7, 94

Dionysius of
 Halicarnasus
Antiquitates romanae
2.26.2–4, 46
4.26.2, 182–83

Epictetus
Discourses
2.16.39, 125
2.16.44–45, 125
3.22.67–82, 140
3.22.68–76, 139
3.24.8–13, 125
3.24.9, 125

The Epistle of Diogenes
44, 139
47, 139

Favorinus
Corinthian Orations
8, 79, 80
12, 19
22, 79, 174
23, 79
24, 81
25–27, 81
25, 79, 80
26, 81
32, 79
33–34, 80
46, 79

Galen
De semine
2.5, 41

*De alimentorum
 facultabus*
1.471–72, 44
7.678, 129

De locis affectis
6.5, 137–38

*De naturalibus
 facultatibus*
1.6, 49

De usu partium
14.6–7, 41, 49

Hygiene
2.3, 43
3.4, 42

Gellius
Noctes atticae
3.1.11–15, 127
3.1.18, 127
3.1.20, 127

Herodotus
Historiae
1.10, 48
7.222–24, 101

Hippocrates
Genitals
4.2, 41

Horace
Epodi
9.12–14, 95

Isocrates
Panegyricus
11, 176

Julian
Mispogen, 38

Orations 3
127B, 190

Juvenal
Satirae
2.143–45, 93

2.165–70, 94
3.109–14, 92
4.15–20, 185
9.85, 144

Libanius
Orations
13–15, 3

Livy
Histories
1.11–12, 37
2.23.4–7, 46

Lucan
De Bello Civili
5.170, 219

Lucian
Anacharsis
15, 190

Demonax
12–13, 77
12, 78
13, 78

Eunuchus
13, 190

Imagines
6, 217

Judicium vocalium
12, 120

Martial
Epigrammata
7.210, 134
8.12, 47

Musonius Rufus
Discourses
12.5–6, 137
12.6–8, 137
12.24–25, 137

Ocellus
On the Nature of the Universe
IV, 137

Ovid
Fasti
3.545–46, 142

Tristia
2.514–15, 74
2.497–540, 74

Oxyrhnchus Papyri
188–208, 170
413, 170

Paulus
Sententiae
5.4.14

Philostratus
Imagines
1.2.10, 190

Vitae Apollonii
1.13, 140

Vitae sophistarum
208, 118–19
481, 76
489, 76, 77
490–91, 77, 80
491, 77
578–80, 118

Plato
Phaedrus
234, 170

Symposium
201–12, 27–28

Plautus
Casina,
1015–1018, 36–37

Pseudolus
1180–81, 36

Pliny the Elder
Naturalis historia
10.145, 73

Pliny the Younger
Epistulae
7.29, 115

Panegyricus
83.4, 47

Plutarch
Quomodo adulator ab amico internoscatur
69C, 122–23

Antonius
10.3, 47
67, 163

Amatorius, 28

Aratus
24.5, 182

Brutus
1.7, 115

Camillus
27.3–4, 95

Cato major
8.2, 95

Conjugalia Praecepta
16, 187–88
46, 188

Moralia
146, 38–39
452c–d, 39
825A, 175

Mulierum virtutes
242E–F, 19
246A, 53
257C–D, 53
257E, 53
258E–F, 53
261D, 53

Quaestiones romanae et graecae
101, 42, 52
266, 218–19
267B, 221
273D, 37
288, 42, 52

De Stoicorum repugnantiis
27, 190

Polemo
Physiognomy
1.151, 79
1.152–56, 79
1.152, 79
1.157–60, 79
1.160–61, 77–78
1.280F, 38
2.191–194F, 48
2.192F, 49

Polybius
Histories
31.25.4–5, 185
31.25.5, 95

Quintillian
Institutio oratoria
1.1.4–5, 127
1.9.9–11, 34–35
1.11.1, 43
1.11.3, 43
2.5.10–12, 185
2.15.7–8, 45
2.20.3–5, 43
4.2..39, 185

5.7.23–24, 4
6.3.24–25, 132
6.11, 180
10.3.1–2, 73
10.5.2, 73
11.3.103, 120
11.1.21–22, 116
11.3.28–32, 185
11.3.57, 43
11.3.76–129, 3
11.3.76, 185
11.3.91, 185
12.1.14, 171
12.2.1–2, 3
12.10.69, 119

Sallust
Bellum catalinae
6.1–9.5, 72
10.1–13.5, 72
11.3, 72
11.5, 186
11.7, 52
13.3, 185
14.1–7, 72
37.6, 52

Seneca
De benefiiis
7.9, 185–86

Epistulae morales
5.2, 38
13.1–3, 122
52.12, 44
52.12–14, 50
83.20, 51
108.98.22, 185
114, 186

Naturales quaestiones
7.32.4, 94

Seneca the Elder
Controversaie
10.1.2, 173

Soranus
Gynecology
2.9.14, 41
2.9.15, 41
2.16.32–33, 41
2.16.34, 41
7.14, 138
8, 138

Thysetes
4, 37

Suetonius
Divus Augustus
40.5, 72–73

Divus Claudius
15.4, 178
26, 188
29, 188

Divus Julius
43.1, 72

Seneca the Elder
Controversaie
1.1.8–9, 42, 95
1.1.10, 42

Tacitus
Annales
2.34, 173
3.28, 144

13.45, 45
14.35, 92

Dialogus de oratoribus
28, 127–28
29, 127–29

Germania
19, 221
20.1, 127

Historiae
5.13, 102

Valerius Maximus
Facta et Dieta
Memorabilia
6.3.10, 48
8.3, 174

Virgil
Aeneid
1.566–67, 50
4.215–17, 53
4.215, 94
6.676, 52
6.790–95, 53
6.875, 52
8.675–80, 53
9.614–20
12.99, 94

Xenophon
Anabasis
3.3.34, 190
5.8.15, 190

Oeconomicus
5.4, 190

About the Author

Born in 1983 in Philadelphia, PA, **Brian J. Robinson** completed his Bachelor of Arts degree at Cairn University in 2006 with a major in Biblical Studies. He received dual Master of Arts degrees in New Testament and Hebrew Bible in 2011 from Biblical Theological Seminary and his Ph.D. in New Testament from Fuller Theological Seminary in 2018. Brian currently lives in Monrovia, CA with Laurie and their son, Sam, and teaches as an adjunct faculty member at Azusa Pacific University. His interests include the application of critical theory so as to better understand the use of discourse and power in the creation and interpretation of texts.

www.ingramcontent.com/pod-product-compliance
Lightning Source LLC
Chambersburg PA
CBHW050900300426
44111CB00010B/1315